Christina

ENGLISH FILE

Upper-intermediate Student's Book

OXFORD

UNIVERSITY PRESS

Paul Seligson and Clive Oxenden are the original co-authors of
English File 1 and *English File 2*

Contents

G question formation
V working out meaning from context
P friendly intonation, showing interest

"I'm not thrilled about answering questions like 'If you were being mugged, and you had a light sabre in one pocket and a whip in the other, which would you use?'

Harrison Ford, US actor"

1A Questions and answers

1 READING & SPEAKING

a Look at the photos of Benedict Cumberbatch and Elisabeth Moss and read their biographical info. Have you seen any of the TV series or films that they have been in? What did you think of them?

b Now read the interviews and match questions A–G with their answers.

A **How do you relax?**
B **What don't you like about your appearance?**
C **What's your earliest memory?**
D **What makes you unhappy?**
E **If you could edit your past, what do you think you would change?**
F **What was your most embarrassing moment?**
G **Who would you most like to say sorry to?**

c Read the interviews again using the glossary to help you. Answer the questions with **BC** (Benedict Cumberbatch) or **EM** (Elisabeth Moss).

Who...?

1 ☐ had an embarrassing experience as a child
2 ☐ finds it hard to make decisions
3 ☐ avoids answering one of the questions
4 ☐ had a dangerous experience when they were travelling abroad
5 ☐ had a dangerous experience when they were young
6 ☐ often hesitates when they're speaking
7 ☐ was fond of a kind of flower when they were a child
8 ☐ has a favourite decade

d Which of the questions in the interviews do you think is...?

- the most interesting
- the most boring
- too personal to ask a person who you don't know well

e Choose six questions from *Q&A* to ask your partner.

Every week the British newspaper, *The Guardian*, chooses people who have been in the news recently, and publishes a short interview with them called Q&A.

The actor **Benedict Cumberbatch** was born in London in 1976. He has starred in many successful TV series and films, including *Sherlock*, *War Horse*, *Star Trek*, and *The Hobbit*.

1 What's one of your happiest memories?
Sitting with the sun on my face and a beer in my hand, the morning after I had been in a car-jacking in South Africa.

2 _____
When I was six, I got stung by a wasp in a Greek market. A woman pulled down my pants and rubbed an onion on my bottom.

3 What don't you like about your personality?
I'm impatient, but also indecisive.

4 What is your greatest fear?
Forgetting people's names.

5 _____
The size and shape of my head. People say I look like Sid from *Ice Age*.

6 What costume would you wear to a fancy dress party?
I rather enjoyed wearing bandages round my face as the Invisible Man at the last one I went to. People got to know me without recognizing me.

7 Which words or phrases do you most overuse?
I say "Erm…" too much.

8 What one thing would improve the quality of your life?
Better time management.

9 _____
I might not have called Trevor Nunn, the famous director, 'Adrian' at my first audition for him.

The actress **Elisabeth Moss** was born in California in 1982. She has been in several very successful US TV dramas, including *The West Wing* and *Mad Men* for which she won an Emmy award.

1 _____
Going out into the backyard of my home in LA and pretending to build a vegetable garden with sticks and rocks. I must have been five.

2 **Which living person do you most admire?**
This is kind of cheesy, but my mum.

3 **Which living person do you most despise, and why?**
I won't say his name.

4 _____
Not getting enough sleep.

5 **What is your favourite smell?**
Jasmine. I grew up in Los Angeles, in the hills, and there was always jasmine growing.

6 _____
To a really good girlfriend with whom I lost touch when I was little. I would love to see her again.

7 **If you could go back in time, where would you go?**
To a 1930s jazz club in New York City. I love the art deco period – the jewellery, the clothes, the music.

8 _____
I am big fan of getting a box set and watching the entire show in two or three weeks. I'm watching *The Sopranos* at the moment, because I missed it when it first came out.

9 **What has been your most frightening experience?**
When I was little, I was on a lake in the US and got caught underneath a rowing boat. That was pretty scary.

> **Glossary**
> **car-jacking** the crime of forcing the driver of a car to take you somewhere or give you their car
> **Emmy** a US award similar to the Oscars, but for TV
> **backyard** *AmE* back garden
> **cheesy** *informal* too emotional or romantic in a way that is embarrassing, e.g. a cheesy love song

Adapted from The Guardian

2 GRAMMAR question formation

a Now read the questions in **1b** again and answer the questions below with a partner.

  1 Which questions are examples of…?
- a subject question, where there is no auxiliary verb
- a question which ends with a preposition
- a question which uses a negative auxiliary verb

  2 What happens to the word order in the question *What would you change?* when you add *do you think* after *what*?

b ➤ p.132 Grammar Bank 1A. Learn more about question formation, and practise it.

3 PRONUNCIATION
friendly intonation, showing interest

a (1 4)) Listen to some people asking questions 1–5. Who sounds friendlier and more interested each time, **a** or **b**?

> 1 Do you **have** a **big family**?
> 2 **What don't** you **like** about the **place** where you **live**?
> 3 **What sports** or **games** are you **good at**?
> 4 Do you **think** you **have** a **healthy diet**?
> 5 **What makes** you **feel happy**?

b (1 5)) Listen and repeat the questions with friendly intonation. Focus on sentence stress and linking.

> 🔍 **Reacting to what someone says**
> When you ask someone a question and they answer, it is normal to show interest by saying, e.g. *Really?* or *Oh yes?* with a friendly intonation, or by asking a question.

c (1 6)) Now listen to the questions in a conversation. Complete the expressions or questions that the man or woman use to react to the answers.

  1 *Wow* ! That's a huge family.
  2 _____? What's wrong with them?
  3 _____! We could have a game one day.
  4 _____! How long have you been a vegan?
  5 _____? I can't think of anything worse!

d (1 7)) Listen and repeat the responses. Copy the intonation.

e Ask and answer the questions with a partner. Use friendly intonation, and react to your partner's answers.

4 READING & VOCABULARY

a Look at the photo with the article. What do you think is happening? Do you think the question is one which someone might really ask in this situation? Why (not)?

b Read the article once and find out. How would *you* answer the question?

HOME / NEWS / UK NEWS / SOCIETY

Extreme interviews

WHAT sort of dinosaur are you? If you answered Tyrannosaurus rex, then the bad news is that you probably won't get the job you're applying for.

💬 Comment   🖶 Print

1 Welcome to the strange world of 'extreme interviewing', the latest trend from America in which interviewers throw bizarre questions at candidates to see how they react.

5 It may seem like a game, but extreme interviewing is deadly serious. The idea is to see how quickly job-seekers think on their feet and, at a time when 25% of recent graduates are unemployed, it offers employers a new way 10 of separating the brilliant candidates from the merely very good.

This new approach to selecting candidates comes from Silicon Valley in California — where else? Google, famous for its demanding 15 interview process, asked a recent candidate: 'You are stranded on a desert island. You have 60 seconds to choose people of 10 professions to come with you. Who do you choose? Go!'

So, what sort of dinosaur would you be?

A Tyrannosaurus rex!

One of the early pioneers of extreme interviewing was Steve Jobs, co-founder of Apple, who could 20 be famously cruel with job seekers. Faced once with a candidate he considered boring, Jobs suddenly pretended to be a chicken, flapping his arms and making clucking noises round the unfortunate applicant, waiting to see what he would do. In fact, the secret to extreme interviewing is neither in the question nor the answer. It is in the candidate's reaction.

David Moyle, a headhunter with the recruitment agency Eximius Group in London, who admits to using 25 the dinosaur question when selecting candidates, said: 'Essentially, that kind of interviewing is used by us to give someone an opportunity to show they are smart and not easily flustered.'

'Most candidates actually get something out of it, it's not about trying to crush them. We are trying to give them an opportunity to show their personality, rather than just showing how they perform in an interview.'

Of course, getting the job is just the start. In the modern business world, survival will depend on what sort 30 of dinosaur you really are.

Glossary

Silicon Valley the informal name for the region in northern California where many of the world's largest technology corporations are based

headhunter a person whose job it is to find people with the necessary skills to work for a company (often in executive posts), and to persuade them to join that company

Adapted from The Sunday Times

c Read the article again carefully. With a partner, try to work out what the highlighted words and phrases might mean, and how you think they are pronounced.

d Now match the words and phrases with 1–10.

> 1 _____ *adj* needing a lot of effort and skill
> 2 _____ *adj* nervous and confused, especially because you have been given a lot to do or are in a hurry
> 3 _____ *adj* very strange or unusual
> 4 _____ **IDM** to be able to think and react to things very quickly without any preparation
> 5 _____ *noun* a way of doing or thinking about something
> 6 _____ *phrase* instead of
> 7 _____ *verb* to destroy somebody's confidence
> 8 _____ *noun* a specialist company which finds and interviews candidates to fill job vacancies in other companies
> 9 _____ *noun* people who are looking for a job
> 10 _____ *verb* moving sth quickly up and down, e.g. wings

e (1 8)))) Listen and check. Under<u>line</u> the stressed syllables.

f Using your own words, answer the questions with a partner.

1 What are extreme interviews?
2 What kind of companies first started using them?
3 Why do some people think that they are better than normal interviews?

g Do you think extreme interviews are a good way of choosing candidates? Which of the questions below (used in real interviews) do you think would work well? Why?

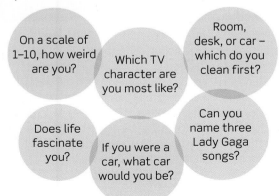

On a scale of 1–10, how weird are you?

Which TV character are you most like?

Room, desk, or car – which do you clean first?

Does life fascinate you?

If you were a car, what car would you be?

Can you name three Lady Gaga songs?

5 LISTENING

a Have you ever been for a job interview? What kind of questions did they ask you? Did you get the job?

b (1 9)))) Listen to five people talking about a strange question they were asked in job interviews. Complete the questions in the first column.

What strange question were they asked?	How did they answer?	What happened in the end?
1 Do you still _____ _____?		
2 What would make you _____ a _____?		
3 _____ _____ are you? How much _____ you _____?		
4 _____ _____ would you like to be reincarnated as?		
5 Are you planning to _____ _____?		

c Listen again and make notes in the rest of the chart.

d Which of the questions did you think were good or bad to ask at an interview?

6 SPEAKING

a ➤ **Communication** *Extreme interviews* **A** *p.104* **B** *p.108.* Ask your partner 'extreme interview' questions.

b Write three extreme interview questions of your own, which you think might tell you something interesting about another person.

c Ask your questions to as many other students as possible and answer theirs.

d Which questions did you think were the most interesting? Why?

G auxiliary verbs; *the...the...* + comparatives
V compound adjectives, modifiers
P intonation and sentence rhythm

" For those who believe,
no proof is necessary. For those who
don't believe, no proof is possible.

*Stuart Chase,
US author* "

1B Do you believe in it?

1 READING & LISTENING

a Look at the beginning of two true stories. What do you think they might have in common?

b ➤ **Communication** Work in pairs **A** and **B** and read two stories.
A read *Noises in the Night* on *p.104*. **B** go to *p.109* and read *The Strange Object on the Hill*.

HARD TO BELIEVE? BUT IT HAPPENED TO ME...
Have you ever experienced a paranormal happening? Write and tell us about it.

NOISES IN THE NIGHT

About six months ago, my husband Russ and I moved into a house in the country. Our house is the middle one of three terraced houses and it's more than a hundred years old. A young couple live in the house on our right, but the house on our left was empty and for sale.

THE STRANGE OBJECT ON THE HILL

This happened when I was 16, and I can still remember it vividly. It was a clear morning, sunny but with a breeze. I was going to meet a school friend to go walking in the hills where there were some wonderful views. I'd agreed to meet him at the top of one of the hills.

c Now read the beginning of another true story. Would you have been happy for Fatos to read *your* coffee cup? Why (not)?

THE COFFEE CUP READING

I went to Turkey a few years ago with a colleague called Chris. We'd been sent there by the British Council to train secondary school teachers in a school on the outskirts of Istanbul. While I was there I decided to go and see an old friend of mine, a young Turkish woman called Fatos, who I hadn't seen for several years. I called her and we agreed to meet in a hotel in the centre of Istanbul. Chris came too, and the three of us had a very pleasant dinner together. After dinner we ordered Turkish coffee and we chatted for a while, until Fatos suddenly asked me, 'Would you like me to read your coffee cup?' I refused politely because, to be honest, I don't really believe in clairvoyants and fortune-telling. But Chris immediately said he would be happy for her to read his coffee cup... *Adam, London*

d (**1 10**)) Listen to the rest of *The Coffee Cup Reading* and answer the questions.

1 What were the first two things Fatos saw in Chris's coffee cup? Were they accurate?
2 What was the third thing she saw?
3 How did Chris and Adam react to this?
4 Who did Chris's mother live with?
5 Where did Chris go the next morning?
6 Who called Adam? Why?
7 What was the bad news?
8 How did Fatos react to what had happened?
9 How does Adam feel about the experience?

e (**1 11**)) Listen to some extracts from the story and complete the missing words. Try to work out what they mean.

1 Well, Carla, Chris's girlfriend at the time, was blonde, so that was ____ ____, too.
2 But Chris is quite a ____-____ sort of person and he didn't seem to be too worried by what she'd said.
3 It was a slightly ____ end to what *had* been a very enjoyable evening.
4 So, was it just a ____ ____…?
5 I always used to be very ____ about fortune-telling…

2 SPEAKING

Talk in small groups.

Which of the three stories do you find the spookiest?
Can you think of any possible explanation for what happened in each story?

Have you (or anybody you know)...?
• seen or heard something which can't be explained, e.g. a UFO or a ghost
• visited a fortune-teller, psychic, or faith healer
• had a surprising coincidence

> 🔍 **Reacting to a story about something strange**
> When somebody talks about something strange or difficult to explain we often react with these phrases.
> *How / That's   strange; bizarre; odd; weird; spooky*

3 GRAMMAR auxiliary verbs

a Look at the dialogues and try to complete the gaps with a ⊞ or ⊟ auxiliary (*do, did, is, was*, etc.).

1 **A** I heard a noise in the middle of the night.
  B ¹____ you? What kind of noise?

2 **A** You don't believe in ghosts, ²____ you?
  B No, I don't.

3 **A** I don't believe you really saw a UFO.
  B I ³____ see one! It couldn't have been anything else.

4 **A** I've never been to a fortune-teller.
  B Neither ⁴____ I.
  C I ⁵____. It was really interesting.

b (**1 12**)) Listen and check. In pairs, decide which auxiliary (1–5) is used…

A ☐ to add emphasis
B ☐ to say that you are different
C ☐ to check information
D ☐ to show surprise
E ☐ to say that you are the same

c ➤ p.133 Grammar Bank 1B. Learn more about using auxiliary verbs, and practise them.

4 PRONUNCIATION
intonation and sentence rhythm

a (**1 14**)) Listen to the dialogues. Notice the stressed auxiliary verbs.

> **A** I **dreamt** that I **saw** a **ghost last night**.
> **B** **Did** you? So **did** I. **How spooky**!
>
> **A** I **don't believe** in **fortune-telling**.
> **B** **Don't** you? **I do**.

b Repeat the dialogues with a partner, copying the rhythm and intonation.

c Complete sentences 1–8 so that they are true for you.

1 I'm not very good at ____. (activity)
2 I'm going to ____ tonight. (verb phrase)
3 I love ____. (a kind of music)
4 I don't like ____. (a kind of food)
5 I've never read ____. (a famous book)
6 I'd love to live in ____. (a town or country)
7 I was very ____ as a child. (adj of personality)
8 I didn't ____ last night. (verb phrase)

d Work in pairs **A** and **B**. **A** read your sentences to **B**.
B respond with a reply question and then say whether you are the same or different. Then swap roles.

e (**1 15**)) Listen to another dialogue. Is *do* stressed in the highlighted phrases?

> **A** You don't like horror films, do you?
> **B** I do like them. It's just that sometimes they're too scary!

f Repeat the dialogue with a partner, copying the rhythm and intonation.

g ➤ **Communication** *You're psychic, aren't you?* **A** p.105 **B** p.109. Make guesses about your partner.

5 (**1 16**)) SONG *Unbelievable* ♫

6 LISTENING & SPEAKING

a On a piece of paper write the sentence *I look forward to hearing from you*. Then sign your name underneath and give the piece of paper to your partner.

b Look at the signatures of some famous people. Can you identify any of them? Do you know anything about these people's personalities?

c Read an extract from a book about graphology. Do you believe that our signature might say something about our personality?

What your *signature* says about you

Your signature is the part of your handwriting that says the most about your personality. It is quite common for your signature to change during your life because it reflects how you develop and evolve as a person. You may have more than one signature, for example a more formal signature (name and surname) when you sign a credit card or your passport, and an informal signature (just your first name) when you sign a birthday card.

Our signature is very much part of the way in which we present ourselves to the world, so it can give some important clues about the kind of person we are and how we feel about ourselves.

d (1 17, 18, 19, 20)) Listen to an expert in graphology talking about how to interpret somebody's personality from their signature. Complete the notes on the right.

> 🔍 **Taking notes**
> We often need to take notes when we are listening, for example to somebody giving a lecture. If you need to take notes when you are listening to someone speaking in English, try to write down key words or phrases because you won't have time to write complete sentences. Afterwards you could expand your notes into full sentences.

e In pairs, interpret the signatures of the famous people. Do any of the interpretations coincide with what you already thought?

f Now look at your partner's signature and try to interpret it. Do you agree with your partner's interpretation of *your* signature?

g Do you believe that you can learn anything about someone's personality by…?

- analysing their handwriting (graphology)
- looking at their hands (palmistry)
- analysing the position of the sun, moon, and planets at the exact time of their birth (astrology)
- another similar method

(1 17))) What's in your signature?

Your name =	*your private self*
Your surname =	
You use only initials either for your first name or your surname =	
There is a space between your name and surname =	

(1 18))) The size of your signature

Your first name is bigger than your surname =
Your surname is bigger than your first name =
Your whole signature is big =
You sign in capital letters =
Your signature is small =

(1 19))) The legibility of your signature

Your signature is legible =
Your signature is illegible =
The more illegible your signature is…

(1 20))) The angle of your signature

A rising signature =
A descending signature =
A horizontal signature =
The angle of a signature may change depending on…

7 MINI GRAMMAR
the...the... + comparatives

> The more space there is between your name and surname, the more you wish to keep separate these two parts of your personality.
>
> The more illegible your signature is, the less assertive you probably are as a person.

Use *the* + comparative adjective or adverb to show that one thing depends on another, e.g.

- *The sooner we start, the earlier we'll finish.* = how soon we will finish depends on when we start.
- *The colder it is, the more clothes you need to wear to keep warm.* = how many clothes you need to wear depends on how cold it is.

a Rewrite the sentences using *the...the* + comparative.

1 If you study a lot, you learn a lot.
The _____, the _____.
2 If we leave soon, we'll get there earlier.
The _____, the _____.
3 If you have a lot of time, you do things slowly.
The _____, the _____.
4 If you are fit, you feel good.
The _____, the _____.

b Complete the sentences in your own words.

1 The more money you have,...
2 The sooner you start your homework,...
3 The faster I speak in English,...
4 The less you sleep,...

8 VOCABULARY compound adjectives

a Look at some extracts from the listening in **6**. Can you remember what the gapped words were?

1 Some people actually sign in capital letters, which suggests that they may be big-_____ or even arrogant.
2 A descending signature...suggests that you are the kind of person who gets disheartened or depressed when you are faced with problems, perhaps because you are not very self-_____.
3 A horizontal signature usually indicates a person who is well-_____ and emotionally stable.

b (1 21)) Listen and check. Do the compound adjectives have a positive or negative meaning?

> **Compound adjectives**
> Compound adjectives are adjectives that have two parts. The second part often ends in *-ed* or *-ing*, e.g. *well-behaved, hard-working*. The words are normally linked by hyphens. The main stress is on the second word.

c With a partner, look at some more compound adjectives to describe a person's character. Use the two parts of the word to try to work out their meaning, and say if they are positive or negative characteristics.

bad-<u>tem</u>pered good-<u>tem</u>pered open-<u>mind</u>ed
narrow-<u>mind</u>ed absent-<u>mind</u>ed easy-<u>go</u>ing laid-<u>back</u>
tight-<u>fist</u>ed two-<u>faced</u> strong-<u>willed</u> self-<u>cen</u>tred

> *I think bad-tempered means somebody who gets angry very easily...*

d (1 22)) Listen and repeat the compound adjectives in **c**.

e Read the information on adjective modifiers.

> **Modifiers**
> We often use modifiers with adjectives of personality.
>
> **With positive characteristics**
>
> | My mum is | quite / pretty
very
really / incredibly | good-tempered |
> |---|---|---|
>
> **With negative characteristics**
>
> | My sister is | a bit
quite / rather / pretty
very
really / incredibly | bad-tempered |
> |---|---|---|

I SAID,'DON'T TALK TO ME!'

PEANUTS © 1966 Peanuts Worldwide LLC. Dist. By UNIVERSAL UCLICK. Reprinted with permission. All rights reserved.

f Tell the partner about people with the characteristics below. Give examples of their behaviour.

Do you know somebody who is...?

rather bad-tempered	a bit two-faced
extremely absent-minded	very good-tempered
a bit tight-fisted	incredibly strong-willed
pretty laid-back	quite self-centred

> *One of my cousins is a bit two-faced. She says one thing to me, and then I find out she said the exact opposite to somebody else in the family...*

1 ◼◀ THE INTERVIEW Part 1
VIDEO

a Read the biographical information about Ryan Judd. What do you think the HR department of a company does?

> **Ryan Judd** was born in 1976. He has been working as a recruitment advisor in the HR (Human Resources) department at Oxford University Press since 2010.

b (1 23)) Watch or listen to **Part 1** of an interview with him. Tick (✓) the things he says candidates for a job interview should do.

1 ☐ Be enthusiastic about the job
2 ☐ Call the interviewer by their first name
3 ☐ Ask questions about the job
4 ☐ Ask questions about the salary
5 ☐ Include a photograph on your CV
6 ☐ Write a good cover letter
7 ☐ Check everything is correct on your CV
8 ☐ Dress appropriately
9 ☐ Be prepared for the interview
10 ☐ Arrive on time

> **Glossary**
> **CV** the abbreviation for Curriculum Vitae, a written record of your education and the jobs you have done that you send when you are applying for a job
> **cover(ing) letter** a letter containing extra information which candidates send with their CV
> **recruiter** /rɪˈkruːtə/ the person who finds new people to join a company
> **salary banding** the level of pay given for certain jobs within a company

c Now listen again and answer the questions.

1 What kind of things does he ask candidates about to relax them before the interview?
2 What kind of things does he ask candidates at the beginning the interview?
3 What information should be given in a covering letter?

◼◀ Part 2
VIDEO

a (1 24)) Now watch or listen to **Part 2**. Which three interview situations did he find difficult or surprised him?

b Listen again and answer the questions.

1 What choice did he have with the first candidate he talks about?
2 What explanation for her behaviour did the second candidate give?
3 What kind of clothes does he think candidates should wear?
4 Why did the third candidate arrive in the wrong kind of clothes? Did he get the job?

> **Glossary**
> **A blazer** /ˈbleɪzə/ a smart jacket which is not worn with matching trousers

◼◀ Part 3
VIDEO

a (1 25)) Now watch or listen to **Part 3**. Complete the two 'extreme interview' questions he mentions.

1 How would you describe _____ to your _____?
2 Would you rather fight a horse-sized _____ or a hundred duck-sized _____?

b Listen again. Mark the sentences **T** (true) or **F** (false). Say why the **F** ones are false.

1 Ryan thinks the purpose of extreme interviewing is to see how candidates react in a strange situation.
2 He has used extreme interviewing on several occasions.
3 The first 'extreme' question he mentions was asked to see if the candidate had technical and communication skills.
4 The second 'extreme' question was asked to see if candidates had leadership potential.
5 Ryan thought that was a good question.
6 He would have chosen the first option.

interviews

2 ◼◣ LOOKING AT LANGUAGE
VIDEO

> 🔍 **Formal language**
> Ryan often uses more formal words and expressions than would normally be used in conversation, but would often be used in a more formal setting, e.g. a job interview.

①26)) Watch or listen to some extracts from the interview and replace the highlighted words or phrases with the more formal equivalent used by Ryan.

1 '…you're also looking for them to **show** experience relevant to the position.'
_____

2 'During an interview, once it has **begun**, I will always try to start the interview with some general questions…'
_____

3 'First thing is obviously, make mistakes on their application, um, that's always **seen** negatively…'
_____

4 '…but again during the interview when she hadn't **said** that's why she was doing it, it was a bit of a surprise.'
_____

5 '…you would expect, expect to see **suitable shoes** and the same for a, **a woman** as well…'
_____ _____ / _____

6 'It's not something that I have direct experience of, but I **know about** some of the techniques that they use…'
_____ _____

7 '…I'm not even sure if I would have been able to give an immediate **answer**…'
_____

3 ◼◣ IN THE STREET
VIDEO

a ①27)) Watch or listen to five people talking about job interviews. How many of them say they definitely got the job?

Jeanine, *South African*   Jo, *English*   Ivan, *American*   Yasuko, *American*   Joost, *Dutch*

b Watch or listen again. Who (**Je, Jo, I, Y,** or **Jst**)…?

☐ didn't get the job because of his / her age
☐ had their interview the most recently
☐ prepared for the interview by assessing how suitable he / she was for the job
☐ took some medicine to help make him / her feel less nervous
☐ tried to find out what the company believed in

c ①28)) Watch or listen and complete the highlighted Colloquial English phrases. What do you think they mean?

1 'I just practised every question that they could ask me in my _____.'
2 '…and then tried to _____ my experience to the various different points on the job interview…'
3 'I think it went well because they _____ up with an email.'
4 '… their philosophy, the history and the _____ of the company.'
5 'In the end, um, they said I was too young, um, so they didn't _____ me.'

4 SPEAKING

Answer the questions with a partner.

1 Have you ever been interviewed for a job or a place on a course? What was it for? How did you prepare for it? How did it go?
2 Have you ever interviewed another person? What for?
3 What do you think is the most important advice to give to someone who is going for a job interview?

G present perfect simple and continuous
V illnesses and injuries
P /ʃ/, /dʒ/, /tʃ/, and /k/; word stress

> My doctor gave me six months to live, but when I said I couldn't pay he gave me six months more.
>
> *Walter Matthau, US actor*

2A Call the doctor?

1 VOCABULARY illnesses and injuries

a Look at the six quiz questions. With a partner, decide what the highlighted words might mean. Use the pictures to help you.

b Now do the quiz with a partner.

c ➤ **Communication** *First aid quiz* **A** *p.105* **B** *p.109.* Read the answers to half of the quiz and the reasons why, and tell each other.

d ➤ **p.152 Vocabulary Bank** *Illnesses and injuries.*

Help save lives! The British Red Cross first aid quiz
www.redcross.org.uk/firstaid

Would you know what to do in these common medical emergencies?

1 **If someone is choking, you should…**
a) hit them on the back
b) lean them backwards
c) lie them on their side

2 **What is the best thing to put on a burn at first?**
a) warm running water
b) cold running water
c) kitchen film

3 **If someone has a cut which is bleeding badly, you should first…**
a) press on the wound
b) cover the wound
c) wash the wound under running water

4 **Which of these is the best way to treat a nose bleed?**
a) lean your head forwards and pinch the soft part of the nose
b) lean your head forwards and pinch the hard part of the nose
c) lean your head backwards and pinch the soft part of the nose

5 **If you find someone collapsed on the ground, what should you do first?**
a) put your jacket over them to keep them warm
b) check if they are breathing
c) run off to find someone else to help

6 **If someone has fallen and you think they may have broken their leg, you should…**
a) try to move their leg into a straight position
b) make sure the leg is supported to prevent unnecessary movement
c) put a bandage on their leg where you think the break is

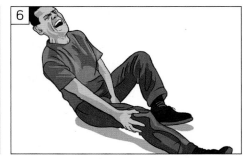

2 PRONUNCIATION & SPEAKING

/ʃ/, /dʒ/, /tʃ/, and /k/; word stress

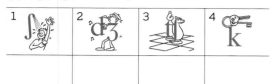

1 ʃ	2 dʒ	3	4 k

a How do you pronounce sounds 1–4 above? Write the words from the list in the correct column.

ache   allergy   ankle   bandage   choking
pressure   rash   stomach   temperature
unconscious

b ⓵ 33 ›)) Listen and check. Practise saying the words.

c ➤ p.167 Sound Bank. Look at the typical spellings for /ʃ/, /dʒ/, /tʃ/, and /k/.

d Look at some more words related to illness and injury. Which ones are similar in your language? Do you know what the other ones mean?

an|ti|bi|o|tics /ˌæntibaɪˈɒtɪks/   symp|tom /ˈsɪmptəm/
medi|cine /ˈmedsn/   e|mer|gen|cy /iˈmɜːdʒənsi/
o|pe|ra|tion /ɒpəˈreɪʃn/   as|pi|rin /ˈæspərɪn/
spe|cial|ist /ˈspeʃəlɪst/   pa|ra|ce|ta|mol /ˌpærəˈsiːtəmɒl/
X-|ray /ˈeks reɪ/   cho|les|te|rol /kəˈlestərɒl/
in|jec|tion /ɪnˈdʒekʃn/   scan /skæn/

e ⓵ 34 ›)) Listen and under<u>line</u> the stressed syllable. Practise saying the words.

f Ask and answer the questions with a partner.

1 **What injuries or illnesses might you get when you are...?**
a) cooking
b) doing sport
c) eating in a restaurant
Have any of these things ever happened to you?

2 **Have you ever been in a situation where you had to give first aid? Who to? Why? What happened?**
How much do you know about first aid? Where did you learn it?
Has anyone ever had to give you first aid? What happened?

3 **What do you think you should do if...?**
a) someone has a very high temperature
b) someone is stung by a wasp and has an allergic reaction
c) someone has very bad sunburn

3 GRAMMAR   present perfect simple and continuous

a ⓵ 35 ›)) Listen to a conversation between a doctor and patient. What symptoms does the patient have? What does the doctor suggest?

b Listen again and complete the gaps with a verb in the present perfect simple or present perfect continuous.

> **Doctor** Good morning, Mr Blaine. What's the problem?
> **Patient** I ¹_____ well for a few days. I keep getting headaches, and I ²_____ a lot, too. And I have a temperature.
> **D** ³_____ anything for the headaches?
> **P** Yes, paracetamol. But they don't really help. I read on the internet that headaches can be the first symptom of a brain tumour...
> **D** How many tablets ⁴_____ so far today?
> **P** I took two this morning.
> **D** And have you taken your temperature this morning?
> **P** Yes. I ⁵_____ it five or six times. It's high.
> **D** Let me see... Well, your temperature seems to be perfectly normal now.
> **P** I think I need a blood test. I ⁶_____ one for two months.
> **D** Well, Mr Blaine, you know I think we should wait for a few days and see how your symptoms develop. Can you send the next patient in please, nurse?

c ⓵ 36 ›)) Listen to what the doctor and nurse say after Mr Blaine has left. What do they think of him?

d Look at the sentences and (circle) the right verb form. Tick (✓) if you think both forms are possible.

1 Have you *been taking* / *taken* anything for the headaches?
2 How many tablets have you *been taking* / *taken* so far today?

e ➤ p.134 Grammar Bank 2A. Learn more about the present perfect simple and continuous, and practise them.

f In pairs, use the prompts to ask and answer the questions. The first question should be present simple or continuous, and the second should be present perfect simple or continuous.

1 | often *get* colds? How many colds | *have* in the last three months?
2 | *take* any vitamins or supplements at the moment? How long | *take* them?
3 | *drink* much water? How many glasses | *drink* today?
4 | *do* any exercise? What? How long | *do* it?
5 | *eat* a lot of fruit and vegetables? How many portions | *have* today?
6 | *walk* to school (or work or university)? How far | *walk* today?
7 How many hours | *sleep* a night? | *sleep* well recently?
8 | *allergic* anything? | ever *have* a serious allergic reaction?

4 WRITING

➤ p.113 Writing *An informal email.* Write an email to a friend explaining that you haven't been well, and saying what you've been doing recently.

5 READING & VOCABULARY

a Look at the title of the article. How would you define a hypochondriac? What do you think a 'cyberchondriac' is?

Oh no! Just what I have!

b Read the article once and check. Then complete the paragraphs with topic sentences A–E.

> 🔍 **Topic sentences**
> In a well written article each paragraph usually begins with a 'topic sentence' which tells you what the paragraph is about.

A Another problem for cyberchondriacs is that online medical information may be from an unreliable source or be out of date.

B Sadly, the problem with Dr Google is that he isn't exactly a comfort in times of crisis.

C The Microsoft study also revealed another serious problem – that online information often doesn't discriminate between common and very rare conditions.

D Unfortunately, once you have it cyberchondria can be hard to cure.

E Four hours later I got a diagnosis.

CONFESSIONS OF A
cyberchondriac

A few weeks ago I was feeling under the weather. After days of intensive internet diagnosis, I finally went to see my GP. After examining me she told me that my heart rate was a bit fast and sent me off to A&E to have some tests. Did I go straight there? Of course not. First I took out my phone, logged on to Google, and found out that the technical term for a fast heart rate is supraventricular tachycardia. Then I typed these two words into Google.

1 _____

For example, *wrongdiagnosis.com* immediately scared me with a list of 407 possible causes. I raced to the hospital, convinced that I probably needed open-heart surgery.

2 _____

I had a chest infection…and a bad case of cyberchondria. The only consolation for the latter condition is that I'm in good company. A Microsoft survey of one million internet users last year found that 2% of all searches were health-related.

3 _____

Since my trip to hospital, I have been obsessively checking my pulse, swapping symptoms in chatrooms, and reading all about worst-case scenarios. What if the doctors got it wrong? What if the ECG machine was faulty? It's exhausting trying to convince yourself that you might have a life-threatening illness.

4 _____

One in four of all articles thrown up by an internet search for 'headache' suggested a brain tumour as a possible cause. Although it is true that this <u>may</u> be the cause, in fact brain tumours develop in fewer than one in 50,000 people. People also assume that the first answers that come up in searches refer to the most common causes, so if you type in 'mouth ulcer' and see that 'mouth cancer' has several mentions near the top, you think that it must be very common. However, this is not the case at all.

5 _____

A recent American study showed that 75% of the people who use the internet to look up information about their health do not check where that information came from, or the date it was created. 'Once something has been put up on the internet, even if it's wrong, it's difficult to remove,' says Sarah Jarvis, a doctor. 'This is a problem especially with scare stories, and also with some alternative remedies which claim to be miracle cures, but which may actually do you harm.'

Check the information? Sorry, I don't have time – I'm off to buy a heart rate monitor!

> **Glossary**
> **GP** general practitioner (= family doctor)
> **A&E** Accident and Emergency department of a hospital
> **ECG machine** electrocardiogram machine used to test people's heart rate
> **scare stories** stories in the news, e.g. 'Mobile phones give you cancer' which make people worry about their health

Adapted from The Sunday Times

c With a partner, look at the highlighted words and phrases and guess what they mean. Then match them with definitions 1–11.

More medical vocabulary		
1	_____ *adj*	sth very serious, which could kill you
2	_____ *noun*	a small blister in the mouth that can be very painful, but is not serious
3	_____ *noun*	ways of curing illnesses that are not traditional medicine, e.g. herbal medicine
4	_____ **IDM**	not feeling very well
5	_____ *noun*	a serious illness in which malignant cells form in the body and kill normal body cells
6	_____ *noun*	an illness that is caused by bacteria or a virus
7	_____ *noun*	the speed at which your heart beats
8	_____ *noun*	the medical treatment of an illness or injury that involves an operation
9	_____ *noun*	the number of times your heart beats in a minute
10	_____ *noun*	a group of cells that are growing in a place where they should not be
11	_____ *noun*	successful treatments for illnesses that were thought to be impossible to cure

d (1 40)) Listen and check.

e Read the article again carefully. Choose a, b, or c.

1 The first thing the journalist did after leaving her GP was…
   a go and see a specialist
   b go to A&E
   c find out what her condition was called

2 After realizing that she was a cyberchondriac, she…
   a stopped worrying
   b worried just as much as before
   c stopped visiting health-related websites

3 One problem with health-related websites on the internet is that…
   a they make unusual illnesses seem more common than they really are
   b they often describe conditions which don't really exist
   c they give more information about rare illnesses than about common ones

4 Another problem with these websites is that…
   a they encourage people to go to the doctor more often
   b they make people believe in miracle cures
   c the information may not be right

6 LISTENING & SPEAKING

a (1 41)) Listen to a radio interview with a doctor about cyberchondria. What's her general opinion of patients using health websites?

b Listen again. Then answer the questions with a partner.

1 What did a patient she saw recently think he had? What did he really have?

2 What four things does she say that diagnosis depends on apart from symptoms?

3 What kind of website forums does she recommend?

4 Complete the three tips she gives to cyberchondriacs:
   i *Only look online…*
   ii *Make sure that the website you are using is…*
   iii *Remember that common symptoms usually…*

c With a partner, or in small groups, answer the questions. Ask for and give as much information as possible.

1 Which of the doctor's three tips do you think is the most important?

2 How often do you look up information about health and illness on the internet? What websites do you usually go to? How useful is the information?

3 Do you know anyone who you think is a hyperchondriac or cyberchondriac?

4 Do you think people in your country worry a lot about…?
   a their blood pressure
   b their cholesterol level
   c their eyesight
   Do they worry about anything else related to health?

7 (1 42)) **SONG** *Just Like a Pill* ♫

G using adjectives as nouns, adjective order
V clothes and fashion
P vowel sounds

"It's true, some wines improve with age. But only if the grapes were good in the first place.

Abigail Van Buren,
US journalist"

2B Older and wiser?

1 SPEAKING

a Look at some adjectives which are commonly used to describe teenagers or elderly people. With a partner, write them in the column where you think they belong. Are the majority of the adjectives positive or negative?

---

absent-minded adventurous bad-tempered
clumsy kind lazy moody narrow-minded
self-centred stubborn unenthusiastic
vulnerable weak wise

---

teenagers	elderly people

> 🔍 **old** or **elderly**?
> *Old* and *elderly* mean the same thing, but *elderly* is only used for people and is more polite.

b In pairs or small groups, discuss the questions.

1 Do you think the adjectives in **a** truly describe most teenagers and elderly people or do you think these are stereotypes?

2 In what way might these stereotypes be damaging?

3 Do you know people in these two age groups who a) conform to the stereotypes b) don't conform to the stereotypes? How?

2 READING

a Look at the photos of Nick Sydney and Karoline Bell. What do you think has been done to them and why?

b Read the first paragraph of the article once and check your answer. Look at the highlighted phrases related to the body. With a partner, say what you think they mean.

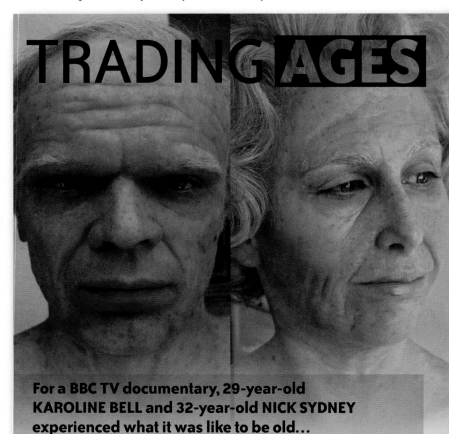

TRADING AGES

For a BBC TV documentary, 29-year-old KAROLINE BELL and 32-year-old NICK SYDNEY experienced what it was like to be old…

It took five hours every morning to make Karoline and Nick look like elderly people in their seventies. They were given synthetic wrinkled skin, false teeth, and grey wigs. They also wore body suits to make them look fatter and contact lenses to make their eyes look older. The discomfort of the make-up, the heavy suits, and the contact lenses (which made their eyesight worse) gave them a small taste of the physical problems of old  age. They were also coached to walk and speak like people in their seventies. Then they had to live each day, for a month, as an old person, with a video diary to record their experiences and hidden cameras to record how other people reacted to them.

c You are going to read about what happened in the programme. Before you read, talk to a partner.

1 In what way do you think people treated them differently because they appeared to be old people?

2 What do you think they learnt about what old age is really like?

3 How do you think they felt after making the programme?

d Now read the rest of the article and check.

1 **A**fterwards both of them described the 'invisibility' of being old. Karoline was astonished to be ignored by some workmen, who only hours before had been wolf-whistling
5 at her when she had been an attractive young woman. Nick said 'I learnt that how people [1]treat you depends on what you look like.' On one occasion a bus driver treated him very rudely when he tried to pay his fare with a large note. 'I was amazed. He
10 wouldn't have talked like that to my young self.' Nick was also nearly robbed when he was taking money out of a cash machine.

There is a point in the documentary when Karoline [2]breaks down and cries. It comes at the end
15 of a day out with her two new pensioner friends, Betty and Sylvia, who she met at a day centre. It is partly because she feels guilty that she is tricking them, but mainly because she realizes that they are individuals, and not just members of what she had
20 previously thought of as 'the elderly'. 'They were talking about real things and I felt unqualified. I didn't have that life experience. They had [3]been through so much. It made me realize how ignorant I was. It was as if I was seeing the young
25 people inside them. Before I would have just seen the wrinkles.'

At the start of the documentary Karoline had said that old people scared her, and that in spite of loving her 86-year-old grandmother, who lives in a
30 home, she had found it difficult to visit her.

Both she and Nick found making the programme life-changing. Nick said 'I'd never thought about getting old before.' Karoline said 'The whole experience of living as an old person helped me to understand
35 them far better and also to understand myself. One of the things that surprised me most was how important relationships still were to elderly people. I was shocked by the fact that older people could still have their hearts broken. After a while I felt like
40 one of them. I felt in a way that they were just young people in an old body trying to [4]deal with the problems of old age. [5]I'm not ready to be 73, but I'm not scared like I was.'

Adapted from The Times

e Read the article again and answer the questions with **K** (Karoline), **N** (Nick), or **B** (both of them).

Who...?

1 ☐ found the physical preparation for their role very uncomfortable

2 ☐ was given classes on how to move like an elderly person

3 ☐ was surprised not be noticed by people who had previously reacted to him / her

4 ☐ noticed that people were less polite to older people

5 ☐ found that playing the role of an older person made him / her more emotional

6 ☐ realized that old people were very different from what he / she had previously imagined

7 ☐ used to be frightened of old people

8 ☐ had never worried about what it would be like to be old

9 ☐ hadn't expected love and friendship to be so important to old people

f Now look at the highlighted verb phrases and match them with their meaning.

☐ be prepared ☐ loses control of his / her feelings
☐ behave towards you ☐ solve a problem or do a task
☐ experienced

g How much contact do you normally have with elderly people? Do you think that they are treated well in your country?

3 GRAMMAR
using adjectives as nouns, adjective order

a Look at the sentences in 1 and 2 below and decide if you think they are right (✔) or wrong (✘). Compare with a partner and say why you think the crossed ones are wrong.

1 a ☐ The old have a harder life than the young.
  b ☐ The old people have a harder life than the young people.
  c ☐ Old people have a harder life than young people.
2 a ☐ The man was with a blonde tall Swedish woman.
  b ☐ The man was with a tall Swedish blonde woman.
  c ☐ The man was with a tall blonde Swedish woman.

b ➤ **p.135 Grammar Bank 2B.** Learn more about using adjective as nouns, and adjective order, and practise them.

c Discuss the statements below in pairs or small groups. Do you agree? Why (not)?

- The elderly are best looked after in residential homes, not at home.
- Politicians should be at least 40 years old – younger people don't have enough experience for such a responsible job.
- Society doesn't sufficiently value the wisdom that elderly people have.
- Rich people are usually meaner than poor people.
- The government could and should do more for the unemployed.
- The homeless should be allowed to live rent-free in empty second homes.

4 LISTENING

BEST DRESSED LIST

Adele

Jane Fonda

Gareth Malone

Mick Jagger

a Look at the photos. How old do you think these people are? Do you like the way they are dressed? Why (not)?

b (1 45)) Listen to a radio programme where two fashion journalists are talking about 'dressing your age'. Do they agree that men and women should dress their age? Complete their two fashion rules.

Liza	Wear whatever you think _____ and makes you _____ .
Adrian	Dress for _____ , not for _____ .

c Listen again and make notes. Why do the journalists mention the following?

Liza	Adrian
• a warm cardigan and slippers	• men in their 20s who
• a leather miniskirt	wear blazers and
• teenagers	chinos or suits
• women of 30+	• men in their 30s
• very short shorts	

d Who do you agree with most, Liza or Adrian?

5 VOCABULARY clothes and fashion

a In two minutes write down as many items of clothing or jewellery as you can that you can wear…

• on your hands and arms • round your neck • on your feet • on your head

b ➤ p.153 Vocabulary Bank *Clothes and fashion.*

c Do the quiz with a partner.

CLOTHES QUIZ

1 **What are the opposites of these adjectives and verbs?**

get dressed   short-sleeved
smart   tight   trendy

2 **What material are the following usually made of?**

cycling shorts   jeans   shoes
a sweater   a tie   tights

3 **Complete the sentence you say if something, e.g. a sweater…**

a   is too big   *It doesn't* [____] *me.*
b   looks awful on you   *It doesn't* [____] *me.*
c   goes perfectly with your trousers   *It* [____] *my trousers.*

4 **In what situations do you normally…?**

a   try clothes on   c   hang clothes up
b   dress up   d   get changed

6 PRONUNCIATION
vowel sounds

a Look at the sound pictures below. Which are short sounds, which are long, and which are diphthongs?

boot	bull	fish

bird	bike	train

b (1 50)) In pairs, put two words in each column. Listen and check.

fur hooded lace linen loose lycra
plain put on shirt shoes silk skirt
slippers striped suede suit tight wool

c ➤ **p.166 Sound Bank.** Look at the typical spellings for these sounds.

d Practise saying these phrases.

- a loose linen suit
- pink silk slippers
- blue suede shoes
- a tight lycra skirt
- a red and white striped tie
- a pale grey suede jacket

7 SPEAKING

Talk in small groups.

1 At what age do you think it is OK for men or women to have…?

grey or white hair   very long hair   pink streaked hair   a piercing
an earring in one ear   a tattoo

I think pink streaked hair looks great at any age.

I don't agree. I think it looks ridiculous unless you're under 20.

2 In what situations do you think it is <u>not</u> OK to wear…?

torn denim jeans   a baseball cap worn backwards
very short shorts   large sunglasses   a mini-skirt   no shirt

3 Do you agree or disagree with the following statements? Say why.

You shouldn't judge other people by the way they dress.

It's better to buy cheap clothes that don't last because then you can buy new ones more often.

People who follow fashion are usually vain and selfish.

It's very risky to buy clothes online.

Only sheep follow fashion. Good dressers have their own style.

Fur coats should be banned.

Women, but not men, are always expected to dress smartly for work or on TV.

8 WRITING

a Imagine you were given two items of clothing for your birthday which you don't like. You have decided to sell them on eBay. Write a detailed description, making them sound as attractive as possible. Set a starting price.

For sale! Blue and white striped cotton skirt – never worn! Size 40. Would look great with white T-shirt. Perfect for the summer.

£3.99
1 bid

+£3.00 postage

7 days left
Thursday 24 April 15:36

b Now read some other students' adverts. Are there any things that you'd like to bid for?

1&2 Revise and Check

GRAMMAR

a Complete the sentences with one word.

1 What were you and Sarah talking _____?
2 You didn't like her latest novel, _____ you?
3 My father loves opera and so _____ my mother.
4 **A** I've been to India twice. **B** _____ you? I'd love to go.
5 What have you _____ doing since I last saw you?

b Circle a, b, or c.

1 Could you tell me what time _____?
a the bus leaves b leaves the bus c does the bus leave
2 How many people _____ this computer?
a do use b use c does use
3 You're not eating much. _____ like the food?
a You don't b Don't you c Aren't you
4 **A** Why didn't you call me?
B I _____, but your phone was switched off.
a do call b did called c did call
5 The slower you work, _____ you'll finish.
a later b the later c the later than
6 _____ three cups of coffee already this morning.
a I've been having b I've had c I have
7 That was probably the worst film_____!
a I've ever seen b I've never seen
c I've ever been seeing
8 I met _____ at my language class today.
a a Swiss b the Swiss c a Swiss girl
9 Some people think that _____ don't pay enough tax.
a the rich b the rich people c rich
10 I got a _____ bag for my birthday.
a beautiful leather Italian b Italian leather beautiful
c beautiful Italian leather

VOCABULARY

a Complete the compound adjectives.

1 My boss is very bad-_____. When things go wrong he starts shouting at everyone.
2 I'm very _____-minded. I tend to forget things .
3 I think Paul is a bit tight-_____. He never spends money unless he absolutely has to.
4 Sylvia won't have any problems at the interview – she's very self-_____.
5 That dress is very old-_____. It looks like the kind of thing my granny would wear.

b Write words for the definitions.

1 **bl**_____ *verb* to lose blood, from a wound or injury
2 **sw**_____ *adj* bigger than normal, especially because of an injury or infection
3 **b**_____ *noun* a piece of cloth used to tie round a part of the body that has been hurt
4 **t**_____ *noun* a pain in one of your teeth
5 **r**_____ *noun* an area of red spots caused by an illness or allergy

c Circle the right verb or verb phrase.

1 I *have | feel* a bit dizzy. I need to sit down.
2 She *burnt | sprained* her ankle when she was jogging.
3 It was so hot in the room that I nearly *fainted | choked*.
4 This skirt doesn't *fit | suit* me. It's a bit too big.
5 Can I go in jeans? I don't feel like *getting dressed | getting changed*.

d Circle the word that is different.

1 striped spotted plain patterned
2 silk cotton fur smart
3 collar sleeveless hooded long-sleeved
4 lycra scarf vest cardigan
5 fashionable scruffy stylish trendy

e Complete with one word.

1 My mother had very bad flu last week, but she's beginning to get _____ it now.
2 Please lie _____ on the couch over there.
3 I'm feeling sick. I think I'm going to _____ up.
4 Do we really need to dress _____ for the party tonight?
5 Please _____ up your clothes in the wardrobe.

PRONUNCIATION

a Circle the word with a different sound.

1 ache choke checked matches
2 unconscious rash fashion suede
3 injury striped silk blister
4 allergic burnt wear fur
5 cough flu suit loose

b Underline the main stressed syllable.

1 in|cre|di|bly 2 big-|hea|ded 3 an|ti|bi|o|tics
4 swim|suit 5 fa|shio|na|ble

CAN YOU UNDERSTAND THIS TEXT?

a Read the article once. What do shamans do?

b Read the article again and choose a, b, or c.

1 According to the article, shamans help people to…
   a communicate with dead relatives
   b solve their health problems
   c enter a parallel reality

2 Shamans heal people by…
   a curing their depression
   b helping them to find something they have lost
   c dealing with their deep emotional problems

3 Harnam Sidhu and Shelly Khanna…
   a both had serious diseases
   b did not initially believe that shamanism could help them
   c have both become more deeply interested in shamanism

4 According to Klinger-Paul, shamanism…
   a requires time to work
   b only works if people believe in it
   c may work only because of the placebo effect

c Choose five words or phrases from the text. Check their meaning and pronunciation and try to learn them.

◼◀ CAN YOU UNDERSTAND THIS FILM?

VIDEO

① 51)) Watch or listen to a short film on the History of Surgery and mark the sentences **T** (true) or **F** (false).

1 St Thomas' hospital had a very early operating theatre.
2 In a modern operating theatre there is a monitor to measure a patient's brain activity.
3 The room where the operating theatre used to be is now a church.
4 The rooms where operations took place were called theatres because the public came to watch.
5 The theatre was usually full for an operation.
6 Most operations at St Thomas' were done on rich people.
7 Surgeons used primitive forms of anaesthetic.
8 Surgeons could cut off a limb very quickly.
9 When there was a lot of blood during an operation, it was collected in a space under the floor.
10 If patients died, their bodies were given back to their families.

The rise of the shamans

The sound of drumbeats reverberates in the small conference room as the shaman goes into a trance. The others present, their eyes closed, focus on the rhythmic sounds of the drums. The shaman, in his trance, makes the journey to a parallel reality in search of solutions to the various problems the group has brought with it.

For most people this may seem weird, but it is becoming a fairly common experience for others. People from many different professions – students, businessmen, housewives, even former soldiers – are turning to shamanism, an ancient spiritual practice where the practitioner communes with 'spirit guides' to gain access to information and healing.

Cosima Klinger-Paul, an Austrian who moved to India in 2000 and has started a school of shamanism, says that the interest in the practice is not surprising. 'Shamanism has always been there in every culture. It is the oldest healing method of mankind.'

How exactly does shamanism work? Shamans believe that all illnesses have a spiritual cause, which is reflected in the physical body. Healing the spiritual cause heals the physical body. An important shamanic belief is the concept of 'soul loss'. Shamanic cultures around the world believe that whenever someone suffers an extreme physical or emotional trauma, a piece of his soul 'falls off'. Soul loss manifests in most people through feelings of emptiness and depression. Once the person gets the missing part of his soul back, shamans believe that the lost vitality and health also comes back.

But is it really as simplistic as this? Those who have undergone shamanic healing sessions seem to think so. Harnam Sidhu, a 46-year-old marketing executive, swears by the practice. 'It helped reverse my disease,' he says. Sidhu was suffering from glaucoma – a degenerative condition that causes the loss of optic nerves leading to blindness. Doctors had told him it was a matter of months before he went completely blind in the bad eye. As a last resort, he tried out shamanism. After a few sessions, when he went for a check-up, his doctor told him that a miracle had happened – his condition was starting to reverse. Shelly Khanna, who took shamanic healing for a frozen shoulder condition, says 80% of her pain vanished after the session. 'I went as a sceptic, but I was so amazed by the experience that I resolved to learn shamanism myself.'

Was it really shamanism at work or simply the placebo effect? Believers stress that shamanic healing is an established tradition that has been tested time and again over centuries. 'Shamanism is not a religion, but an adventure into one's own mind,' says Klinger-Paul. 'It takes time to become familiar and to deal with the spirit world. I tend to say no to requests for quick healing. This is not a spiritual aspirin that you can take and be healed.'

Atul Sethi in The Times of India

G narrative tenses, past perfect continuous; *so / such...that*
V air travel
P regular and irregular past forms, sentence rhythm

"
I don't have a fear of flying,
I have a fear of crashing.

*Billy Bob Thornton,
US actor and singer* "

3A The truth about air travel

1 LISTENING & VOCABULARY air travel

a 🔊 **2 2))** Listen to some in-flight announcements and match them to pictures A–D. What information or instructions are the passengers being given?

 A 4
 B 2
 C 3
 D 1

Air Travel: *the inside story*

Air Babylon is a best-selling book, co-written by Imogen Edwards-Jones and anonymous airline staff whose identities must remain secret. It tells the 'inside story' about flying and answers all these questions and many more...

- Is it really worth listening to the safety demonstration telling you how to put your life jacket on?
- Why is there usually a big mirror when you are going through Customs?
- Why can you sometimes smell roast chicken in a plane when they are serving you fish?
- Why do airport staff get annoyed with some passengers who ask for a wheelchair?

ISBN ...716-6

b Listen again. What word or phrase do the flight attendants use to mean…?

1 *small bags and cases* hand head luggage
2 *the cupboards above your seat* overhead
3 *put on* your seat belt fasten compartments.
4 *phones, tablets*, etc. Personal electronic devices.
5 *the doors* where you can get out of the plane quickly if there is a problem emergency exits
6 the *thing you have to put on* if the plane is going to land on the sea life jacket
7 to *blow air* inside something Inflate

c ▶ p.154 Vocabulary Bank *Air travel.*

2 READING

a Read the back cover of a book about air travel. Can you guess the answers to any of the questions?

b Now read the extract from *Air Babylon*. What are the answers to the questions, according to the text?

c Now read the extract again and mark the sentences **T** (true) or **F** (false). Underline the part of the text that gave you the answer.

1 Most airline passengers believe that the life jacket could save their life.
2 The passengers who inflated their life jackets too early didn't survive.
3 Customs officers can see through the mirror in Customs.
4 Passengers are often caught by customs officers because of their body language.
5 Small birds are more dangerous for planes than big birds.
6 Passengers get confused because what they can smell is not on the menu.
7 There aren't enough wheelchairs for all the people who need them.
8 One flight attendant sometimes makes sarcastic comments about passengers who don't really need a wheelchair.

d Did you find any of the information surprising? Which? Do you believe it at all?

1 **M**ost airline passengers think it is laughable that a small yellow life jacket with a whistle will make any difference if the plane crashes into the sea. However, in some cases, like when
5 a hijacked Ethiopian Airlines Boeing 767 landed in the Indian Ocean in 1996, it did. Despite instructions from the cabin crew not to pre-inflate their lifejackets inside the plane, several passengers did. They were unable to escape the
10 rising water inside the plane. But others, who followed the pilot's instructions, survived. So it is probably a good idea to look up from your magazine when the flight attendant is giving the safety demonstration.

15 **C**ustoms officers are watching everywhere. They are watching you from the moment you walk off the plane, while you are standing in Baggage Reclaim waiting for your bag, and especially when you come out the other side of
20 Customs, which is when people who are trying to smuggle something finally let their guard down and get caught. The large two-way mirror in Customs, (behind which customs officers sit and watch) is part of that process. As you walk
25 past, it makes you look taller and thinner. So you feel good about yourself and you relax and smile. That's when a customs officer suddenly appears and asks you to open your case…

Birds are one of the major problems for any
30 airport when planes are taking off and landing. Any large bird can easily cause an accident. It flies into the engine, totally destroying itself and the machinery. Smaller birds are less of a problem. In some cases they can do some
35 damage, but usually they are just roasted. When this happens, there is often such a strong smell of roast bird that passengers on the plane think that chicken is being cooked, and they are often surprised when they're given a choice of fish or
40 beef at dinner!

Wheelchairs are a big problem for airline staff. Not only is there always a shortage of them for the people who really need them, but worse still, some of the people who request
45 them often don't need them at all. I've lost count of the number of times I have pushed someone through the airport, taken them through Customs and Passport Control, got a porter to pick up their luggage, and then seen the person jump up in
50 Arrivals and move quickly towards their waiting relatives. One flight attendant I know gets so annoyed when this happens that as soon as the passenger gets out of the chair she shouts to the other passengers, 'Ladies and gentlemen!
55 Another miracle, courtesy of the airline industry! After years in a wheelchair, he walks again!' The passenger is normally so embarrassed that he (and it's usually a 'he') disappears as quickly as he can.

From Air Babylon *by Imogen Edwards-Jones*

3 MINI GRAMMAR *so / such…that*

a Look at these two sentences from the *Air Babylon* extract.

> The passenger is normally so embarrassed that he disappears as quickly as possible.

> When this happens there is often such a strong smell of roast bird that passengers on the plane think that chicken is being cooked.

We often use *so / such…that* to express a consequence.
- Use *so* + adjective
  The flight was so bumpy (that) we all felt sick.
- Use *so* + adverb
  The taxi driver drove so quickly (that) we got to the airport on time.
- Use *so much / so many* + noun
  There was so much traffic that we nearly missed our flight.
- Use *such a* + adjective + single countable noun
  It was such a great hotel (that) we want to go back there next year.
- Use *such* + adjective + uncountable noun
  We had such terrible weather that we didn't really enjoy the holiday.
- Use *such* + adjective + plural noun
  They were such uncomfortable seats (that) I couldn't sleep at all.

b Complete the sentences with *so, so much | many, such,* or *such a.*
1 The flight was ~~so~~ long that I got really bored.
2 I had ~~such a~~ noisy child sitting beside me that I couldn't sleep at all.
3 My suitcase was ~~so~~ heavy that I had to pay excess baggage.
4 I slept ~~so~~ badly on the flight from New York that the jet lag was worse than usual.
5 We were served ~~such~~ terrible food that I couldn't eat a thing.
6 There were ~~so many~~ people at check-in that we had to queue for ages.
7 We had ~~so much~~ luggage that we had to get another trolley.
8 The people we met on holiday were ~~such~~ nice people that we kept in touch with them.

4 SPEAKING

In pairs, ask and answer the questions.
1 How do you feel about flying?
2 How often do you fly? What for?
3 When was the last flight you took? Where did you fly to?
4 Have you ever…
   - been very delayed at an airport? How long for?
   - missed a flight? Why?
   - been stopped in Customs? Were you carrying anything that you shouldn't have?
   - had very bad turbulence on a flight? How did you feel? Was anyone on the flight injured?
   - flown long haul? Did you get jet lag?
   - flown or been upgraded to business class? What was it like?
   - been on a flight where there was an emergency? What happened?
   - sat next to a screaming baby on a flight (or a child that kept kicking your seat)? What did you do?

5 LISTENING

a You are going to listen to an airline pilot and an air traffic controller talking on a radio programme. Before you listen, discuss questions 1–8 with a partner and imagine what the answers will be.

1 What weather conditions are the most dangerous when you are flying a plane?
2 Is turbulence really dangerous?
3 Which is more dangerous, taking off or landing?
4 Are some airports more dangerous than others?
5 What personal qualities does an air traffic controller need?
6 Is the job really very stressful?
7 Why is it important for air traffic controllers and pilots to speak English well?
8 Are there more men than women working as pilots and air traffic controllers?

b (2 7)» Listen to the programme. How many of the questions did you answer correctly?

c Listen again for more detail and make notes for each of the questions.

d Which job would you prefer, to work as a pilot or as an air traffic controller? Why?

6 GRAMMAR

narrative tenses, past perfect continuous

a Read a newspaper story about an incident that happened during a flight. What exactly happened?

Last updated at 09:12

Nightmare over the Atlantic!

At 11.35 on January 13th 2012 British Airways flight BA 0206 ¹***took off / was taking off* from Miami to London.** It had been flying for about three hours, and was over the Atlantic, when suddenly a voice ²*came out / had come out* of the loudspeakers: 'This is an emergency announcement. We may shortly have to make an emergency landing on water.'

Immediately panic ³*broke out / was breaking out*. One passenger on the flight said, 'My wife and I looked at each other and we feared the worst. We imagined that we were about to crash into the Atlantic. It was awful. Everybody ⁴*screamed / was screaming*.' complete

But about 30 seconds later the cabin crew started to run up and down the aisle saying that the message ⁵*had been played / was being played* by accident, and that everything was OK. By this time a lot of the passengers were in tears, and ⁶*tried / were trying* to get their life jackets out from under their seats.

Another passenger said, 'The captain didn't even say anything about it until just before we started to land and even then he didn't explain what ⁷*happened / had happened*. It was very traumatic. Everybody was terrified. I can't think of anything worse than being told your plane's about to crash. It ⁸*was / had been* the worst experience of my life.'

Later a British Airways spokesman ⁹*said / had said*, 'A pre-recorded emergency announcement was activated by error on our flight from Miami to Heathrow. We would like to apologize to passengers on this flight.'

Adapted from the Daily Telegraph

b Read the story again and circle the right form of the verbs 1–9.

c Now look at two sentences about the story. What do you think is the difference between the two highlighted verbs?

The pilot was very experienced and had flown this route many times before.
When the announcement was made the plane had been flying for about three hours.

d ➤ p.136 Grammar Bank 3A. Learn more about narrative tenses and the past perfect continuous, and practise them.

e In pairs or groups, try to complete the two sentences in four different ways using the four narrative tenses.

1 The police stopped the driver because he…
2 I couldn't sleep last night because…

7 PRONUNCIATION

irregular past forms, sentence rhythm

a Write the past simple of the following verbs in the chart according to the pronunciation of the vowel sound.

| ~~become~~ ~~catch~~ cut drive fall fly hear |
| hide fight hold hurt keep leave lie read |
| ride say sleep tell think throw write |

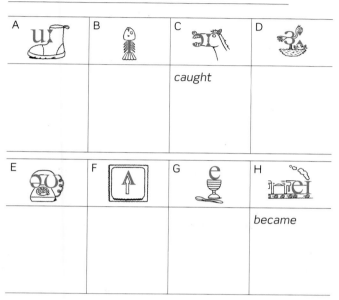

A	B	C	D
		caught	

E	F	G	H
			became

b Look at the verbs in **a** again. Which ones have a past participle which is different from the past simple form? Write these past participles in the chart.

c (2 10)) Listen and check. Then listen and repeat.

d (2 11)) Listen to an extract from a narrative. Notice which are the stressed and unstressed words.

We were on a **flight** to **Tokyo**, and we'd been **flying** for about **five hours**. I was **reading** and my **wife** was **watching** a **film** when **suddenly** we **heard** a **very loud noise**. It **sounded** as if an **engine** had **exploded**. The **pilot didn't tell** us what had **happened** until **half** an **hour later**.

e Practise reading the extract with the right rhythm.

8 SPEAKING

a ➤ **Communication** *Flight stories* **A** *p.105* **B** *p.110.* Read a newspaper story. Then imagine you were a passenger on the plane, and tell your partner the story.

b You are going to tell an anecdote. The story can either be true or invented. If it's invented, you must try to tell it in such a convincing way that your partner thinks it's true. Choose <u>one</u> of the topics below and plan what you're going to say. Use the language in the **Telling an anecdote** box to help you, and ask your teacher for any other words you need.

Talk about a time when you...

had a frightening experience when you were travelling or on holiday

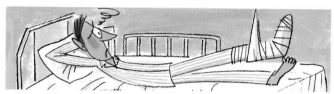

got ill or had an accident while travelling

arrived home from a trip and had a surprise

> 🔍 **Telling an anecdote**
>
> **Setting the scene**
> *This happened to me when I was...*
> *I was...-ing when...*   *I...because I had / hadn't...*
>
> **The main events**
> *I decided to...because...*   *So then I...*
> *Suddenly / At that moment...*
>
> **What happened in the end**
> *In the end / eventually...*   *I felt...*

c In pairs, **A** tell **B** your story. **B** show interest and ask for more details. Then decide whether you think the story is true or not. Then swap roles.

This happened to me a few years ago when I was on holiday in Florida. I was swimming in the sea one day when I saw a shark.

Really? How big was it?

9 (2 12)) **SONG** *The Airplane Song* 🎵

G the position of adverbs and adverbial phrases
V adverbs and adverbial phrases
P word stress and intonation

> If you want a happy ending, that depends, of course, on where you stop your story.
>
> *Orson Welles*
> *US actor and director*

3B Incredibly short stories

1 GRAMMAR the position of adverbs and adverbial phrases

a Read the four fifty-word stories, using the glossary to help you. Match each one to its title.

The story of my life   Generation gap   Revenge is sweet   Hooligans

fiftywordstories.com

Fiftywordstories.com is a website to which people from all over the world contribute fifty-word stories in English.

A _____

The young men walked aggressively through the crowded shopping centre. They had their target in their sights, and wouldn't stop until they had done what they had set out to do.

Now she felt scared. She ran from the hooded gang, stopped, and was cornered.

'Miss, you forgot your handbag.'

C _____

He was worried. Unfortunately, since his wife's death his teenage daughter had become extremely difficult. They had agreed 2.00 a.m. as the latest return time from nightclubs. Now it was 3.30. He prepared himself for confrontation as the door opened. 'Dad,' she shouted angrily. 'I've been frantic. You're late again.'

Glossary

A
target *noun* objective, goal
hooded *adj* with the hood of a coat covering your face
set out to do sth PV to begin an action with a particular goal in mind

B
stab *verb* to push a knife into sb or sth
cliff *noun* a high area of rock often at the edge of the sea
brakes *noun* the things that you use to stop a car

C
frantic *adj* very worried

D
fabulous *adj* wonderful
intake *noun* the amount of food and drink that you take into your body
pudding *noun* dessert

B _____

They had been arguing bitterly the night before. He had come in from the garage with oil on his shoes. Fed up, desperate, she stabbed him. Horrified by what she had done, she drove away from the house along the cliff road. Suddenly she realized that the brakes weren't working.

D _____

Stage one: Feel fat. Go on diet. Lose weight. Feel fabulous. Buy new clothes.

Stage two: Eat normally but controlling intake. Look fabulous. New clothes slightly tight.

Stage three: Eat and drink normally (potatoes, bread, pudding AND wine). New clothes don't fit. Old clothes thrown away.

Back to stage one.

b Look at the highlighted adverbs or adverbial phrases in the stories. Think about what they mean and notice their position in the sentence. Write them in the correct place in the chart.

Types of adverbs
Time (when things happen, e.g. *immediately*)
~~now~~ *suddenly*
Manner (how you do something, e.g. *slowly*)
~~angrily~~ *aggressively* *bitterly* *normally*
Degree (describing / modifying an adjective, e.g. *very*)
slightly *extremely*
Comment (giving an opinion, e.g. *luckily*)
Unfortunately

c With a partner, decide where the **bold** adverbs should go in these sentences.

1 He speaks French and Spanish. **fluently**
2 I use public transport. **hardly ever** (*rarely*)
3 I thought I'd lost my phone, but it was in my bag. **fortunately**
4 It's important that you arrive on time. **extremely**
5 As soon as I know, I'll tell you. **straightaway**

d ➤ **p.137 Grammar Bank 3B.** Learn more about adverbs and adverbial phrases, and practise them.

e ② 14)) Listen to some sound effects and short dialogues. Then use the **bold** adverb to complete the sentence.

1 When she got to the bus stop, the bus… **just**

_____

2 They were having a party when… **suddenly**

_____

3 He thought he had lost his boarding pass, but… **luckily**

_____

4 The woman thought Andrea and Tom were friends, but in fact… **hardly**

_____

5 The driver couldn't see where he was going because… **hard**

_____

6 Alain couldn't understand the man because… **incredibly**

_____

2 VOCABULARY adverbs and adverbial

a Read another fifty-word story. Who is it about?

Exam nerves

It was nearly 4 a.m. and she c
keep her eyes open. She had been working
hard since lunchtime, but the exam was near.
Would she be able to finish in time? At nine
the next morning she was in the classroom.
'OK,' she said. 'You can start now.'

b Look at the highlighted adverbs. What's the difference between…?

a *hard* and *hardly*   b *near* and *nearly*

c ➤ **p.155 Vocabulary Bank** *Adverbs and adverbial phrases.*

3 PRONUNCIATION word stress and intonation

a ② 17)) Underline the stressed syllables in these adverbs. Listen and check.

ac|tua|lly al|most a|ppar|ent|ly ba|sic|ally def|in|ite|ly
e|ven e|ven|tual|ly for|tu|nate|ly gra|dua|lly i|dea|lly
in|cre|dib|ly luck|il|ly ob|vi|ous|ly un|for|tu|nate|ly

b ② 18)) Listen and repeat the sentences, copying the stress and intonation of the adverbs.

1 There was a lot of traffic, and unfortunately we arrived extremely late.
2 We definitely want to go abroad this summer, ideally somewhere hot.
3 It's incredibly easy – even a child could do it!
4 Mark gradually began to realize that Lily didn't love him any more.
5 I thought Roberto was Portuguese, but actually he's Brazilian.
6 Apparently Jack has been offered a promotion at work, but it will mean moving to New York.
7 I absolutely love Italian food, especially pasta.

4 WRITING

a You are going to write a fifty-word story. It must be 50 words exactly (not including the title) and you must include at least two adverbs. Contracted forms (e.g. *I'd*) count as one word. First, in pairs, choose two of the titles below.

A holiday romance   **A day to forget**
The lie   **Never again**

b Brainstorm ideas for the two plots, and each write a first draft without worrying about the number of words.

c Swap your drafts then edit the stories, making sure they are exactly 50 words.

d Read two other pairs' stories. Which do you like best?

e ➤ **p.114 Writing** *A short story.* Write a 120–180 word short story.

...AKING

Ask and answer the questions in the *Reading habits* questionnaire with a partner.

b How similar are your reading habits?

Reading habits

The press

national newspapers	free papers
local papers	comics
sports papers	academic journals

Books

novels	non-fiction, e.g. self-help books
classics	short stories
textbooks	manuals

Online

web pages	academic or work-related websites
blogs	news websites
chat forums	song lyrics

General reading

- Which of the above do you read? How often?
- Do you ever read any of them in English?
- Do you read anything specifically to improve your English?
- Do you prefer reading on paper or on screen?
- Do you read more or less than you used to (or about the same)?

Do you read books for pleasure?

⟩ YES

- What was the last book you read?
- Why did you choose to read it?
- What are you reading at the moment?
- Do you have a favourite author or authors?
- What's the best book you've read recently?

⟩ NO

- Would you read more if you had more time?
- Did you use to read more when you were younger? When did you stop? Did you have a favourite children's book?
- What do you do to pass the time when you are travelling?

Reading and listening

Do you ever...?

- listen to a song and read the lyrics at the same time
- watch films or TV in English with English subtitles
- read books and listen to them on audio at the same time, e.g. Graded Readers

6 READING & LISTENING

a **2 19))** Read and listen to **Part 1** of an American short story. Answer the questions with a partner.

1 Where does Susan want Stan to take her? To do what? *shooting range protect herself*
2 Why is Stan surprised? *because she always hate guns.*
3 What had happened to Susan the previous week? *she was robbed*
4 Why does the writer say about Susan 'She was right, of course, except about the 'hard-earned' part.'? *She didn't work hard.*

Lazy Susan

BY NANCY PICKARD

' I want you to teach me how to shoot a gun,' Susan Carpenter said to her husband at breakfast.

'You want me to do *what?*' Stan Carpenter stared at her, a piece of toast in his hand.

'Take me to a shooting range.' Susan placed a couple of mushrooms and a fried egg carefully onto her bread to make a sandwich. It seemed a silly waste of effort to eat only one thing at a time. Her husband's surprise turned to delight.

'I think that's a wonderful idea!'

Ever since she'd been robbed the week before on a dark night in the parking lot of the Mulberry Street Shopping Center, Stan had been telling her to learn how to protect herself, preferably with a gun.

'Are you serious about this? You've always hated guns.'

'Well, it looks like you win, dear.'

'We'll go to a range tonight,' Stan promised.

Susan had been more angry than scared when she was robbed that night. He hadn't hurt her much, just a light knock on the head with his gun before he took her purse. It was only a little injury added to the greater insult. She was so angry about it!

'Fifty dollars!' she said incredulously to the nice police officer. 'One minute I had fifty dollars in my purse and the next minute I had nothing. Fifty hard-earned dollars gone, just gone! I have to work *hours* to earn that much money, and he comes along and takes it just like that!'

She was right, of course, except about the 'hard-earned' part. That was a bit of an exaggeration. True, she did have a job as a receptionist in a sales office, but she didn't exactly work hard for her money. Oh, she was at work for eight hours every day, and she smiled at all the customers, and her bosses liked her, most people liked her. But there was more work that didn't get done than did. As she was always saying to her friends, 'Oh, well, you know me ... "Lazy Susan".'

Glossary
parking lot noun *AmE* for car park
purse noun *AmE* for a woman's bag

b (2 20)» Look at the glossary and make sure you know how the words are pronounced, and what they mean. Now listen to **Part 2**. Then answer the questions with a partner.

> **Glossary**
> **aimed** /eɪmd/ *verb* pointed a weapon at sth
> **mugging** /'mʌgɪŋ/ *noun* the crime of attacking sb, or threatening to do so, in order to steal from them
> **trigger** /'trɪgə/ *noun* the part of a gun that you press in order to fire it
> **John Wayne** an American actor who often starred in Western and war films
> **tough** /tʌf/ *adj* strong enough to deal with a difficult situation
> **bushes** /'bʊʃɪz/ *noun* medium-sized plants like small trees

1 Where are Susan and Stan at the beginning of **Part 2**?
2 How does Susan feel about shooting? *Smill pheasent*
3 According to the instructor, who is the typical victim of a mugging? *little Old women whoable week*
4 What kind of person does the mugger avoid? *a strong fit hands free.*
5 How does the instructor recommend they should walk in order to look tough and confident? *confidly shede free Pwse ewnn*
6 How does the instructor say they can recognize a mugger? *→ Dark dother hide at the bushes.*
7 What did he teach them in the previous two classes?
8 What surprises Stan about Susan? *Delighot, confidice has Susa. Doing very well.*

c (2 21)» Read and listen to **Part 3**. Answer the questions with a partner.

The shops were closed when the movie-goers came out into the dark Mulberry Street Shopping Center parking lot. It had been one of the Superman films and Susan felt inspired. Stan would not have approved of her going to the movies alone, especially not back to the place where she was robbed. But he was away and she'd taken all those self-defense lessons. Now she knew a thing or two.

A group of dark bushes were between her and her car. She walked confidently straight through them, then she stopped. She bent down slightly, and turned to look carefully behind her. She saw the man before he saw her. Everything she'd learned in her classes went through her mind: she looked at his walk, the look on his shadowed face, the object in his hands. Her breathing got quicker. She thought of the hours she'd worked to earn those fifty dollars, and of the so-and-so who had stolen it from her so easily. She took from her pocket the little gun that Stan had taught her to use. Then, just as the man walked past the bushes, she jumped behind him so he couldn't see her.

1 What effect did watching *Superman* have on Susan? *She felt inspired.*
2 How did Susan feel about going to the cinema alone this time?
3 What did she think about when she saw the man? *Confidence.*
4 Look at the highlighted words and phrases and try to work out their meaning from the context.
5 What do you think is going to happen next? →

d (2 22)» Listen to the end of the story. In pairs, discuss what you think happened, and what Susan is going to do in the future. Do you like the way the story ended? Did it end the way you expected?

> 🔍 **Graded Readers**
> This story is in a Graded Reader (from the Oxford Bookworm series level 6) called American Crime Stories. Remember that the more you read, the more vocabulary you learn, and the better your English will become.

1 ◼◀ THE INTERVIEW Part 1
VIDEO

a Read the biographical information about Julia Eccleshare and look at the book covers: have you read any of them?

> **Julia Eccleshare** is a well-known British journalist and writer on the subject of children's books. She has been children's book editor for the *Guardian* newspaper since 2000. She regularly appears as a judge or Chair of judges on some of the major children's book prizes, and is particularly interested in how to encourage children and young people to read. Julia was awarded the Eleanor Farjeon Prize in 2000 in recognition of her outstanding contribution to children's books. She has four children and lives in London.

b (2 23))) Watch or listen to **Part 1** of an interview with her. Why does she mention these four books?

Warrior Scarlet   Little House on the Prairie (author)
Mouse House   Northern Lights
(author),   (author)

c Now listen again and mark the sentences **T** (true) or **F** (false). Say why the **F** sentences are false.

1 Julia has only re-read *Warrior Scarlet* once since she was a child. F
2 She thinks people have very clear memories about books they loved as children. T
3 Her parents read to her a lot when she was a child. F
4 Her husband didn't want to read to the children at the end of a long day. F
5 One of the things she loves about Philip Pullman's books is that they make children think. T

> **Glossary**
> **warrior** /ˈwɒriə/ a person who fights in a battle or war (especially in the past)
> **His Dark Materials trilogy** a series of three fantasy novels by the author Philip Pullman consisting of *Northern Lights*, *The Subtle Knife*, and *The Amber Spyglass*. A film based on *Northern Lights* was released in 2007 called *The Golden Compass*.

◼◀ Part 2
VIDEO

a (2 24))) Now watch or listen to **Part 2**. Number the photos in the order she mentions them.

b Listen again. Circle the right answer.

1 The one big thing that she thinks makes a child a reader is *learning to read early | finding the right book*.
2 When teenagers have seen a film it *often | rarely* makes them want to read the book.
3 Parents sometimes think that children *should | shouldn't* read books which are difficult.
4 Jacqueline Wilson is an example of an author who *parents | children* used to think was very good but *parents | children* didn't.
5 Julia thinks that children *should | shouldn't* only read books which are of high literary quality.

> **Glossary**
> **a teen anthem** a song which young people strongly identify with. Here Julia uses the expression to describe a novel.
> **a literary stylist** a writer who writes in a very literary style

children's books

a **(2 25)》** Now watch or listen to **Part 3**. Answer the
questions.

1 Does she read print books, e-books, or both?
2 Does she think people will read fewer books because
of all the new technology?
3 Does she still read for pleasure?

b Listen again. What is she referring to when she says the
following things?

1 'I think we are, ought to, sort of, stop seeing the two in
polarity, I think, you know. Everybody is going to read
both.'
2 'So the book has always been under threat from these
other media…'
3 '…I know you can do both, but most people don't…'
4 '…but as you get older it's just harder to carve out time
like that and there's always something else pressing…'
5 '…and you have that kind of chemical moment when
the story grabs you…'

2 ▶◀ LOOKING AT LANGUAGE
VIDEO

> 🔍 **Ways of giving yourself time to think**
> Julia often gives herself time to think when she's
> answering questions, either by stopping and starting
> again, sometimes in a slightly different way, or by using
> 'filler' sounds, e.g. 'um' and 'er', and certain words or
> phrases, e.g. 'well', 'I mean', etc. that don't add meaning
> but which we use for this purpose.

(2 26)》 Watch or listen to some extracts from the
interview and complete the missing words or phrases.

1 '_Well_, that's interesting, because if I think back to it…'
2 '…I think, there's a lot of, of talk about how children
learn to read and all of this but _____ , and what
strategy might be best, but actually what makes a
reader…'
3 'Well, I think the biggest inspiration that I, I would,
_____ I would like to say again…'
4 'You take a book like _The Beach_, _____ it wasn't a
book that was written for children…'
5 '…it was a _____ almost a teen anthem novel…'
6 'And what do you say about someone like JK Rowling
who is, _____ , not a great literary stylist…'

3 ▶◀ IN THE STREET
VIDEO

a **(2 27)》** Watch or listen to three people talking about
children's books. Match the speakers (**C**, **S**, and **L**)
with the book titles they mention.

Charlie, _English_   Sean, _English_   Lucy, _English_

☐ _Northern Lights_   ☐ The Famous Five
☐ _The Lion, the Witch and the Wardrobe_
☐ _Dear Zoo_   ☐ The Roald Dahl books

b Watch or listen again. Who (**C**, **S**, or **L**)…?

☐ had favourite authors rather than favourite books
☐ heard their favourite book before reading it
☐ identified with a particular situation rather than
specific characters
☐ identified with naughty children in general
☐ liked a book because it was about something he / she
wasn't allowed to have
☐ liked an author's books especially because of the
pictures in them

c **(2 28)》** Watch or listen and complete the highlighted
Colloquial English phrases. What do you think they
mean?

1 'I liked the _____ that the boy got lots of different
animals through the post…'
2 '…she was like a tomboy, so I _____ liked the idea
of being quite adventurous…'
3 'I remember we had a teacher at school who read it
_____ to us…'
4 '…so whenever there was a, a boy who got into lots
of _____…'
5 '…I loved because it just offered a really detailed other
world, to just _____ into…'

4 SPEAKING

Answer the questions with a partner. Practise using
'fillers' to give yourself time to think.

1 What was your favourite book when you were a child?
Why did you like it so much?
2 Was there a character in a children's book that you
identified with when you were a child?
3 Did your parents use to read to you? When and where?
4 Do you read more print books or more e-books? Why?

G future perfect and future continuous
V the environment, the weather
P vowel sounds

4A Eco-guilt

1 READING & SPEAKING

a Look at the title of the lesson. What do you think it means?

b Read the introduction to the article and check. Then do the questionnaire and add up your score.

c Now compare your answers with a partner. Explain why you do or don't do these things. See what your score means. Do you agree with it?

How ECO-GUILTY are you?

I committed a crime last Tuesday, which just happened to be Earth Day*, a day that invites people to think about their eco-sins. I turned on the shower, intending to get straight in even though the water takes a while to warm up. But then I decided to brush my teeth, and suddenly the water had been running for over two minutes. By the time I got in, I was drowning in eco-guilt! I had wasted water…

Should you feel eco-guilty, too? Take the test.

SHOPPING BAGS

☐ I have a reusable shopping bag made of recyclable materials, which I always use when I'm shopping. ♻♻♻♻ (+4 eco-points)

☐ I own several reusable shopping bags, but I often forget to bring them with me. ♻♻♻ (-3 eco-points)

☐ I always ask for plastic bags because they're convenient. They can be recycled, can't they? ♻♻♻♻ (-4)

WASHING TOWELS

☐ I wash my towels immediately after I use them. ♻♻♻♻♻ (-5)

☐ I use a towel for several days before I put it in the washing machine. ♻ (+1)

☐ That reminds me, I must wash my towels! ♻♻♻ (+3)

RUNNING WATER

☐ I never leave the water running when I brush my teeth, nor before getting into the shower. ♻♻ (+2)

☐ I'm allergic to cold water, so I have to leave the shower to run for a while before I get in. ♻♻ (-2)

☐ I hate showers. I need a hot bath every day to relax. ♻♻♻ (-3)

BUYING FRUIT AND VEGETABLES

☐ I never buy fruit and vegetables at supermarkets. I buy organic fruit and vegetables in markets or small shops. ♻♻♻ (+3)

☐ I buy some fruit and vegetables in a market, but the supermarket is more convenient. ♻♻ (-2)

☐ I shop at the cheapest places – who cares about eco-guilt, I feel guiltier if I spend too much money on food!. ♻♻♻♻♻ (-5)

*Earth Day an annual day (22nd April) on which events are held worldwide to increase awareness and appreciation of the environment

RECYCLING

☐ I throw everything in the same bin. ♻♻♻♻♻ (-6)

☐ I sometimes recycle glass bottles, especially after a party! But that's probably all. ♻♻♻♻ (-4)

☐ I recycle all my newspapers, bottles, and plastic containers. ♻♻♻♻♻ (+5)

GETTING AROUND

☐ I walk, use public transport or cycle because cars pollute the planet. ♻♻♻♻♻ (+5)

☐ I walk, use public transport or cycle because I can't afford to buy a car. ♻ (-1)

☐ Vroom vroom here I come! ♻♻♻♻♻ (-5)

So how guilty should you feel?

Below 0: You should feel very guilty.

0–12 points: You should feel quite guilty.

Above 10: You are too good to be true!

Adapted from the Chicago Times

2 GRAMMAR future perfect and future continuous

a Read some predictions that have been made about the next 20 years. Which ones do you think…?

1 are already happening
2 are likely to happen
3 probably won't happen

How we will be living in 20 years' time… (or will we?)

At home

Most people will have installed solar panels or wind turbines on their houses or blocks of flats to generate their electricity.

People will be recycling nearly 100% of their waste (and those who don't will have to pay a fine).

Transport

Cars that use a lot of petrol (e.g. four-by-four cars) will have been banned and many people will be driving electric cars.

Low-cost airlines will have disappeared and flights will be much more expensive.

The environment

Paper books will no longer be produced to save trees from being cut down, and all books will be electronic.

Fresh water will be running out in many parts of the world and we will be getting much of our water from the sea (through desalination plants).

The weather

Temperatures worldwide will have risen even further. Many ski resorts will have closed because of a lack of winter snow and some beaches and holiday resorts will have disappeared completely.

We will be having even more extreme weather, and heatwaves, hurricanes, floods, etc. will be frequent occurrences.

b Read the predictions again. Which two would you most and least like to come true?

c Look at the highlighted verbs in the predictions. Which ones refer to…?

a an action or situation that will be finished in the future (*future perfect*)

b an action or situation which will be in progress in the future (*future continuous*)

d ➤ p.138 Grammar Bank 4A. Learn more about the future perfect and the continuous, and practise them.

e Talk to a partner and say if you think the following predictions will happen. Explain why (not).

IN TWENTY YEARS' TIME…

- Most people in office jobs will be working from home.
- All private swimming pools and golf courses will have been banned.
- Most people will be using public transport or bikes to get to work.
- People will be having more holidays in their own country and fewer abroad.
- People will be retiring at 70 or even later.
- The teaching of handwriting will have disappeared from the school curriculum because students will only be writing on tablets or laptops.

> 🔍 *definitely, probably,* and *likely / unlikely*
> We often use *definitely, probably,* and *likely / unlikely* when talking about the future, especially when we are making predictions.
> *I think*   *it'll definitely happen /*
> *it definitely won't happen.*
> *it'll probably happen /*
> *it probably won't happen.*
> *it's (very) likely (to happen) /*
> *it's (very) unlikely (to happen).*

3 READING & VOCABULARY
the weather

a Look at the cartoon. What does it say about British weather? Would it be true about your country?

We're all going on a... summer holiday...

www.CartoonStock.com

b Read the article once. At what time of year was the article written? What is an Indian summer?

c Read the article again and mark the sentences **T** (true) or **F** (false). <u>Underline</u> the sentence or part of the article that gives you the answer.

1 British people talk about the weather more than they used to.
2 People had mixed feelings about the hot weather.
3 Some weather experts said that the warm weather was not an Indian summer because it happened in September.
4 The older English term for Indian summers is still used in some parts of the UK.
5 Kate Fox says that the British talk about the weather because they are shy.
6 Sir John Mortimer believes that the British talk about the weather to avoid saying what they really think.

d Look at the highlighted phrases related to the weather. With a partner, say what you think they mean.

e ➤ p.156 Vocabulary Bank *Weather.*

f Do you have an expression for Indian summer in your language? Do people in your country often talk about the weather? Why (not)?

Don't know what to say?
Talk about the weather!

1 'It is commonly observed,' wrote Dr Johnson in 1758, 'that when two Englishmen meet, their first talk is of the weather; they are in haste to tell each other, what each must already know, that it is hot or cold, bright or cloudy, windy or calm.' Not much has
5 changed. A survey published earlier this year found that the average British person mentions the weather at least once every six hours, and that 70 per cent of us check the weather forecast every day, even when nothing unusual is happening.

Last week, as temperatures soared to 29°C – the highest recorded
10 end-of-September temperature for 116 years – there was a sense of both delight (at the lovely hot weather) and worry (about the threat of global warming). On television and in the newspapers, experts argued earnestly over what such extreme weather meant, and if there was even a term for it. While many called it an Indian summer, the
15 Met Office ruled that it couldn't be properly called an Indian summer, which only occurs 'as a warm spell in autumn, especially in October and November'. The BBC's main weatherman also agreed that the heat had arrived a bit too early to be described as an Indian summer.

Indian summer has different names across the globe. In Britain, until
20 around the end of the First World War, late heatwaves were known as 'St Martin's summers' – the feast of St Martin falling on 11th November – and in much of Europe they still are. Other countries have their own names – in Russia it's an 'Old Ladies' summer'; in Bulgaria a 'Gipsy summer'; and in China a 'Tiger autumn'.

25 But the big difference between the British and other nationalities is that they talk about Indian summers much more. 'Britons need weather-talk to help us overcome our reserve,' explains Kate Fox, author of *Watching the English*. 'We talk about it a lot, but not because it is an intrinsically interesting topic. People use weather-talk to
30 facilitate social interaction.'

The writer Sir John Mortimer saw a deeper reason for Britain's peculiar obsession with the weather. 'There's nothing personal about it,' he wrote. 'It gives away no secrets. Talking to our next-door neighbours over the fence, we, as a nation, are reluctant to make
35 such uncomfortable confessions as 'I can't stand your children', or 'I'm passionately in love with your wife'. It's far easier to say, 'I think we'll be having rain over the weekend'.'

Lovely weather for ducks!

Glossary
Dr Johnson a very influential 18th century writer and editor
the Met Office the UK's national weather service

4 PRONUNCIATION
vowel sounds

> **🔍 Spelling and pronunciation**
> Most vowels, or combinations of vowels, can be pronounced in more than one way. If you are unsure what the vowel sound is in a new word, check with your dictionary.

a Look at the groups of words below and (circle) the word you think is different.

1 blow   snow   showers   below
2 weather   sweat   heavy   heat
3 drizzle   blizzard   chilly   mild
4 hard   warm   dark   garden
5 flood   cool   soon   loose
6 fought   ought   drought   brought
7 thunder   sunny   hurricane   humid
8 scorching   world   tornado   storm

b **2 34**))) Listen and check.

c **2 35**))) Listen and write five sentences. Then practise saying them.

d Talk to a partner.

- What kind of weather do you associate with the different seasons where you live?
- What's the weather like today? Have you heard the forecast for tomorrow / next weekend?
- What's your favourite weather? Does the weather affect your mood? What do you like doing when the weather is bad?
- What kind of weather do you think is the best and the worst for…?
  a camping
  b going for a walk in the mountains
  c driving
  d running a marathon
  e shopping
  f sightseeing
- Do you think global warming is affecting the climate? In what ways has climate change affected the weather in your country?

5 LISTENING & SPEAKING

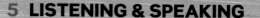

a **2 36**))) You're going to listen to three people talking about their experiences of extreme weather in the UK. Listen once. Which speaker…?

3 was both frightened and excited by the weather
2 got quite stressed because of the weather
1 really enjoyed themselves in spite of the bad weather

b Listen again and make notes in the chart.

	Speaker 1	Speaker 2	Speaker 3
When did it happen?	New year's eve.	so ptober In the summer of 2003	In october 1987.
Where were they at the time?	North of England in the pub in Yorkshire	London	Boarding school
What kind of weather was it?	Snow Blizzard. snowstorm	boiling heatwave scorching	drizzling, thunder. windy Hurricane
What happened as a result?	They had to stay 4 days.	they had to go to a clinic	they have to stay at home, broke window, 17. flabours car falls.

> **🔍 Modifiers with strong adjectives**
> When you are talking about extreme situations, e.g. very bad weather you can use:
> 1 Normal adjectives with a modifier (*very, really, extremely, incredibly, unbelievably*), e.g. *It was incredibly cold, extremely hot, unbelievably windy*, etc.
> 2 Strong adjectives, e.g. *It's boiling here – 40 degrees, It's freezing today*, etc.
> 3 Strong adjectives with *absolutely*, e.g. *It was absolutely freezing. The midday heat was absolutely scorching.*
> Remember that we often use *a bit* or *rather* + adjective to express a negative idea, e.g. *It's a bit too hot. It's rather chilly today.*

c In small groups, talk about a time when you were somewhere when…

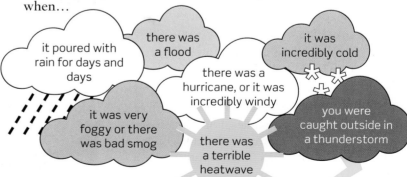

it poured with rain for days and days

there was a flood

it was incredibly cold

there was a hurricane, or it was incredibly windy

it was very foggy or there was bad smog

there was a terrible heatwave

you were caught outside in a thunderstorm

Where were you and what were you doing?
What did you do to protect yourself from the weather?
Did you ever feel scared or in danger?

6 **2 37**))) **SONG** *Heatwave* 🎵

G zero and first conditionals, future time clauses
V expressions with *take*
P sentence rhythm

"
In a world that's changing really quickly, the only strategy that is guaranteed to fail is not taking risks.

Mark Zuckerberg,
US internet entrepreneur "

4B Are you a risk taker?

1 LISTENING & SPEAKING

a Talk to a partner.

1 Imagine that you had a dream where you were standing on the edge of a precipice. What sort of dream would it be for you?

    a an exciting one

    b a nightmare

    c an interesting one, which you might try to interpret

2 What do you think your answer says about your attitude to risk?

b (2 38)) Listen to six people answering the question *Are you a risk taker?* How many of the speakers consider themselves risk takers?

c Listen again. Who…?

[2] says that some activities are enjoyable because they are a bit risky

[1] thinks that his / her attitude to risk is different from what it was before

[3] thinks that taking risks means losing control

[5] had to pay some money because of his / her risky behaviour

[6] worries about his / her personal safety

[4] does something which most people think of as very risky, but which he / she says is not

d Listen again for more detail. What examples of risks do the speakers say they would take, or have taken? What things wouldn't they do? Do you identify with any of the speakers? Why?

e Work with a partner. **A** interview **B** with the questions in the red circles. For each circle, write **R** if you think that in that area **B** is prepared to take risks. Then **B** interview **A** with the blue circles.

f Look at what you have written in the circles. In which areas of his / her life would you say your partner was a risk taker? Does he / she agree? Which of you is the bigger risk taker?

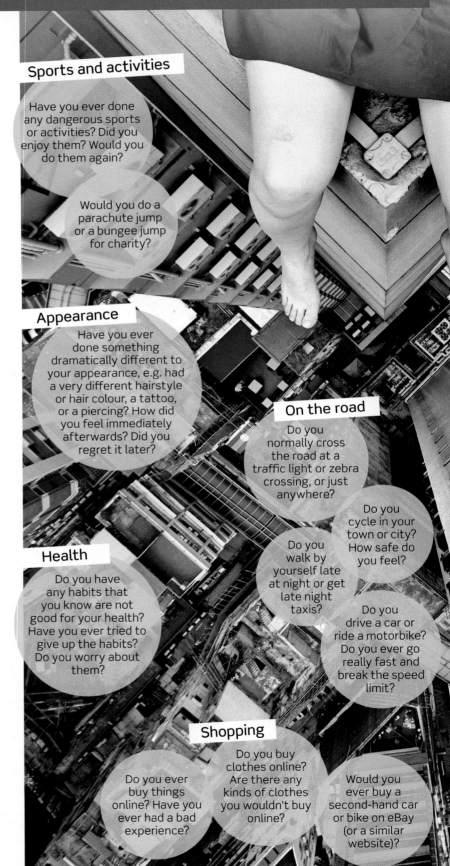

Sports and activities

Have you ever done any dangerous sports or activities? Did you enjoy them? Would you do them again?

Would you do a parachute jump or a bungee jump for charity?

Appearance

Have you ever done something dramatically different to your appearance, e.g. had a very different hairstyle or hair colour, a tattoo, or a piercing? How did you feel immediately afterwards? Did you regret it later?

On the road

Do you normally cross the road at a traffic light or zebra crossing, or just anywhere?

Do you cycle in your town or city? How safe do you feel?

Do you walk by yourself late at night or get late night taxis?

Do you drive a car or ride a motorbike? Do you ever go really fast and break the speed limit?

Health

Do you have any habits that you know are not good for your health? Have you ever tried to give up the habits? Do you worry about them?

Shopping

Do you buy clothes online? Are there any kinds of clothes you wouldn't buy online?

Do you ever buy things online? Have you ever had a bad experience?

Would you ever buy a second-hand car or bike on eBay (or a similar website)?

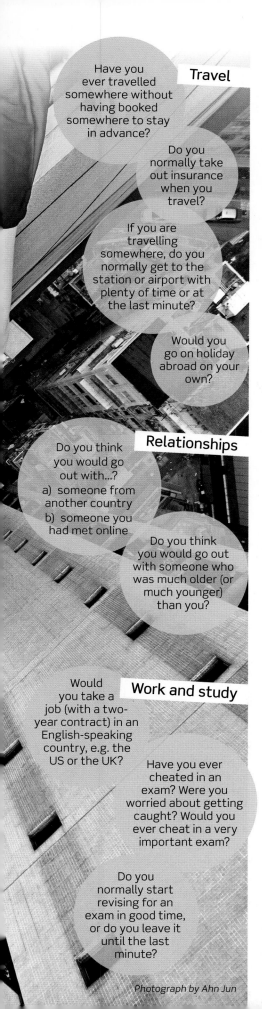

2 GRAMMAR zero and first conditionals, future time clauses

a Match the sentence halves.

1 **B** If my dad **finds out** I've been hitchhiking,
2 **D** When **you're crossing** the road in the UK,
3 **C** As soon as **I've passed** my driving test,
4 **G** If **it's still raining** this afternoon,
5 **F** When **I've booked** the flights,
6 **E** If **you don't ask her** to pay you back,
7 **H** If **I'm not feeling** better tomorrow,
8 **A** If **you carry on** with the diet,

A you'll have lost ten kilos by Christmas.
B he'll be furious.
C I'm going to buy a car.
D make sure you look right and then left.
E she'll have forgotten she borrowed it.
F we can start looking for hotels.
G we're calling off the match.
H I won't be going to work.

b Look at the highlighted verbs. In first conditional sentences and future time clauses, what forms or tenses can you use a) after *if, when,* etc. (1–8) b) in the main clause (A–H)? → Any present tense

c Now look at two more conditional sentences. Do the main clauses refer to a) something which might be a consequence of the *if*-clause, or b) something which is always a consequence of the *if*-clause?

If people drive when they are tired, they often have accidents.
If roads are wet or icy, the number of accidents goes up.

d ➤ p.139 Grammar Bank 4B. Learn more about conditionals and future time clauses, and practise them.

e In pairs, complete each sentence in your own words.

1 Don't let children play near a swimming pool unless…
2 Never leave a dog locked up in a car if…
3 Keep a first aid kit in your house in case…
4 Children shouldn't be left alone in the house until…
5 Always unplug electrical appliances (e.g. a hairdryer) as soon as…
6 Always keep medicines in a safe place in case…
7 Don't allow strangers into your house unless…
8 If you are frying something and the oil catches fire,…

3 PRONUNCIATION sentence rhythm

a ② 42)) Listen and write six sentences in the dialogues.

1 A If we rent a house in the mountains, will you come skiing with us?
  B ¹_____. How much do you think it'll cost?
  A ²_____.
  B Well, I'll have to check my dates first.
  A OK, but ³_____.

2 A How will I find you at the theatre?
  B ⁴_____.
  A ⁵_____? I don't finish work until 7.00.
  B I'll wait for you until 7.20 and then I'll go to my seat.
  A ⁶_____.

b ② 43)) Listen to both dialogues and <u>underline</u> the stressed words you have written.

c In pairs, practise the dialogues. Try to say the sentences smoothly with a natural rhythm.

4 READING

a Have you ever travelled very fast in a car or on a motorbike? Do you know how fast you were going? How did you feel?

b Look at the article. Can you explain the title? Read the article once and answer the questions.

1 What two alternatives are offered to speedaholics if they are caught?

2 What's the main thing that participants learn on the course?

3 Do you think the course will make John Earl go more slowly?

c Read the article again and complete the gaps with A–E.

A the speeders are asked to explain why they were stopped and to give details of any accidents they've had

B so before leaving, each of them is given a metal key ring engraved with a cross-section of a head inside a helmet

C programmes used to treat alcoholics and drug addicts

D although other people get injured and even die, 'It's not going to happen to me'

E the class to write down their worst experience on the road, their potential risk areas, and what they need to remember to keep themselves alive

d Look at the highlighted phrases. With a partner, use your own words to say what they mean.

e Which of the two punishments for speeding (doing the course or getting points on your licence) do you think would be more effective in your country? Why?

Glossary
speed *noun* the rate at which something moves or travels
speed *noun (informal)* an illegal amphetamine drug
points on your licence in the UK (and many other countries) if you commit a driving offence you may get penalty points on your licence. If you get more than 12 points in three years, you can be banned from driving.
Valentino Rossi an Italian motorcyclist who has won nine Grand Prix World Championships

I'M JOHN, I'M A SPEEDAHOLIC

ADDICTION THERAPY IS THE NEW WAY TO STOP SPEEDING BIKERS AND CAR DRIVERS.

John Earl is 25 and addicted to speed. Not the drug, but a mixture that is just as powerful – an intoxicating combination of high-powered engines, testosterone and youth. 'It's not the speed exactly,' he says. 'It's the adrenaline. It's the buzz you get when you go fast.'

But if you regularly drive at 120mph (190kph) on a public road, sooner or later you're going to get caught, and today John is one of a dozen speeders attending a new programme designed to cure them of their need for speed. It is similar to [1]_____. At the beginning of the course the participants are asked to introduce themselves and admit that they have a problem. 'Hello, my name's John, and I'm a speedaholic.'

The speedaholics course is for serious and habitual offenders, and is offered as an alternative to getting points on your licence. 'It is based on research into the attitudes of young drivers and bikers,' says Chris Burgess, a psychology lecturer at Exeter University, who created the programme. There are courses for both car drivers and motorcyclists. 'There is an element of addiction in this sort of behaviour,' says Burgess. 'It's sensation-seeking, it's taking risks, looking for that buzz, but ignoring the potentially fatal consequences. They all have the feeling that [2]_____.

Today's course, which is for motorcyclists, is led by Inspector Robin Derges, a police officer who is a senior investigator of road deaths and a keen biker himself. After introducing themselves, [3]_____. They range in age from 18 to mid-forties and most were caught doing at least 20mph (36kph) over the speed limit. Derges gets straight to the point. 'Motorcyclists make up just 1% of all the vehicles on the road, but 33% of all deaths and serious injuries happen to motorcyclists. Unless something changes, if we meet up here in a year's time, one of you will be dead.'

Says Derges 'We want to give them a sense of their own vulnerability, their human limitations, and to help them make a realistic assessment of the risks involved. It's not about stopping people from enjoying riding, it's about preventing deaths.' Towards the end of the day he asks [4]_____. 'The problem is that people get on their bikes and suddenly think they're Valentino Rossi,' says John.

Standing in the car park at the end of the course, the bikers seem to have taken everything they have heard very seriously. John admits 'It's certainly made me more aware. I know I sometimes behave like an idiot. But that's not to say I won't forget all about it in a few weeks' time.' Burgess knows this, [5]_____. It is to remind them of a part of the course that explained what can happen to the brain in a collision.

'The idea is that they will see the key ring when they are riding and it will make them think twice,' says Burgess.

Adapted from The Sunday Times

5 LISTENING

a You are going to listen to an expert talking about the risks of driving. Before you listen, choose which you think is the right option, a, b, or c. Compare with a partner and give reasons for your choice.

1 The most dangerous thing to be on the road is….
  (a) a pedestrian   b a driver   **(c)** a motorcyclist

2 Most fatal accidents happen because drivers….
  a fall asleep at the wheel   b are drunk   **(c)** drive too fast

3 Driving at night is … as dangerous as driving during the day.
  a three times   **(b)** four times   c ten times

4 You're most likely to have an accident on a….
  a Monday morning
  (b) Friday afternoon
  c Saturday night

5 Most accidents happen….
  a on long-distance journeys
  b in the city centre
  (c) very near your house

6 The worst roads for fatal accidents are….
  a motorways   b urban roads   **(c)** country roads

7 Mile for mile, women have more…than men.
  (a) minor accidents
  b serious accidents
  c fatal accidents

8 The age at which a driver is at most risk is….
  a over 25   b between 21 and 26   **(c)** under 25

b **(2 44)))** Listen once and check your answers.

c Listen for more details for each question in **a**.

d Talk to a partner.

1 Would these statistics probably be similar in your country?

2 Do you think the age limit for having a driving licence should be raised?

3 Do you think punishments for dangerous driving should be more severe?

4 What else do you think would help to reduce accidents in your country?

5 Do *you* or does anybody you know often drive too fast?

6 VOCABULARY expression...

a Look at three sentences from the les... highlighted phrases with *take* mean... phrasal verb?

Do you normally take out insurance whe...
It's sensation-seeking, it's taking risks…
…we need to take the risks involved in driving very seriously

b Match some more expressions and phrasal verbs with *take* to their meanings.

Expressions with *take*
1 take care of
2 take advantage of
3 take part in
4 take place
5 take (your) time
6 take into account

Phrasal verbs with *take*
7 take after
8 take off
9 take up

A [A] look after
B [9] begin a new activity
C [3] participate in
D [4] happen
E [8] 1 (*for planes*) leave the ground; 2 (*for clothes*) remove
F [5] do sth slowly, not in a hurry
G [7] be similar to sb
H [2] make use of an opportunity
I [6] think about sb / sth when you are making a decision

c Complete the questions with a phrasal verb or expression from **b**. Then ask and answer with a partner. Give examples to explain your answers.

1 Who do you take _after_ more, your father or your mother?

2 Do you worry about your health? Do you take _take care of_ yourself?

3 Do you get up very quickly in the morning or do you take _your time_?

4 Have you ever not taken _advantage of_ a good opportunity (and regretted it)?

5 Have you ever taken _part in_ a demonstration?

6 Have you taken _up_ a new sport or hobby recently?

7 Has any big sporting event ever taken _place_ in your (nearest big) city?

8 If you were thinking of buying a new computer or mobile phone, what factors would you take _into account_?

> 🔍 **Giving examples**
> We often use *for example* or *for instance* to give examples.
> *I take after my mother,* **for example** / **for instance** *we both have the same sense of humour.*

7 WRITING

➤ **p.115 Writing** *For and against.* Write a blog post.

GRAMMAR

a (Circle) a, b, or c.

1 When we got to Terminal 2, the flight from London _____.
   a had already landed b had already been landing c already landed

2 As soon as we arrived at the airport, we _____.
   a had checked in b were checking in c checked in

3 We _____ for about an hour when suddenly the plane began to lose height.
   a had been flying b were flying c flew

4 It was _____ boring film that we left in the middle of it.
   a so b such a c a such

5 Nico's father _____.
   a speaks English fluently b speaks English fluent c speaks fluently English

6 _____. I just need another five minutes.
   a I've finished nearly b Nearly I've finished c I've nearly finished

7 The driver _____ in the accident.
   a seriously was injured b was injured seriously c was seriously injured

8 The car _____ 50,000 km – we'll need to get it serviced.
   a will soon have done b will soon do c will soon be doing

9 You can watch TV as soon as _____ your homework.
   a you'll finish b you're finishing c you've finished

10 If the tickets cost more than 100 euros, _____.
   a I don't go b I'm not going to go c I won't have gone

b Complete the sentences with the correct form of the verb in **bold**.

1 Imagine! This time tomorrow we _____ on the beach. **lie**
2 The match starts at 7.00. By the time I get home it _____ already _____. **start**
3 You mustn't use your mobile phone until the plane _____. **land**
4 Many people have problems sleeping if they _____ coffee after midday. **drink**
5 I want to spend a year travelling when I _____ university. **finish**

VOCABULARY

a Write words for the definitions.

1 **g**_____ the door outside which you wait to board your flight
2 **b**_____ **r**_____ the place where you pick up your luggage after you've arrived
3 **a**_____ the passage between the rows of seats inside a plane
4 **t**_____ a series of sudden and violent changes in wind direction which affects flights
5 **j**_____ **l**_____ the feeling of being tired and confused after a long flight

b (Circle) the correct word.

1 Gina and I haven't seen each other much *late | lately*.
2 Our hotel has a great view! We can *even | ever* see the Eiffel Tower!
3 I've been working too *hard | hardly* lately.
4 How much *cases | luggage* are you going to take?
5 I love all pasta, but *especially | specially* lasagne.

c Complete with the verb in the past tense.

1 The wind **bl**_____ so hard that two trees fell down.
2 The taxi **dr**_____ me off outside the terminal.
3 It **p**_____ with rain last night and I got soaked coming home from work.
4 She **g**_____ on the bus but there was nowhere to sit.
5 We **t**_____ advantage of the good weather and spent the day at the beach.

d (Circle) the word that is different.

1	breeze	wind	hurricane	blizzard
2	chilly	boiling	hot	scorching
3	fog	damp	mist	smog
4	cold	freezing	bright	icy
5	hail	thunder	lightning	drought

e Complete with one word.

1 We checked _____ as soon as we got to the airport.
2 The most dangerous moment during a flight is when the plane is taking _____ or landing.
3 I've decided to take _____ running. I need to lose some weight.
4 Who do you take _____ most in your family?
5 The final will take _____ in Stockholm next Saturday.

PRONUNCIATION

a (Circle) the word with a different sound.

1 pouring   storm   hardly   warm
2 weather   heavy   clear   pleasant
3 lounge   snow   cold   closed
4 luggage   flood   thunder   humid
5 rain   trolley   lately   delayed

b Under<u>line</u> the main stressed syllable.

1 e|ven|tua|lly   2 gra|dua|lly   3 e|spe|cia|lly
4 pa|ssen|ger   5 hu|rri|cane

CAN YOU UNDERSTAND THIS TEXT?

a Read the article once. Is wingsuit flying a popular hobby?

b Read the article again and complete it with phrases A–F. There is one sentence you do not need.

A But the sport truly took off in 1997
B Some wingsuit flyers attach cameras to their helmets
C For me, the crazy thing isn't continuing to do it
D With practice, some wingsuiters can stay in the air for more than three minutes
E The acronym stands for the potential jump off points
F But wingsuiters are not easily deterred

c Choose five words or phrases from the text. Check their meaning and pronunciation and try to learn them.

◄ CAN YOU UNDERSTAND THIS FILM?

VIDEO

(2 45)) Watch or listen to a short film on The British and the Weather. Complete the sentences with one or two words.

1 A _____ of British people begin a conversation by talking about the weather.
2 People talk even more about the weather nowadays, because in Britain it's becoming _____ _____.
3 2012 was the _____ year since records began.
4 British weather is quite _____ compared to other countries.
5 The British weather has an influence on its _____ and _____.
6 Former Prime Minister Gordon Brown blamed Britain's bad economic performance on the _____ _____.
7 In the UK, elections are nearly always held in the _____ or _____.
8 Some experts say that the weather is the reason why Britain has never had a _____.
9 Turner and Constable are famous British _____ who were inspired by the weather.
10 The expression 'to weather the _____' means to survive something.

They believe they can fly

Some people just won't be satisfied till they can fly. This primal urge has given rise to wingsuit fliers, thrill-seekers who leap off cliffs or out of aeroplanes wearing winged jumpsuits. [1]_____, and hit speeds of over 100 miles an hour, achieving what they say is the closest thing to engineless flight that humans have ever experienced.

'It's a weird, risky thing to do,' said Tanya Weiss, 35, a professional wingsuit pilot, 'but the dream of flight is ancient, and some of us feel like it's something we were born with.'

In addition to the dozen or so professionals like Ms Weiss, who spend their workdays filming adverts and doing movie stunts, there are only a handful of people who have ever actually tried it. Most are elite skydivers, also known as BASE jumpers. [2]_____ – **B**uildings, **A**ntennas, **S**pans (bridges), and **E**arth (i.e. hills and cliffs).

There have been many attempts at wingsuit flying throughout history, dating from the German engineer Otto Lilienthal, who in the late 1800s designed winged gliders that allowed him to fly up to 1,000 feet without an engine. [3]_____, when the French skydiver Patrick de Gayardon successfully jumped from a plane wearing nothing but a modified jumpsuit.

Wingsuit flying as a spectator sport derives much of its thrill from people putting their lives at risk, and at extremely high speeds. Both Otto Lilienthal and Patrick de Gayardon died trying to achieve flight with winged outfits, as did Eric Stephenson, Tanya Weiss's mentor and fiancé.

[4]_____. Despite the death of the man she planned to marry, Ms Weiss, who recently led the successful effort to set a world record for the largest wingsuit skydive formation with 99 others in California, still pursues her dream of flying.

'I thought about quitting,' she said. 'But we're pushing the boundaries of what humans can do. [5]_____. The crazy thing would be to walk away from this thing that has brought me together with some of the most incredible people in the world.'

Adapted from The New York Times

G unreal conditionals
V feelings
P word stress in 3- or 4-syllable adjectives

> To survive, it is often necessary to fight,
> and to fight you have to get dirty.
>
> *George Orwell,*
> *UK author*

5A The survivors' club

1 SPEAKING & READING

a Answer the questions with a partner. Give reasons for your answers.

1 How do you think you would react in a life or death emergency situation?
   a I'd panic and become hysterical.
   b I'd 'freeze' and wouldn't be able to do anything.
   c I'd act coolly and calmly.

2 If you caught a plane tomorrow and the flight attendant began giving the safety information, would you…?
   a listen, but not take it very seriously
   b carry on reading your book or magazine
   c pay attention and also read the safety information in the seat pocket

3 What would you do if you were hiking alone in the mountains and you got completely lost (without phone coverage)?
   a I'd stay where I was and wait to be rescued.
   b I'd keep walking and try to find my way to my destination.
   c I'd try to find my way back to where I'd started from.

4 What would you do if you woke up in the middle of the night and thought that you could hear an intruder in your home? If you would do something different, say what.
   a I'd confront the intruder.
   b I'd keep still and quiet and hope that the intruder would go away.
   c I'd lock myself in a room and call the police.

b Read the article *How to eat an elephant* and answer the questions.
   1 What is the key to surviving in a life or death crisis?
   2 What is the *10–80–10 principle*?
   3 What is the other important factor apart from keeping calm?

c Look at the highlighted words and phrases try to work out their meaning. Then match them to 1–8.
   1 *overwhelmed*
       adj unable to react because the emotion is too strong
   2 Stunned
       adj so shocked that you cannot think clearly or act
   3 challenge
       noun a new or difficult thing that tests your abilities
   4 bewildered
       adj very confused
   5 rational
       adj based on reason and not emotion
   6 overcome
       verb to succeed in dealing with or controlling a problem
   7 keep calm
       to not get excited or nervous, to not panic
   8 manageable tasks
       pieces of work that it is possible to deal with or control

d Work in groups of three. ➤ **Communication** *It's an emergency!* **A** *p.106* **B** *p.110* **C** *p.112.* Read about what to do in three different emergency situations. Then take turns to say what you should and shouldn't do.

e Now look back at the questions in **a**. Did you choose the right answers?

HOW TO EAT AN ELEPHANT
THE LESSONS OF THE SURVIVORS CLUB

1   At least 80% of us react in the same way to a life or death crisis or emergency: we're simply overwhelmed – the challenge seems too great, the problem insolvable. In Air
5 Force survival school, they try to teach you how to overcome this feeling. One of the things they ask new cadets, is 'How would you eat an elephant?', and they make them memorize the right answer, which is: 'You eat an elephant one bite at a time.' Survival means
10 dealing with a huge life-or-death problem, one which you may not be able to solve quickly or all at once. The key to survival is to slow down and divide the challenges into small, manageable tasks, one goal at a time, one decision at a time. When an avalanche
15 buried the survivors of a plane crash in the Andes, the survivors whispered to each other 'Breathe. Breathe again. With every breath you are alive.' In a hopeless situation without oxygen or light this approach kept them going until they found a way out.

20 This and much more is what survival expert Ben Sherwood tells us in his best-selling book *The Survivors Club,* which brings together stories of real-life survivors from all kinds of disasters. He begins by explaining the 10–80–10 principle. When faced with
25 an emergency 80% of people freeze. They are stunned and 'turn into statues' or are so bewildered by what is happening around them that they can't react. Ten per cent lose control. These people scream and cry, and often make the situation worse. But 10% keep calm and
30 behave in a rational way. They don't panic and they assess the situation clearly and take decisions. These people have the best chance of survival in a crisis, and Sherwood explains how you can try to become more like them.

35 He also reminds us that, apart from staying calm and not despairing, knowing the right thing to do in a crisis is also vital, and that in most emergencies many more people survive than don't. For example, most
40 people think that you can't survive a plane crash, but American research has shown that the survival rate in all air crashes is historically 95.7%. Sherwood not only tries to show us how to behave rationally and calmly, he also gives us the information we need to join 'The Survivors Club'.

2 VOCABULARY feelings

a Look at four adjectives in **1c**. Which three describe how people are feeling?

b ➤ **p.157 Vocabulary Bank** *Feelings.*

3 PRONUNCIATION
word stress in 3- or 4-syllable adjectives

a Read the dialogues and underline the stressed syllable in the **bold** adjectives.

> 1   **A**   Hi, Sue. What's the matter?
>   **B**   I've just been robbed! Please come quickly. I'm **des|per|ate**.

> 2   **A**   You weren't **of|fend|ed** by what I said, were you?
>   **B**   Yes, actually I was.

> 3   **A**   What did you think of the film?
>   **B**   To be honest, I was a bit **dis|ap|point|ed**.

> 4   **A**   What don't you understand in the report?
>   **B**   I'm just completely **be|wil|dered** by so many facts and figures.

> 5   **A**   Were you surprised to hear that the boss is leaving?
>   **B**   I was **as|ton|ished**. I really wasn't expecting it.

> 6   **A**   So can you come to dinner next week?
>   **B**   Yes, we'd be **de|light|ed** to.

> 7   **A**   How did your parents react when you told them you and Susan had separated?
>   **B**   They were **dev|as|ta|ted**.

> 8   **A**   How did you feel when you heard the news?
>   **B**   I was absolutely **hor|ri|fied**. It was such an awful accident.

> 9   **A**   So do you like the watch?
>   **B**   I love it. I'm completely **o|ver|whelmed** – I don't know what to say!

b **3 5))** Listen and check. Practise the conversations, copying the intonation and stressing the right syllable in the adjectives.

c Choose two adjectives from **a** and tell your partner about a time or a situation when you felt like that.

4 READING & LISTENING

a Answer the questions in pairs.

1 Imagine you were going to go backpacking in the Amazon rainforest, what do you think would be the main problems you would need to overcome, e.g. the heat, insects, the food, etc.?

2 What would you be most afraid of?

b Read the beginning of a true survival story and then answer the questions below.

1 What was the three friends' original plan? How did this change?

2 What caused tensions between…?
   a the three men and the guide
   b Kevin and Marcus

3 Why did they finally separate?

4 Which pair would *you* have chosen to go with? Why?

5 How would you have felt if you had been in Marcus's situation?

[handwritten notes: They will end of Village. Went backpacking - go to an undiscovered Indian Village, and raft nearly 200 km... Marcus was complaining all the time, and he go his own way.]

LOST IN THE

Four young men went into the jungle on the adventure of a lifetime. Only two of them would come out alive…

The Amazon rainforest is roughly the size of Europe or Australia. It is the home of more than half the plant and animal species known to man, many of which are lethal.

In 1981 three friends went backpacking in a remote area of Bolivia: Yossi Ghinsberg, 22, and his two friends Kevin Wallace, 29, and Marcus Stamm, 29. They hired an experienced guide, an Austrian called Karl, who promised that he could take them deep into the rainforest to an undiscovered Indian village. Then they would raft nearly 200 kilometres back down river. Karl said that the journey to the village would take them about seven days. Before they entered the jungle, the three friends made a promise that they would 'go in together and come out together'.

c You are going to listen to part of a documentary and find out what happened to the four men. After each part answer the questions with a partner.

3 6))) 1 What happened to Kevin and Yossi on the raft?
2 What piece of luck did Yossi have?

Whose situation would you rather have been in, Kevin's or Yossi's? Why?

3 7))) 3 How were Kevin and Yossi feeling?
4 What happened to Yossi on his first night alone in the jungle?

What would you have done if you had been in Yossi's situation?

3 8))) 5 Why did Yossi's spirits change from desperate to optimistic, and then to desperate again?

How would you have felt at this point? What do you think had happened to Kevin?

3 9))) 6 What had Kevin been doing all this time?
7 What did Kevin decide to do?
8 Why was he incredibly lucky?

If you had been Kevin, what would you have done now?

JUNGLE

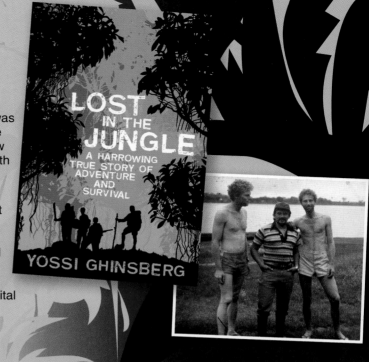

LOST IN THE JUNGLE
A HARROWING TRUE STORY OF ADVENTURE AND SURVIVAL
YOSSI GHINSBERG

The four men set off from the town of Apolo and soon they had left civilization far behind. But after walking for more than a week there was no sign of the village and tensions began to appear in the group. The three friends started to suspect that Karl, the guide, didn't really know where the Indian village was. Yossi and Kevin began to get fed up with their friend Marcus because he was complaining about everything, especially his feet, which had become infected and were hurting.

Eventually they decided to abandon the search for the village and just to hike back to Apolo (instead of rafting) the way they had come. But Kevin was furious because he thought that it was Marcus's fault that they had had to cut short their adventure. So he decided that he would raft down the river, and he persuaded Yossi to join him, but he didn't want Marcus to come with them. Marcus and Karl decided to go back to Apolo on foot. The three friends agreed to meet in a hotel in the capital La Paz in a week's time.

Early next morning the two pairs of travellers said goodbye and set off on their different journeys…

(3 10)) 9 How did Kevin first try to get help?
10 Why was it unsuccessful?
11 What was his last attempt to find his friend?

(3 11)) 12 How long had Yossi been on his own in the jungle? How was he?
13 What did he think the buzzing noise was? What was it?

What do you think might have happened to Marcus and Karl?

d Do you think you would have survived if you had been in Yossi's situation? Would you have done anything differently?

5 GRAMMAR unreal conditionals

a Look at four sentences, and complete the gaps with the verbs in the right tense.
1 What would you do if you ___were___ (be) in the mountains and you ___got lost___ (get lost)?
2 If I thought that somebody was in my house, I ___would call___ (call) the police and I ___wait___ (not confront) the intruder.
3 What would you have done if you ___were___ (be) in Yossi's situation?
4 If Kevin hadn't looked for his friend, Yossi ___would have died___ (die).

b Look at sentences 1–4 again. Which two refer to a hypothetical situation in the past? Which two refer to a hypothetical situation in the present or future?

c ➤ p.140 Grammar Bank 5A. Learn more about unreal conditionals, and practise them.

d Complete the two sentences in your own words with a positive ⊕ and negative clause ⊖.
1 If I lived in the city centre…
⊕ ___I would live near to a station___
⊖ ___
2 My phone bill wouldn't have been so high if…
⊕ ___
⊖ ___

e ➤ **Communication** *Guess the conditionals* **A** *p.106* **B** *p.111.*

6 WRITING

➤ **p.116 Writing** *An article.* Write an article about how to keep safe.

G structures after *wish*
V expressing feelings with verbs or *-ed* / *-ing* adjectives
P sentence rhythm and intonation

> Some people want things to happen, some wish things would happen, others make things happen.
>
> *Michael Jordan, US basketball player*

5B It drives me mad!

1 GRAMMAR wish + would

a Look at a Twitter thread where people tweeted about things that annoy them. Tick (✓) the things that annoy you, too.

b Compare the things you've ticked with a partner. Which are your top three, and why?

> 🔍 **Useful language**
> *I agree with this one.*
> *It really annoys me when...*
> *It's so annoying when...*   people shout
> *It drives me mad when...*   on mobile phones.

c ➤ **p.141 Grammar Bank 5B.** Learn more about *wish + would*, and practise it.

d Write three more things that annoy you and that you would like people to change, to add to the Twitter thread. Begin...

I wish...would / wouldn't...

e In pairs or small groups, compare your tweets.

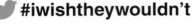 **#iwishtheywouldn't**

Tweets Top / All

 I wish people wouldn't start stupid rumours that aren't true. #iwishtheywouldn't

 I wish my boyfriend wouldn't fall asleep every time I want to talk to him. ☹ #iwishtheywouldn't

 I wish my son wouldn't always leave the car with no petrol every time he borrows it. #iwishtheywouldn't

 I wish people would turn up when they say they're going to. #iwishtheywouldn't

 I wish people would stop using emoticons and smiley faces. They just annoy me. :(#iwishtheywouldn't

 I wish my family would put DVDs back in their cases. I hate finding empty cases when I'm looking for something to watch. #iwishtheywouldn't

 I wish my friends would put their phones away when we're having a meal. You shouldn't text at the dinner table! #iwishtheywouldn't

 I wish my children would take their tissues out of their pockets before they put their clothes in the washing machine. #iwishtheywouldn't

 I wish my boss wouldn't always arrange meetings during my lunch hour. #iwishtheywouldn't

 I wish people wouldn't ask me 'What are you doing?' when it's completely obvious what I'm doing. #iwishtheywouldn't

 I wish advertising companies wouldn't use songs I really love to advertise something I hate. #iwishtheywouldn't

 I wish people wouldn't leave supermarket trolleys in the car park just because they can't be bothered to take them back. #iwishtheywouldn't

 I wish shop assistants would serve me when I'm waiting instead of chatting with their friends. #iwishtheywouldn't

 I wish people would throw away pens when they don't work any more!!! #iwishtheywouldn't

2 VOCABULARY & SPEAKING expressing feelings with verbs or -ed / -ing adjectives

Ways of talking about feelings

We often talk about feelings in three different ways:

1 by using a **verb** (e.g. *annoy*)
That noise is starting to annoy me.
2 by using an **-ing adjective** (e.g. *annoying*)
That noise is really annoying.
3 by using an **-ed adjective** (e.g. *annoyed*)
I'm getting really annoyed by that noise.

Remember that the rules for pronouncing *-ed* adjectives are the same as for regular past tense verbs, e.g. *annoyed* = /d/, *irritated* = /ɪd/ and *depressed* = /t/.

a Complete the sentences with the correct form of the word in **bold**.

1 It really __infuriates__ me when people drive close behind me.   **infuriate**

2 I get very __frustrated__ when something goes wrong with my internet connection and I don't know how to fix it.   **frustrate**

3 It's so __embarrassing__ when I can't remember someone's name, but they can remember mine.   **embarrass**

4 I used to love shopping in the sales, but now I find it __exhausting__. After an hour I just want to go home.   **exhaust**

5 I'm often __disappointed__ with my birthday presents. My expectations are obviously too high!   **disappoint**

✱6 It __amazes__ me that some people still don't buy things like books and music online.   **amaze**

7 I find speaking in public absolutely __terrifying__. I hate doing it.   **terrify**

8 I've often been __inspired__ by reading about how some successful people have overcome difficulties.   **inspire**

9 I never find instructions for electronic devices helpful, in fact usually they just __confusing__ me. confused   **confuse**

10 When I travel I'm always __thrilled__ if I manage to communicate something in a foreign language.   **thrill**

b (3 16)) Listen and check. Then with a partner, say if the sentences are true for you or not. Give examples or reasons.

Feelings adjectives that have an -ed form, but not an -ing form

A few *-ed* adjectives describing feelings don't have an *-ing* form, e.g. *impressed – impressive* NOT *impressing*

c Complete the sentences below with a form of the adjective in **bold**.

1 We are extremely **impressed** by your CV. Your CV is extremely *impressive*.

2 I'm very **stressed** by my job. My job is very __stressful__

3 I was really **scared** during the film. The ending was especially __scary__.

4 I was **delighted** to meet Jane. She really is a __delightful__ person.

5 I was really **offended** by what you said. What you said was really __offensive__.

d In pairs, choose three circles to talk about.

- an embarrassing mistake you once made
- a film or a book that you found really disappointing
- something that sometimes frustrates you about learning English
- something that makes you feel depressed
- something that really annoys you when you're shopping
- something that really stresses you in your daily life

e Are there any things that make you feel exactly the same way as your partner?

3 READING & SPEAKING

a You are going to read an article about some research that has been done about what people regret in life. Before you read, with a partner say whether you think the following sentences are true or not.

1 Most people spend some time every day thinking about things that they regret having done or not having done. T

2 The main area of life where people have regrets is relationships. T

3 On average people have one major regret in life. F

4 Most people think that the things they regret having done (or not done) are other people's fault. F

5 Most people believe that regrets are positive, because you learn from your mistakes. T

b Read the first part of the article (to line 16) once and check.

c Without looking back at the article, can you remember another way of saying…?

1 75%
2 66.6%
3 25%

d Now read *Some of the top 20 regrets*. With a partner, number what you think the top five regrets were in the survey (1= the most common regret).

e (3 17)》 Listen and check. How many did you get right? Which do you think would be the top regrets for people in your age group?

> 🔍 *regret doing* or *regret having done*?
> After *regret* the following verb must be in the gerund, but you can normally use either a simple gerund or a perfect gerund.
> *I regret not going to university.* OR *I regret not having gone to university.*

Regrets, we've had a few
(our love lives, health, childhoods...)

A recent survey has shown that we spend almost three quarters of an hour every week dwelling on our regrets.

I wish I hadn't…

1 Three quarters of the people surveyed said they did not believe it was possible to live a life without regrets, perhaps explaining why, on average, we spend 44 minutes a week thinking about things we could or should have done differently. Our main areas of regret are
5 our love lives (20%), family (18%), career (16%), health (14%), and finances (14%).

On average, most people have two main regrets in life – and 17% of those interviewed laid the blame at someone else's door. But two thirds of 2,000 people interviewed said they thought their regrets
10 had led them to act more positively and that they had learnt from their mistakes. A quarter of them said their regrets had made them into the person they are today.

Common regrets range from not getting on the property ladder sooner to not having had more relationships when they were
15 younger. Others include regretting not telling someone we loved them and wishing that we had repaired a damaged friendship.

Some of the top 20 regrets were (not in order):

- Getting married too early T
- Not asking grandparents more about their lives when they were alive F
- Not having done more exercise or eaten more healthily F (3)
- Not having saved enough money T (4)
- Not learning a foreign language or a musical instrument when you were younger
- Not working harder at school
- Not having travelled more and seen more of the world (0)
- Making the wrong career choice
- Not keeping in touch with friends T (2)
- Having taken up smoking (5)
- Falling out with a friend and not making up

Glossary
Regrets, I've had a few… an often-quoted line from the Frank Sinatra song *My Way*
lay the blame at sb else's door IDM say that sb else is responsible for sth
getting on the property ladder IDM buying your first house or flat

From the Daily Mail

4 GRAMMAR
wish + past simple or past perfect

a Now read four comments which people posted on the newspaper website after reading the article. Do you agree with any of them? Why (not)?

I'm almost 23 and saving incredibly hard to travel round the world! I'd hate to reach my 30s and then look back at my 20s and say 'I wish I'd travelled more when I had the time'.
Matthew, Aberdeen

I don't regret anything. There's nothing that I wish was different about my life. Everything I've done, however stupid it seems now, seemed like the right thing at the time... Of course I've made mistakes, but I don't regret anything. And yes, that includes saving money, bad boyfriends, all the usual things! I see them as pure mistakes – something to learn from, something which makes me the person I am today. I never think 'I wish I'd stayed on at university... I wish I'd married my ex...' If I had done these things, then I wouldn't be who I am today.
Cindy, Coggeshall

Regrets? I try not to think about them. What's the point? It's no use crying over spilt milk. But I have a few. Not buying the house I was renting for half the price I eventually paid for it, and smoking. I really wish I hadn't wasted all that money on cigarettes. What a fool. Still, I managed to give it up, which I'm proud of.
Nancy, Norwich

I wish there was a song called 'Je regrette tout'*. That would be my philosophy of life!
Martyn, Oxford

---

*Je regrette tout French for *I regret everything*. There is a very well-known Edith Piaf song called *Je ne regrette rien* (= I don't regret anything).

b Underline the six sentences in the comments with *wish*. What tense is the verb after *wish*? Are they wishes about the present or about the past?

c ➤ **p.141 Grammar Bank 5B.** Learn more about *wish* + past simple and past perfect, and practise it.

5 PRONUNCIATION sentence rhythm and intonation

a **3 19))** Listen and write down six sentences with *wish*.

b Match each sentence from **a** with a sentence below.

A ☐ Do you want me to phone and make an excuse?
B ☐ Well, don't ask me! I've never been here before.
C ☐ Well, it isn't too late. You're only 22.
D ☐ Well, it's not my fault. You've got no self-control!
E ☐ Why don't you go back to the shop and see if they still have them?
F ☐ Sorry, but it is. And I'm getting hungry.

c **3 20))** Listen and check. In pairs, practise the dialogues, copying the rhythm and intonation.

6 LISTENING & SPEAKING

a **3 21))** Listen and match speakers 1–5 with the regrets. There is one sentence you don't need to use.

Who...?
A ☐ wishes he / she had followed somebody's advice
B ☐ wasn't old enough to do something he / she now regrets
C ☐ felt very ashamed about what he / she had done
D ☐ wishes he / she had been more grateful for everything he / she had
E ☐ wishes he / she had been a bit braver
F ☐ regretted what he / she had done immediately after doing it

b Listen again. Why do the speakers mention or say the following:

1 'I really fancied her.'; 'Now it's too late.'
2 'Someone has to say to you that you really don't have to do this.' 'I spent the next 15 years trying to get out of it.'
3 the Russian Revolution; old letters
4 'It was a crazy idea and totally out of character' 'in the long run it was probably a good thing'
5 'My parents were really keen for me to change' 'but I was totally against the idea'

c Work in small groups. Tell the other students about...

• two things you wish you could do but you can't
• two things you wish you had which would improve your life
• two things you wish you had done when you were younger
• two things you wish you hadn't done when you were younger

7 **3 22)) SONG** *Same Mistake* ♫

1 📹 THE INTERVIEW Part 1

a Read the biographical information about Candida Brady. Have you seen *Trashed* or any other documentary film about the environment?

Candida Brady is a British journalist and film-maker. She founded her film company, Blenheim Films, in 1996 and has produced and directed several documentaries on a variety of topics, including youth culture, music, and ballet. In 2012, Candida completed her first documentary feature film, *Trashed*, which follows the actor Jeremy Irons around the world as he discovers the growing environmental and health problems caused by waste – the billions of tons of rubbish that we generate every day – and the way we deal with it. The soundtrack for the film was composed by the Greek composer Vangelis, who wrote the award-winning soundtrack to *Chariots of Fire*. The film had a special screening at the 2012 Cannes Film Festival and has won several awards at film festivals, including the Tokyo International Film Festival.

b (3 23)》 Watch or listen to **Part 1** of an interview with her. Mark the sentences **T** (true) or **F** (false).

1 Candida made the film *Trashed* because she wanted people to know more about the problem of waste.
2 Jeremy Irons is a person who loves buying new things.
3 Candida was surprised that he immediately loved the film proposal.
4 Vangelis is a good friend of Candida's.
5 Vangelis had previous experience of projects related to the environment.
6 She didn't need to do much research before making the film because she was already an expert on the subject.

c Now listen again and say why the **F** sentences are false.

Glossary
rough cut /rʌf kʌt/ the first version of a film after the different scenes have been put together
Jacques Cousteau a well-known French conservationist and film-maker who studied the sea and all forms of life in water.

📹 Part 2

a (3 24)》 Now watch or listen to **Part 2**. Answer the questions.

1 Which was the bigger problem for Candida: making the film visually attractive, or trying not to make it too depressing?
2 What kind of pollution does she think is the most worrying: air, land, or sea?

b Listen again. Complete the sentences with one word.

1 Candida had a _____ DOP (Director of Photography).
2 She wanted to film in beautiful places that had been _____ by man-made rubbish.
3 She would have preferred to make a more _____ documentary.
4 She thinks they were very much aware that they wanted to offer _____ at the end of the film.
5 She says you have to dig down over a foot deep on a beach to find sand that doesn't have any _____ in it.
6 She says the pieces of plastic in the water become so fragmented that they're the same size as the zooplankton, which is in the _____ chain.

Glossary
Saida (or Sidon) a port in Lebanon, its third largest city
a foot UK measurement = 30.5 centimetres
zooplankton microscopic organisms that live in water

BLENHEIM FILMS PRESENTS

JEREMY IRONS
IN
TRASHED

IF YOU THINK WASTE IS SOMEONE ELSE'S PROBLEM
...THINK AGAIN

OFFICIAL SELECTION
FESTIVAL DE CANNES
2012

waste

VIDEO Part 3

a (3 25))) Now watch or listen to **Part 3**. Answer the questions.

1 Who does she blame for the problem of waste?
2 Why does San Francisco offer a positive note at the end of the film?
3 Has the film changed her own habits?

b Listen again. What does she say about…?

1 hotels in San Francisco
2 her grandparents
3 her bicycle

> **Glossary**
> **zero waste** the recycling and re-using of all products
> **bins** containers where people throw their rubbish

2 VIDEO LOOKING AT LANGUAGE

> 🔍 **Comment adverbs**
> Candida uses a lot of comment adverbs (e.g. *unfortunately*) to clarify how she feels about what she is saying.

(3 26))) Watch or listen to some extracts from the interview and write in the missing adverbs.

1 'We ended up _____ filming in 11 countries…'
2 '…but the stories that I've chosen are universal and, _____, I spoke to, to people in communities, um, in more countries, um, than we actually filmed in…'
3 '…and so I sent him the treatment and _____ he, um, he loved it.'
4 'but _____, again, he was very shocked, um, by the film and really wanted to get involved.'
5 '…yes and no, um, _____ enough. Obviously I had a wonderful, DOP, Director of Photography, so, um, he can pretty much make anything look beautiful…'
6 'I did a lot of research and so, _____, these things were repeatable and, and in every country around the world…'
7 '_____ what's happened with the way that soft plastic degrades in water is that, um, the pieces become so fragmented…'

3 VIDEO IN THE STREET

a (3 27))) Watch or listen to four people talking about recycling. Which person seems to have the most positive attitude about recycling?

| Sally, *English* | Jo, *English* | Jill, *American* | Pranjal, *American* |

b Watch or listen again. Who (**S**, **Jo**, **J**, or **Pr**)…?

- ☐ ☐ thinks the government should offer money for recycling and producing less rubbish
- ☐ thinks it's up to people themselves to realize that it's worth recycling
- ☐ thinks the government should provide more containers for recycling
- ☐ thinks the government should do more to show people why recycling is good for the environment

c (3 28))) Watch or listen and complete the highlighted Colloquial English phrases. What do you think they mean?

1 '…people haven't really got an _____ not to recycle any more.'
2 '…well maybe they could offer a _____ incentive for, for recycling.'
3 '…I think we still have a _____ _____ to go.'
4 '…filling it up with cans and bottles, newspapers and all _____ of _____.'
5 '…and so if everyone could just get in that _____ that the smallest change they can make in their lives makes a big difference.'

4 SPEAKING

Answer the questions with a partner. Try to use comment adverbs to show how you feel about what you're saying.

1 How much recycling do people in your country do?
2 How much recycling do you do personally?
3 What do you think the government, or individuals, could do to make people recycle more?
4 What do you think that companies and shops could do to reduce the amount of waste?
5 Are you optimistic or pessimistic about the future of the environment?

G gerunds and infinitives
V music
P words that come from other languages

"Music with dinner is an insult both to the cook and the violinist.

G.K. Chesterton, UK author

6A Music and emotion

1 VOCABULARY & PRONUNCIATION
music, words from other languages

a (3 29)) Listen and match what you hear with a word in the list.

4 a bass guitar	1 a cello	9 a choir	8 a conductor	2 drums
3 a soprano	7 a flute	1 a violin	10 a keyboard	6 a saxophone

an orchestra (appears in list)

b (3 30)) Listen and check. Practise saying the words. What other words do you know for instruments and musicians?

c Read the information box below. Then, in pairs, look at **Borrowed words related to music** and try to pronounce them as they are pronounced in English. Under<u>line</u> the stressed syllable.

> 🔍 **Foreign words that are used in English**
> English has 'borrowed' many words from other languages, for example in the field of music from Italian, Greek, and French. The English pronunciation is often similar to their pronunciation in their original language, e.g. *ch* in words which come from Greek is /k/, e.g. *orchestra*.

Borrowed words related to music	
From Italian	cello /ˈtʃeləʊ/; concerto /kənˈtʃɜːtəʊ/ mezzo-soprano /metsəʊ səˈprɑːnəʊ/
From Greek	orchestra /ˈɔːkɪstrə/; choir /ˈkwaɪə/; chorus /ˈkɔːrəs/ microphone /ˈmaɪkrəfəʊn/; rhythm /ˈrɪðm/; symphony /ˈsɪmfəni/
From French	ballet /ˈbæleɪ/ encore /ˈɒŋkɔː/; genre /ˈʒɒnrə/

d (3 31)) Listen and check. How are the pink letters pronounced?

e With a partner, try to work out which language these words come from, and put them in the right rows. Do you know what they all mean?

architecture barista bouquet cappuccino chauffeur chef chic
croissant fiancé graffiti hypochondriac macchiato paparazzi
philosophy photograph psychic psychologist villa

From Italian	
From Greek	
From French	

f (3 32)) Listen and check. Practise saying the words.

2 SPEAKING

Ask and answer the questions with a partner.

Your music

Do you have a favourite...?
- kind of music
- song
- piece of classical music (symphony, sonata, etc.)
- band
- solo artist
- composer
- conductor

Do you play a musical instrument?
YES
- What instrument, or instruments, do you play?
- How long have you been playing it?
- Have you had or are you having lessons?
- Can you read music?
- Have you ever played in a band / orchestra?

NO
- Have you ever tried to learn to play an instrument? Why did you stop learning?
- Is there an instrument you would like to learn to play?

Have you ever...?
- sung in a choir
- performed in front of a lot of people
- taken part in a musical talent contest

Concerts
- Have you been to a good concert recently?
- Which artist or band would you most like to see in concert?
- What's the best live concert you've ever been to?

3 READING

a Think of a song or piece of music that you remember hearing and liking when you were a child. Where did you first hear it? How old were you? Why did you like it?

b Look at the title of a newspaper article. Then read the article once. Why did the writer choose this title?

c Read the first paragraph again. Find words or phrases meaning:

1 _____ completely
2 _____ behave in a way that makes other people think you are stupid
3 _____ started crying because of strong emotion
4 _____ not thinking that anything positive would happen
5 _____ a mixture of loud and unpleasant sounds

d What kind of sounds do you think *whir*, *hum*, and *clacking* (line 10) are?

e Read the rest of the article again. With a partner, and in your own words, say why the article mentions the following pieces of music or artists.

1 the *Lacrimosa* from Mozart's Requiem
2 the Rolling Stones, Michael Jackson, Sigur Rós, Radiohead, Elvis, and Pink Floyd
3 music from the fifties
4 Guillaume de Machaut's *Agnus Dei*
5 country music
6 Queen's *Bohemian Rhapsody*
7 Beethoven's Ninth Symphony and Sinatra's *Fly Me to the Moon*
8 the Beatles
9 silence

f Talk to a partner.

• Why do you think the journalist says that Austin's experience may help us understand more about musical taste?
• Imagine you were going to recommend music to Austin. Which...

song or piece of music
decade
composer   would you suggest?
band
singer

What music would you play to an alien?

'I can hear music for the first time ever,' wrote Austin Chapman, a 23-year-old film-maker from California. 'What should I listen to?'

1 Austin, you see, was born profoundly deaf. For his whole life, music has been a mystery. 'I had seen people make a fool of themselves, singing or moving wildly on the dance floor,' he says. 'I had also seen people moved to tears by a song, which was probably the hardest
5 thing for me to understand.' Then, just a few weeks ago, his parents suggested that he try a newly developed hearing aid that they had heard about. He went to the doctor's with no great expectations. But when the doctor switched on the hearing aid, he was stunned. 'I sat in the doctor's office, frozen as a cacophony of sounds attacked me. The
10 whir of the computer, the hum of the air conditioning, the clacking of the keyboard, the sound of my friend's voice.' Austin could hear. And for the first time ever the world of music was open to him.

It didn't take him long to decide what to do: he was going to listen to music non-stop. Later that day, he heard his first piece, Mozart's beautiful
15 *Lacrimosa* (from his Requiem), in a friend's car. He wept. So did everybody else in the car. The experience, he says, was 'like the first time you kiss a girl'. His friends went on to play him the Rolling Stones, Michael Jackson, Sigur Rós, Radiohead, Elvis, and Pink Floyd. But Austin knew that there was a vast universe of music to explore, so he decided to seek further
20 help. He described his situation on reddit.com and so far, he's received more than 14,000 suggestions. As a strategy, he has decided to follow the advice of someone who posted this message on the site: 'This is like introducing an alien to the music of Earth. Once you've tired of classical, you could start with music from the fifties and progress through each
25 decade. That way you can really see the growth of modern music.'

Austin Chapman

Austin adopted that system, but chose to start much earlier, with a piece by Guillaume de Machaut called *Agnus Dei*, from the 14th century. Currently, he's listening to four or five hours of music a day. As he had never heard music before Austin isn't influenced by nostalgia and, via the
30 internet, he can listen to just about anything ever composed. Consequently his experience may help us to understand more about musical taste. So what has he been listening to? It seems that no one genre dominates (although he says he's not very keen on country music – too depressing). His favourite piece – for now – is Queen's *Bohemian Rhapsody*. He's also
35 keen on Beethoven's Ninth Symphony and Frank Sinatra's *Fly Me to the Moon*. But so far he has not listened to the most recommended band, the Beatles. 'I'm waiting for a special occasion,' he says.

Austin is also learning how to hear. When we met at a café in West Hollywood, we took a table far from the street to avoid the
40 background noise of traffic. The ability to ignore unwanted noise is something that will take him time. This may help explain why Austin says that 'silence is still my favourite sound. When I turn my hearing aid off, my thoughts become clearer; it's absolutely peaceful.'

Adapted from The Times

4 LISTENING & SPEAKING

a (3 33)》 Listen to some short pieces of music. How do they make you feel? Would you like to carry on listening?

b (3 34)》 Listen to John Sloboda, a music psychologist, talking about why we listen to music. Try to complete the notes below by writing key words or phrases. Then with a partner, try to remember as much as you can of what he said.

c (3 35)》 Now listen to John explaining how music can affect the way we feel. Complete the notes below by giving examples. Then compare with a partner and try to remember what he said.

How does music affect our emotions?

Three important human emotions
1   happiness
2
3

How we feel affects the way we speak, e.g.
1   happy – speak faster / higher
2
3

Music copies this, e.g.
1   fast / high music makes us happy
2
3

Examples (pieces of music)
Music that makes us feel
1   happy, e.g.
2   angry, e.g.
3   sad, e.g.
This is especially exploited in...

Why do we listen to music?

1   to make us...
*   e.g.*

2   to help us to...
*   e.g.*

3   to intensify...
*   e.g.*

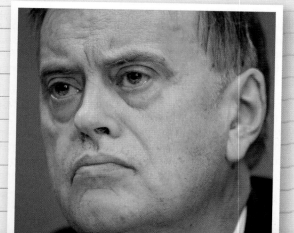

5 GRAMMAR gerunds and infinitives

a Look at some extracts from the listening. Put the verbs in brackets in the infinitive (with or without *to*) or the gerund (*-ing* form).

1 Firstly, we listen to music to make us _____ important moments in the past. (**remember**)

2 When we hear a certain piece of music we remember _____ it for the first time… (**hear**)

3 If we want _____ from one activity to another, we often use music to help us _____ the change. (**go, make**)

b ③36)) Listen and check.

c Look at two sentences with the verb *remember*. Which one is about remembering the past? Which one is about remembering something for the future?

1 I remember meeting him for the first time.
2 Please remember to meet him at the station.

d ➤ **p.142 Grammar Bank 6A.** Find out more about gerunds and infinitives, and practise them.

e Tell your partner one thing that…

- you'll never forget seeing for the first time
- you sometimes forget to do before you leave the house in the mornings
- you remember doing when you were under five years old.
- you must remember to do today or this week
- needs doing in your house / flat (e.g. the kitchen ceiling needs repainting)
- you need to do this evening
- you tried to learn but couldn't
- you have tried doing when you can't sleep at night

6 ③39)) **SONG** *Sing* ♫

d Talk to a partner. Ask for more details where possible.

1 On a typical day, when and where do you listen to music?

2 Do you listen to different kinds of music at different times of day?

3 What music would you play…?
- if you were feeling sad and you wanted to feel more cheerful
- if you were feeling down and you wanted to feel even worse
- if you were feeling furious about something or somebody
- if you were feeling stressed or nervous about something and wanted to calm down
- if you wanted to create a romantic atmosphere for a special dinner
- if you were feeling excited and were getting ready to go out for the evening
- if you were falling in love

OXFORD

Handbook of
Music and
Emotion

Edited by Patrik N. Juslin • John A. Sloboda

G used to, be used to, get used to
V sleep
P sentence stress and linking

"
Laugh and the world laughs with you,
snore and you sleep alone.

*Anthony Burgess,
UK author* "

6B Sleeping Beauty

1 LISTENING & SPEAKING

a Do you have problems sleeping? Why (not)?

b (3 **40, 41, 42**)》 You are going to listen to three people who have problems sleeping at night. Listen and take notes on what their problem is, and what has caused it. Compare with a partner and then listen again to complete your notes.

Speaker 1	Speaker 2	Speaker 3
• Bedroom it's not dark enough. • He gets to bed black out. • He wakes up too ... • the wife ...	• Policeman, he works at night! /shift • main problem: body he's exhausted • e.g a bus pass to ... his ...	• Jet lag night shift flights • ....

c Answer the questions with a partner.

　　1　Do you usually sleep with your bedroom completely dark, or with the curtains or blinds open? Do you have problems sleeping if there is too much or not enough light for you?

　　2　Have you ever worked at night? Did you have any problems sleeping the next day? Why (not)? Do you think you would be able to work at night and sleep during the day?

　　3　Have you ever flown long haul? Where to? Did you get jet lag? How long did it take you to get over it?

2 GRAMMAR

used to, be used to, get used to

a Look at some extracts from the listening. Match the highlighted phrases to their meanings 1–3. What form is the verb after a) *used to* b) *be / get used to*?

　　1　In Spain I always used to sleep in complete darkness.

　　2　It's very hard to get used to being awake all night

　　2　And just when I'm finally used to being on New York time, then it's time to fly home.

　　1　I usually did this in the past.

　　2　It's not a problem for me because it is now a habit.

　　3　It's a problem for me because it hasn't become a habit yet.

b ▶ p.143 **Grammar Bank 6B.** Find out more about *used to*, *be used to* and *get used to* and practise them.

3 PRONUNCIATION

sentence stress and linking

a (3 **45**)》 Listen and repeat three sentences. Notice the rhythm and how the words are linked.

> 1　I'm **used␣to working␣in␣a team**.
> 2　I **can't get used␣to driving␣on the right**.
> 3　I **used␣to get␣up** at **six o'clock␣every day**.

b (3 **46**)》 Now listen and write down three more sentences.

c Practise saying the sentences quickly, getting the stress right and trying to link the words.

d Talk to a partner. Ask for and give more information.

　　1　When you were a child, did you use to…?
　　　　• share a room with a brother or sister
　　　　• have nightmares
　　　　• wake up very early in the morning

　　2　Do you have problems if you have to sleep in a bed that you aren't used to sleeping in (e.g. in a hotel)?

　　3　Do you think you would find it difficult to get used to…?
　　　　• getting up at 5.30 a.m. every day
　　　　• only being able to sleep for six hours a night
　　　　• not having breakfast in the morning

4 READING & SPEAKING

a Read the introductory paragraph of *Three things you (probably) didn't know about sleep.* Do you know the answers to any of the questions?

b Read **Living your dreams** and mark the sentences **T** (true) or **F** (false). <u>Underline</u> the part of the text that gave you the answer.

1 When we have a 'lucid' dream we know that we're dreaming.

2 In a 'lucid' dream the person who is dreaming can never change what is happening.

3 Gamers may be able to control their dreams because dreams are similar to computer games.

4 The reason we have nightmares may be to prepare us for certain dangerous situations.

5 Video gamers have more nightmares than non-gamers because they don't experience dangerous life-threatening situations.

6 Video gamers are braver in their dreams than non-gamers.

c ➤ **Communication** *Three things you (probably) didn't know about sleeping.* A *Sleeping Beauty p.106* **B** *How our ancestors used to sleep p.111.* Tell your partner some more interesting facts about sleep.

d In pairs see if you can remember some of the words and phrases from the articles you have read or heard.

Vocabulary Quiz

1 a medical condition, often an unusual one: a _____

2 an adjective meaning staying faithful to somebody and supporting them: _____

3 an adjective often used with sleep. A person who is in a ~ sleep is difficult to wake: _____

4 a hundred years, e.g. from 1900 to 2000: a _____

5 the time in the evening when it becomes dark: _____

6 the verb meaning to speak to God: _____

7 the word for a person who plays a lot of video games: a video _____

8 an adjective meaning clear, especially after a period of confusion: _____

9 to change position so as to face the other way: _____ _____

e Answer the questions in pairs.

1 Do you play video games? Do you think it has any effect on the way you dream? Do you think it has any positive or negative effects on you?

2 What do you think would be the worst thing for someone with Sleeping Beauty Syndrome?

3 Do you think sleeping in two shorter periods is a better way of sleeping? Do you think it would suit you and your lifestyle?

Three things you (probably) didn't know about

Everybody loves it. Everybody needs it. No-one seems to get enough of it. We all know that most people need eight hours sleep, and that REM* sleep is when you have most dreams, but here are three questions about sleep which you may not know the answer to:

- How can video games help us control our dreams?
- What is Sleeping Beauty Syndrome?
- What did our ancestors use to do in the middle of the night (which we don't)?

Living your dreams

A university psychologist in Canada believes that people who play video games are more likely to be able to control their own dreams. Jayne Gackenbach studied the dreams of regular video gamers and non-gamers and found
5 that people who frequently played video games experienced 'lucid' dreams more often. A lucid dream is one in which we are aware that we are dreaming. In a lucid dream, the dreamer is sometimes able to control or influence what is happening to them in the dream – very similar to controlling
10 the action of a character in a video game.

'Dreams and video games are both parallel universes,' says Gackenbach, 'Gamers spend hours a day in a virtual reality and they are used to controlling their game environments, and this seems to help them to do the
15 same when they are dreaming.'

Gackenbach also discovered that video gamers have fewer nightmares than non-gamers. Some experts believe that we have nightmares to help us practise for life-threatening situations in a safe environment. Since
20 video gamers already practise those situations regularly in games, Gackenbach's research suggests that video gamers may have less need of nightmares. But, interestingly, when gamers *do* have a nightmare they react differently to non-gamers: 'What happens with gamers,' says Gackenbach, 'is
25 that when they have a frightening experience in a dream they don't run away like most of us do, they turn round and fight back.'

*REM is an abbreviation for 'rapid eye movement'

5 LISTENING & SPEAKING

a Look at the picture and the headline of the article. Why do you think the man cooks in the middle of the night?

b (3 47)) Now listen to the first part of a radio programme and check your answers to **a**. What kind of things does he cook? Why is it a problem?

c Read the newspaper article about Robert Wood. Can you remember any of the details about him? Try to complete the gaps with a word or words, then listen again to check.

d You are now going to listen to the second half of the radio programme. Before you listen, work with a partner and discuss if you think the information in sentences 1–10 is **T** (true) or **F** (false).

1 A sleepwalker can drive a car while he is asleep. (T)
2 It is easy to know if someone is sleepwalking or not. (F)
3 About 8% of people sleepwalk from time to time. (F)
4 Sleepwalking is most common among young boys. (T)
5 Stress can cause people to sleepwalk. (T)
6 You should never wake up a sleepwalker. (F)
7 Sleepwalkers cannot hurt themselves. (F)
8 People usually sleepwalk for a short time. (T)
9 Sleepwalkers don't usually remember anything afterwards. (T)
10 Sleepwalking is no excuse if you commit a crime. (F)

e (3 48)) Listen once to check your answers. Then listen again and correct the false statements.

f Have you ever sleepwalked or do you know anyone who sleepwalks? What do they do when they sleepwalk? Where do they go? Does anyone try to wake them up?

The chef who cooks in the middle of the night

ROBERT WOOD, from Fife in Scotland, often gets up in the middle of the night and goes downstairs to the kitchen. Not surprising, you may think. He's probably hungry and looking for something to eat. But you'd be wrong. Robert starts cooking – and he does this while he is fast asleep.

Mr Wood, who is ¹_____ 55 _____ years old and a retired ²_ chef _, has been a sleepwalker for more than 40 years.

'The first time it happened I was ³_____ 14 _____', he said. 'My parents heard me wandering downstairs in the middle of the night. Now I get up ⁴_four a five_ times a week and these days I usually head for the kitchen, although on other occasions I have also turned on the television very loudly and even filled ⁵_bath_ with water.'

His wife Eleanor says that she often wakes up in the night when she hears her husband cooking downstairs. She has seen him laying the table and caught him making ⁶_omelettes_ and spaghetti bolognese and even frying ⁷_chips_. The couple say that because of Mr Wood's sleepwalking they only get a few hours' sleep a night and are getting worried that Robert could start a ⁸_house fire_ without realizing. 'I really am asleep and have no idea I am getting up,' said Mr Wood.

Mrs Wood says that although the food her husband cooks when asleep looks lovely, she has never eaten it. 'Every night, I think "Is Rob going to cook tonight?". The last time he was in the kitchen, he spilt milk all over the place.'

6 VOCABULARY & SPEAKING sleep

a **Vocabulary race.** In pairs, write the correct word from the list in the column on the right.

alarm · blankets · duvet · fall asleep · fast asleep · insomnia · keep you awake · nap · jet-lagged · nightmares · log · oversleep · pillow · sheets · set · sleeping tablets · siesta · sleepy · snore · yawn

1	Most people start feeling ▨ around 11.00 at night.	*sleepy*
2	They often open their mouth and ▨.	~~snore~~ yawn
3	They go to bed and ▨ their ▨ (clock).	set / alarm
4	They get into bed and put their head on the ▨.	pillow
5	They cover themselves up with a ▨, or with ▨ and ▨.	duvet / sheets / blankets
6	Soon they ▨.	fall asleep.
7	Some people make a loud noise when they breathe. In other words, they ▨.	snore
8	During the night some people have bad dreams, called ▨.	nightmares
9	If you don't hear your alarm clock, you might ▨.	oversleep.
10	If you drink coffee in the evening, it may ▨.	keep you awake
11	Some people can't sleep because they suffer from ▨.	insomnia
12	These people often have to take ▨.	sleeping tablets.
13	Some people have a ▨ or ▨ after lunch.	nap / siesta
14	A person who sleeps well 'sleeps like a ▨.'	log
15	Someone who is tired after flying to another time zone is ▨.	jet-lagged
16	Someone who is sleeping very deeply is ▨.	oversleep / fast asleep

b (3 49)》 Listen and check.

c Cover the column of words and test yourself.

d Ask and answer the questions in pairs. **A** asks the blue questions, and **B** asks the red questions. Ask for and give as much information as possible.

Do you sometimes have problems getting to sleep? Do you take, or have you ever taken, sleeping pills? Do you have any tips for people who suffer from insomnia?

Do you prefer to sleep with a duvet or with blankets? How many pillows do you have? What temperature do you like the bedroom to be?

Do you find it difficult to sleep when you're travelling, e.g. in buses or planes? Is there any food or drink that keeps you awake, or that stops you from sleeping well?

Do you ever have a nap after lunch or during the day? How long do you sleep for? How do you feel when you wake up?

Do you often have nightmares or recurring dreams? Do you normally remember what your dreams were about? Do you ever try to interpret your dreams?

Have you ever stayed up all night to revise for an exam the next day? How well did you do in the exam?

Are you a light sleeper or do you sleep like a log? How do you usually wake up in the morning?

Do you have a TV or computer in your bedroom? Do you often watch TV before going to sleep? Do you ever fall asleep on the sofa in front of the TV?

Do you snore? Have you ever had to share a room with someone who snores? Was this a problem?

Have you ever fallen asleep at an embarrassing moment, e.g. during a class or in a meeting?

Have you ever overslept and missed something important? What was it?

5&6 Revise and Check

GRAMMAR

a Complete the second sentence so that it means the same as the first.

1 They escaped from the jungle because they found the river.
They wouldn't have escaped from the jungle if they _____ _____ the river.

2 I can't go to dance classes because I work in the evening.
I would be able to go to dance classes if I _____ _____ in the evening.

3 We went to that restaurant because you recommended it.
We _____ _____ _____ to that restaurant if you hadn't recommended it.

4 Marta goes to bed late, so she's always tired in the morning.
If Marta didn't go to bed late, she _____ _____ so tired in the morning.

5 After living in London for a year I still find driving on the left difficult.
After living in London for a year I still can't get _____ _____ _____ on the left.

6 My hair was very long when I was a child.
When I was a child I used _____ _____ very long hair.

7 I get up very early, but it's not a problem for me now.
I'm used _____ _____ _____ very early.

8 It's a pity I can't speak French.
I wish _____ _____ _____ French.

9 I regret not learning to play the piano when I was younger.
I wish _____ _____ _____ _____ the piano when I was younger.

10 I hate seeing your dirty clothes on the floor.
I wish _____ _____ _____ your dirty clothes on the floor.

b Complete the sentences with the correct form of the **bold** verb.

1 I don't remember _____ you before. **meet**

2 The car needs _____. Shall I take it to the car wash? **clean**

3 We managed to _____ the airport on time. **get**

4 Please try _____ late tomorrow. **not be**

5 My sister isn't used to _____ in such a big city. She'd always lived in the country before. **live**

VOCABULARY

a Complete the sentences with an adjective expressing a feeling.

1 Our son played brilliantly in the concert! We felt very **pr**_____.

2 I'm feeling a bit **h**_____. I really miss my family.

3 Thanks for lending me the money. I'm very **gr**_____.

4 I shouldn't have bought that bag – it was so expensive. Now I feel really **g**_____.

5 When I heard that I had won the prize I was completely **st** _____. I couldn't say anything!

b Complete the sentences with the correct form of the **bold** word.

1 That walk was _____. I need a good rest now. **exhaust**

2 I was really _____ when I read Tim's email. **shock**

3 You really _____ me at the party last night! **embarrass**

4 It's very _____ when you think that you are going to miss your flight. **stress**

5 It _____ me when people who don't know me use my first name. **annoy**

6 Last night's concert was really _____. The orchestra didn't play well at all. **disappoint**

7 It always _____ me that people actually enjoy doing risky sports. **amaze**

8 We were _____ when we heard the news. **horrify**

9 What you said to Ruth was rather _____. I think you should apologize. **offend**

10 It was an incredibly _____ film! **scare**

c Write the words for the definitions.

1 _____ the person who directs an orchestra

2 _____ a group of people who sing together

3 _____ a stringed instrument that you hold between your knees

4 _____ a woman who sings with a very high voice

5 _____ an electronic musical instrument, like a piano

d Complete the missing words.

1 Could I have an extra **p**_____ for my bed, please?

2 My husband says I **sn**_____ really loudly at night.

3 I didn't sleep last night, so I'm going to have a **n**_____ now.

4 Last night I had a horrible **n**_____. I dreamt that I was lost in the jungle.

5 Don't forget to **s**_____ the alarm for tomorrow morning.

PRONUNCIATION

a Circle the word with a different sound.

1 sheets   really   relieved   sleepy

2 alarm   yawn   exhausted   snore

3 chorus   chauffeur   chemist   choir

4 chef   shattered   architect   shocked

5 delighted   inspired   survival   guilty

b Underline the main stressed syllable.

1 up|set   2 de|va|sta|ted   3 or|che|stra   4 in|som|ni|a   5 sleep|walk

CAN YOU UNDERSTAND THIS TEXT?

a Read the article once. What two factors helped Samuel to survive?

b Read it again and choose the best words to fill the gaps.

1   a carrying   b wearing   c holding
2   a take off   b take up   c take out
3   a watching   b finding   c setting
4   a including   b involving   c inviting
5   a search   b film   c shoot
6   a so   b because   c although
7   a understand   b worry   c fear
8   a found   b missing   c injured
9   a career   b course   c degree
10 a underused   b misused   c mispronounced

c Choose five new words or phrases from the text. Check their meaning and pronunciation and try to learn them.

◼️ CAN YOU UNDERSTAND THIS FILM?

VIDEO

3 50)) Watch or listen to a short film on sleep research. Choose a, b, or c.

1 In Britain _____ of people have problems getting to sleep.
   a over 10%   b approximately 10%   c more than 50%

2 One of the more common sleeping disorders mentioned is _____.
   a Sleep paralysis   b somniloquy   c Exploding head syndrome

3 Scientists at the Sleep Unit take measurements in order to analyse people's _____.
   a sleeping patterns   b brain activity   c body movement

4 Many people today are sleep deprived because they _____.
   a sleep too few hours
   b sleep different hours every night
   c wake up a lot during the night

5 Nowadays many people sleep longer hours _____.
   a during the week
   b after a night out
   c at weekends

Survival tastes so sweet for rescued British backpacker

Contact lens solution is not usually considered a survival tool, but if 18-year-old Samuel Woodhead hadn't been [1]_____ it, he might not have survived. The British gap year student went missing in the 40°C heat of the Australian outback on Tuesday. A fitness fanatic hoping to join the Royal Marines, Samuel survived for three days by drinking the saline cleaning solution, which his father had packed in his rucksack, but which he had forgotten to [2]_____ when he went for a run.

Samuel had been working for only two weeks as a ranch hand at Upshot cattle station, near the town of Longreach in the vast state of Queensland. After [3]_____ out for his run, he lost his way. Australian authorities had feared for his survival in a region where heat, a lack of water, poisonous snakes, and the possibility of injury could prove deadly.

Samuel Woodhead and his mother, Claire Derry

After a helicopter rescue mission, [4]_____ hundreds of people, he was found exhausted about six miles from the station. Alex Dorr, a pilot with the North Queensland Rescue Helicopter Service, said that he went in the dark to the area where the teenager had disappeared and used night-vision cameras to [5]_____ for the missing boy. 'Where am I?' was all that he asked his rescuers when they found him in the early hours of the morning. He was immediately taken for a medical assessment before being transferred to a hospital in Longreach, but was found to be suffering from no more than sunburn and dehydration, [6]_____ he had lost 15 kilos.

Claire Derry, his mother, said she heard that he was safe from the captain of the plane as she was flying to Australia to join the hunt for her son. 'I sobbed, absolutely sobbed and I jumped up and hugged the air hostesses and the captain,' she said. 'To be honest, I was beginning to [7]_____ the worst. It's been the worst three days of my life, by a long way, since 5.30 a.m. Tuesday when two policemen knocked on my front door and told me they'd got a message from Australia and told me my son was [8]_____.'

Samuel's training for a [9]_____ in the Armed Services helped him to survive in the hostile conditions, his mother said. 'My father was a war hero and Sam was named after him and he's always wanted to live up to that sort of reputation,' she said. His father, Peter Woodhead, was visibly emotional as he described the ordeal the family had been through while waiting for news that he was safe. 'The word nightmare these days is much [10]_____,' he said. 'This has been a true nightmare.'

Adapted from The Times

G past modals: *must have*, etc.; *would rather*
V verbs often confused
P weak form of *have*

> My parents only had one argument in 45 years. It lasted 43 years.
>
> *Cathy Ladman,*
> *US comedian*

7A Don't argue!

1 GRAMMAR past modals: *must have*, etc.

a **4 2)))** Look at the photos. What do you think the people are arguing about in each photo? What were the arguments about? Listen and check.

b **4 3)))** Listen to some extracts from the conversations again and complete them with *may have, might have, must have, can't have,* or *should have.*

Conversation 1		
1	You _____ finished it.
2	You _____ given it to the cat last night.
3	I _____ given it to the cat.

Conversation 2		
4	Oh no! We _____ gone wrong.
5	We _____ taken the second exit at the roundabout.
6	OK, I _____ made a mistake.

c In pairs, put **A**, **B**, **C**, or **D** in the box before each phrase.

Which phrase (or phrases) in **b** means you think…?

A it's very probable (or almost certain) that something happened or somebody did something

B it's possible that something happened or somebody did something

C it's impossible that something happened or somebody did something

D somebody did something wrong

d ➤ **p.144 Grammar Bank 7A.** Learn more about past modals, and practise them.

2 PRONUNCIATION
weak form of *have*

a **4 6)))** Listen to the extracts from the conversations in **1b** again. Underline the stressed words. How is *have* pronounced?

b In pairs, read the conversations and complete **B**'s responses with your own ideas (for responses 5–8 you also need to use *must have, might have, should have,* or *can't have*). Then practise the conversations.

1 **A** It was my birthday yesterday!
  B You should have _told me_.

2 **A** I can't find my phone anywhere.
  B You must have _____.

3 **A** I definitely said we were meeting them at 7.00.
  B They may have _____.

4 **A** I'm so tired. I can't keep my eyes open.
  B You shouldn't have _____.

5 **A** I failed my piano exam.
  B _____.

6 **A** Why do you think Fiona and Brian broke up?
  B _____.

7 **A** Alberto didn't come to class yesterday.
  B _____.

8 **A** We're going to be late. There's so much traffic.
  B _____.

3 READING & SPEAKING

a In your experience, what do couples typically argue about? Do you think men and women use different strategies when they argue? In what way?

b Read an article about how men and women argue. Does it mention any of the strategies you talked about?

c Now read the article again and mark the sentences **T** (true) or **F** (false). Underline the parts of the article that give you the answers.

1. The argument Deborah Cameron describes happened because a wife considered her husband responsible for an accident she had.
2. In Papua New Guinea when a woman is arguing with her husband, he's supposed to reply to his wife's insults.
3. John Gray says that men are more assertive in arguments than women.
4. Edward thinks that he could win arguments more often if he were better prepared.
5. Christine Northam says that older men are less able than younger men to talk about their feelings.
6. She says that some women start crying during arguments only because they get truly upset.
7. Sarah thinks that her boyfriend is insensitive to her crying.
8. Christine Northam believes it is not difficult to learn new ways of dealing with arguments.

d Look at the highlighted words and phrases which are related to arguing. With a partner, try to work out what they mean and then check with a dictionary or the teacher.

e Do you agree with what the text says about the different way men and women argue?

HOW MEN AND WOMEN ARGUE

Damian Whitworth investigates gender differences when couples argue.

1 In Gapun, a remote village in Papua New Guinea, the women take a very direct approach to arguing. Linguist Deborah Cameron tells of an argument between a husband and wife. It started after the woman fell through a hole in the rotten floor of their home and she blamed
5 her husband. He hit her with a piece of sugar cane, so she threatened to attack him with a machete and burn the house to the ground. At this point the husband decided to leave and she launched into a *kros* – a traditional angry tirade of insults and swear words – directed at a
9 husband with the intention of it being heard by everyone in the village.

'YOU ARE A ?!&#@.!! YOU ARE A ?!&#@.! RUBBISH MAN, YOU HEAR? YOU BUILT ME A HOUSE THAT I JUST FALL DOWN IN, THEN YOU GET UP AND HIT ME WITH A PIECE OF SUGAR CANE, YOU ?!&#@.!!'

13 The fury can last for up to 45 minutes, during which time the husband is expected to keep quiet. Such a domestic scene may be familiar to some
15 readers, but, for most of us, arguing with our partners is not quite such an explosive business!

Human beings argue about everything but are there any differences between the sexes in the way that we argue?

In fact, according to John Gray, author of *Men are from Mars, Women*
20 *are from Venus* (the 1990s best-seller) – men prefer not to argue at all, wherever possible. 'To avoid confrontation men may retire into their caves and never come out. They refuse to talk and nothing gets resolved. Men would rather keep quiet and avoid talking about any topics that may cause an argument.' Women, however, are quite happy
25 to bring up relationship matters that they would like to change.

Edward, 37, a writer, says 'I'm useless at arguing. There are things that bother me about my partner, but when I finally say something I am too slow to win the argument. I can only argue properly when I have all the evidence to back up my argument ready to use, but I'm too lazy to do
30 that. I think women, on the whole, are more practised at arguing, or more interested.'

Christine Northam, a counsellor with Relate, the marriage-counselling service, agrees with the view that men have a greater tendency to withdraw. 'Women say: "He won't respond to me, he won't listen, he
35 thinks he's right all the time." However, the younger men that I see tend to be much more willing to understand their own feelings and talk about them. Older men find it more difficult.'

However she adds that women are also capable of the withdrawal technique. 'Oh yes, women are quite good at doing that as well. They
40 change the subject or cry. Crying is a good tactic and then the poor man says: "Oh, my God, she's in tears".'

'I don't argue a lot, but I do cry a lot,' says Sarah, 32, an advertising executive. 'I'll say something hurtful to him and he'll say something equally hurtful back and then I'll be in floods of tears. I call my friend
45 and she says: "Where are you?" "In the loo*," I say. And then, when I finally come out after half an hour, he's just watching TV as if nothing has happened.'

Northam says, 'Everything goes back to our upbringing, the stereotypical stuff we have all been fed. We are very influenced by the way our parents
50 were, or even our grandparents. The way you deal with emotions is learnt in your family. To understand this, and then make a conscious decision that you will do it differently requires a lot of maturity.'

*loo *informal* = toilet

Adapted from The Times

4 LISTENING & SPEAKING

a (**4 7**))) You're going to listen to a psychologist giving some tips to help people when they disagree with somebody about something. Listen once and tick (✔) the six things she says.

1 ☐ Think carefully what to say when you begin a discussion.

2 ☐ Try to 'win' the argument as quickly as you can.

3 ☐ Say sorry if something really is your fault.

4 ☐ Never avoid an argument by refusing to talk.

5 ☐ Don't say things that aren't completely true.

6 ☐ Don't shout.

7 ☐ Don't talk about things that aren't relevant to the argument.

8 ☐ Use another person to mediate.

9 ☐ Postpone the argument until later when you have both calmed down.

10 ☐ It's a bad thing for a couple to argue.

b Listen again and with a partner, try to add more detail to the tips you ticked.

c (**4 8**))) Look at the sentences from the listening and try to work out what the missing words are. Then listen and check.

1 But of course it's **easier said** ____ ____.

2 If you're the person who's ____ **the** ____, just admit it!

3 …it's important to ____ **things** ____ **control**…

4 Raising your voice will just make the other person ____ **their** ____, too.

5 …stop for a moment and ____ **a** ____ **breath**.

6 It's also very important to ____ ____ **the point**.

7 There's much more chance that you'll be able to ____ **an** ____.

8 …____ ____ **conflict** is an important part of any relationship…

d With a partner, decide which two of the psychologist's tips you think are the most useful, and why they're useful.

e ➤ **Communication** *Argument!* **A** *p.107* **B** *p.110*. Role-play two arguments with a partner.

f Did you follow any of the psychologist's advice about how to argue? Was there anything you should / shouldn't have done? Is there anything your partner should / shouldn't have said?

5 MINI GRAMMAR *would rather*

> *Men would rather keep quiet and avoid talking about any topics that may cause an argument.*
>
> *Listen, I'd rather talk about this tomorrow when we've both calmed down.*
>
> - We use *would rather* with the infinitive without *to* as an alternative to *would prefer*, e.g.
>   *I'd rather go on holiday in July than August.*
>   *Would you rather stay in or go out tonight?*
>   *I'd rather not go out tonight. I'm really tired.*
>   NOT ~~I'd not rather.~~
>
> - We can also use *would rather* + person + past tense to talk about what we would prefer another person to do.
>   *I'd rather you didn't smoke in here, if you don't mind.*

a Re-write the sentences using *would rather*.

1 I'd prefer to go to the cinema than to a club.
2 I'd prefer not to go to the party if my ex is going to be there.
3 Would you prefer to meet on Thursday morning or afternoon?
4 My wife would prefer not to fly. She had a bad experience once.
5 My husband would prefer to get a train to Manchester, not take the car.
6 I'd prefer to come on Sunday, if that's OK.

b Work in pairs. Look at the options and take turns to ask and answer with *Would you rather…?* Say why.

1 do an English course in London or New York
2 have a summer holiday or a winter holiday
3 work for yourself or work for a company
4 go to a foreign restaurant for dinner or to a restaurant which serves food from your country
5 read an e-book or a normal book
6 have a four-by-four or a small sports car
7 go to a concert or a sporting event
8 live on your own or share a flat with friends

> *Would you rather do an English course in London or New York?*

> *I'd rather do a course in New York because…*

6 VOCABULARY verbs often confused

a Look at some extracts from the listening in **4**. Circle the correct verb. What does the other verb mean?

1 Try not to say…you never *remind / remember* to buy the toothpaste.
2 If you follow these tips, you may often be able to *prevent / avoid* an argument.
3 The most important thing is not to *rise / raise* your voice.

b ➤ **p.158 Vocabulary Bank** *Verbs often confused.*

c Complete the questions with the verbs from each pair in the right form. Then ask and answer with a partner.

1 Do you _____ if people are a bit late when you have arranged to meet them, or do you think it doesn't _____? **matter / mind**
2 Can you usually _____ family birthdays, or do you need somebody to _____ you? **remember / remind**
3 Have you ever been _____ when you were on holiday? What was _____? **steal / rob**
4 What would you _____ people to do if they want to come to your country in the summer? What might you _____ them to be careful about? **advise / warn**
5 Do you think taking vitamin C helps to _____ colds? What other things can people do to _____ catching colds? **avoid / prevent**

7 ④10»» SONG *My Girl* ♫

G verbs of the senses; *as*
V the body
P silent letters

> Botox should be banned for actors…
> Acting is all about expression; why would
> you want to iron out a frown?
>
> *Rachel Weisz,*
> *UK actress*

7B Actors acting

1 GRAMMAR verbs of the senses

a Read the introduction to Howard Schatz's books. Then look at the photo of actress Fran Drescher playing a role. In pairs, choose **a**, **b**, or **c**.

> In Character: *Actors Acting*
> Caught in the Act: *Actors Acting*
>
> The photographer Howard Schatz had a very unusual idea for his books. He invited actors into his studio, and asked them to 'be' certain characters in certain situations, and then he photographed them.

Fran Drescher

1 I think she **looks**…
   a scared
   b miserable
   c embarrassed

2 I think she **looks like**…
   a a teenage student
   b a young mother
   c a young business woman

3 I think she **looks as if**…
   a she has just had some bad news
   b she is watching something on TV
   c she has just heard a noise

b 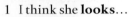 **(4 11)** Now listen to someone talking about the photo. Were you right?

c Look at the sentences in **a**. What kind of words or phrases do you use after *looks*, *looks like*, and *looks as if*?

d ➤ **p.145 Grammar Bank 7B.** Learn more about using the verbs of the senses, and practise them.

e **(4 13)** Listen to these sounds. What do you think is happening? Use *It sounds as if…* or *It sounds like…*

(*It sounds as if somebody's scored a goal.*

(*It sounds like a football match.*

f ➤ **Communication** *Guess what it is* **A** *p107* **B** *p111*. Describe objects for your partner to identify using *looks, feels, smells,* or *tastes* + an adjective or + *like* + noun.

2 SPEAKING & LISTENING

a Look at some more photos from the book. Describe how you think the characters are feeling.

(*I think she looks very pleased with herself…*

b Answer the questions with a partner.

Who do you think looks …?
1 like a child who's doing something naughty
2 like somebody who's apologizing to someone
3 like a very proud parent or teacher
4 as if they have just seen something awful
5 as if they are eating or drinking something that tastes terrible
6 as if they're going to hit somebody

c **(4 14)** Listen and check.

d Listen again. What exactly were the roles each actor was asked to play?

e How do you think acting is different when you are working in…?

   a film and TV   b theatre   c radio

Cheryl Hines

Jason Schwartzman

Ellen Burstyn

Dan Hedaya

Jane Lynch

Steve Guttenberg

f (4 15)) Now listen to an interview with Tim Bentinck, who has been working as a radio actor for many years. What is the main way in which he says radio acting is different from other kinds of acting?

g Listen again and answer the questions.

1 What two things does he say radio actors use to convey feelings?

2 Complete the tip that a radio actor once gave him: You have to be able to _____ one eyebrow with your _____.

3 What technique does he use to help convey the feeling of happiness?

4 What are radio actors trying to do when they read a script?

h Do you have radio dramas in your country? Do you ever listen to them?

3 MINI GRAMMAR *as*

a Look at some extracts from **2f**, and then read the rules about *as*.

Tim Bentinck has been working as a radio actor for many years.

'It's as naturalistic as you can make it sound – to lift it off the page, to make it sound as though you're not reading it.'

We can use *as* in many different ways:
1 to describe somebody or something's job or function: *She works as a nurse. You can use that box as a chair.*
2 to compare people or things: *She's as tall as me now.*
3 to talk about how something appears, sounds, feels, etc.: *It looks as if it's going to snow.*
4 to give a reason: *As it was raining, we didn't go out.* (as = because)
5 to say that something happened while something else was happening: *As they were leaving the postman arrived.* (as = when / at the same time)

b Decide how *as* is used in each sentence and match them to uses 1–5 above.

A ☐ I don't think his performance in this series was as good as in the last one.

B ☐ That picture looks as if it has been painted by a child.

C ☐ You can use that glass as a vase for the flowers.

D ☐ I got to the airport really quickly as there was hardly any traffic.

E ☐ As he was driving home it started to rain.

F ☐ You sound as if you've got a bad cold.

G ☐ His hair went greyer as he got older.

H ☐ He got a job with the BBC as a programme researcher.

4 VOCABULARY the body

a (4 16)》 Look at a picture of another actress, Dame Helen Mirren. Match the words in the list with 1–9 in the photo. Listen and check.

☐ cheek ☐ chin ☐ eyebrow ☐ eyelash ☐ eyelid
☐ forehead ☐ lips ☐ neck ☐ wrinkles

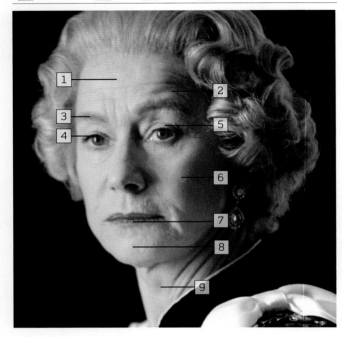

b ➤ p.159 Vocabulary Bank *The body.*

c (4 20)》 Listen and mime the action.

5 PRONUNCIATION silent letters

a Cross out the 'silent' consonant in these words.

calf wrist palm wrinkles comb kneel thumb

b (4 21)》 Listen and check. What can you deduce about the pronunciation of…?
- *wr* and *kn* at the beginning of a word
- *mb* at the end of a word

c Look at some more words with silent consonants. In pairs, decide which they are and cross them out. Use the phonetics to help you.

aisle /aɪl/ calm /kɑːm/ climb /klaɪm/ design /dɪˈzaɪn/
doubt /daʊt/ fasten /ˈfɑːsn/ half /hɑːf/ honest /ˈɒnɪst/
knock /nɒk/ muscle /ˈmʌsl/ whistle /ˈwɪsl/ whole /həʊl/

d (4 22)》 Listen and check. Then practise saying the phrases below.

half an hour I doubt it calm down an aisle seat, please
designer clothes anti-wrinkle cream kneel down

6 READING & LISTENING

a Look at the title of the article and read the subheading. Why do you think the writer called his book *What **Every Body** is Saying* and not *What **Everybody** is Saying*?

b Read the article once and then in pairs, answer the questions.

1 Why wasn't the man being questioned one of the main suspects?
2 Why did the agent ask him the question about four different murder weapons?
3 How did the man show that he committed the murder?
4 Why was Joe Navarro a very successful FBI agent?
5 What are the two kinds of communication he mentions?
6 Why can't we usually identify non-verbal signs?

WHAT EVERY BODY IS SAYING

IT'S ESTIMATED THAT AS MUCH AS 80% OF OUR INTERACTION WITH OTHERS IS THROUGH NON-VERBAL COMMUNICATION, OR BODY LANGUAGE.

[1] The man sat at one end of the table, carefully planning his replies. He wasn't considered a major suspect in the murder case. He had an alibi which was credible, and he sounded sincere, but the agent pressed on, and asked a series of questions about the murder weapons:

'IF YOU HAD COMMITTED THE CRIME, WOULD YOU HAVE USED A GUN?'

'IF YOU HAD COMMITTED THE CRIME, WOULD YOU HAVE USED A KNIFE?'

'IF YOU HAD COMMITTED THE CRIME, WOULD YOU HAVE USED AN ICE PICK?'

'IF YOU HAD COMMITTED THE CRIME, WOULD YOU HAVE USED A HAMMER?'

c Read the article again, and find synonyms for the words and phrases below.

Paragraph 1
1 believable _____
2 honest, not pretending _____
3 continued in a determined way *(verb)* _____

Paragraph 2
1 watched _____
2 meaning *(noun)* _____
3 seen _____

Paragraph 3
1 thought to be responsible for _____
2 find the meaning of _____
3 make it possible for _____

Paragraph 4
1 identify _____
2 succeed in getting _____
3 join together _____

2 One of the weapons, the ice pick, had actually been used in the crime, but that information had been kept from the public. So, only the killer would know which object was the real murder weapon. As Joe Navarro, the FBI agent, went through the list of weapons, he observed the suspect carefully. When the ice pick was mentioned, the man's eyelids came down hard, and stayed down until the next weapon was named. Joe immediately understood the significance of the eyelid movement he had witnessed, and from that moment the man became the chief suspect. He later confessed to the crime.

3 Joe Navarro is credited with catching many criminals in his 25-year career with the FBI. If you ask him how he has been able to do this, he says, 'I owe it to being able to read people'. In his best-selling book *What Every Body is Saying*, he teaches us how to decipher other people's non-verbal behaviour, and thus to enable us to interact with them more successfully.

4 'When it comes to human behaviours,' he says, 'there are basically two kinds of signs, verbal and non-verbal, e.g. facial expressions, gestures, etc. All of us have been taught to look for the verbal signs. Then there are the non-verbal signs, the ones that have always been there but that many of us have not learnt to spot because we haven't been trained to look for them. It is my hope that through an understanding of non-verbal behaviour, you will achieve a deeper, more meaningful view of the world around you – able to hear and see the two languages, spoken and silent, that combine to present human experience in all its complexity.'

d Look at the pictures. With a partner, say how you think the people are feeling.

e Now try to match the gestures to the feelings.

☐ dominant   ☐ friendly and interested   ☐ in a good mood
☐ insecure   ☐ nervous   ☐ relaxed   ☐ stressed

f (4 23)) Listen and check. Then listen again for more detail, and make notes.

> 🔍 **-wards**
> We often add the suffix *-wards* to a preposition or adverb of movement to mean 'in this direction', e.g. *forwards, backwards, inwards, outwards, upwards, downwards.*

g Test a partner. **A** make the gestures, one-by-one, but in a different order. **B** say what the gestures mean. Then swap roles.

h Is there any gesture that you know you do a lot, like folding your arms or standing with your hands on your hips? Why do you think you do it?

7 SPEAKING & WRITING

a ➤ **Communication** *Two photos* **A** *p.108* **B** *p.112.* Describe your picture for your partner to visualize. Describe the people's body language, and how you think they are feeling.

b ➤ **p.117 Writing** *Describing a photo.* Write a description of a picture speculating about what the people are doing, feeling, etc.

1 ◀ VIDEO THE INTERVIEW Part 1

a Read the biographical information about Simon Callow. Have you seen any of his films?

> **Simon Callow** is an English actor, writer, and theatre director. He was born in London in 1949 and studied at Queen's University, Belfast, and the Drama Centre in London. As a young actor he made his name when he played the part of Mozart in Peter Shaffer's production of *Amadeus* at the Royal National Theatre in London in 1979 and he later appeared in the film version. As well as acting in the theatre he has also appeared in TV dramas and comedies and in many films including *Four Weddings and a Funeral* and *Shakespeare in Love*. He has directed both plays and musicals and was awarded the Laurence Olivier award for Best Musical for *Carmen Jones* in 1992. He has written biographies of the Irish writer Oscar Wilde and Orson Welles, the American actor and film director. He was awarded the CBE in 1999 for his services to drama.

b ◀4 24)) Watch or listen to **Part 1** of an interview with him. Mark the sentences **T** (true) or **F** (false).

1 His first job was as an actor at The Old Vic theatre.
2 When he watched rehearsals he was fascinated by how good the actors were.
3 Acting attracted him because it involved problem solving.
4 Playing the part of Mozart in *Amadeus* was a challenge because he wasn't a fictional character.
5 Mozart was the most exciting role he has had because it was his first.

c Now listen again and say why the **F** sentences are false.

> **Glossary**
> **The Old Vic** one of the oldest and most famous of the London theatres
> *Amadeus* is a play by Peter Shaffer about the life of the composer Wolfgang Amadeus Mozart. It was also made into a film of the same name. In the play, Mozart is portrayed as having a very childish personality, which contrasts with the genius and sophistication of his music.
> *The Marriage of Figaro* one of Mozart's best-known operas
> **box office** the place at a theatre or cinema where tickets are sold
> **rehearsals** /rɪˈhɜːslz/ time that is spent practising a play or a piece of music
> **auditorium** /ˌɔːdɪˈtɔːriəm/ the part of a theatre where the audience sits

◀ VIDEO Part 2

a ◀4 25)) Now watch or listen to **Part 2**. Answer the questions.

1 Which does he prefer, acting in the theatre or in films?
2 Complete the two crucial differences he mentions about acting in the theatre:
There's an _____.
Every single performance is utterly _____.
3 Who does he say are the most important people in the making of a film, the director, the editor, or the actors? Why?
4 Does he think acting in film is more natural and realistic than theatre acting? Why (not)?

b Listen again. What is he referring to when he says…?

1 'It's important because you have to reach out to them, make sure that everybody can hear and see what you're doing.'
2 '…I mean you never do, you never can.'
3 'So, in that sense, the actor is rather powerless.'
4 '…there are some, you know, little metal objects right in front of you, sort of, staring at you as you're doing your love scene…'

> **Glossary**
> **(film) editor** the person whose job it is to decide what to include and what to cut in a film
> **editing suite** /ˈedɪtɪŋ swiːt/ a room containing electronic equipment for editing video material

acting

◄ Part 3

4 26)) Now watch or listen to
Part 3. What does he say about…?

1 watching other actors acting
2 the first great actors he saw
3 Daniel Day-Lewis
4 wearing make-up
5 the first night of a play

Daniel Day-Lewis

Laurence Olivier

Glossary
John Gielgud a famous stage and film actor
(1904 – 2000)
Ralph Richardson a famous stage and film
actor (1902 – 1983)
Laurence Olivier a famous stage and film
actor (1907 – 1989)
Edith Evans a famous stage and film actor
(1888 – 1976)
Peggy Ashcroft a famous stage and film actor (1907 – 1991)
Daniel Day-Lewis a famous film actor (1957–)
stage fright nervous feelings felt by actors before they appear in
front of an audience

2 ◄ LOOKING AT LANGUAGE

> 🔍 **Modifiers**
> Simon Callow uses a wide variety of modifiers (*really,
> incredibly*, etc.) to make his language more expressive.

4 27)) Watch or listen to some extracts from the
interview and complete the missing adjective or modifier.

1 '…I thought what a wonderful job, what a _____
interesting job…'
2 'My job was to reconcile that with the fact that
he wrote *The Marriage of Figaro*, and that was
tremendously _____.'
3 '…its fame, almost from the moment it was
announced, was **overwhelmingly** _____ than
anything I had ever done…'
4 'They're _____ **different** media, they require
different things from you as an actor…'
5 '…you bring _____ **different** things to them.'
6 'The beauty of the theatre is that every single
performance is **utterly** _____ from every other
one.'
7 'As a young man, and a boy, I was _____ **lucky** to
see that fabled generation of actors, of, of Gielgud and
Richardson, Olivier,…'

3 ◄ IN THE STREET
VIDEO

a **4 28))** Watch or listen to four people talking about
their favourite actors. Match the speakers (**N, S, J,** or
M) to the actors.

Nathan,   Sean,   Jo,   Mairi,
English   *English*   *English*   *Scottish*

☐ Audrey Hepburn   ☐ Jodie Foster
☐ Judi Dench   ☐ Kevin Spacey
☐ Matt Smith   ☐ Natalie Portman
☐ Olivia Colman   ☐, ☐ Robert De Niro
☐ Russell Crowe

b Watch or listen again. Who (**N, S, J,** or **M**)…?

☐ likes one of the actors he / she mentions because he/
she is very versatile
☐ has seen one of the actors he / she mentions in the
theatre
☐ thinks his / her favourite actors express feelings very
well
☐ says the actor he / she likes best was also in the film
he / she likes best

c **4 29))** Watch or listen and complete the highlighted
Colloquial English phrases. What do you think they
mean?

1 '…actors who are that famous have some sort of
star _____,…'
2 'I think he just has an intensity, and a _____ that
makes you want to watch him.'
3 '…my favourite film and my favourite performance
of _____ _____ is *The Deer Hunter*.'
4 '… I feel like she put her _____ into everything,…'

4 SPEAKING

Answer the questions with a partner. Try to use a variety
of modifiers.

1 What actors do you particularly enjoy watching? Why
do you like them? Which performances particularly?
2 What's one of the best films you've seen recently? Why
did you like it so much?
3 Do you ever go to the theatre? Do you prefer it to the
cinema? Why (not)? What plays have you seen?
4 Have you ever acted in a play or film? What was it, and
what part did you play? Did you get stage fright?

> The reason there is so little crime in Germany is that it is against the law.
>
> *Alex Levin, US writer*

8A Beat the robbers...and the burglars

HOW **NOT** TO
GET ROBBED IN THE STREET

1

You dramatically increase your chances of being robbed if you look as if you might have a lot of money on you. You don't have to look like a tramp, but you should try to look as if you aren't carrying much of value. If you're a tourist, keep your expensive camera or phone hidden.

2

This is especially true in countries where there are big income differences, and particularly in urban areas. Children are sadly often the most dangerous people on the street because they have nothing to lose. If you see a group of children coming towards you, ignore them completely and walk quickly to an area where there are plenty of other people.

3

If you see that people are watching you in a suspicious way, look straight back at them and make eye contact. If they were thinking of robbing you, it will make them realize that you may not be an easy target.

4

If you are a tourist and somebody in the street tells you to put your phone away, do it. Sometimes the locals can be overprotective because they want you to see the best side of their town, but it's always a good idea to take their advice. If they say don't go somewhere, don't.

5

The safest thing to do is to phone a reputable company every time you need one (your hotel can normally help with this). If you do have to get a taxi in the street, make sure it looks like a regulated one (e.g. one which has an official number or company phone number on it) and never ever get into a cab that has another person in the front passenger seat.

6

What's the first thing tourists do when they come out of Westminster Tube station in London? They look up at Big Ben, and then they pose to have their photo taken. When they're looking up, or looking at the camera, that's the moment when a pickpocket steals their wallet. Thieves also love the posters you see that warn tourists: 'Watch out! Pickpockets about!' When men read that their natural reaction is to immediately put their hand on the pocket where their wallet is, to make sure it's still there. The pickpockets are watching and so they see exactly where the man is carrying his wallet.

1 READING & LISTENING

a Have you ever been robbed in the street? Where were you? What was stolen?

b Read the article *How not to get robbed in the street*. Match the headings to the paragraphs.

  A **Be careful when you're sightseeing**
  B **Be smart about cabs**
  C **Don't look too well off**
  D **Keep an eye on the kids**
  E **Listen to the locals**
  F **Look confident**

c Read the article again. Then cover the text and look at A–F. Can you remember the advice? What advice would you give someone to avoid being robbed in your town?

d Look at the questions and predict the answers.

How to beat the burglars

1 How long do you think a burglar normally takes to search someone's house?
2 Which are the most common things that burglars steal, apart from money?
3 What one thing would be likely to stop a burglar coming into your house?
4 What factors influence a burglar to choose a house?
5 Why do some burglars prefer it if the owners are at home?
6 When are you most likely to be burgled, during the day or night?
7 How are burglars more likely to get into a house?
8 What is the best room in the house to hide your valuables?

Adapted from CNN

e (4 30))) Listen to an interview with an ex-burglar. Check your answers to d.

f Listen again for more detail. What reasons does he give for each answer? What tips can you learn from what he says to protect yourself from being burgled?

g Of all the tips for keeping safe at home and in the street, which one do you think is the most useful? Why?

2 VOCABULARY crime and punishment

a Match the words for people who steal with the definitions in the list.

> burglar mugger pickpocket robber shoplifter thief

1 A _____ is someone who breaks in and steals from a private house.
2 A _____ is someone who steals from a person or place, e.g. a bank, using or threatening violence.
3 A _____ is someone who steals something from a shop.
4 A _____ is someone who steals from you in the street, usually without you noticing.
5 A _____ is someone who uses violence to steal from you in the street.
6 A _____ is the general word for someone who steals from a person.

b (4 31))) Listen and check. Underline the stressed syllables.

c ➤ p.160 Vocabulary Bank *Crime and punishment.*

3 PRONUNCIATION & SPEAKING the letter *u*

> accuse burglar caught court drugs fraud judge
> jury mugger murderer punishment smuggling

a Look at the words in the list, which all have the letter *u* in them. Put them in the correct column below according to how the vowel sound is pronounced.

↑	🦆	🐴	juː	🦉

b (4 34))) Listen and check. Which two words are pronounced exactly the same?

c Practise saying the sentences.
1 Luke was accused of smuggling drugs.
2 'Murderers must be punished,' said the judge.
3 The burglar is doing community service.
4 The jury said he was guilty of fraud.
5 The mugger was caught and taken to court.

d Talk to a partner.

What are the most common crimes in your town or city?

What has been the biggest crime story in your country in the last few weeks?

Do you have trial by jury in your country? Do you think it's a good system?

Do you have capital punishment in your country? If not, would you re-introduce it?

Do you know anyone...? What happened?
- who has been burgled
- who has been mugged
- whose car has been stolen
- who has been unfairly accused of shoplifting
- who has been stopped by the police while driving
- who has been robbed while on holiday
- who has been offered a bribe
- who has been kidnapped

4 MINI GRAMMAR
have something done

> *They look up at Big Ben, and then they pose to have their photo taken.*
>
> - Use *have (something) done* when you get another person to do something for you. Compare:
>   *I took a photo of Westminster Bridge* = I took the photo myself.
>   *I had my photo taken on Westminster Bridge* = I asked someone to take my photo.
> - *Have* is the main verb so it changes according to the tense.
>   *I'm going to have my hair cut tomorrow. I had my car repaired after the accident.*
> - You can also use *get* instead of *have*, e.g. *I'm going to get my hair cut tomorrow.*

a Complete the sentences with the right form of *have* + the past participle of a verb from the list.

> cut install renew repair take

1 How often do you _____ your hair _____?
2 Have you ever had a problem with your laptop? Where did you _____ it _____?
3 Do you usually _____ your passport or ID card _____ in plenty of time before it runs out?
4 Have you _____ a burglar alarm _____ in your house or flat? What kind is it?
5 Have you ever _____ your photo _____ in front of a famous monument? Where?

b Ask and answer the questions with a partner.

5 GRAMMAR the passive (all forms); *it is said that..., he is thought to...,* etc.

a Read a true crime story. What does it advise us to be careful with? What happened to the woman?

Not her best buy

If a man approaches you outside a Best Buy store* with a complicated story about needing money to get home, and a surprisingly cheap iPad for sale, don't believe him!

A woman in Daytona Beach, Florida, ¹*learnt / was learnt* this the hard way after handing over $400 for what turned out to be a square piece of wood with a piece of glass stuck to the front. When the man, 39-year-old Torrance Canady, who ²*had / was had* a long criminal record, ³*later caught / was later caught* by the police, several more fake Apple products ⁴*found / were found* in his car. There were two MacBooks which ⁵*had made / had been made* from wood and which were covered in silver tape. An Apple logo ⁶*had cut / had been cut* out in the middle, and a Best Buy price tag stuck on the back. Canady insisted that he ⁷*didn't know / wasn't known* the computers were fake and said he'd 'bought them in a nearby town for his girlfriend'. He ⁸*has charged / has been charged* with selling fake electrical equipment and ⁹*is holding / is being held* in Volusia County jail.

* Best Buy store = a US store selling electronic equipment

b Read the story again. (Circle) the right form of the verb.

c (4 35)) Now listen to another crime story. Answer the questions.

1 Where were the burglaries taking place?
2 What did he steal?
3 What did Cooper do apart from stealing?
4 What did he do if he found people at home?
5 How was he caught?
6 Where did the police find him?

d Listen again and complete the extracts with the missing words. How is the structure different after *he is thought* and after *it is thought*?

1 ...he is thought _____ _____ _____ between 50 and 100 burglaries in the area.
2 It is believed _____ _____ _____ mainly interested in finding drugs...
3 Cooper is also said _____ _____ _____ himself at home in the houses.
4 ...it is thought _____ _____ _____ _____ to know someone there.

e ➤ **p.146 Grammar Bank 8A.** Learn more about the passive, and practise it.

f Use the notes below to complete a newspaper crime story.

Britain's most polite robber

Police in Stockport in the UK are looking for a man who ¹_____. (**believe / be Britain's most polite armed robber**)

The robber, who always says 'please' and 'thank you' when he orders shop staff to give him the money in the till, ²_____. (**say / be a tall man in his early forties**)

He wears a mask and washing-up gloves during robberies. It ³_____ at least four shops in Stockport in recent weeks. (**think / he / rob**)

A police officer said, 'He ⁴_____ (**report / be polite to his victims**), but there is nothing polite about armed robbery. Last week this man used a knife to threaten shop staff. They were terrified. Saying "please" and "thank you" cannot change that.'

6 READING

a Look at the title of the article. What kind of crime(s) do you think it will be about?

b Read the article once. Choose the best summary of the writer's opinion.

A Illegal downloading of music is not necessarily bad for the music industry. In some ways it benefits it.
B There is no way of stopping illegal downloading. We will just have to learn to live with it.
C Illegally downloading music is the same as stealing it from a shop and it will ultimately harm the people who are committing the crime.

c Read the article again. Answer the questions with a partner.

1 According to the writer, in what way do people have a different attitude to the online world?
2 In what way is people's attitude to online music illogical?
3 What did the government want to do? Who opposed this, and why?
4 What is the writer's view about illegal downloading?
5 Why does she compare fans who illegally download their idols' music to 'lovers' who 'watch you as you drown'?
6 Why does she think that the people who download will be the losers in the long run?

d Look at the highlighted words and phrases related to crime. In pairs, work out their meaning.

Crime online

What is the world online? Is it real? Are we safe there? How should we behave there?

1   The answer is: it's just the internet. Our internet. The internet we made. It's exactly like the real world – just a place with shops, and information, where people chat – but on a computer. But for some reason, we won't accept so simple an answer. We think that, as soon as
5   something is on the internet, it turns into something else, that it's not quite real.

Take for instance a song. When is a song not a song? When it's on the internet. If a song is on a CD, in a shop, we would not hesitate to pay for it. But if you put the same song on the internet, millions of people think
10 that you can take the same song without paying for it. It's still the same song, written by the same people, who spent the same hours and same money recording it, but press a button and it's yours.

There are plenty of justifications for taking things for free on the internet. In fact, when the government proposed punishing illegal
15 downloaders with internet disconnection, a lobby group of artists and musicians actually campaigned against it saying that 'it would reduce the civil liberties of every one of us in this country.'

But how can this be true? How is being banned from using the internet because you have committed a crime any different to being banned
20 from a library because you stole some books from there? The internet isn't a necessity. It's thrilling and brilliant and useful most of the time, but it's not a right to be able to use it. We don't have a right to listen to the music we want, or watch the films we like, for free. These things are treats, pleasures, luxuries. Why is it considered a right? Because it's the
25 internet. And why is the internet different from the rest of the world, where luxuries have to be paid for? Because...it's the internet.

There is also the argument that it's good for artists to be heard and seen. But what use are 9 million people who love your work, but not enough to want to pay you for your song or your film? Fans who don't
30 pay their idols are like lovers who promise everlasting love but then sit and watch you as you drown.

Do you know who will end up suffering the most from all this? Young people, the ones who themselves are doing it. The music industry has shrunk 40% since 2000. Famous music magazines, like *Melody Maker* and
35 *The Face*, have now closed. And young people who try to get jobs in the music industry complain about the low salaries, while they download hundreds of pounds worth of albums for free.

By The Times journalist Caitlin Moran

7 SPEAKING

a In groups, discuss the questions below:

Are these activities against the law in your country? Do you think they should be illegal? Why (not)? How do you think they should be punished?

Online world
- Downloading music, books, and films
- Hacking into somebody else's computer
- Posting aggressive or threatening 'tweets' or messages
- Photographing someone and posting the photo on the internet without their permission
- Using a false identity online
- Creating a computer virus

Real world
- Owning an aggressive breed of dog
- Squatting in an unoccupied house (living there without paying rent)
- Going on strike without having previously agreed / announced it
- Ill-treating an animal in any way
- Painting attractive graffiti on a wall or fence

> 🔍 **Useful language: saying what you think (1)**
> When we are giving our opinion about the right way to punish someone, we often use *should* + passive infinitive.
>
> | I think
I don't think | it should be | illegal /
against the law. |
> |---|---|---|
> | I think people who
do this should be | fined.
sent to prison.
banned from using
the internet.
made to... | |

b Compare your ideas with other groups. Do you agree?

8 WRITING

➤ **p.118 Writing** *Expressing your opinion.*
Write an article for a magazine saying what you think about either downloading music and films, or about squatting.

G reporting verbs
V the media
P word stress

> For most people no news is good news,
> but for journalists good news is not news.
>
> *Gloria Borger,*
> *US political commentator*

8B Breaking news

Home | World | UK | Business | Politics | Health | Education | Sci/Environment | Technology | Entertainment & Arts

1 SPEAKING & LISTENING

a Talk to a partner.

1 How do you normally find out…?
* the latest news
* what the weather's going to be like
* sports results and match reports
* what's on TV
* your horoscope
* film and book reviews
* job / accommodation adverts

2 Which sections of a newspaper do you normally read?
Which sections do you usually skip?
* politics
* sport
* crime
* business
* foreign news
* celebrity gossip
* food & lifestyle
* local / national news

3 What stories are in the news at the moment in your
country?

b Look at the photo and the headline from a news story.
What do you think the story is about?

Last updated 07:52

Love at first bite

c (4 38)) Listen and check. Were you right?

d Listen again and answer the questions.

1 Who is Soundari, and how old is she?
2 Why did the keepers build the snowmen?
3 What was inside one of the snowmen?
4 What did Soundari do when she saw the snowman?
5 Why is the film recorded on the camera very unusual?
6 What useful information did the keepers get from the
film?

e Look at the photos and headlines from two more
stories. What do you think they are about?

Last updated 15:09

Lost tourist finds herself

Dog phones for help

f ➤ **Communication** *Strange, but true* **A** *p.107,* **B** *p.112.*
Read the other two stories and tell each other what
happened.

2 GRAMMAR reporting verbs

a Read a news story called *Chicken fight*. What was the
'chicken fight'? How did the local paper resolve the
dispute? Would you like to try the dish?

b Read it again and match the highlighted phrases 1–6 in
the text with the direct speech below.

A ☐ 'I'll say sorry.'
B ☐ 'It's not true.'
C ☐ 'OK. I *did* see it there.'
D ☐ 'Would you like to make it for us?'
E ☐ 'OK, we'll do it.'
F ☐ 'You stole it.'

c Three of the four stories on these pages are true, but
one was invented. Which do you think is the invented
one?

d ➤ **p.147 Grammar Bank 8B.** Learn more about
reporting verbs, and practise them.

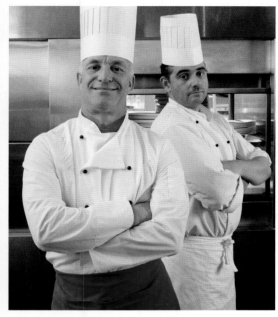

Last updated 14:33 ✉ 🖶

Chicken fight

By Sam Urban

Two chefs got into a fight last week after Andrew Palmer [1]accused Geoff Lewis of stealing one of his recipes and publishing it in a local newspaper.

Andrew Palmer, 28, claimed that he had invented the dish of cold chicken with strawberry mayonnaise at his Kent gastropub, The King's Head. However, restaurant chef Geoff Lewis, 30, who writes a weekly newspaper column on cooking, [2]denied copying the recipe and said the dish was his own creation.

So, the local newspaper, the *Sidcup Echo*, [3]invited both chefs to prepare the dish at their offices to see whose recipe it really was. They [4]agreed to come, and the 'cook-off' took place yesterday. Newspaper staff tried both dishes and unanimously declared Andrew's to be the winner. Geoff's dish was said to be 'lacking in flavour'. He later [5]admitted having seen the dish on the menu at Andrew's pub and he has [6]offered to publish an apology in the following issue of the *Echo*. 'In any case,' he said later, 'I've decided that it works better with raspberries.'

3 PRONUNCIATION word stress

a Look at the two-syllable reporting verbs in the list. All of them except four are stressed on the second syllable. (Circle) the four exceptions.

a|ccuse	ad|mit	ad|vise	a|gree	con|vince	de|ny
in|sist	in|vite	o|ffer	or|der	per|suade	pro|mise
re|fuse	re|gret	re|mind	su|ggest	threa|ten	

b (4 40)》 Listen and check.

> 🔍 **Spelling of two-syllable verbs**
> If a two-syllable verb ends in consonant, vowel, consonant, and is stressed on the second syllable, the final consonant is doubled before an *-ed* ending, e.g. *regret* > *regretted*, *admit* > *admitted* BUT *offer* > *offered*, *threaten* > *threatened*.

c Complete the sentences below with the correct reporting verb in the past tense.

1 'Shall I make some coffee?'   He *offered* to make some coffee.
2 'No, I won't go.'   He _____ to go.
3 'OK, I'll help you.'   He _____ to help me.
4 'I'll call you. Believe me.'   He _____ to call me.
5 'Remember to lock the door!'   He _____ me to lock the door.
6 'You should buy a new car.'   He _____ me to buy a new car.
7 'Would you like to have dinner?'   He _____ me to have dinner.
8 'I didn't break the window!'   He _____ breaking the window.
9 'Yes, it was me. I stole the money.'   He _____ stealing the money.
10 'I wish I hadn't married Susan.'   He _____ marrying Susan.
11 'Let's go to a club.'   He _____ going to a club.
12 'You killed your boss.'   The police _____ him of killing his boss.

d (4 41)》 Listen and check.

e (4 42)》 Cover the examples in **c**. Now listen to the sentences in direct speech in a different order. Say the reported sentence.

OK. I'll help you.   *He agreed to help me.*

iTutor **8B** 79

4 READING & VOCABULARY the media

a Read an extract from *24 Hours in Journalism*, showing what six different people are doing between 6.00 and 8.00 in the morning. Match the extracts with the kind of journalists below.

☐ a war reporter ☐ the online editor of the magazine *Marie Claire* ☐ a paparazzo (pl *papparazzi*)
☐ a radio news presenter ☐ an agony aunt ☐ a freelance journalist

When reporter and author John Dale wanted to show his readers what the life of a journalist was really like, he wrote to journalists from all different types of media and asked them to describe a typical day in their working life.

6 a.m. – 8 a.m.

1 Helen Russell wakes up excited, with a Frank Sinatra song running through her head like a mantra…*New York, New York.*

The first thing she reaches for is her BlackBerry. She's got all her complex life locked up in that electronic matchbox. Well-manicured fingers tap keys, and she starts looking at her diary. She sees meetings, meetings…

In her head Helen is already choosing the wardrobe she needs to wear, to look like her ¹_____ would like to look themselves. When you're this kind of journalist you have to look ²_____.

2 *'You're listening to Today on Radio 4 with Justin Webb and James Naughtie. The ³_____ this morning…The Chancellor has warned that the row about paying bonuses threatens to put jobs at risk… but Labour have accused him of putting the economy into reverse…A new ⁴_____ says that old people who need care have been let down by social services which pass them round like a parcel…'*

3 *'Anything happening?'*
'Two IEDs have exploded this morning.'
'How many have you found?'
'Fourteen.'

It's a bad start to the day, and a warning. Sommerville climbs into a British armoured vehicle. It is a dangerous ⁵_____, although he is well used to that. His life is one of bloody headlines. Wherever he is, that's the Big Story. The army convoy moves forward. Sommerville knows it's not *if* another bomb will ⁶_____, it's *when.*

4 A limousine sweeps along Wilshire Boulevard, Los Angeles, and turns in between the palm trees which mark the driveway of an undistinguished chain hotel. It pulls up, and a uniformed commissionaire steps forward and reaches for the handle of the rear door.

He pulls it open, and a woman's legs appear. He ⁷_____ her face and says, 'Good evening, Madam.' The woman smiles and walks through the door into the lobby.

Outside in the hotel grounds a man carrying several large cameras ⁸_____ a call on his mobile.
'She's here'.

5 Samantha Booth gets out of bed, goes into the kitchen and makes the first coffee of the day. She sits at her computer and opens her emails.
Gimme work, gimme work.

She's been sending out lots of ideas, hoping that at least one of her stories would be accepted. She ⁹_____ down the screen. Nothing. Zilch. Samantha is starting to feel sidelined. She ¹⁰_____ the TV and stares at the news, hardly taking it in. Why don't editors reply?

6 While organizing her three children for school, Katie Fraser switches on her computer. She ¹¹_____ dozens of Facebook groups dealing with everything, from drugs to abandoned wives, to panic attacks and premature babies.

She ¹²_____ her messages. The first one says *'I've had enough of feeling like this now. Doctors keep giving me pills but they don't work…'*

Fraser has to take the dog for a walk as well as get her kids ready for school. 'Come on, everyone,' she keeps saying, 'Time to go.'

> **Glossary**
> **The Chancellor (of the Exchequer)** The senior finance minister in the British government
> **IED** Improvized Explosive Device (small home-made bomb)
> **commissionaire** attendant, a person whose job it is to help or serve
> **gimme** *slang*, contraction of 'give me'
> **zilch** nothing (informal, US English)

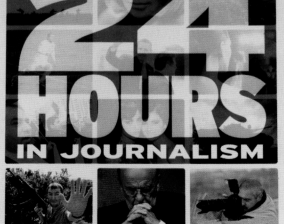
ONE DAY. ONE MILLION STORIES.
24 HOURS IN JOURNALISM

b Read the extract again. Choose the best option a, b, or c to complete the gap.

	a	b	c
1	readers	viewers	audience
2	hard-working	intelligent	glamorous
3	titles	headlines	story
4	report	article	news
5	arrangement	assignment	attachment
6	go off	take off	be off
7	reminds	recognizes	realizes
8	makes	does	phones
9	downloads	scrolls	clicks
10	turns down	turns off	turns on
11	leads	posts	runs
12	controls	checks	saves

c Which of the six jobs in the book extract sounds…?

- the most interesting
- the most stressful
- the most insecure
- the most fun

Which job would you most / least like to have?

d ▶ p.161 **Vocabulary Bank** *The media.*

5 SPEAKING

Talk in small groups.

1 Do you have a favourite…?
   a newsreader
   b film or TV critic
   c sports writer or commentator
   d TV or radio presenter
   e newspaper journalist

   What do you like about them? Are there any that you can't stand?

2 Which newspapers, TV channels, or radio stations in your country do you think are…?
   a biased   b reliable   c sensational

3 Is there much censorship in your country?

4 Look at the topics below and decide if you personally agree or disagree with them. Then, in your groups, discuss them. What is the majority opinion on each topic?

> It's not acceptable for journalists to listen in on politicians' phone calls and hack into their email accounts.

> The print newspaper is dead. We will soon read all our news online.

> Celebrities have to accept that the media publishes stories and photos about their private lives. That is the price they pay for being rich and famous.

🔍 **Useful language: saying what you think (2)**

In my opinion / view…
If you ask me…   celebrities should…
Personally I think…

Agreeing / disagreeing
I completely agree. / I don't agree at all.
I think / don't think you're right.

---

6 LISTENING

a (4 46)) Look at photos of six celebrities. Do you know anything about them? Listen to an interview with Jennifer Buhl, one of the paparazzi who work in the Hollywood area. Why are the celebrities mentioned?

Brad Pitt   Britney Spears   Lindsay Lohan

Julia Roberts   Kate Bosworth   Paris Hilton

b Listen again and tick (✓) the things that Jennifer says.

1 Many celebrities work with the paparazzi.
2 There are far more male paparazzi than female.
3 Most celebrities have a favourite paparazzo or paparazza.
4 It's easy for celebrities to avoid the paparazzi if they want to.
5 If celebrities are not photographed, the public become less interested in them.
6 There is no need to have stricter laws to protect people from paparazzi.
7 Nowadays many paparazzi use their phones to take photos.
8 There are some places where paparazzi won't go to try and get photographs.
9 Being followed by paparazzi is not stressful for most celebrities.

c Who do the paparazzi follow a lot in your country? Why? Are there any celebrities who rarely appear in the press?

7 (4 47)) **SONG** *News of the World* ♫

GRAMMAR

Complete the second sentence so that it means the same as the first.

1 I'm almost sure you left your phone in the restaurant.
You _____ _____ left your phone in the restaurant.

2 Why didn't you tell me it was your birthday?
You _____ _____ _____ me it was your birthday!

3 I'm sure the backpackers haven't got lost.
The backpackers _____ _____ _____ lost.

4 What would you prefer to do tonight, go out or stay in?
What would you _____ _____ tonight, go out or stay in?

5 I think somebody has tried to break in.
It looks _____ _____ somebody has tried to break in.

6 This meat has a very similar taste to beef.
This meat _____ _____ beef.

7 My brother is a waiter in a restaurant.
My brother works _____ _____ _____ in a restaurant.

8 The accident happened when they were repairing the road.
The accident happened when the road _____ _____ _____.

9 They'll probably never find the murderer.
The murderer will probably _____ _____ _____.

10 People think the burglar is a teenager.
The burglar is thought _____ _____ a teenager.

11 People say that crime doesn't pay.
It _____ _____ that crime doesn't pay.

12 We need to install a burglar alarm in our house.
We need to have a _____ _____ _____ in our house.

13 'I think you should talk to a lawyer,' I said to Sarah.
I advised Sarah _____ _____ to a lawyer.

14 'I didn't kill my husband,' Margaret said.
Margaret denied _____ _____ _____.

15 'I'm sorry I'm late,' James said.
James _____ _____ _____ late.

VOCABULARY

a (Circle) the correct verb.

1 Please *remind* / *remember* the children to do their homework.

2 **A** I'm terribly sorry.
B Don't worry. It doesn't *mind* / *matter*.

3 The robbers *stole* / *robbed* €50,000 from the bank.

4 If you know the answer, *raise* / *rise* your hand, don't shout.

5 Don't *discuss* / *argue* about it! You know that I'm right.

6 My brother *refuses* / *denies* to admit that he has a problem.

b (Circle) the word that is different.

1 palm   calf   wrist   thumb
2 kidney   lung   hip   liver
3 wink   wave   hold   touch
4 robber   vandal   burglar   pickpocket
5 fraud   smuggler theft   terrorism
6 evidence judge   jury   witness

c Write the verbs for the definitions.

1 _____ to bite food into small pieces in your mouth
2 _____ to rub your skin with your nails
3 _____ to look at sth or sb for a long time
4 _____ to make a serious, angry, or worried expression
5 _____ to find a way of entering sb's computer
6 _____ to demand money from sb by threatening to tell a secret about them
7 _____ to give sb money so that they help you especially if it's dishonest
8 _____ to leave your job (esp. in newspaper headlines)

d Complete the missing words.

1 The Sunday Times TV **cr**_____ wrote a very negative review of the programme.

2 This paper always supports the government. It's very **b**_____.

3 The journalist's report was **c**_____ by the newspaper. They cut some of the things he had wanted to say because of government rules.

4 My favourite **n**_____ is the woman on the six o'clock news on BBC1.

5 The article in the newspaper wasn't very **acc**_____ – a lot of the facts were completely wrong.

PRONUNCIATION

a (Circle) the word with a different sound.

1 elbow   frown   shoulders   hold
2 lay   nails   raise   biased
3 fraud   murder   burglar   journalist
4 aunt   heart   charge   stare
5 /juː/ argue refuse   news   jury

b Underline the main stressed syllable.

1 re|a|lize   2 kid|ney   3 kid|nap
4 co|mmen|ta|tor 5 ob|jec|tive

CAN YOU UNDERSTAND THIS TEXT?

a Read the article once. What was ironic about Jill Dando's murder?

b Read the article again. Mark the sentences **T** (true) or **F** (false).

1 Ex-criminals reconstruct their crimes on *Crimewatch*.

2 The objective of the programme is to solve crime.

3 More than 50% of the crimes featured on *Crimewatch* are solved as a result of the show.

4 A neighbour discovered Jill Dando's body about 15 minutes after she died.

5 The press thought that her murder was possibly connected to her job.

6 The programme itself was used to try to catch Dando's murderer.

7 The police arrested Barry George immediately after the reconstruction.

8 Barry George was known to stalk women.

9 George had said that he was innocent.

10 All the jury believed he was responsible for the murder.

c Choose five new words or phrases from the text. Check their meaning and pronunciation and try to learn them.

◼◀ CAN YOU UNDERSTAND THIS FILM?

VIDEO

(4 48)) Watch or listen to a short film on the Speed of News and answer the questions.

The Boston News-Letter.

New-England. Numb. 767

Published by Authority.

From Monday December 22. to Monday December 29. 1718.

1 How can ordinary people become journalists nowadays?

2 How many newspapers are there in the Newseum?

3 Which famous person appeared in the Boston Newsletter in 1718?

4 In the early days of journalism how did journalists get their stories to the nearest printing press?

5 Why was the news out of date by the time it reached the public?

6 Which invention changed the history of journalism?

7 What were two reasons why the news reporting on the American Civil war wasn't very accurate?

8 Which inventions created the age of mass media?

9 How do visitors to the HP New Media Gallery see the day's latest news stories?

10 Why did the news of the plane landing on the Hudson River reach the world so quickly?

crime watch

Who murdered Jill Dando?

The killing of a popular BBC journalist and TV presenter has baffled police and crime experts for many years.

One of the strangest unsolved crimes in the UK in recent years was the murder of Jill Dando, a well-known and much-loved presenter on the BBC programme *Crimewatch*.

On *Crimewatch*, major crimes are reconstructed by actors in the hope that members of the public will come forward with new information to help the police catch the criminals involved. According to the producers of the show, about a third of its cases are solved, half of which as a direct result of viewers' calls. These have included some of Britain's most notorious crimes, such as kidnappings and murders.

But on the morning of 26th April 1999 Jill Dando herself became a victim of a violent crime. As she was about to open the front door of her house in West London she was shot once in the head. Her body was discovered about a quarter of an hour later by her next-door neighbour.

At first there was great media speculation that the murderer might have been a criminal who had previously been convicted and imprisoned because of Jill Dando's investigative work on *Crimewatch*, but the police later discounted this theory. In fact, *Crimewatch* reconstructed the presenter's murder in an attempt to aid the police in the search for her killer, but a year later, despite an intensive police investigation no arrest had been made. The police began to focus their attention on 38-year-old Barry George, who lived about half a mile from Dando's house. He had a history of stalking women and other anti-social and attention-seeking behaviour. George was put under police surveillance, and on 25 May 2000 he was arrested and charged with Dando's murder. He was tried at the Old Bailey court in London and he pleaded not guilty to murder. The jury reached a majority verdict – George was found guilty and sentenced to life imprisonment, despite the fact that the only forensic evidence linking him to the crime was a tiny microscopic particle in his pocket, which experts believed could be gunpowder. George appealed unsuccessfully against the sentence on two occasions, but after a third appeal he was acquitted and released from prison, after serving eight years of his life sentence. Jill Dando's murder remains unsolved.

G clauses of contrast and purpose; *whatever, whenever,* etc.
V advertising, business
P changing stress on nouns and verbs

> Advertising is the art of convincing people to spend money they don't have on something they don't need.
>
> *Will Rogers,*
> *US humorist*

9A Truth and lies

1 READING & VOCABULARY

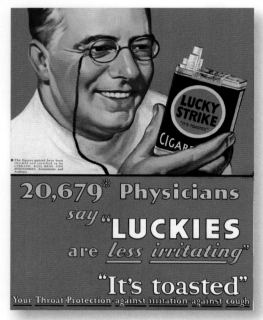

20,679* Physicians say "**LUCKIES** are *less irritating*"

"It's toasted"

Your Throat Protection - against irritation - against cough

a Look at the advert and answer the questions with a partner.

1 What is being advertised?
2 What decade do you think it's from?
3 Why do you think they used a doctor in the advert?

b Read the first paragraph of the article and check your answers to **a**.

c Read the whole article and answer the questions. Write **1–4** next to sentences A–F.

Which company (or companies)…?

A ☐☐ deceived the public by pretending that their product had properties which it didn't really have

B ☐☐ used a celebrity or a professional person in order for them to associate their product with a healthy lifestyle

C ☐ used technology to create a false impression

D ☐ admitted that they had made a claim that wasn't true

E ☐ admitted that they had done something wrong

F ☐ was punished for their misleading advert

FOUR OF THE MOST MISLEADING ADVERTS OF ALL TIME

1 Cigarettes are not harmful to your health
Hard to believe, but there was a time when tobacco companies actually tried to make us believe that doctors approved of smoking, or that certain brands were better for your throat than others. This advert for Lucky Strike from the 1920s is just one of dozens of ads featuring doctors recommending or 'preferring' one brand over another. Tobacco companies continued to use doctors to convince the public to smoke until the 1950s when evidence showing the link between smoking and lung cancer became too strong to ignore.

2 The thinner the better
In 2009 fashion retailer Ralph Lauren made a series of advertisements using a model who was so heavily airbrushed that her waist appeared to be smaller than her head. The ads were widely criticized in the press and experts warned of the negative effect these kinds of images might have on young girls. Lauren threatened to sue a blogger, who was the first person to publish and comment on the image online. But later he made a statement apologizing and admitting that 'we are responsible for the poor imaging and retouching that resulted in a very distorted image of a woman's body.' However, he later fired the model in the advert, Fillipa Hamilton, because she was 'overweight' (she weighed 54 kilos).

3 Vitamins prevent cancer
In 2010 the pharmaceutical company Bayer was sued by the Center for Science in the Public Interest for running TV and radio commercials that suggested one of the ingredients in its *One A Day* vitamin supplement brand prevented prostate cancer. In fact, there is no scientific evidence that vitamins fight cancer in any way. Bayer eventually paid a fine and signed a legal agreement which banned it from claiming that vitamins can cure cancer.

4 You can lose weight without dieting or doing exercise
During the 1990s Enforma, a US fitness company, ran an advertising campaign using TV commercials in which baseball player Steve Garvey promoted two diet supplements, a 'Fat Trapper' that supposedly blocked the absorption of fat, and a product named 'Exercise In A Bottle'. These two products together, according to the ad, would allow you to lose weight without dieting or exercise and promised consumers that 'they would never have to diet again'. The Federal Trade Commission* (the FTC) took Garvey to court for making false claims about the product. So began an epic legal battle which the FTC ultimately lost when a federal court ruled that celebrity endorsers were not responsible for misleading statements in ads. However, this ruling eventually led to the passing of new regulations making it illegal for celebrities to make false statements of fact in advertisements.

* The Federal Trade Commission is an independent agency in the US which helps to protect consumers.

From CBS News website

d Look at the highlighted words and phrases. With a partner, try to work out what they mean. Then match them with their meanings 1–11.

1 _advertisements_ notices, pictures, or films telling people about a product
2 _____ noun advertisements on the radio or TV
3 _____, _____ noun two abbreviations for advertisements
4 _____ verb saying that sth is true
5 _____ famous people who promote a product
6 _____ verb digitally changed details in a photograph
7 _____ noun types of product made by a particular company
8 _____ verb took a person or company to court to ask for money because of something they said or did to harm you
9 _____ adj giving the wrong idea or impression, making you believe sth that is not true
10 _____ noun people who buy goods or use services
11 _____ a series of advertising messages with the same theme

e Do adverts or commercials in your country use any of the tricks mentioned in the text? Which ones?

2 LISTENING & SPEAKING

a Look at the advertisement for mascara. The ad campaign for this product was withdrawn because it was misleading. Why do you think it was misleading?

b (5 2)) Now listen to a radio programme about five tricks used by advertisers. Tick (✓) the things that the woman mentions that are often used in adverts:

- [ ] free gifts
- [ ] limited supplies of the product
- [ ] two for one offers
- [ ] animals and nature
- [ ] crowds of people
- [ ] a good slogan
- [ ] attractive models
- [ ] doctors and celebrities
- [ ] smiling, happy families
- [ ] good music or a good song
- [ ] recent studies
- [ ] humour

c Listen again. Why are the things you have ticked often a trick? Make notes.

d Talk in small groups.

1 Which of the marketing techniques in **b** might influence you to buy (or not buy) the product?
2 Have you bought something recently which wasn't as good as the advertisement made you think? How was the advert misleading?
3 What are viral adverts? Have you ever forwarded one to other people? Do you have a favourite one?
4 Can you think of a recent advert which made you not want to ever buy the product? Why did the advert have this effect on you?
5 Are there any brands which you think have a really good logo or slogan? Does it make you want to buy the products?

3 GRAMMAR
clauses of contrast and purpose

a Look at some extracts from the listening in **2**, and complete them with the phrases A–G.

1 In spite of _____, its price was really included in the magazine subscription.
2 Even though _____, and maybe don't even like them, we immediately want to be among the lucky few who have them.
3 So as to _____, they use expressions like, 'It's a must-have'…
4 …and they combine this with a photograph of a large group of people, so that _____.
5 The photo has been airbrushed in order to _____, with perfect skin, and even more attractive than they are in real life.
6 Although _____, do you really think she colours her hair with it at home?
7 It was probably produced for _____, and paid for by them, too.

A the company itself
B the actress is holding the product in the photo
C we can't fail to get the message
D make us believe it
E we don't really need the products
F what the advert said
G make the models look even slimmer

b (5 3)) Listen and check. Then look at the seven phrases again, and the highlighted word(s) immediately before them. Which ones express a contrast? Which ones express a purpose?

c ▶ p.148 Grammar Bank 9A. Find out more about clauses of contrast and purpose, and practise them.

d Sentence race: Try to complete as many sentences as you can in two minutes.

1 I think the advertising of expensive toys should be banned, so that…
2 In spite of a huge marketing campaign,…
3 Although they have banned most cigarette advertising,…
4 She applied for a job with a company in London so as to…
5 He's decided to carry on working despite…
6 Even though the advert said I would notice the effect after a week,…
7 I took my new laptop back to the shop to…
8 We went to our head office in New York for…

4 READING & LISTENING

a Look at the title of the article and the photos. What do you think the 'bagel test' is?

b Read the article and check. Then in pairs say what you can remember about…

1 Paul Feldman's original job
2 the incident that made him decide to change his job
3 how the 'bagel habit' started, and what it consisted of
4 why he started asking for money, and the proportion of people who paid
5 his friends' and family's reaction to his change of job
6 how his business progressed
7 the economic experiment he had (unintentionally) designed

c You are going to hear an American economist talking about Paul Feldman's experiment. Before you listen, in pairs, predict the answers to the questions:

1 What was the average payment rate?
    a 70%–80%   b 80%–90%   c 90%–100%
2 Were smaller offices more or less honest than big ones?
3 How often has the cash box been stolen?
4 Did people 'cheat' more during good or bad weather?
5 Did people 'cheat' more or less at Christmas? Why?
6 Who cheated more, executives or lower status employees?

d (5 6)) Listen and check your answers to **c**.

e Listen again and choose **a**, **b**, or **c**.

1 More people paid in Feldman's own office…
    a after he had caught somebody stealing
    b because he asked them personally for the money
    c because the workers were his colleagues
2 Feldman eventually stopped selling bagels to…
    a a company where less than 80% paid for their bagels
    b a company where the money box got stolen
    c a company where less than 90% paid for their bagels
3 People are more honest in smaller companies because…
    a they are more likely to get caught
    b they would be more embarrassed about being caught
    c there is more control over what goes on
4 People 'cheat' more…
    a after a day off
    b before all public holidays
    c before some public holidays
5 Which of these people is most likely to pay?
    a an administrative worker who doesn't like his boss
    b an executive who is very popular with his staff
    c an employee who likes the company where he works

f If Feldman left a basket of bagels in your school or work place, what proportion do you think would pay?

What The Bagel Man Saw
Would you pass the bagel test?

Once upon a time, Paul Feldman dreamed big dreams. While studying agricultural economics at Cornell, he wanted to end world hunger. Instead, he ended up taking a job with a research institute in Washington, analysing the weapons expenditures of the United States Navy. He was well paid and unfulfilled. 'I'd go to the office Christmas party, and people would introduce me to their wives or husbands as the guy who brings in the bagels,' he says. 'Oh! You're the guy who brings in the bagels!' Nobody ever said, 'This is the guy in charge of the public research group."

The bagels had begun as a casual gesture: a boss treating his employees whenever they won a new research contract. Then he made it a habit. Every Friday, he would bring half a dozen bagels, a serrated knife, some cream cheese. When employees from neighbouring floors heard about the bagels, they wanted some, too. Eventually he was bringing in 15 dozen bagels a week. He set out a cash basket to recoup his costs. His collection rate was about 95 per cent; he attributed the underpayment to oversight.

In 1984, when his research institute fell under new management, Feldman said to management: 'I'm getting out of this. I'm going to sell bagels.'

His economist friends thought he had lost his mind. But his wife supported his decision. Driving around the office parks that encircle Washington, he solicited customers with a simple pitch: early in the morning, he would deliver some bagels and a cash basket to a company's snack room; he would return before lunch to pick up the money and the leftovers. Within a few years, he was delivering 700 dozen bagels a week to 140 companies and earning as much as he had ever made as a research analyst.

He had also – quite without meaning to – designed a beautiful economic experiment. By measuring the money collected against the bagels taken, he could tell, down to the penny, just how honest his customers were. Did they steal from him? If so, what were the characteristics of a company that stole versus a company that did not? Under what circumstances did people tend to steal more, or less?

Adapted from The New York Times

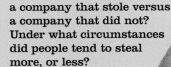
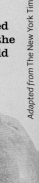

5 MINI GRAMMAR
whatever, whenever, etc.

*...a boss treating his employees **whenever** they won a new research contract.*

We use *whenever* to mean *at any time* or *it doesn't matter when*, e.g. *Come and see me whenever you like.*

We can also use:

whatever (= anything), *whichever* (=anything, from a limited number), *whoever* (= any person), *however* (= in any way), *wherever* (= any place). They also mean *it doesn't matter what / which / who / how / where*, etc.

Complete the sentences with *whatever, whichever, whoever, whenever, however,* or *wherever.*

1 Please sit _____ you like.
2 There is a prize for _____ can answer the question.
3 _____ she opens her mouth she says something stupid.
4 I'm going to buy it _____ expensive it is!
5 _____ I give her, it's always the wrong thing.
6 I'll go by bus or train, _____ is cheaper.

6 VOCABULARY business

a Look at some words from the *What the bagel man saw* article. With a partner, say what they mean.

- research
- in charge of
- employees
- won a contract
- under new management
- customers

b ➤ p.162 Vocabulary Bank *Business.*

c Answer the questions with a partner.

What's the difference between...?

1 a customer and a client
2 a boom and a recession
3 increase and improve
4 rise and fall
5 export a product and import a product
6 a manager and an owner

7 PRONUNCIATION & SPEAKING
changing stress on nouns and verbs

> 🔍 **Changing stress on two-syllable nouns and verbs**
> Some words change their stress depending on whether they are verbs or nouns. The nouns are usually stressed on the first syllable, e.g. *an export, a record* and the verbs on the second syllable, e.g. *to export, to record.* Words like this include: *increase, decrease, import, progress, permit, produce, refund, transport.*

a Read the information in the box and practise saying each word both ways, as a verb and as a noun.

b Underline the stressed syllable on the **bold** word.

1 We're making good **pro|gress** with the report.
2 The new building is **pro|gre|ssing** well.
3 We **ex|port** to customers all over the world.
4 One of our main **ex|ports** is wine.
5 **A** Can you **re|fund** me the cost of my ticket?
   B Sorry, we don't give **re|funds**.
6 Sales have **in|creased** by 10% this month, so there has been an **in|crease** in profits.
7 The demand for organic **pro|duce** has grown enormously.
8 Most toys nowadays are **pro|duced** in China.
9 They're planning to **trans|port** the goods by sea.
10 There has been a rise in the number of people using public **trans|port**.

c **5 10))** Listen and check. Practise saying the sentences.

d Talk to a partner.

In your country...

1 What agricultural products are produced or grown? What products are manufactured?
2 What are the main exports to other countries? What kind of products are usually imported to your country?
3 Is your country in a boom period, in a recession, or somewhere in between? How easy is it to find a job at the moment? Has the number of unemployed increased or decreased recently?

8 **5 11)) SONG** *The Truth* ♫

G uncountable and plural nouns
V word building: prefixes and suffixes
P word stress with prefixes and suffixes

9B Megacities

1 READING & SPEAKING

a What do you think a 'megacity' is? Read the introduction to the text to check your answer. With a partner, in two minutes, list what you think are probably the biggest problems for people who live in a megacity.

b Read the article once. In which city are the things you discussed in **a** a problem: Tokyo, Mexico City, both, or neither?

c Read the article again. Then, in pairs, using your own words, say why the following are mentioned.

TOKYO
33 million   eight million   a letter from the train company
driving schools   25 square metres   the *Hikikomori*
rent a friend   the *Hashiriya*

MEXICO CITY
taco stands   Mariachi bands   two-and-a-half hours
social imbalance   kidnapping   Kevlar

d Find words in the article which mean…

TOKYO
1 _____ *adj* operated by machines not people (paragraph 1)
2 _____ *adj* impossible to imagine (paragraph 1)
3 _____ *noun* the number of people who don't have a job (paragraph 1)
4 _____ *adj* with too many people in it (paragraph 2)
5 _____ *noun* a feeling that you don't belong to a community (paragraph 3)
6 _____ *noun* the feeling of not having any friends (paragraph 3)

MEXICO CITY
7 _____ *noun* the process of making air (and water) dirty (paragraph 2)
8 _____ *noun* the state of being very rich
9 _____ *noun* the state of being poor
10 _____ *adjective* not having a house

e Talk to a partner.

1 If you had to go to work or study in either Mexico City or Tokyo, which would you choose, and why?
2 What do you think are the main advantages of living in a big city?
3 What's the biggest city you've ever been to? Why did you go there? What did you think of it?

Andrew Marr's Megacities

BBC 1 Wednesday 8.00 p.m.

By 2050, 70% of the world will live in cities, and by the end of the century three-quarters of the entire planet will be urban. There are now 21 cities called 'megacities', i.e. they have more than 10 million inhabitants. In Andrew Marr's BBC series *Megacities* he travelled to five of these cities, including Tokyo and Mexico City.

TOKYO

Tokyo, with a population of 33 million people, is by far the largest city in world. It's also the most technologically advanced, and the city runs like digital clockwork. The automated subway*, for example, is so efficient that it is able to transport almost eight million commuters every day and on the rare occasions that it goes wrong, nobody believes it. If you are late for work in Tokyo and, as an excuse, you say that your train was late, you need to provide written proof from the train company. The idea of late trains is almost unthinkable. There is very little crime, violence, or vandalism in Tokyo and the streets are safe to walk by day or night. There is also relatively low unemployment compared to other big cities in the world.

But such a huge population creates serious problems of space, and as Marr flew over Tokyo in a helicopter he saw football pitches, playgrounds, even driving schools constructed on top of buildings. Streets, parks, and subways are extremely overcrowded. Property prices are so high and space is so short that a family of six people may live in a tiny flat of only 25 square metres.

There are other problems too, of alienation and loneliness. The *Hikikomori* are inhabitants of Tokyo who cannot cope with 'the mechanical coldness and robotic uniformity' of a megacity and have become recluses, rarely or never leaving their homes. There is also a new business that has grown up in Tokyo which allows friendless people to 'rent a friend' to accompany them to a wedding or just to sit and chat to them in a bar after work.

Another strange group of people are the *Hashiriya*, Tokyo's street racers who risk their lives driving at ridiculous speeds along the city streets. During the week these men have ordinary jobs and they're model citizens. But on Saturday nights they spend the evening driving though the city as fast as they possibly can. It's a deadly game, but it's just one way of escaping the daily pressures of life in the metropolis.

* the underground or metro system

TOKYO

MEXICO CITY

MEXICO CITY

As a complete contrast to Tokyo, Marr takes us to Mexico City, a colourful and vibrant city of about 20 million people where people live their lives in the street. Marr says that 'in Mexico City, food and friendship go hand in hand'. The city is full of taco stands and cafés where people meet and socialize and Mariachi bands stroll through the boulevards and squares playing songs for money. And on Sundays people of all ages gather to dance in the street.

But it's a city with problems of its own, too. It can take two-and-a-half hours for commuters to drive to and from work in the rush hour through choking traffic fumes, and pollution levels are high. And, looking down from a helicopter, Marr shows us the huge social divide. On one hillside we see massive, luxurious houses and on the next hill, slums. It's a city of great wealth but also extreme poverty, and there are many homeless people. Because of this social imbalance it can be a dangerous city too, with high levels of crime, especially kidnapping. In fact, there are boutiques which sell a rather special line in men's clothes: the shirts, sweaters, and jackets look completely normal but are in fact bulletproof, made of reinforced Kevlar.

But despite the crime, the traffic, and the pollution Andrew Marr describes Mexico City as 'a friendly, liveable place' and the most enjoyable megacity of all that he visited.

2 VOCABULARY
word building: prefixes and suffixes

> 🔍 **Prefixes and suffixes**
> A **prefix** is something that you add to the beginning of a word, usually to change its meaning, e.g. *pre* = before (**pre**-*war*), or a negative prefix like *un-* or *dis-* (**un**healthy, **dis**honest). A **suffix** is something you add to the end of a word, usually to change its grammatical form, e.g. *-ment* and *-ness* are typical noun suffixes (*enjoy**ment**, *happi**ness***). However, some suffixes also add meaning to a word, e.g. *-ful* = full of (*stress**ful**, *beauti**ful***).

a Read the information about prefixes and suffixes. What prefix can you add to *city* meaning *big*? What suffix can you add to *home* meaning *without*? Can you think of any other examples of words with this suffix?

b ➤ p.163 **Vocabulary Bank** *Word building.*

3 PRONUNCIATION & SPEAKING
word stress with prefixes and suffixes

> 🔍 **Word stress on words with prefixes and suffixes**
> We don't put main stress on prefixes and suffixes that are added to nouns and adjectives. However, there is usually secondary stress on prefixes, e.g. *un* in *unemployment*.

a Underline the main stressed syllable in these multi-syllable nouns and adjectives.

ac|com|mo|da|tion   an|ti|so|cial   bi|ling|ual
en|ter|tain|ment   go|vern|ment   home|less
lone|li|ness   mul|ti|cul|tu|ral   neigh|bour|hood
o|ver|crow|ded   po|ver|ty   un|der|de|ve|loped
un|em|ploy|ment   van|dal|ism

b 🔊 **5 16**))) Listen and check. Practise saying the words.

c Answer the questions below with a partner.

Which city (or region) in your country do you think...?
- is the most multicultural
- offers the best entertainment (for tourists / for locals)
- has a bilingual or trilingual population
- is very overcrowded
- has very serious pollution problems
- has a lot of homeless people
- has some very dangerous neighbourhoods
- has the highest rate of unemployment
- has the worst levels of poverty
- suffers from the worst vandalism and antisocial behaviour

4 LISTENING & SPEAKING

a When you travel to another country or city, do you normally try to find out about it before you go? Where from? What kind of information do you look for?

b You are going to listen to an interview with Miles Roddis, a travel writer for the Lonely Planet guidebook series, talking about his five favourite cities. Look at the photos, and try to guess which continent or country they were taken in.

c (5 17))) Listen once and find out where they are. What personal connection does Miles have to each place?

d Listen again and make notes. What does Miles say is special about each place?

e (5 18))) Now listen to some extracts from the interview. Try to write in the missing words. What do you think they mean?

1 …there's wonderful surfing on Bondi beach and plenty of great little _____ for sunbathing and swimming.

2 …the choice of places to eat is _____.

3 But what gives the city a special _____ during the festival is 'the Fringe'.

4 And the Museum of Islamic Art has a whole lot of _____ pieces from Muslim times.

5 Tuscany's two major tourist towns, Florence and Pisa, are absolutely _____ - _____ with tourists all year round…

6 These walls are amazing – they're completely intact, and you can _____ into people's living rooms as you walk past.

7 The Laotians are a lovely, _____, laid-back people.

8 I remember looking down on it from one of the restaurants along its banks, and feeling that it was _____ _____ all my troubles.

f Talk in small groups.

1 Which of the five places Miles mentions would you most like to go to? Why?

2 What other cities would you really like to go to? Why?

3 What are your two favourite cities (not including your own)?

4 Of the cities you've been to, which one(s) have you liked least? Why?

5 GRAMMAR uncountable and plural nouns

a Circle the correct form. Tick (✓) if you think both are possible.

1 A good guidebook will give you *advice | advices* about what to see.
2 You may have *some bad weather | a bad weather* if you go to London in March.
3 When I was in Rome and Paris, *the accommodation was | the accommodations were* extremely expensive.
4 It's best not to take *too much luggage | too many luggages* if you go on a city break.
5 The old town centre is amazing, but *the outskirts is | the outskirts are* a bit depressing.
6 I really liked the hotel. The rooms were beautiful, and *the staff was | the staff were* incredibly friendly.

b ➤ p.149 Grammar Bank 9B. Learn more about uncountable nouns and plural and collective nouns, and practise them.

c Play **Just a minute** in small groups.

Just a minute

> **RULES**
>
> One person starts. He / she has to try to talk for a minute about the first subject below.
>
> If he or she hesitates for more than five seconds, he / she loses his / her turn and the next student continues.
>
> The person who is talking when one minute is up gets a point.

modern furniture
good advice you've been given
what's in the news at the moment
tourist accommodation in your country
the weather you like most
the most beautiful scenery you've seen
the traffic in your town / city

chocolate

the police in your country
clothes you love wearing

6 WRITING

➤ p.119 Writing Bank *A report.* Write a report for a website about good places for eating out or entertainment in your city.

1 ◄ THE INTERVIEW Part 1
VIDEO

a Read the biographical information about George Tannenbaum. Have you seen any adverts for the companies he has worked with?

> **George Tannenbaum** was born in 1957 in Yonkers, New York and was educated at Columbia University in New York. He has worked on advertising campaigns for many well-known companies such as IBM, Mercedes-Benz, Gillette, Citibank, and FedEx. Today he is the Executive Creative Director at R/GA, an international advertising agency.

b (5 21)) Watch or listen to **Part 1** of an interview with him and answer the questions.

1 Which other members of his family have worked in advertising?
2 When did George start working in advertising?
3 What wasn't he allowed to do when the family were watching TV?
4 Why does he think jingles are so memorable?
5 What kind of adverts were the H.O. Farina TV commercials?
6 What happens in the story of Wilhelmina and Willie?

Glossary
jingle a short song or tune that is easy to remember and is used in advertising on radio or television.
H.O. Farina a company which has been making cereals since the 1940s. They ran an advertising campaign in the 50s based on a cartoon character called Wilhelmina.

◄ Part 2
VIDEO

Tommy Lee Jones in a BOSS advertising campaign

(5 22)) Watch or listen to **Part 2**. Complete the notes with one or two words.

1 George says that a commercial is made up of three elements
  1 _____
  2 _____
  3 _____

2 The acronym AIDA stands for
  A _____
  I _____
  D _____
  A _____

3 According to George, using a celebrity in advertising is a way of _____, but he isn't a _____ of it.

4 George thinks that humour in advertising is _____.

Glossary
a depilatory /ə dɪˈpɪlətri/ a product used for removing unwanted hair
Tommy Lee Jones a US actor born in 1946, winner of an Oscar in the 1993 film *The Fugitive*.
Mad Men a well-known US TV series about advertising executives in the 1960s who worked in offices in Madison Avenue in New York

advertising

◄ Part 3
VIDEO

(5 23)⟩ Watch or listen to **Part 3** and (circle) the correct phrase.

1 He thinks that billboard and TV advertising will *remain important | slowly decline.*

2 He tends to notice *both good and bad adverts | only well-made adverts.*

3 He thinks Nike adverts are very successful *because of their logo and slogan | because they make people feel good about themselves.*

4 He thinks Apple's approach to advertising was very *innovative | repetitive.*

5 Their advertising message was *honest and clear | modern and informative.*

billboard /ˈbɪlbɔːd/ a large board on the outside of a building or at the side of the road, used for putting advertisements on

2 ◄ LOOKING AT LANGUAGE
VIDEO

🔍 **Metaphors and idiomatic expressions**
George Tannenbaum uses a lot of metaphors and idiomatic expressions to make his language more colourful, e.g. *took the baton* = carry on in the family tradition, (from relay races in athletics) .

a (5 24)⟩ Watch or listen to some extracts from the interview and complete the missing words.

1 'You know they, what do they call them, _____ **worms**?'

2 'They **get into your** _____ and you can't get them out sometimes…'

3 'And I bet you I'm getting this _____ **for word** if you could find it.'

4 '…we do live in a celebrity culture and people, you know, **their ears** _____ **up** when they see a celebrity.'

5 'Have billboards and TV commercials **had their** _____?'

6 '…because you've got **a captive** _____.'

7 'they became kind of the gold standard and they rarely **hit a** _____ **note**.'

b Look at the expressions with a partner. What do you think they mean?

3 ◄ IN THE STREET
VIDEO

a (5 25)⟩ Watch or listen to five people talking about advertising. How many of them say they are influenced by advertising campaigns?

Jeanine, *South African* | Dustin, *American* | Elvira, *American* | Ivan, *American* | Yasuko, *American*

b Watch or listen again. Who (**J**, **D**, **E**, **I**, or **Y**)…?

☐ is against adverts which can make smoking seem attractive to young people

☐ prefers to do their own research before they buy a product

☐ ☐ say that they are concerned about young people's health

☐ is not sure we should ban the advertising of unhealthy products

☐ thinks that women are sometimes exploited in advertising

c (5 26)⟩ Watch or listen and complete the **highlighted** Colloquial English phrases. What do you think they mean?

1 '…when they see it they're very _____ to the adverts and then they want it immediately and it's a problem.'

2 'I'm sure I am, probably not consciously, but I'm sure _____.'

3 'The only thing that _____ to _____ that should be banned from advertisements is…'

4 'That's _____ _____ the only thing that I can think of.'

5 '…so I think that anything that causes health _____ or bad influences or addiction should be banned from being on commercials.'

4 SPEAKING

Answer the questions with a partner.

1 Do you think you're influenced by advertising campaigns?

2 Is there any product that you think shouldn't be advertised?

3 Are there any brands that you think make very good or very bad adverts?

4 Are there any jingles or slogans that you remember from your childhood? Why do you think they were so memorable? Are there any others that have got into your head since then?

5 Are there many billboards in your country? Do you think they make the streets uglier or more attractive?

6 How important do you think humour and celebrities are in advertising?

G quantifiers: *all, every, both*, etc.
V science
P stress in word families

> We live in a society exquisitely dependent on science and technology, in which hardly anyone knows anything about science and technology.
>
> *Carl Sagan,
> US scientist and writer*

10A The dark side of the moon

1 SPEAKING & LISTENING

a With a partner, discuss the statements below. Do you think they are **F** (facts) or **M** (myths)? Say why.

b (5 27)) Listen to a scientist on a radio programme discussing each statement. Were you right?

c With a partner, see if you can remember any of the explanations the scientist gave. Then listen again and make notes for each statement.

d Do you know any other things that some people think are scientific facts, but are really myths?

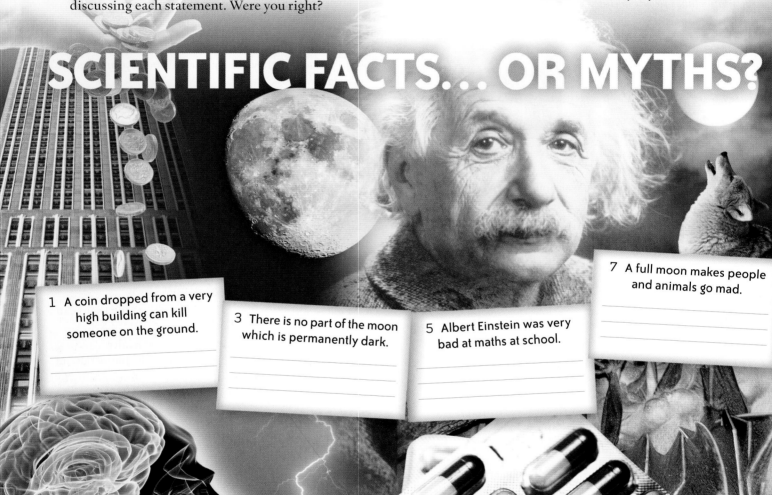

SCIENTIFIC FACTS… OR MYTHS?

1 A coin dropped from a very high building can kill someone on the ground.

3 There is no part of the moon which is permanently dark.

5 Albert Einstein was very bad at maths at school.

7 A full moon makes people and animals go mad.

2 We only use ten per cent of our brains.

4 Rubber tyres protect a car from lightning.

6 Antibiotics don't kill viruses.

8 Bats are blind.

2 VOCABULARY & PRONUNCIATION
stress in word families, science

a Look at these extracts from the listening in **1b** and write the highlighted words in the table below.

This is one of the most popular scientific myths…
He got very high marks in maths and science.

person	adjective	subject
scientist		
chemist		
biologist		
physicist		
geneticist		

b Now complete the chart for the other four words.

> 🔍 **Stress in word families**
> In some word groups the stressed syllable changes in the different parts of speech, e.g. *geographer, geographic, geography*.

c ⑤ 28))) Listen and check. Then listen again and under<u>line</u> the stressed syllables in the words. In which groups does the stress change?

d Practise saying the word groups.

e Complete the sentences with a word from the list.

discovery   drugs   ~~experiments~~   guinea pigs   laboratory
research   side effects   tests   theory

1 Scientists **carry out** *experiments* in a _____.
2 Archimedes **made** an important _____ in his bath.
3 Isaac Newton's experiments **proved** his _____ that gravity existed.
4 Before a **pharmaceutical company** can sell new _____, they have to do _____ to make sure they are safe.
5 Scientists have to **do** a lot of _____ into the possible _____ of new drugs.
6 People can **volunteer** to be _____ in **clinical trials**.

f ⑤ 29))) Listen and check, and mark the stress on all the multi-syllable words in **bold**. Practise saying the sentences.

3 SPEAKING

Work with a partner. A interview B with the questions in the red circles. Then B interview A with the blue circles.

Which scientific subjects do / did you study at school? What do / did you enjoy the most / the least?

Which scientific subjects do you think have actually taught you something useful?

Is there a scientist (living or dead) who you admire? Who?

What do you think is the most important scientific discovery of recent years? Why?

Are there any scientific discoveries that you wish <u>hadn't</u> been made?

If you were ill, would you agree to be a guinea pig for a new kind of treatment?

Do you think it is acceptable for animals to be used in experiments? Does it make a difference if the experiments are for medical research or for cosmetics testing?

Are you happy to eat genetically modified food? Why (not)?

Are there any scientific stories in the news at the moment?

Are you worried about any of the things scientists are currently experimenting with?

What would you most like scientists to discover in the near future?

4 READING

a You are going to read about four scientists who suffered to make their discoveries. Read the article once. How many of the scientists were killed by their experiments or inventions?

b Read the extracts again and answer questions 1–8 from memory. Write **A–D** in the right box.

Which scientist or scientists...?

1 ☐ got ill after trying to show that his discovery was harmless
2 ☐☐ made a fatal mistake during an experiment
3 ☐ died of diseases he caught as a result of his experiment
4 ☐ caused the death of other scientists
5 ☐☐ used to breathe in toxic substances
6 ☐ was doing his experiments to reverse / stop the ageing process
7 ☐ is remembered today for the negative effects of his discovery
8 ☐ was not very successful in his first job

Suffering scientists

Four scientists who were injured or killed by their own experiments.

A Sir Humphry Davy
(1778–1829)

Sir Humphry Davy, the British chemist and inventor, had a very bumpy start to his science career – as a young apprentice he was fired from his job as an apothecary* because he caused too many explosions! When he eventually took up the field of chemistry, he had a habit of inhaling the various gases he was dealing with. Fortunately, this bad habit led to his discovery of the anaesthetic properties of nitrous oxide. Unfortunately, the same habit led him to nearly kill himself on many occasions and the frequent poisonings left him an invalid for the last two decades of his life. During this time he also permanently damaged his eyes in a nitrogen trichloride explosion.

* apothecary = person who in the past used to make and sell medicines

B Alexander Bogdanov
(1873–1928)

Alexander Bogdanov was a Russian physician, philosopher, economist, science fiction writer, and revolutionary. In 1924, he began experiments with blood transfusion – in a search for eternal youth. After 11 transfusions (which he performed on himself), he declared that he had stopped going bald, and had improved his eyesight. Unfortunately for Bogdanov, the science of transfusion was not very advanced and Bogdanov had not been testing the health of the blood he was using, or of the donors. In 1928, Bogdanov took a transfusion of blood infected with malaria and tuberculosis, and died soon after.

C Thomas Midgley
(1889–1944)

Thomas Midgley was an American chemist who helped to develop leaded petrol (lead was added to petrol to make car engines less noisy). General Motors commercialized Midgley's discovery, but there were several deaths from lead poisoning at the factory where the additive was produced. In 1924, Midgley took part in a press conference to demonstrate the safety of his product and he inhaled its vapour for a minute. It took him a year to recover from the harmful effects! Weakened by lead poisoning, he contracted polio at the age of 51, which left him disabled. He invented a system of ropes and pulleys so that he could pull himself out of bed, but his invention caused his death when he was strangled by the ropes. The negative impact on the environment of leaded petrol seriously damaged his reputation and he has been described as 'the human responsible for most deaths in history'.

c (5 30)) Look at the highlighted words, which are all related to science and medicine. Do you know what they mean? Are they similar in your language? How do you think they are pronounced? Listen and check.

D Louis Slotin
(1910–1946)

Louis Slotin, a Canadian physicist, worked on the Manhattan project (the American project which designed the first nuclear bomb). In 1946, during an experiment with plutonium, he accidentally dropped a container causing a critical reaction. Other scientists in the room witnessed a 'blue glow' and felt a 'heat wave'. Slotin had been exposed to a lethal dose of radiation. He rushed outside and was sick and then was taken to hospital. Although volunteers donated blood for transfusions, he died nine days later. Three of the other scientists who were present died later of illnesses related to radiation.

5 GRAMMAR quantifiers: *all, every, both,* etc.

a With a partner circle the right word or phrase.

1 *Both | Both of* Sir Humphry Davy and Thomas Midgley damaged their health as a result of inhaling chemicals.
2 *Either | Neither* Thomas Midgley nor General Motors were prepared to admit how dangerous lead was.
3 Until 1973, *all | every* cars used leaded petrol.
4 *All the | All* blood Bogdanov used in his experiments might have been contaminated, because he never tested any of it.
5 Sir Humphry Davy was fascinated by *all | everything* to do with gases.

b ➤ **p.150 Grammar Bank 10A.** Learn more about quantifiers, and practise them.

c Do the Science quiz with a partner.

1 In Direct current, the electrons...
   a move in only one direction
   b move in both directions
   c don't move at all

2 Helium gas can be found...
   a only in liquid form
   b in neither liquid nor solid form
   c in both liquid and solid form

3 Adult giraffes remain standing...
   a some of the day
   b all day
   c most of the day

4 Of all the water on our planet, ... is found underground.
   a hardly any of it
   b about half of it
   c most of it

5 Snakes eat...
   a only other animals
   b either other animals or eggs
   c either other animals or fruit

6 A diamond can be destroyed...
   a by either intense heat or acid
   b by both intense heat and acid
   c only by intense heat

7 The human brain can continue to live without oxygen for...
   a nearly two minutes
   b nearly six minutes
   c a few hours

8 In our solar system,...
   a neither Pluto nor Neptune are now considered to be planets
   b both Pluto and Neptune are considered to be planets
   c Pluto is no longer considered to be a planet

9 When we breathe out,...
   a most of that air is oxygen
   b none of that air is oxygen
   c some of that air is oxygen

10 An individual blood cell makes a whole circuit of the body in...
   a nearly 60 seconds
   b nearly 45 seconds
   c a few minutes

d (5 34)) Listen and check.

G articles
V collocation: word pairs
P pausing and sentence stress

> Today's politicians can no longer write their own speeches, and there is some evidence that they can't read them either.
>
> *Gore Vidal,*
> *US writer*

10B The power of words

1 GRAMMAR articles

a Who was the first man to land on the moon? In what year?

b (5 35)) Listen to him saying the first words spoken from the moon. With a partner, try to complete the sentence and answer the questions.

> That's one _____ step for _____,
> one giant leap for _____.

1 What do you think the difference is between *a step* and *a leap*?
2 What do you think *mankind* means?

c (5 36)) Listen to an interview about the moon landing. What was the controversy about the words Armstrong actually said? What's the difference in meaning between *a man* and *man*? Did new technology prove him right or wrong?

d Listen again and answer the questions.

1 When did Armstrong write the words he was planning to say when he first stepped on the moon?
2 Does Armstrong say he wrote *'That's one small step for man…'* or *'One small step for a man…'*?
3 Why doesn't the sentence everybody heard make sense?
4 What did Armstrong think he said?
5 Who is Peter Shann Ford? What did he discover?
6 How did Armstrong feel when he heard about this?

e Read some more facts about Armstrong. Are the highlighted phrases right or wrong grammatically? Correct the mistakes.

1 Neil Armstrong was born in the USA.
2 He was a shy boy, who loved the books and the music.
3 He studied aeronautical engineering at the university.
4 He was the first man who set foot on moon.
5 His famous words were heard by people all over the world.
6 Before becoming a astronaut, he worked for the US navy.
7 After 1994 he refused to give the autographs.
8 In 2005 he was involved in a lawsuit with an ex-barber, who tried to sell some of the Armstrong's hair.

f ➤ p.151 Grammar Bank 10B. Learn more about articles, and practise them.

g ➤ **Communication** *Geography true or false* A *p.108* B *p.111*. Complete sentences about geography with articles.

2 READING

a Read extracts from four famous inspirational speeches. Match the summary of what they are saying to each speaker **EP**, **WC**, **NM**, and **BO**.

1 Although people don't believe we are capable of succeeding, if we really want to, we will be able to do it.
2 We are prepared to starve ourselves in order to draw attention to inequality.
3 However long it takes, we will carry on resisting the enemy and we will never give up.
4 I have fought all my life to end racial inequality.

b Read the speeches again and find words or phrases in the text for these definitions.

Emmeline Pankhurst
1 _____ *noun* refusing to eat to protest about something
2 _____ IDM about to die
3 _____ *noun* the people in power, e.g. in government
4 _____ *adj* very important, to be treated with great respect

Winston Churchill
1 _____ PHR V continue
2 _____ *adj* getting bigger
3 _____ *verb* give up, stop fighting

Nelson Mandela
1 _____ *verb* formal to love sth very much
2 _____ IDM formal if necessary

Barack Obama
1 _____ *verb* resist
2 _____ *noun* a person who doesn't believe that anything good can happen
3 _____ IDM when you have to think about how things really are, not how you would like them to be
4 _____ *noun* belief

c Which speeches seem to you to be the most / least inspirational? Why?

d (5 40)) Now listen to the extracts spoken by the people themselves (except Emmeline Pankhurst's which is read by an actress). Do you respond to any of them differently? Which do you think is more important, the words themselves or the way they were spoken?

EMMELINE PANKHURST

She was leader of the suffragette movement. In 1913, when women were campaigning for the right to vote. She gave the speech after several suffragettes had been imprisoned for attacking a policeman and chaining themselves to railings outside the Prime Minister's house in London.

❝I have been in audiences where I have seen men smile when they heard the words "hunger strike", and yet I think there are very few men today who would be prepared to adopt a "hunger strike" for any cause. It is only people who feel an intolerable sense of oppression who would adopt a means of that kind. Well, our women decided to terminate those unjust sentences at the earliest possible moment by the terrible means* of the hunger strike. It means you refuse food until you are at death's door, and then the authorities have to choose between letting you die, and letting you go.

Human life for us is sacred, but we say if any life is to be sacrificed it shall be ours; we won't do it ourselves, but we will put the enemy in the position where they will have to choose between giving us freedom or giving us death.❞

*means = method

BARACK OBAMA

He made this speech during his first presidential campaign in 2008, which he won to become the first ever black president of the United States.

❝We know the battle ahead will be long, but always remember that no matter what obstacles stand in our way, nothing can stand in the way of the power of millions of voices calling for change.

We have been told we cannot do this by a chorus of cynics, and they will only grow louder and more dissonant in the weeks and months to come. We've been asked to pause for a reality check. We've been warned against offering the people of this nation false hope.

But in the unlikely story that is America, there has never been anything false about hope. For when we have faced down impossible odds*; when we've been told we're not ready, or that we shouldn't try, or that we can't, generations of Americans have responded with a simple creed that sums up the spirit of a people.

Yes, we can! Yes, we can! Yes, we can!❞

*faced down impossible odds = had to deal with very difficult situations

WINSTON CHURCHILL

He was British Prime Minister during the second World War. He gave this speech to the House of Commons in 1940 when a German invasion of Britain was expected at any moment.

❝We shall go on to the end. We shall fight in France, we shall fight on the seas and oceans, we shall fight with growing confidence and growing strength in the air, we shall defend our island, whatever the cost may be. We shall fight on the beaches, we shall fight on the landing grounds, we shall fight in the fields and in the streets, we shall fight in the hills; we shall never surrender...❞

NELSON MANDELA

He made this speech in 1990 on his release from jail, where he had spent 27 years for being an activist in the fight against apartheid. He later became the first black president of South Africa.

❝In conclusion, I wish to quote my own words during my trial in 1964. They are as true today as they were then. I wrote: I have fought against white domination, and I have fought against black domination. I have cherished the ideal of a democratic and free society in which all persons live together in harmony and...and with equal opportunities. It is an ideal which I hope to live for and to achieve. But, if needs be, it is an ideal for which I am prepared to die.❞

3 LISTENING & SPEAKING

a Have you ever had to make a speech or give a talk or presentation in front of a lot of people? When? Where? How did you feel? Was it a success?

b Read part of an article about presentation disasters. Which tip from 'Ten Top Tips' below should the speaker have remembered?

Presentation Disasters!

However bad you think your presentation has been, take some comfort from the fact that at least it probably wasn't as bad as these true stories...

A few years ago I had to give a presentation to the Belgian management team of an international IT company. Not wishing to be the typical 'Brit' presenting in English, I had carefully prepared my presentation in French. I intended it as a surprise, so I didn't say anything beforehand. After speaking in French for 45 minutes, I was halfway through my presentation and we had a break for coffee. At this point the manager of the company came up to me and asked me if I would change to speaking in English. "Is my French that bad?" I said. "No," he replied, "it's just that we are all from the Dutch-speaking part of Belgium."

TEN TOP TIPS FOR SPEAKING IN PUBLIC

1 Prepare your presentation carefully, and if possible practise it beforehand.

2 If you are using e.g. PowerPoint or Prezi, make sure that your text is clear and easy to read, and that there are not too many distracting graphics.

3 Get to know as much as possible about your audience beforehand, and about any important or sensitive local issues.

4 Dress carefully so that you feel confident about your appearance in front of an audience.

5 Get to the place where you are going to speak in plenty of time.

6 Make sure that you check that all your equipment is working properly before you start.

7 If you are given a time limit, keep to it.

8 Sound enthusiastic, even passionate, about what you are saying.

9 Look at your audience. Try to make eye contact with individual people as you speak.

10 It's good to make your audience laugh, but make sure any jokes or stories you tell are appropriate.

c **5 41))** Listen to four other people talking about a disastrous presentation. Complete the first column of the chart.

Speaker	What the disaster was	How and why it happened	Which tip the speaker should have remembered
1			
2			
3			
4			

d Listen to the people again, one by one, and complete the second and third columns.

e Which of the **Ten Top Tips** do you think are the most important? Have you ever been to a talk or presentation where something went badly wrong?

4 VOCABULARY collocation: word pairs

Word pairs
Some pairs of words in English which go together always come in a certain order, for example we always say 'Ladies and Gentlemen' at the beginning of a speech, but never the other way round, and we always say 'black and white' not 'white and black.' This order may sometimes be different in your language.

a How do you say 'Ladies and Gentlemen' and 'black and white' in your language? Are the words in the same order?

b Take one word from **circle A** and match it with another from **circle B**. Then decide which word comes first. They are all joined with *and*.

Circle A: pepper bread ice thunder fork quiet bed forwards

Circle B: knife peace lemon butter lightning salt breakfast backwards

c Look at some common word pairs joined with *or*. What is the second word?

right or _____   sooner or _____   dead or _____
now or _____   all or _____
more or _____   once or _____

d (5 42)) Listen and check your answers to **b** and **c**, and notice how the phrases are linked and how *and* is pronounced. Practise saying them.

e Match the word pair idioms with their meanings.

1 I'm sick and tired of hearing you complain.
2 I didn't buy much, just a few bits and pieces.
3 I've been having headaches now and again.
4 **A** What are you making for lunch? **B** Wait and see.
5 Every relationship needs a bit of give and take.
6 We've had our ups and downs, but now we get on really well.
7 The army were called in to restore law and order.
8 Despite flying through a storm we arrived safe and sound.

A good times and bad times   E compromise
B a situation in which the law is obeyed   F occasionally
C fed up with   G small things
D without problem or injury   H You'll soon find out.

f Complete the sentences with a word pair from this page.

1 I see my uncle _____, but not very often.
2 I think this is our last chance. It's _____.
3 I much prefer _____ photos to colour ones. They're more atmospheric.
4 After lots of adventure, she arrived home _____.
5 Could you stop making so much noise? I need a bit of _____.
6 _____ Naomi will realize that Henry is not the man for her.
7 **A** Have you finished?
  B _____. I just have one sentence left.
8 After the riots, the government sent soldiers in to try to establish _____.
9 I'm _____ of my boss! I'm going to look for a new job.
10 It was an amazing storm. There was a lot of _____.

5 PRONUNCIATION & SPEAKING pausing and sentence stress

a (5 43)) When people give a talk they usually divide what they say into small chunks, with a brief pause between each chunk. Listen to the beginning of a talk and mark the pauses.

Good afternoon everyone / and thank you for coming. I'm going to talk to you today about one of my hobbies, collecting adult comics. Since I was a child I've been mad about comics and comic books. I started reading Tintin and Asterix when I was seven or eight. Later when I was a teenager some friends at school introduced me to Manga, which are Japanese comics. I've been collecting them now for about five years and I'm also learning to draw them.

b Now practise giving the beginning of the talk, pausing and trying to get the right rhythm.

c You are going to give a five-minute presentation to other students. You can choose what to talk about, for example:

a hobby you have or a sport you play
an interesting person in your family
a famous person you admire
the good and bad side of your job

Decide what you are going to talk about and make a plan of what you want to say.

d In groups, take turns to give your presentation. While they are listening the other students should write down at least one question to ask the speaker after the presentation is over. Then have a short question and answer session.

Giving a presentation
Read through the tips in **3** again to help you to prepare your presentation and to give it successfully. When you give your presentation, don't speak too quickly. Remember to pause and take a breath from time to time. This will help the audience to follow what you are saying.

6 (5 44)) SONG *World* ♫

GRAMMAR

Choose a, b, or c.

1 He got a good job, _____ not having the right degree.
   a although   b despite   c in spite
2 My uncle still works, _____ he won the lottery last year.
   a in spite of   b despite   c even though
3 I called my sister to remind her _____ the flowers.
   a to buy   b for buy   c for buying
4 Jane opened the door quietly _____ her parents up.
   a to not wake   b so that she not wake
   c so as not to wake
5 _____ she goes out the paparazzi are always there.
   a Whatever   b However   c Whenever
6 Adrian is looking for _____ in London.
   a some cheap accommodations   b some cheap
   accommodation   c a cheap accommodation
7 Let me give you _____ – don't marry him!
   a a piece of advice   b an advice   c some advices
8 I need to buy a new _____.
   a trouser   b trousers   c pair of trousers
9 There's _____ milk. I'll have to get some from the shop.
   a no   b any   c none
10 _____ in that shop is incredibly expensive.
   a All   b All of them   c Everything
11 They shouldn't go sailing because _____ of them can swim.
   a both   b either   c neither
12 I was in _____ hospital for two weeks with a broken leg.
   a the   b –   c a
13 I now live next door to _____ school where I used to go.
   a the   b –   c a
14 _____ Lake Constance is the biggest lake in Switzerland.
   a The   b –   c A
15 _____ British Museum is in central London.
   a The   b –   c A

VOCABULARY

a Complete with the correct form of the **bold** word.

1 A lot of research is being done into human _____. **gene**
2 Many important _____ discoveries were made in the 19th century. **science**
3 We live in a very safe _____. **neighbour**
4 Many people in big cities suffer from _____. **lonely**
5 His _____ came as a terrible shock. **die**

b Add a prefix to the **bold** word.

1 New Delhi in India is a very _____**populated** city.
2 I asked for an aspirin, but the receptionist didn't understand me because I had _____**pronounced** it.
3 A _____**national** company is a large company that operates in several different countries.
4 Gandhi wrote most of his _____**biography** in 1929.
5 Anne is unhappy with her job, because she's _____**paid**.

c Complete the missing words.

1 Will the company make a l_____ this year?
2 He borrowed £10,000 to s_____ _____ his own business.
3 Ikea is probably the market l_____ in cheap furniture.
4 The company are planning to l_____ their new product in the spring.
5 It's a large bank which has **br**_____ all over the country.
6 It's a large company with over 1,000 s_____.
7 When there's a property boom, house prices r_____.
8 The new drug has some very unpleasant s_____ effects.
9 We need to c_____ out some more experiments.
10 Would you ever be a g_____ pig in a clinical trial?

d Complete the two-word phrases.

1 I'm going to the mountains for some peace and _____.
2 He arrived back from his adventure safe and _____.
3 Sooner or _____ we're going to have to make a decision.
4 It's a very dangerous city. There's no law and _____.
5 This is our last chance to do this. It's now or _____.

PRONUNCIATION

a (Circle) the word with a different sound.

1   neighbourhood   bilingual   science   neither
2   government   prove   slums   discovery
3   volunteer   theory   research   idea
4   staff   branch   launch   market
5   geologist   colleague   genes   biology

b Underline the main stressed syllable.

1 bi|o|lo|gi|cal   2 phy|si|cist   3 mul|ti|cul|tu|ral
4 in|crease (*verb*)   5 man|u|fac|ture

CAN YOU UNDERSTAND THIS TEXT?

a Read the article once. How does Billy Ray Harris feel about the incident?

b Read it again and choose the best words to fill the gaps.

1 a lost   b dropped   c fallen
2 a relieved   b infuriated   c shocked
3 a expensive   b serious   c genuine
4 a often   b occasionally   c rarely
5 a realized   b noticed   c expected
6 a apparently   b unluckily   c fortunately
7 a appreciation b happiness   c luck
8 a according to b related to   c belonging to
9 a losing   b finding   c returning
10 a obviously   b actually   c eventually

c Choose five new words or phrases from the text. Check their meaning and pronunciation and try to learn them.

▶ CAN YOU UNDERSTAND THIS FILM?

VIDEO

5 45))) Watch or listen to a short film on The Museum of the History of Science. Complete the sentences with a number, or one or two words.

1 There is a device used by Marconi to show how _____ _____ worked.
2 You can see apparatus used by _____ who were developing penicillin.
3 The most popular exhibit in the museum is a _____. Einstein used it to give a class in _____.
4 The museum was opened in _____, when Lewis Evans donated his collection of _____ _____. He collected things related to mathematics, _____ and navigation.
5 The astrolabes are instruments which predict the position of the _____, the _____ and the _____.
6 The sundials were used for telling the _____ and the quadrants were used for measuring _____.
7 There are two beautiful globes which show maps of the _____ and the _____.
8 There is also a _____ microscope which belonged to King _____ _____.

The return of the ring

A homeless man in Kansas City, Missouri is anticipating a windfall of more than $100,000 for his kindness after he returned a diamond engagement ring to its rightful owner, which she had accidentally [1]_____ into his donation cup.

Billy Ray Harris, who is homeless and often sleeps under a bridge, was [2]_____ to find a diamond ring in his collection cup while begging last Friday. 'The ring was so big I knew that if it was real then it must be [3]_____,' he said. Rather than sell it, Harris had a hunch that the owner would return for it and so he stored it in a safe place.

The ring belonged to Sarah Darling, who was devastated the next day when she realized she had lost it. She [4]_____ takes the ring off, but that day she had put it in her purse for safe keeping after she had developed a slight rash on her finger. She [5]_____ that she must have given Harris the ring by mistake along with some coins when she took out her purse to give him some money.

She went back to look for Harris on the Saturday, but couldn't find him. She tried again the next day and [6]_____ he was in the same spot. 'I said to him "I don't know if you remember me, but I think I gave you something that's very precious to me," and he said, "Was it a ring? Yeah, I have it, I kept it for you"'.

To show their [7]_____, Darling and her husband set up an online fundraising page for Harris on giveforward.com. So far, more than 3,800 donations have been made, totalling over $100,000. The money will be given to Harris at the end of a 90-day campaign. Darling's husband, Bill Krejci, met Harris to tell him about the flood of donations and to get to know him better. 'We talked about a lot of things [8]_____ my family's ring and about the many donations. We talked about how one day in the future the ring may be passed down to my daughter.'

Harris told Krejci that he has found a place to stay where he is 'safe and sound'. He has spoken about the attention he has received since [9]_____ the ring. 'I like it, but I don't think I deserve it. What I [10]_____ feel like is, "What has the world come to when a person returns something that doesn't belong to him and all this happens?"' he said.

Adapted from the Mail Online

Communication

1A EXTREME INTERVIEWS
Student A

a You are giving **B** an extreme interview for a job in your company. Ask **B** the questions and ask him / her to give reasons for his / her answers. Then say if you would give him / her the job and why (not).

1 Which one aspect of your personality would you change if you could, and why?
2 If you could have dinner with anyone from history, who would you choose?
3 If you were an animal, which animal would you be?
4 What kind of things make you angry?
5 If you had to spend the rest of your life on a deserted island (with plenty of food and water), what two things would you want to have with you?
6 Which TV or film character would you most like to be?
7 What's the best (or worst) decision you've ever made?
8 If I came to your house for dinner, what would you cook for me?

b Now answer **B**'s questions. Try to think quickly and make a good impression. Give good reasons for your answers.

1B HARD TO BELIEVE? Student A

a Read the story below. Guess the meaning of the highlighted words and then complete the glossary.

b Tell **B** the important details from the story you read. Explain any new words if necessary.

- When did it happen and what was the background to the story?
- What was the strange happening? What did Carol do afterwards?
- How do they feel now about what they heard?

This happened to a woman called Carol and her husband Russ...

c Now listen to **B**'s story. If **B** uses a word or phrase you don't know, ask what it means, and ask questions where necessary to clarify the details of the story.

NOISES IN THE NIGHT

About six months ago, my husband Russ and I moved into a house in the country. Our house is the middle one of three terraced houses and it's more than a hundred years old. A young couple live in the house on our right, but the house on our left was empty and for sale.

We had been living in the house for about two months when we were both suddenly woken up in the middle of the night by a loud noise. We could hear the sound of furniture being moved in the empty house next door. It sounded as if somebody was moving something very heavy, like a table or a bed, by dragging it across the floor. I looked at my watch. I said to Russ 'What are they doing moving furniture at this time of the night? It must be the new owners. I'll complain to them tomorrow.' Just then the noise stopped, but five minutes later it started again and this time it carried on for several minutes. Finally it stopped completely, and we were able to go back to sleep.

The next morning I rang the doorbell next door, but there was no answer, and when I looked through the curtains the house still looked completely empty. I called the estate agent and asked him if he had come to the house the previous night to move furniture. He said that he hadn't and he was as mystified as us about the noises.

I asked the estate agent who had lived in the house previously and he told me that an old lady had been living there for many years, but she had suddenly died a few months ago. I don't really believe in ghosts, but Russ and I can find no logical explanation for the noises we heard that night. *Carol, Kent*

Glossary
1 _____ /ˈkɜːtnz/ *noun* pieces of cloth that are used to cover a window
2 _____ /ɪsˈteɪt ˌeɪdʒənt/ *noun* a person whose job is to sell houses for people
3 _____ /ˈdræɡɪŋ/ *verb* pulling something with effort or difficulty
4 _____ /ˌkærɪd ˈɒn/ *pv* continued
5 _____ /ˈterəst/ *adj* used to describe houses that are joined together in one block

1B YOU'RE PSYCHIC, AREN'T YOU?
Student A

a Imagine you're a psychic. Use your psychic powers to complete the sentences below about **B**.

1 Your favourite colour is _____,...?
2 You were born in _____ (place),...?
3 You really like _____, (a sport or hobby),...?
4 You _____ (an activity) last weekend,...?
5 You haven't been to _____ (a city or country),...?
6 You would like to be able to _____,...?
7 You can't _____ very well,...?
8 You're very good at _____,...?

b Check if your guesses are true by saying the sentences to **B** and checking with a question tag, e.g. *Your favourite colour is pink, isn't it?* Try to use falling intonation.

c Now **B** will check his / her guesses about you. Respond with a short answer. If the guess is wrong, tell **B** the real answer.

d Count your correct guesses. Who was the best psychic?

2A FIRST AID QUIZ Student A

1 a You should hit the person firmly on the back between the shoulder blades to remove the object. This is often enough to clear the blockage, letting the person breathe again. If necessary, call the emergency services or get someone else to do it.

2 b The first thing to do is cool the burn under cold running water for at least ten minutes. This will make the burn less painful, and reduce swelling and scarring. Then cover the burn with cling film, or a clean plastic bag if your foot or hand is burned. This prevents infection and keeps air from the surface of the skin, which reduces pain. If it's a serious burn, call the emergency services because it may need urgent medical treatment.

3 a You should immediately put pressure on the wound to stop or slow down the bleeding. Use whatever is available – like a T-shirt or other clean cloth, or even your hand. Get help as soon as possible by calling the emergency services. Keep pressure on the wound until help arrives.

3A FLIGHT STORIES Student A

a Read a newspaper article about a flight. Imagine that you were one of the passengers on the plane. Think about:

- why you were flying to North Carolina
- who you were with
- what you did during the emergency and how you felt.

BRAVE PILOT LANDS PLANE ON THE HUDSON RIVER

On 15th January US Airways flight 1549 took off from La Guardia airport in New York at 3.26 p.m. heading for North Carolina, with 150 passengers and five crew on board. Less than two minutes after take off, passengers near the wings heard strange noises coming from the engines. The plane started shaking, and then suddenly began to lose height. Both engines had stopped making any noise, and the plane was strangely quiet – the only sound was some people who were crying quietly. Most people were looking out of the window in horror. Moments later the captain made an announcement: 'This is the captain, brace for impact.' He had decided to try to land the plane on the only large flat empty area that he could reach – the Hudson River. The plane landed on the river, and one passenger shouted 'We're in the water!' People stood up and starting pushing towards the emergency exits, which the crew had managed to open. It was freezing cold outside. Some passengers jumped into life rafts, and others stood on the wings waiting for help. Amazingly, after only ten minutes ferries arrived and rescued all the passengers and crew. It was later discovered that birds had flown into both engines on the plane which had caused them to stop working.

b Tell **B** your story in your own words, e.g. *It was in January a few years ago and I was on a flight from New York to North Carolina…*

c Now listen to **B**'s story.

d What two details do the stories have in common? Have you ever been on a flight where there was a medical or technical emergency?

Communication

5A IT'S AN EMERGENCY! Student A

a Read your survival tips and <u>underline</u> things you should and shouldn't do, and why. Try to remember the information.

WHAT TO DO IF...THERE'S AN EMERGENCY ON A PLANE

Your plane is very unlikely to crash, but if it does, the most important thing is to be ready for it. Eighty per cent of all accidents take place during take-off or landing, and if there is an emergency, such as a fire, you will probably only have about 90 seconds to get off. So when you get on the plane (and when it starts the descent) you need to be thinking about what you would do.

Pay attention to the safety card and the flight attendant's safety briefing. Memorize where the emergency exits are and count how many rows you are away from them. Don't do what many people do which is to relax, take off their shoes, and start reading or listening to music. If something does happen you need to be ready to take action. In fact this is one of the reasons why people are told to switch off electronic devices during take off and landing. Above all don't go to sleep. But once the plane is flying and the seat belt signs have gone off, you can start to relax and enjoy the flight.

b Now in your own words tell **B** and **C** how to survive if there's an emergency on a plane.

5A GUESS THE CONDITIONALS Student A

a Read through sentences 1–6 and think how you could complete the gaps. They are either second or third conditionals. ⊞ = a positive verb phrase, ⊟ = a negative verb phrase.

b Say your complete sentence 1 to **B**. If **B** says *That's right*, write in the words. If **B** says *Try again*, think of another possible completion and say the sentence again. You can have three tries.

c Now listen to **B** say sentences 7–12. If **B** says exactly what you have, say *That's right*. If **B** says something different, say *Try again*.

1 The cat wouldn't have got out if you _____. ⊞
2 If I spent a month in the UK, _____. ⊞
3 We wouldn't have lost the match if our best player _____. ⊟
4 If you'd told me earlier about the concert, _____. ⊞
5 If I'd known the traffic was going to be so bad, _____. ⊟
6 My husband and I would go out more if we _____. ⊟

7 We would have played tennis if it hadn't been so windy.
8 If you hadn't reminded me, I would have forgotten.
9 I would have bought the flat if it had been cheaper.
10 I wouldn't use public transport if I had a car.
11 If you had watered the plants, they wouldn't have died.
12 If I knew the answer, I'd tell you.

6B THREE THINGS YOU (PROBABLY) DIDN'T KNOW ABOUT SLEEPING Student A

Sleeping Beauty

In 2008, when Louisa Ball was fourteen, she had the symptoms of flu and soon after she began falling asleep in class. Then one day she went to sleep and didn't wake up...for ten days. Doctors diagnosed her as having a rare neurological disorder called Kleine-Levin Syndrome, also known as 'Sleeping Beauty Syndrome.' People who have this medical condition often sleep for long periods without waking up.

Louisa regularly misses long periods of school, her weekly dance lessons (and, once, a whole week of a family holiday) because she is asleep. On one occasion she even missed her final exams. When she sleeps for several days her parents have to wake her up once a day to give her something to eat and take her to the bathroom. But then she immediately falls back into a deep sleep.

People who have this syndrome often complain that they lose their friends because they disappear for such long periods of time. Fortunately, Louisa's friends have stayed loyal and they even visit her on days when she is asleep.

Although she sometimes feels frustrated Louisa says, 'I've got used to it now and I've learnt to live with it.' Doctors have told her that the syndrome will eventually disappear, but maybe not for ten or fifteen years.

a Read the article and answer the questions.

1 What exactly is the syndrome?
2 What were the early symptoms of Louisa's medical problem?
3 What affect does the syndrome have on her life? How have her friends reacted?
4 What do her parents do when she has one of her long sleeps?
5 How does she feel about her problem?

b Use the questions to help you to tell **B** about the Sleeping Beauty Syndrome.

c Then listen to **B** telling you about how our ancestors used to sleep.

7A ARGUMENT! Student A

Role-play two arguments with a partner.

1 WIFE

It's your birthday today. Your husband (**Student B**) had promised to come home early. You have prepared a great dinner. You have been dropping hints for the past month that what you really want for your birthday is some jewellery, as your partner is usually very unimaginative about choosing presents. Last Christmas he bought you the *Lord of the Rings* DVDs which you didn't particularly like and he ended up watching more than you.

Tonight he arrives home late from work (the dinner is cold) and gives you a box of chocolates (you're on a diet, and he knows this) and some flowers which look as if they were bought at a petrol station.

Your husband (**Student B**) starts the conversation by giving you the chocolates.

2 MOTHER / FATHER

Your son / daughter (**Student B**) is in his / her first year of university studying medicine. You are a doctor, and you have always encouraged your child to follow in your footsteps, and he / she was good at science at school, and you think he / she would make an excellent doctor. He / she was quite keen on studying journalism, but you think that this was a 'lazy option' and nowadays it's very difficult to get a good job in journalism. So you persuaded him / her to study medicine. Although he / she worked hard at school, this year at university he / she seems to be out with friends all the time and spends a lot less time studying than you did at the same age. You have just discovered that he / she has failed all the first year exams.

You start the conversation: *I think we need to talk about your exam results...*

7B GUESS WHAT IT IS Student A

a Look at the pictures below. You are going to describe them to **B**. Say what kind of thing each one is, and then use *looks*, *smells*, *feels*, or *tastes*.

 cabbage mango rose ice-lolly fur coat

b Describe your first thing to **B** in as much detail as possible. **B** can then ask you questions to identify what the thing is.

> It's a kind of vegetable. It looks a bit like a green ball. It tastes quite strong and I think it smells awful when it's being cooked. You can use it to make...

c Now listen to **B** describe his / her first thing. Don't interrupt until he / she has finished describing. You can ask **B** questions to identify what the thing is.

d Continue taking turns to describe all your things.

8B STRANGE, BUT TRUE
Student A

a Read the article and highlight the key information that will help you remember the story.

Lost tourist finds herself

More than 50 people were involved in a search and rescue operation in the volcanic region of Eldgjá in south Iceland on Saturday.

Police were called to the area after it was reported that a female member of a tour party who were travelling around the region had failed to return to the bus.

The tourist was described as being 'of Asian origin, aged 20–30, and about 160 cm.' She was wearing 'dark clothing' and spoke fluent English. The police asked for a helicopter to assist the rescue operation but it was too foggy for it to fly. So the police, helped by the tourists themselves, began to look for the missing woman on foot.

The search continued through the night, but at 3.00 in the morning the search was called off when it was discovered that the missing woman was not only alive and well but was actually assisting in the search.

What had happened was that the woman had got off the bus for some fresh air and had changed her clothes. Because of that other people didn't recognize her and thought that she was missing. The tour organizer had counted the tourists but had miscounted. Police said that the woman had not recognized that the description of the missing person was her. The police said, 'She did not realize that she was the person everybody (including herself) was searching for until several hours later.'

b Tell **B** your story in your own words, e.g. *This happened in Iceland. The police were called because someone had reported that a tourist was missing...*

c Now listen to **B**'s story, and ask **B** to clarify or rephrase if there's anything you don't understand.

Communication

7B TWO PHOTOS
Student A

a Look carefully at your photo. Then describe it in detail to **B**, focusing especially on the people and their body language. Say who you think they are and what you think they're doing.

b Show your photo to **B** and see if he / she agrees with you.

c Listen to **B** describe another photo. Try to visualize it.

d **B** will now show you the photo to see if you agree with his / her description and interpretation.

> 🔍 **Describing a photo**
> This photo looks as if it was taken (in the summer, in the 1990s, etc.)
> In the centre
> In the foreground   (of the photo) there is / there are...
> In the background
> The child has his head in his hands. He looks as if...

1A EXTREME INTERVIEWS
Student B

a **A** is going to give you an extreme interview for a job in his / her company. Answer the questions. Try to think quickly and make a good impression. Give good reasons for your answers.

b Now give **A** an extreme interview for a job in your company, using the questions below. Ask him / her to give reasons for his / her answers. Then say if you would give him / her the job, and why (not).

1 Which three adjectives describe you best?
2 If you were a type of food, what type of food would you be?
3 How do you normally treat animals?
4 Who do you admire most, and why?
5 If you could be a super hero, what would you want your superpowers to be?
6 Tell me about something in your life that you are really proud of.
7 If Hollywood made a movie about your life, who would you like to see play the lead role as you?
8 If you could have six months with no obligations or financial limitations, what would you do with the time?

10B GEOGRAPHY TRUE OR FALSE Student A

a Complete the gaps in your sentences with *the* where necessary.

1 ___ Andes is ___ longest mountain range in ___ world. (**T**)
2 ___ Loch Ness is ___ largest lake in Scotland. (**F** – It's the second largest. Loch Lomond is the largest)
3 ___ capital of ___ United States is ___ New York City. (**F** – It's Washington DC)
4 ___ Mallorca is an island in ___ Mediterranean sea. (**T**)
5 ___ Uffizi gallery is ___ famous art museum in ___ Rome. (**F** – It's in Florence)
6 ___ South America is larger than ___ North America. (**F**)
7 ___ Mount Vesuvius is a volcano in ___ north west Italy. (**F** – It's in south west Italy)
8 ___ Brooklyn Bridge connects ___ Brooklyn and ___ Manhattan. (**T**)

b Now read your sentence 1 to **B**. He / She must say if the information true or false. Correct his / her answer if necessary.

c Now listen to **B**'s sentence 1 and say if you think it's true or false. If you think it's false, say what you think the right answer is.

d Continue taking turns to say your sentences. Who got the most right answers?

1B HARD TO BELIEVE? Student B

a Read the story below. Guess the meaning of the highlighted words and then complete the glossary.

THE STRANGE OBJECT ON THE HILL

This happened when I was 16, and I can still remember it vividly. It was a clear morning, sunny but with a breeze. I was going to meet a school friend to go walking in the hills where there were some wonderful views. I'd agreed to meet him at the top of one of the hills.

I knew those hills really well, but that morning there was a strange shape in the familiar landscape. It was a mile or so to the north, on the top of the next hill. It was a white object and it looked like a dome or an igloo. I was carrying binoculars, so I could see it clearly. It was big, the size of a small house, but it didn't seem to have any doors or windows, and it wasn't moving in spite of the wind.

Then I noticed that some sheep which were on that hill were running away from it. They seemed really frightened.

I kept staring at the dome. Then, suddenly, it began to move. It moved slowly, not in the direction of the wind but almost directly against it. It looked as if it might be gliding a few inches above the grass.

A few seconds later the dome disappeared. I never saw it again. I had watched it for 15 minutes.

When my friend arrived I asked him if he had seen the object, too, but he hadn't. He had been coming from a different direction.

I have told only a few people about what I saw. One of them, a friend of mine who is a doctor, is convinced that I was hallucinating. But I am sure that what I saw wasn't a hallucination. It was really there. *Carl, Winchester*

Glossary
1 _____ /dəʊm/ *noun* a circular thing or a building with a round roof and a flat base
2 _____ /ˈɡlaɪdɪŋ/ *verb* moving smoothly and quietly, as if with no effort
3 _____ /həˈluːsɪneɪtɪŋ/ *verb* seeing or hearing things that are not really there, because of an illness or drugs
4 _____ /ˈvɪvɪdli/ *adv* very clearly
5 _____ /bɪˈnɒkjələz/ *noun* an instrument that makes far away objects seem nearer
6 _____ /briːz/ *noun* a light wind

This happened to a boy called Carl when he was 16…

b Listen to **A**'s story. If **A** uses a word or phrase you don't know, ask what it means, and ask questions where necessary to clarify the details of the story.

c Now tell **A** everything you can remember from the story you read. Explain any new words if necessary.

- When did it happen and what was the background to the story? (*What was the weather like? What was he going to do?*, etc.)
- What was the strange happening? What did Carl do afterwards?
- How does he feel now about what he saw?

1B YOU'RE PSYCHIC, AREN'T YOU? Student B

a Imagine you're a psychic. Use your psychic powers to complete the sentences below about **A**.

1 You were born in _____ (month),…?
2 You don't like _____ (a kind of music),…?
3 You're going to _____ (activity) tonight,…?
4 You've seen _____ (a film),…?
5 Your favourite season is _____,…?
6 You didn't like _____ (kind of food) when you were a child,…?
7 You can play _____ (musical instrument),…?
8 You wouldn't like to live in _____ (a place),…?

b **A** is going to make some guesses about you. Respond with a short answer. If the guess is wrong, tell **A** the real answer.

c Now check if your guesses about **A** are true, by saying the sentences and checking with a question tag, e.g. *You were born in Pisa, weren't you?* Try to use a falling intonation. Check if your guesses were true.

2A FIRST AID QUIZ Student B

4 a If someone you are with has a nosebleed, you should ask them to sit down and lean forward. Ask the person to pinch the soft part of the nose, which they should do for ten minutes. Get medical advice if the bleeding continues for more than thirty minutes.

5 b Tilt their head backwards so that their tongue isn't blocking their airway. Check if they're breathing by looking to see if their chest is moving, and feel for breath on your cheek. Now move them onto their side and tilt their head back. Putting them in this position with their head back helps keep the airway open. As soon as possible, call the emergency services or get someone else to do it.

6 b Use a cushion or items of clothing to prevent unnecessary movement. Call the emergency services or get someone else to do it. Don't try to straighten the person's leg, but continue supporting the injury until help arrives.

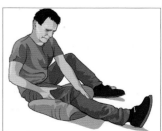

Communication

3A FLIGHT STORIES Student B

a Read a newspaper article about a flight. Imagine that you were one of the passengers on the flight, and were sitting just behind Mrs Fletcher. Think about:

- why you were travelling to Florida
- who you were with
- what you saw and how you felt.

IS THERE A DOCTOR ON BOARD?

Mrs Dorothy Fletcher was travelling with her daughter and her daughter's fiancé on a US Airways flight from London to Florida. Her daughter was going to be married there the following week. They had to get a connecting flight in Philadelphia, but the flight landed late and they had to rush between terminals. On their way to the gate, Mrs Fletcher began to feel ill. She didn't say anything to her daughter because she didn't want to worry her. However when the flight from Philadelphia to Florida took off, she suddenly got a terrible pain in her chest, back, and arm – she was having a heart attack.

The cabin crew put out a call to passengers: 'We have a medical emergency. If there is a doctor on board, could you please press the call bell.' Incredibly, not just one bell sounded but fifteen! There were fifteen doctors on board, and what was even better news, they were all cardiologists! They were travelling to Florida for a conference.

The doctors immediately gave Mrs Fletcher emergency treatment and they managed to save her life. The plane made an emergency landing in North Carolina and she was taken to hospital there. Fortunately she recovered quickly enough to be able to attend her daughter's wedding.

b Now listen to **A**'s story.

c Tell **A** your story in your own words, e.g. *A few years ago I was flying from London to Florida on a US Airways flight…*

d What two details do the stories have in common? Have you ever been on a flight where there was a medical or technical emergency?

5A IT'S AN EMERGENCY! Student B

a Read your survival tips and underline things you should and shouldn't do, and why. Try to remember the information.

WHAT TO DO IF...YOU GET LOST ON A HIKE IN THE MOUNTAINS

According to experts, people who get lost when they are out hiking typically keep walking (or even running), desperately trying to find the right path to safety, but this is absolutely the wrong thing to do. As a survival expert says, 'Fear is the enemy. Lost people want to run.' They lose their heads and start to panic. Sometimes they even forget to look in their backpacks for food and water.

The number one survival tip is to stay where you are or find an open space nearby and wait to be rescued (especially if you have told someone where you were going to walk). In research done in Canada, only two out of 800 lost people actually did this. If the others had stayed in one place, they would have been found much sooner.

Look for a sheltered place nearby in case you have to spend the night there, for example under a rock, or make a shelter with tree branches to keep you warm. But make sure you stay in the open during the day so that you can be seen by a helicopter. Make a fire to attract attention. If you don't have matches, tie a piece of bright clothing to a stick and leave it in a visible place.

b Now in your own words tell **A** and **C** how to survive if you get lost in the mountains.

7A ARGUMENT! Student B

Role-play two arguments with a partner.

1 HUSBAND
It's your wife's (**Student A's**) birthday today. You always try to buy her good birthday presents (last year you bought her the *Lord of the Rings* DVDs!). You know that she really wanted some jewellery but you have been very busy at work and haven't had time to go shopping. You had intended to finish work early this evening and go shopping, but you had to work late. So you stopped at a petrol station on the way home and bought her some chocolates, which you know she usually likes, and some flowers.
    You start the conversation by giving your wife her present. *Happy Birthday, darling. I hope you like them.*

2 SON / DAUGHTER (UNIVERSITY STUDENT)
You're in your first year of university, studying medicine. You haven't enjoyed it at all, and have just failed all your first year exams. In fact, you never really wanted to study medicine but your parents are both doctors and you feel they pushed you into it. You would like to change courses and study journalism, which you think would suit you better. You want to try to convince your mother / father (**Student A**) although you know they're not very pleased with your exam results.
    Your mother / father (**Student A**) will start by asking you about your exam results.

5A GUESS THE CONDITIONALS Student B

a Read through sentences 7–12 and think how you could complete the gaps. They are either second or third conditionals. ⊞ = a positive verb phrase, ⊟ = a negative verb phrase.

1 The cat wouldn't have got out if you'd closed the window.
2 If I spent a month in the UK, my English would improve a lot.
3 We wouldn't have lost the match if our best player hadn't been injured.
4 If you'd told me earlier about the concert, I would have gone.
5 If I'd known the traffic was going to be so bad, I wouldn't have taken the car.
6 My husband and I would go out more if we didn't have children.
7 We would have played tennis if it _____ *hadn't* . ⊟ *rained*.
8 If you hadn't reminded me, I _____ . ⊞ *wouldn't have to able to* *would have forgotten*
9 I would have bought the flat if it _____ . ⊞ *pick up the children.*
10 I wouldn't use public transport if _____ . ⊞ *had won the lottery I had been -...* *I would have lived near my office*
11 If you had watered the plants, _____ . ⊟ *you would have had a ar.* *had a ur.* *it wouldn't have died.* ✓
12 If I knew the answer, I _____ . ⊞ *and it wouldn't have died.* ✓ *would have passed the exam*

b Listen to **A** saying sentences 1–6. If **A** says exactly what you have, say *That's right*. If **A** says something different, say *Try again*.

c Say your complete sentences 7–12 to **A**. If **A** says *That's right*, write in the words. If **A** says *Try again*, think of another possible completion and say the sentence again. You can have three tries.

6B THREE THINGS YOU (PROBABLY) DIDN'T KNOW ABOUT SLEEPING Student B

How our ancestors used to sleep

An American historian, Roger Ekirch, has done a lot of research (based mainly on literature and diaries) which shows that until the end of the 18th century humans used to sleep in two distinct periods, called 'First sleep' and 'Second sleep'.

First sleep began about two hours after nightfall, and lasted for about four hours. It was followed by a period of between one or two hours when people were awake. During the waking period people were quite active. Most people stayed in bed reading, writing, or praying, etc. but others got up and even used the time to visit neighbours. They then went back to sleep for another four hours.

This research is backed up by an experiment done by a psychiatrist, Thomas Wehr, in the early 1990s, in which a group of people were left in total darkness for 14 hours every day for a month. By the fourth week the people had begun to sleep in a very clear pattern. They slept first for four hours, then woke for one or two hours before falling into a second four-hour sleep, in exactly the same way as people had slept in the 18th century. The research suggests that today's habit of sleeping seven to eight consecutive hours may not be the most natural way to sleep.

a Read the text and answer the questions.

1 What did the historian's research show?
2 What was the typical sleep routine in those days?
3 What did people do during the period between sleeps?
4 What was Thomas Wehr's experiment, and what did it show?

b Listen to **A** tell you about the Sleeping Beauty Syndrome.

c Use the questions in **a** to tell **A** about how our ancestors used to sleep.

7B GUESS WHAT IT IS Student B

a Look at the pictures below. You are going to describe them to **A**. Say what kind of thing each one is, and then use *looks, smells, feels,* or *tastes*.

chilli pepper

camembert · jasmine · kitten · vinegar

b Now listen to **A** describe his / her first thing. Don't interrupt until he / she has finished describing. You can ask **A** questions.

c Now describe your first thing in as much detail as possible. **A** can then ask you questions to identify what the thing is.

> It's a kind of vegetable. It's very popular in Mexico. It's very hot...

d Continue taking turns to describe all your things. Who guessed the most right?

10B GEOGRAPHY TRUE OR FALSE Student B

a Complete the gaps in your sentences with *the* where necessary.

1 ___ capital of ___ Netherlands is ___ Amsterdam. (**F** – It's The Hague)
2 ___ Amazon is ___ longest river in ___ world. (**F** – It's the Nile)
3 ___ Panama Canal connects ___ Atlantic Ocean to ___ Pacific Ocean. (**T**)
4 ___ Atacama desert is in ___ north of ___ Chile. (**T**)
5 ___ Black Sea is in ___ south west Europe. (**F** – It's in south east Europe)
6 ___ biggest lake in ___ world is ___ Lake Victoria in ___ Africa. (**F** – It's Lake Superior in Canada / the USA)
7 ___ Mont Blanc is ___ highest mountain in ___ Alps. (**T**)
8 ___ Hyde Park is in ___ central London. (**T**)

b Now listen to **A**'s sentence 1 and say if you think it's true or false. If you think it's false, say what you think the right answer is.

c Now read your sentence 1 to **A**. Correct his / her answer if necessary.

d Continue taking turns to say your sentences. Who got the most right answers?

Communication

5A IT'S AN EMERGENCY! Student C

a Read your survival tips and <u>underline</u> things you should and shouldn't do, and why. Try to remember the information.

WHAT TO DO IF... SOMEBODY BREAKS INTO YOUR HOUSE.

Imagine that you wake up in the middle of the night because you can hear somebody moving around in the kitchen. What should you do?

Even if you are brave, it is usually a mistake to go and confront the intruder. You could find yourself face to face with somebody who may have a weapon and who is likely to react violently.

The most important thing is to have a plan to follow: lock yourself and your family in a safe place, e.g. your bedroom or bathroom. Move a piece of furniture against the door to make it impossible for the intruder to open it. Next, call the police (you should always have a fully charged phone close to hand at night with the emergency number programmed in) and wait for help to arrive.

b Now in your own words tell **A** and **B** how to survive if somebody breaks into your house.

7B TWO PHOTOS Student B

a Listen to **A** describe his / her photo. Try to visualize it.

b **A** will now show you the photo to see if you agree with his / her description and interpretation.

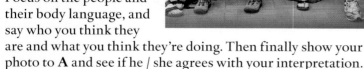

c Now describe your photo. Focus on the people and their body language, and say who you think they are and what you think they're doing. Then finally show your photo to **A** and see if he / she agrees with your interpretation.

> 🔍 **Describing a photo**
> This photo looks as if it was taken (in the summer, in the 1990s, etc.)
> In the centre
> In the foreground | (of the photo) there is / there are...
> In the background
> The woman on the left has her eyes closed. She looks as if...

8B STRANGE, BUT TRUE Student B

a Read the article and highlight the key information that will help you remember the story.

Dog phones for help

Dogs are often called 'Man's best friend' because they sometimes help save their owner's life. But George, a two-year-old basset hound in Yorkshire in the north of England, managed to save his own life by dialling 999.

George had been left at home on his own and had knocked the phone on the floor. He became entangled with the cord of the phone and was choking. Somehow he must have touched the number 9 key of the phone with his paws a few times, and as a result, he dialled the UK emergency number: 999. All the operator could hear was the sound of somebody choking and breathing heavily, so she sent the police to the house. The police got in with the help of a neighbour, Paul Walker, who had a spare key. To their amazement they found George with the cord round his neck. He was absolutely terrified, and couldn't free himself. They quickly pulled the phone cord out of the wall. Mr Walker said, 'It was incredible. You could see his paw print on the key of the phone. He literally saved his own life.'

George's owners, Steve Brown and his daughter Lydia, 18, were as amazed as everybody else. Lydia said, 'It's not as if George is particularly clever. In fact, he's really dopey – he just likes to chew socks most of the time.'

b Listen to **A**'s story, and ask **A** to clarify or rephrase if there's anything you don't understand.

c Tell **A** your story in your own words, e.g. *A dog called George who lives with a family in Yorkshire in the UK was left alone in the house when his owners went out…*

Writing

AN INFORMAL EMAIL

From: Anna
To: johnston586@gmail.com
Subject: News!

Hi Sue,

Sorry that I havent been in touch for a while, but I've been ill. I got flu last week and I had a temprature of 39°C, so I've been in bed since four days. I'm feeling a bit better today, so I've been catching up on my emails. Luckly my classes at university don't start till next week.

How are you? What have you been doing? Anything exciting. Here everyone are fine (apart from me and my flu!). My brother Ian has just started his new job with a software-company – I think I told you about it when I last wrote – anyway, he's really enjoying it. How are your family? I hope their well.

I have some good news – I'm going to a conference in your town in may, from 16th to 20th. Could you recomend a hotel where I could stay in the centre of town? It needs to be somewhere not too expensive because the university is paying. I'll have a free half-day for siteseeing. Do you think you'll be able show me around? That would be great.

Well, that's all for now. Please give my regards to your family.

Hope to hear from you soon.

Take care,

Anna

🔍 **Beginning an informal email**
When you are writing an informal email, it is more usual to start with *Hi* than with *Dear*.

---

a Read the email from Anna. It has 12 highlighted mistakes, four grammar or vocabulary, four punctuation, and four spelling. With a partner, decide what kind of mistake each one is and correct it.

b Read Anna's email again and find sentences that mean…

I haven't written or phoned.
I've been reading and replying to my emails.
Have you been doing anything exciting?

c You're going to answer Anna's email. Look at the **Useful language** expressions and try to complete them.

🔍 **Useful language: an informal email**
Opening expressions
Thanks 1_____ your email / letter.
It was great 2_____ hear from you.
Sorry for 3_____ writing earlier / sorry that I haven't been in touch for a while.
I 4_____ you and your family are well.

Responding to news
Sorry 5_____ hear about your exam results.
Glad to 6_____ that you're all well.
Good 7_____ with the new job.
Hope you 8_____ better soon.

Closing expressions
Anyway, / Well, that's all 9_____ now.
Hope to hear from you soon. / Looking 10_____ to hearing from you soon.
11_____ my regards (love) to…
Take 12_____ / 13_____ wishes / Regards / (Lots of) love from…
14_____ (= something you forgot and want to add) Please send me the photos you promised.

d **Plan** the content of your email.

1 Underline the questions in the email that Anna wants you to answer.
2 Underline other places in the email where you think you need to respond, e.g. *I've been ill.*
3 Think about how to respond to each of the things you've underlined.

e **Write** 120–180 words, in two or three paragraphs. Use informal language (contractions, etc.), and expressions from **Useful language**.

f **Check** your email for mistakes (grammar, punctuation, and spelling).

◀ p.15

Writing

A SHORT STORY

a Read the story. What was the 'small mistake'? What happened in the end?

It was only a small mistake, but it changed my life for ever. I had been working at JB Simpson's for ten years. It was a small ¹*family-run* company which exported garden furniture. I was ² ~~quite~~ happy with my job. I got on ³ *well* with the owner, Arthur Simpson, but not with his wife, Linda. She was a loud, ⁴ *aggressive* woman, who ⁵ *frequently* used to turn up at the office and start criticizing us for no reason. Everyone disliked her.

One afternoon Mrs Simpson came in while I was finishing writing a report. She looked at me and said, 'If I were you, I wouldn't wear that colour. It doesn't suit you at all.' I was wearing a ⁶ *new* pink shirt that I was very ⁷ *fond* of, and her comment really annoyed me. I typed a ⁸ *quick* email to Alan Simmonds in Sales. 'Watch out! The old witch is here!' and pressed 'send'. A couple of minutes later I was surprised to receive an email from Mr Simpson asking me to come to his office ⁹ *immediately*. When I opened the door I saw his wife glaring at the computer screen. I realized, to my horror, what I had done. I had clicked on Simpson instead of Simmonds. ¹⁰ *An hour later* I was packing my things. I had been sacked!

b Using adverbs and adjectives helps to make a story come alive and makes it more enjoyable to read. Complete the story with an adjective or adverb from the list.

---

aggressive   an hour later   quite   family-run   fond
frequently   immediately   new   quick   well

---

c You may want to write some dialogue as part of your story. Re-write the following with the correct punctuation. Use the dialogue in the story to help you.

> i want to talk to you about an email you sent
> Mr Simpson said coldly

d Look at the highlighted time expressions in **Useful language** and complete them.

> ### 🔍 Useful language: time expressions
> _____ that moment the door opened.
> As soon _____ I saw him, I knew something was wrong.
> Ten minutes _____, I went back to sleep.
> _____ morning in September I got to work early.
> We got to the station just _____ time to catch the train.

e You are going to write a story beginning with one of the sentences below. With a partner, choose which story to write and discuss what the plot could be.

1 **It was eleven o'clock at night when the phone rang.**
2 **Alex had been working hard all day, and was looking forward to going home.**
3 **We had been driving for four hours when we saw the sign for a small hotel and decided to stop.**

f **Plan** the content.
1 Write what happened simply, in about 50 words.
2 Think about how you could improve your story by adding more details, e.g. with adjectives and adverbs.
3 Think about what tenses you need for each part of the story, e.g. how to set the scene, what significant events happened before the story starts.

g **Write** 120–180 words, organized in two or three paragraphs. Use a variety of narrative tenses and adverbs and adjectives to make your story more vivid. Use time expressions to make the sequence of events clear.

h **Check** your short story for mistakes (grammar, punctuation, and spelling).

◀ p.29

FOR AND AGAINST

a Read a post about adventure sports on a blog site called *For and Against?* Do you think there are more advantages or more disadvantages?

b Read the blog post again and complete it with the linking expressions from the list (two of them are interchangeable).

> although   another advantage   because of
> for example (x2)   furthermore   in addition
> on the other hand   ~~the main advantage~~
> to sum up

c Put the linking expressions from **b** in the **Useful language** chart below.

> 🔍 **Useful language: linking expressions**
>
> **To list advantages / disadvantages**
> *the main advantage*
>
> _____
>
> **To add more points to the same topic**
>
> _____
>
> _____
>
> **To introduce an example**
> *For instance,...*
>
> _____
>
> **To make contrasting points**
> *However,...*
> *In spite of (the fact that)...*
>
> _____
>
> _____
>
> **To give a reason**
> *Because (+ clause)...*
> _____ *(+ noun)...*
>
> **To introduce the conclusion**
> *In conclusion,...*
>
> _____

d You are going to write a post for the site. Choose one of the titles below.

Going to work abroad: an exciting opportunity or a scary one?

Being a celebrity: a dream or a nightmare?

Everything has two sides to it, a positive one and a negative one. Post your opinions on our blog...

Adventure sports – fun or too risky?

Every year, more and more people are tempted by the idea of going on an adventure sports holiday, especially during the summer months.

Spending your holiday being active and enjoying the outdoors has a lot of advantages. 1*The main advantage* is that adventure sports, like many other physical activities, offer health benefits. 2_____, when you practise extreme sports your brain releases endorphins because of the adrenalin rush and that makes you feel happy. 3_____ is the self-confidence that you gain from doing these activities. 4_____, the lessons learnt from facing the difficulties and the risks of these extreme sports may be very valuable in everyday life.

5_____, there are also some important disadvantages. 6_____ they make you feel good, risky sports can be extremely dangerous. The possibility of getting seriously injured while performing these activities is quite high, and some adventure sports, 7_____ skydiving or cliff jumping can even have fatal consequences. 8_____ these risks, you need to be extremely fit to practise these sports during a holiday, which means that they are not for everyone. 9_____, they are likely to be expensive because they require a lot of equipment, safety measures, and well-trained and qualified instructors.

10_____, adventure sports holidays have both advantages and disadvantages. Whether they suit you or not depends on your level of fitness, your personality, and how much you can afford.

👍 Like | ◀ Share | 💬 Comment

e **Plan** the content.

1 Decide what you could say either about how many young people today choose or are forced to go and work abroad, or about how people today are interested in famous people or want to be famous themselves. This will give you material for the introduction.

2 List two or three advantages and disadvantages, and number them in order of importance.

3 Decide if you think there are more advantages than disadvantages.

f **Write** 120–180 words, organized in four paragraphs: introduction, advantages, disadvantages (or disadvantages then advantages), and conclusion. Use a formal style (no contractions or colloquial expressions). Use the linking expressions in **Useful language**.

g **Check** for mistakes (grammar, punctuation, and spelling).

◀ p.41

Writing

AN ARTICLE

a Look at the three pictures. What do you think the parents should and shouldn't have done? Read the article and check.

Make your home a safer place for children!

You probably think that your home is a very safe place. But this may not be true if you have children coming to stay. Here are some tips to prevent accidents./First look at the bedroom, where the children are going to sleep. Make sure the beds are <u>not</u> under a window, in case a child tries to climb out. If a very small child is going to sleep in the bed, you could put some pillows on the floor next to the bed, in case the child falls out. The next place to check is the bathroom. Many people keep medicines in a drawer or on a shelf above the washbasin. But this can be dangerous, as children may find them and think they are sweets. You should leave them in a locked cupboard. Finally, have a look at the kitchen, which is the most dangerous room in the house for children. Knives should be kept in drawers which children can't reach, and make sure that all cleaning liquids are in high cupboards. If you follow this simple advice, children who come to stay will never be at risk in your home.

b This article was originally written in five short paragraphs. Mark / where each new paragraph should begin.

c You are going to write an article for a school magazine. With a partner, choose one of the titles below.

How to keep safe if you go walking in the mountains.
How to keep safe on a day at the beach.
How to keep safe online.

d **Plan** the content.

1 Think of at least three useful tips.
2 Think of a good introductory sentence (or sentences).

e **Write** 120–180 words. Use expressions from **Useful language** below, and write in a neutral or informal style.

> **Useful language: giving advice**
> *Don't forget to... / Remember to...*
> *Make sure you...*
> *You should...*
> *Never...*
>
> **Reasons**
> *...in case*
> *...so (that)*
> *...because it might...*

f **Check** your article for mistakes (grammar, punctuation, and spelling).

 p.47

116

DESCRIBING A PHOTO

a Look at the photo and read the description. Do you agree with what the writer says about the people?

I think this is a family photo, although none of the family members is actually looking at the camera. ¹*In the foreground* we see the inside of a room with a glass door leading into a garden. ²_____ of the photo there is a girl sitting at the table, resting her head on one hand, with an open book ³_____ her. There are two other empty chairs around the table. The girl is smiling; she looks as if she's daydreaming, maybe about something she's read in the book. ⁴_____, there is another woman, who looks older than the girl, perhaps her mother. She's standing with her arms folded, looking out of the glass doors into the garden. She seems to be watching what's happening ⁵_____, and she looks a bit worried.

⁶_____, we can see a terrace, and ⁷_____ that a beautiful garden. Outside the glass doors on the right you can see a boy and a man who may be father and son. The boy is standing looking at the man, who is crouching ⁸_____ him. It looks as though they're having a serious conversation. Maybe the boy has been naughty, because it seems as if he's looking at the ground. This photo reminds me of a David Hockney or Edward Hopper painting, and it immediately makes you speculate about who the people are and what they are thinking.

b Complete the description with a word or phrase from the list.

behind   in front of   in the background   in the centre
~~in the foreground~~   to her right   opposite   outside

> 🔍 **Useful language: describing a photo or picture**
> *In the foreground / background / centre of the photo...*
> *The (man) looks as if / looks as though...*
> *It looks as if / as though...*
> *The (woman) may / might be... / Perhaps the woman is...*
> *The photo reminds me of...*

c You are going to write a description of the photo below. **Plan** the content. With a partner, look at the photo carefully and decide what you think the people are thinking or feeling. Decide how to organize what you want to say into two paragraphs.

d **Write** 120–180 words. Use the phrases in **Useful language** to help you.

e **Check** your description for mistakes (grammar, punctuation, and spelling).

◀ p.71

EXPRESSING YOUR OPINION

a Read the title of the magazine article. Do you agree or disagree? Then quickly read the article and see if the writer's opinion is the same as yours.

b Complete the article with a word or phrase from the list below.

finally	firstly	for instance	in addition	in conclusion
in most cases	nowadays	secondly	so	whereas

c You are going to write an article for a magazine. With a partner, choose one of the titles below.

Downloading music or films without paying is as much of a crime as stealing from a shop.

Squatters who live in an unoccupied property should not be forced to leave it.

d **Plan** the content. The article should have four or five paragraphs.

1 **The introduction**: Think about what the current situation is and what your opinion is.

2 **The main paragraphs**: Try to think of at least two or three clear reasons to support your opinion. You could also include examples to back up your reasons.

3 **The conclusion**: Think of how to express your conclusion (a summary of your opinion).

e **Write** 120–180 words, organized in four or five paragraphs (introduction, reasons, and conclusion). Use a formal style (no contractions or colloquial expressions). Use the phrases in **b** and in **Useful language**.

> 🔍 **Useful language: ways of giving your opinion**
> (Personally) I think… / I believe…
> In my opinion…
> In addition / Also
> In conclusion / To sum up
>
> **Ways of giving examples**
> There are several things we can do, for example / for instance / such as…
> Another thing we can do is…
> We can also…

f **Check** your article for mistakes (grammar, punctuation, and spelling).

◀ p.77

Community service is the best punishment for young people who commit a minor offence.

[1] *Nowadays* in the UK when a young person commits a minor offence, he or she is normally sentenced to prison, given a fine, or community service. [2] _____ I believe that community service is the best option.

[3] _____, community service often persuades a young person not to re-offend. [4] _____ working with sick children or old people makes young offenders realize that there are people who have more difficult lives than they do. So community service can be an educational experience, [5] _____ going to prison or paying a fine is not.

[6] _____, spending time in prison results in young people meeting other criminals and learning more about the criminal world, which may tempt them into committing more crimes. [7] _____, in prisons many of the inmates take drugs and this is a terrible example for young offenders.

[8] _____, I do not think that a fine is a suitable punishment for young people. They do not usually have much money themselves, [9] _____ it is often their parents who pay the fine for them.

[10] _____, I believe that community service has important advantages both for minor offenders and for the community.

A REPORT

a Read the report on restaurants. With a partner, think of suitable headings for paragraphs 1, 3, and 4.

b You have been asked to write a report on either **good places for eating out** or **entertainment in your town** for an English language magazine. With a partner, **plan** the content.

1 Decide which report you are going to write.
2 Decide what headings you can use to divide up your report.
3 Decide what information to include under each heading.

c **Write** 120–180 words, organized in three or four paragraphs with a heading. Use a neutral / formal style, and use expressions from **Useful language** for generalizing.

> 🔍 **Useful language: talking in general**
> *Most / The majority of (cinemas in my town…)*
> *(Cinemas) are usually / tend to be (quite cheap)*
> *In general… / Generally speaking…*
> *almost always… / nearly always…*

d **Check** your report for mistakes (grammar, punctuation, and spelling).

◀ *p.91*

Eating out in London

This report describes various options for students who want to eat out while staying in London.

1 _____

Fast food – The majority of fast-food restaurants are cheap and clean and the service is fast, but they are often noisy and crowded, and of course the food is the same all over the world.

World food – London has restaurants offering food from many parts of the world, for example India, and China. These are often relatively inexpensive and have good-quality food and a nice atmosphere.

2 *Value for money*

Gastropubs – These are pubs which serve high-quality food but tend to be slightly cheaper than the majority of mid-range restaurants. Generally speaking, the food is well-cooked and some have very imaginative menus.

Italian restaurants – You can normally get a good pasta dish and a salad in most Italian restaurants without spending too much, but be careful, some restaurants have very expensive wine lists.

3 _____

There are many options if you want to try somewhere special, but be aware that this nearly always means spending a lot of money. French restaurants, for example, are often expensive, and also restaurants run by celebrity chefs.

4 _____

- Don't make your meal cost more by ordering expensive drinks.
- If you have a special restaurant in mind, don't forget to book in advance because the best restaurants are usually full, especially at weekends.
- Even if you have a limited budget, take advantage of the different restaurants that London has to offer.

Listening

(1 9))

1 I was being interviewed for a job with an advertising agency and um, the interviewer kept checking information on my CV and then asking me about it, and he saw that I'd studied philosophy at university, and he said, 'Oh, I see that you studied Philosophy at university. Do you still practise philosophy?' So I said, 'Well, I still think a lot'. Anyway he obviously liked the answer because I got the job.

2 At my job interview to become an editor with a publishing company, there were three people asking questions: two managers, and a woman from Human Resources. All the questions had been pretty normal, they were about my studies and experience, and then suddenly the woman from Human Resources asked me, 'What would make you kick a dog?' I was totally flustered but I managed to answer – I said, 'I'd only kick it if the dog had bad grammar and couldn't punctuate properly'. I thought it was quite a clever answer and, in fact, I got the job!

3 When I was applying for a teaching job in Korea, they were doing the interviews by phone because I was in the US. And because of the time difference they were all very early in the morning, which is not my best time. Anyway, the Director of Studies of this particular school asked me, 'How tall are you?' and, 'How much do you weigh?' I answered his questions but after the interview, when I thought about it, I decided that I didn't want to work in a school that would judge me by my height or my weight. So later, when they offered me the job, I turned it down.

4 I was being interviewed for a job with a company in Switzerland and the interviewer asked me, 'What animal would you like to be reincarnated as?' So I said a cat, because it was the first thing I thought of and because cats have a good life – well at least in Britain they do. And then the interviewer immediately looked a bit embarrassed and said that he had been told to ask me that question to see how I would react, but that he thought it was a stupid question. In the end I didn't get the job, so maybe the interviewer wasn't very fond of cats…

5 I went for a job in a lawyer's office. There were two of us waiting to be interviewed – me and a man about the same age as me – and he was nice so we were chatting before we went in, and we agreed to have a coffee afterwards. Well, I went in first, and they asked me the usual sorts of questions about my previous job. They had all my personal information on my CV and so they knew I was married and suddenly they asked me, 'Are you planning to have children?' I said 'not in the immediate future but maybe one day'. Afterwards when I was having coffee with the other candidate, I asked him if he'd been asked the same question, and he said no, even though he was married, too. In fact we both got offered jobs, but I still think it was a very sexist question to ask.

(1 10))

Fatos began to look very carefully at the coffee grounds in Chris's cup and to tell him what she could see. I remember that the first thing she said was that she could see 'sacks of money' – and this was very accurate because Chris had worked in Saudi Arabia for several years and had earned a lot of money there. She also said that she could see 'a blonde lady'. Well, Carla, Chris's girlfriend at the time, was blonde so that was spot on, too. But then Fatos suddenly looked very serious and she said, 'I can see somebody in your family who is ill, very ill, at this moment.'

I remember thinking, 'Oh no! Don't ruin a nice evening!' But Chris is quite a laid-back sort of person and he didn't seem to be too worried by what she'd said. He just said, 'Well, as far as I know the people in my family are OK'. Chris is an only child and his mother lived with her sister in London. They were both in their seventies.

Fatos said one or two more things and then we asked the waiter for the bill and said our goodbyes. It was a slightly weird end to what had been a very enjoyable evening. I can remember feeling quite relieved that I had said 'no' when Fatos asked me if she could read my coffee cup.

Chris and I got a taxi back to our hotel. The next day Chris had a free morning, because it was my turn to do the teacher training session in the hotel, so he went off early to go sightseeing in Istanbul. Around nine o'clock I got a call on my mobile. It was Chris's girlfriend, Carla, calling from the UK. She told me that she needed to talk to Chris urgently but that he wasn't answering his mobile. I could tell by her voice that she had some very bad news for him and I immediately thought of what Fatos had said the night before and I felt a shiver run down my spine.

I asked Carla what had happened and she told me that Chris's aunt had died suddenly in the night. So, was it just a spooky coincidence, or did Fatos really see what she said she saw in the coffee cup? I spoke to her before I left Istanbul and I told her that Chris's aunt had died the night that we had dinner. She wasn't at all surprised and she just said, 'Yes, I saw in the cup that someone in his family was near to death, but I didn't want to frighten him so I just said that the person was very ill.' All I can say is that I always used to be very sceptical about fortune telling but now, well, I'm not so sure.

(1 17))

What's in your signature?

Our signature is very much part of the way in which we present ourselves to the world, so it can definitely give us some clues about the kind of person we are and how we feel about ourselves.

As you know, a person's signature usually consists of a first name and a surname, or an initial and a surname. Your first name represents your private self – how you are with your family; and your surname represents your public self – the way you are at work or school, and in your social life.

If you use only initials either for your first name or your surname in your signature, this means that you are more secretive and protective about either your private or public self.

Now look at the space between your name and surname. Are the two names very close together, or is there a reasonable space between them? The more space there is between your name and your surname, the more you wish to keep these two parts of your personality separate.

(1 18))

The size of your signature

Now let's look at the size of your signature. If your first name is bigger and more prominent in your signature this normally means that your 'private' self is more important to you than your 'public' self. If your surname is bigger and more prominent, this probably means that your 'public' self is more important to you.

If your whole signature is very big compared with the rest of your writing this normally means that you are quite a self-confident person. Some people actually sign in capital letters, which suggests that they may be big-headed or even arrogant rather than just self-confident. On the other hand, people who sign their name with a very small signature tend to be insecure and have low self-esteem.

(1 19))

The legibility of your signature

Another important factor is how legible your signature is – in other words how easy it is to read. A legible signature tends to mean that you're a person with clear ideas and objectives. On the other hand if your signature is difficult to read this may imply that you're somebody who doesn't think very clearly and that you may be disorganized or indecisive. It can also mean that you're quite secretive.

Generally speaking the more illegible your signature is, the less assertive you probably are as a person.

(1 20))

The angle of your signature

Finally I want to say something about the angle of your signature, that's to say whether your signature is horizontal, or goes up or goes down on the page.

A rising signature, one which goes up, means that you are the kind of person who, when you're faced with problems, will work hard to overcome them. You're a determined person and probably optimistic and ambitious. A descending signature, that is one which goes down, suggests that you're the kind of person who gets disheartened or depressed when you're faced with problems, perhaps because you are not very self-confident. A horizontal signature, one which goes straight across the page, usually indicates a person who is well-balanced and emotionally stable, and someone who is generally satisfied with the way their life is going.

But it's worth bearing in mind that the angle of our signature may change at different times of our lives, depending on how we are feeling.

(1 23))

Part 1

Interviewer What's the first thing you're looking for in a candidate for a job?

Ryan The first thing you're looking for with a job candidate is an enthusiasm for the role, you're also looking for them to demonstrate experience, er, relevant to the position.

Interviewer How do you get candidates to relax in the interview?

Ryan It's important to engage with the candidate straight away, so when you collect them from reception or from the, the front of the building whatever it may be, you want to kind of greet them in a friendly manner, you want to ask them some general questions, just talking about their journey into the interview or, um, the weather or have they been to the city before.

Interviewer And during the interview?

Ryan During an interview, once it has commenced I will always try to start the interview with some general questions, just to allow the candidate to talk about themselves, to talk about their CV, their background, um, and often when a candidate is talking about something they know, which is themselves and what they've been doing, um, they're able to settle down much more quickly and have an element of confidence around, er, what they're talking.

Interviewer Is it important for candidates to ask the interviewer questions and if so what kind of questions should candidates ask?

Ryan Questions can be related to anything, so I personally would encourage candidates to ask questions rated to any aspect of employment and most recruiters would welcome that sort of interaction as an opportunity to actually give a little bit more information about the company.

Interviewer Is it OK for candidates to ask about the money or the salary at the interview?

Ryan Of course, and candidates should be honest and realistic about their expectations too; an interview is an appropriate environment to ask such a question especially if salary or, er, salary banding was not identified in the job advert.

Interviewer How important are CVs and covering letters?

Ryan CVs are very important to a recruiter because it actually provides an overview of a candidate's background, their employment, what they've been doing to date, but a cover letter can actually be more important because that's where a candidate will actually list and identify how they meet the criteria for the post, so it allows a candidate to be very specific about demonstrating what skills and experience they have that would be relevant and often that skill and experience may be missed on a CV when you're looking at a wider career history.

Interviewer What's the worst thing a job candidate can do when they're applying for a job?

Ryan First thing is obviously, make mistakes on their application, um, that's always viewed negatively depending on the role they're applying for. Um, also coming to an interview late, coming to an interview unprepared.

1 24

Part 2

Interviewer Can you give us an example of some of the more difficult interviews you've been involved in?

Ryan I've been in interviews where candidates haven't been prepared and have not been able to, from the start, answer some of the questions, um, one particular situation was when a candidate actually thought they were being interviewed for something completely different, um, so again you have to actually think how do you deal with that situation, do you stop the interview or do you carry on?

Interviewer Anything else that has surprised you during an interview?

Ryan There was another situation where, er, a candidate actually produced food during the interview, er, in the middle of answering a question, they stopped and rummaged in their bag to pull out a KitKat, um, which took both myself and the interviewing manager by surprise, we did ask and enquire as to what she was doing, er, at which point she actually advised that she was a diabetic and just felt at that particular moment, um, that she just needed a little, er, something to eat to, to calm things, which was absolutely fine, but again during the interview when she hadn't announced that's why she was doing it, it was a bit of a surprise.

Interviewer How important is the way a candidate dresses for an interview?

Ryan A candidate's dress for interview is important because it shows how serious they take the situation. Um, however, I would always recommend that candidates would come to interview, um, in a dress that is appropriate for the role they're applying for. In today's modern, er, recruitment, er, environment it's not always necessary for a, a guy to wear a suit to an interview, however you would expect to see a shirt, you would expect to see a blazer, you would expect, expect to see appropriate footwear and the same for a, a lady as well, um, certain clothes, certain types of footwear would be inappropriate to come into an interview and may set a perception of that candidate which is perhaps incorrect.

Interviewer Have you ever had an interview with someone who was dressed very inappropriately?

Ryan I had an interview on one occasion where a candidate actually arrived in tennis gear, a white T-shirt and shorts, they'd literally come straight from the tennis court and they had simply forgotten the interview was on that day, had suddenly had the reminder that actually they were due to be at the interview, so they thought they would come anyway as they were, um, I did see the candidate and they were actually very impressive, we just had to move past the, the clothing aspect but actually it was quite funny and allowed a real opportunity to engage with that particular candidate from the start.

Interviewer Did that person get the job?

Ryan No, they didn't.

1 25

Part 3

Interviewer What can you tell us about extreme interviewing, that is asking candidates very strange questions like 'What dinosaur would you be?'?

Ryan OK, um extreme interviewing is a technique used by recruiters to put the candidate in a situation that they may not have been in before, um, or to, put them, give them a scenario where they have to think quickly, where they have to digest information, where they perhaps have to problem solve before giving an answer.

Interviewer Have you used it yourself?

Ryan It's not something that I have direct experience of, but I am aware of some of the techniques that they use and some of the questions that could be used. Um, I was reading recently about, um, extreme interviewing techniques used for an insurance company, they asked candidates to describe, they asked candidates during the interview how they would describe Facebook to their grandmother? What the recruiter was looking for was for that candidate to display an element of, um, technical skills and technical awareness, also to display communications skills and how they would explain Facebook to an audience or to somebody who doesn't understand modern technology or modern social media.

Interviewer Do you have any others?

Ryan One I was reading about recently was posed to candidates during an interview, er, where they were looking to assess a candidate's ability to multitask. The candidates were asked whether they would want to fight a horse-sized duck or a hundred duck-sized horses. Depending on the answer one or a hundred that would potentially dictate whether that candidate was most comfortable multitasking or dealing with one, er, situation or one objective at a time.

Interviewer What would your answer to that question have been?

Ryan I, when I read it I had to re-read it four times, and that's just me reading it. In an interview I would have had to have asked for that question to be repeated and I'm not even sure if I would have been able to give an immediate response because I would still be trying to understand what exactly they were asking of me. I guess for me personally, when I'd thought about it, I would have said one horse-sized duck, um, but that would potentially mean that I'm not able to multitask! So…

1 27

Interviewer When did you last have an interview for a job or a place on a course?

Jeanine Uh, the last time I had an interview for a job was in 2011.

Interviewer How did you prepare for the interview?

Jeanine Ah, I took a lot of Rescue Remedy to help with the nerves and I, I just practised every question that they could ask me in my head.

Interviewer Did the interview go well?

Jeanine No, it didn't. I didn't get the job.

Interviewer When did you last have an interview for a job or a place on a course?

Jo Err, about two months ago.

Interviewer How did you prepare for the interview?

Jo Well, I looked at the job description and thought about my experience, um, and then tried to match my experience to the various different points on the job interview.

Interviewer Did the interview go well?

Jo It did.

Interviewer How do you know it went well?

Jo Because they offered me the job.

Interviewer When did you last have an interview for a job or a place on a course?

Ivan I last had an interview for a job a few weeks ago, um, that's the last time I had an interview for a job.

Interviewer How did you prepare for the interview?

Ivan To prepare for the job interview I read about the company and learnt about what they did and to see if I liked the work that they did.

Interviewer Did the interview go well?

Ivan I think it went well because they followed up with an email, um, to talk about, um, further opportunities at that company.

Interviewer When did you last have an interview for a job or a place on a course?

Yasuko Um, the last interview that I had was for my current company that I work for, and that was about two years ago.

Interviewer How did you prepare for the interview?

Yasuko I prepared for the interview by, um, res… doing a little research on the company, the kind of products that they make, um, the, their philosophy, the history and the background of the company.

Interviewer Did the interview go well?

Yasuko I think that the interview went well because it was actually a long interview. I had a lot of, um, good conversation with the managers there, and I also got a few more interviews afterwards, and eventually got the job, so the, the interviews went well.

Interviewer When did you last have an interview for a job or a place on a course?

Joost Um, about three months ago.

Interviewer How did you prepare for the interview?

Joost Uh, I read about the company and um, I knew what the job content was, and um, yeah I knew everything that I had to know for the interview, I was well-prepared to answer their questions.

Interviewer Did the interview go well?

Joost Uh, it went well. In the end they said I was too young, so they didn't hire me, but, um, yeah, they would have if I was older, they said.

1 41

I So, Dr Cannon, Do you meet a lot of cyberchondriacs in your work?

D All the time, I'm afraid. It's very common nowadays for people to look up their symptoms on health websites on the internet and to diagnose themselves with weird or exotic illnesses! For example the other day I had a patient who came in because his back was very red and itchy. He had been looking on internet medical sites and was absolutely convinced that he had an extremely rare skin condition – he even knew the medical name: nodular panniculitis. But, in fact when I examined him and talked to him it turned out that he had spent the weekend gardening in the sun and his back was sunburnt.

I So you would prefer your patients not to check their symptoms on the internet?

D No, don't get me wrong, I'm not anti health websites, I just want people to use them sensibly. The problem is that diagnosis of a condition or an illness doesn't just depend on one specific symptom that you can type into Google. It depends on all sorts of other things like a patient's appearance, their blood pressure, their heart rate, and so on.

I Of course.

D And diagnosis also depends on where you live. For example, if you live in west London and you haven't travelled abroad, it's very unlikely that you have malaria even if you have some of the symptoms.

I What other problems are there when people use health websites?

D Well, you have to check carefully what kind of site it is that you are looking at. Some websites look as if they have been created by health professionals, but in fact they've been set up by commercial companies that are trying to sell you something. Also, some American healthcare sites recommend expensive treatments or medicine that is not available here in the UK.

I Are there any websites which you would recommend?

D Oh yes, absolutely. For example, people with chronic diseases like asthma can get a lot of help and information from online support groups. These websites have forums where you can talk to other people who have the same condition and illness and you can usually get information about the latest research and new treatments. And there are often online support groups for people who have unusual illnesses, too.

I Finally, do you have any tips for all those cyberchondriacs out there?

D Yes, I have three. First, only look online after you've been to the doctor. If you're not feeling well, make a list of the symptoms you have that are worrying you, and go and see your doctor with this list. Then when your doctor has told you what he or she thinks, you could have a look online. Secondly, make sure you're looking at a reliable and professional medical website. And finally, remember that common symptoms usually have common causes – so if you have diarrhoea, for example, it's much more likely to be food poisoning than the Ebola virus.

I Doctor Cannon, thank you very much.

1 45

P Welcome to today's programme in our series on age. The topic is clothes, and the question is, do people nowadays dress their age, and should they? Our guests are both fashion journalists with well-known magazines. Hello, Liza and Adrian.

L + A Hello. Hi!

P Let's start with you, Liza.

L Well, the first thing I'd like to say to all the young people out there is next time you give your granny a warm cardigan and some slippers for her birthday, don't be surprised if she asks for the receipt, because she'll probably want to go out and change them for something more exciting.

P So you think nowadays women in their sixties and seventies dress much younger than they used to?

L Oh, absolutely. Think of women like Sophia Loren, Catherine Deneuve, Helen Mirren, and Jane Fonda. Jane Fonda is in her late seventies and last month she was on a US talk show wearing a leather mini skirt – she looked fabulous! But, of course, it isn't just famous women who are dressing younger; some recent research says that nine out of ten women say that they try to dress younger than their years.

P Do you think that's true?

L Well, it depends on your age of course. A lot of teenage girls try to dress older than they are, maybe to get into pubs and bars. But I would say that from 30 onwards most women try to dress younger than they are.

P And do you think there's anything wrong with that?

L Actually, I think it's not a question of dressing older or younger, it's a question of wearing what suits you. And if you looked good in jeans when you were 15, if you keep your figure you'll probably look good in them when you're 80. There are a few things which can look a bit ridiculous on an older woman, like, let's see, very short shorts...but not many.

P So your fashion rule would be...?

L Wear whatever you think suits you and makes you feel good.

P Adrian, what about men? Do you think they also try to look younger than their age?

A Well, interestingly, in the research Liza mentioned, only 12 % of the men who were questioned said they had ever thought about dressing to look younger. But actually I think a lot of them weren't telling the truth. Look at all those middle-aged men you see wearing jeans which are too tight and incredibly bright T-shirts.

P You don't approve?

A No, I don't. Personally I think that men should take their age into account when they're buying clothes.

P Do you think that some men actually dress older than their age?

A Yes, definitely, some do. Some men in their twenties look as if they were 20 years older by wearing blazers and chinos, or wearing suits and ties all the time when they don't have to. They've maybe just started work and they want their bosses to take them more seriously. And a lot of men in their thirties realize that they can't dress like a teenager any more, but they go to the opposite extreme and they start buying the sort of clothes that their fathers wear.

P So what would your fashion rule be for men?

A Dress for the age you are, not for the age you wish you were.

P Liza and Adrian, thank you very much.

② 2))

1 Ladies and gentlemen, welcome on board this flight to Hong Kong. Please place all hand luggage in the overhead compartments or underneath the seat in front of you. We ask that you please fasten your seatbelts and, for safety reasons, we advise you to keep them fastened throughout the flight.

2 We also ask that you make sure your seats and table trays are in the upright position for take-off. Please turn off all personal electronic devices, including laptops and cell phones. We remind you that smoking is prohibited for the duration of the flight.

3 Ladies and gentlemen, may we have your special attention for the following safety instructions. Please read the safety instructions card which is located in the pocket of the seat in front of you. There are six emergency exits on this aircraft, all marked with exit signs. Take a minute to locate the exit closest to you. Note that the nearest exit may be behind you.

4 The safety instruction card is in the pocket of the seat in front of you. Please read it. It shows you the equipment carried on this aircraft for your safety. Your life jacket is located under your seat. In the unlikely event of the aircraft landing on water, place the life jacket over your head, fasten the straps at the front, and pull them tight. Do not inflate the jacket inside the aircraft. As you leave the aircraft, pull down the red tabs to inflate the vest. If necessary, the life jacket can be inflated by blowing through these tubes.

② 7))

Interviewer With me in the studio today I have Richard, who's a pilot, and Brynn, who's an air traffic controller, and they are going to answer some of the most frequently asked questions about flying and air travel. Hello to both of you.

Richard and Brynn Hello.

Interviewer Right, we're going to start with you, Richard. The first question is what weather conditions are the most dangerous when flying a plane?

Richard Probably the most dangerous weather conditions are when the wind changes direction very suddenly. Er… this tends to happen during thunderstorms and typhoons and it's especially dangerous during take-off and landing. But it's quite unusual – I've been flying for 37 years now and I've only experienced this three or four times.

Interviewer What about turbulence? Is that dangerous?

Richard It can very bumpy and very uncomfortable but it isn't dangerous. Even strong turbulence won't damage the plane. Pilots always try to avoid turbulence, but it can sometimes occur without any warning, which is why we always advise passengers to wear their seatbelt all the time during the flight.

Interviewer Which is more dangerous, take-off or landing?

Richard Both take-off and landing can be dangerous. They're the most dangerous moments of a flight. Pilots talk about the 'critical eight minutes' – the three minutes after take-off and the five minutes before landing. Most accidents happen in this period. But I would say that take-off is probably slightly more dangerous than landing. There is a critical moment just before take-off when the plane is accelerating, but it hasn't yet reached the speed to be able to fly. If the pilot has a problem with the plane at this point, he has very little time – maybe only a second – to abort the take-off.

Interviewer Are some airports more dangerous than others?

Richard Yes, some are – particularly airports with high mountains around them and airports in countries with older or more basic navigation equipment. For some difficult airports like, let's say Kathmandu, they only allow very experienced pilots to land there. And for some of these airports, pilots have to practise on a simulator first before they are given permission to land a plane there.

Interviewer Thanks, Richard. Over to you, Brynn. What personal qualities do you think you need to be an air traffic controller?

Brynn I think confidence is number one. You need to be a self-confident person, you have to be sure of yourself and of the decisions you're making.

Interviewer Most people imagine that being an air traffic controller is very stressful. Do you agree?

Brynn Actually, on a daily basis, the job isn't as stressful as people think. Obviously it's true that stressful situations do arise, but when you're very busy, you just don't have time to get stressed.

Interviewer Why is it important for pilots and controllers to have good, clear English?

Brynn English is the official language of air traffic control. We communicate with pilots using very specific phrases like *runway, wind, cleared for take-off, turbulence, traffic ahead, to your left, to your right,* things like that, and it's true that you could just learn these specific phrases. But then in an emergency you don't know what language you might need, it's much less predictable, which is why it's vital for pilots and air traffic controllers to speak really good, clear English.

Richard If I could just interrupt here, in fact there have been several air crashes which happened because the air traffic controller misunderstood something that the pilot had said in English, or vice versa, because their pronunciation wasn't clear enough.

Brynn Yes, that's right.

Interview Finally, people tend to think that most pilots and air traffic controllers are men. Would you say that was true?

Brynn Not in air traffic control – there are lots of women. It may not be fifty-fifty, but there are plenty of us.

Richard It's true about pilots, though. I mean there are some women pilots, but it's still quite a male-dominated job, I'd say.

Interviewer Why do you think that is?

Richard People say it's because men have a better sense of direction.

Brynn Very funny.

Interviewer Richard, Brynn, thank you very much.

② 20))

Part 2

'How does it feel?' shouted Stan.

Susan smiled. The little gun was surprisingly pleasant to hold. She held it in her right hand, aimed it as Stan had instructed her, felt angry once again when she thought of the mugging, and pulled the trigger.

'Hey, that's good!' Stan shouted.

She'd never heard him shout before, but then that was the only possible way to communicate at the Target Shooting Range. Susan wanted to blow the smoke away from the end of the gun like John Wayne.

'I want to shoot another round,' she said, confidently.

'Good evening, ladies.'

The expert in self-defense stood beside a large projected screen.

'The victim of a mugging usually looks like this . . .'

A picture of a little old woman now appeared on the screen. She was carrying a shopping bag in one hand and a purse in the other.

'She looks vulnerable and weak. The mugger likes her – it'll be easy for him to take what he wants and run. He won't choose a victim who looks as if she might fight back.'

A picture of a younger woman now appeared on the screen. She looked strong and fit, and her hands were free.

'If you want to avoid being mugged, walk confidently! Keep your head up. Pull your shoulders back. Don't carry a lot of packages and keep your hands free. Carry your purse under your arm. Look as if you know where you're going, even if you don't. That mugger should think you're tough. Any questions so far?'

Susan raised her hand.

'Is there any way to identify a typical mugger?'

The instructor smiled.

'He's the one wearing dark clothes, hiding in the bushes.'

Everyone but Susan laughed. This was the third week of the self-defense course. The first week, they'd learned to scream loudly and to run away fast. The second, they'd looked at keys and scissors as potential defence weapons. This week the topic was, 'Who Is a Likely Mugging Victim?'

At the end of the class, the women all walked out confidently, with their heads high. They didn't walk near any bushes on their way to their cars.

Stan was delighted at how much stronger and more confident Susan seemed after only three weeks of self-defense classes.

'You're really doing well,' he said, and kissed the top of her head. 'I've never seen you so single-minded.'

'Well, some things in life are important,' Susan said. 'And, anyway, I'm still so angry about being robbed!'

Nobody was going to mistake her for a victim again.

② 23))

Part 1

Interviewer What was your favourite book when you were a child?

Julia It's always very difficult thinking back to one's favourite book as a child because, er, different times were different favourite books, but the book that I remember best that I go back to in times of wanting to have a quiet moment of, er, reflection is a book by Rosemary Sutcliff called *Warrior Scarlet*, and why it appealed to me is very hard to say, it's about a boy with a withered arm in the Iron Age who can't get his place in the tribe because he can't kill a wolf. I probably read it once a year even now.

Interviewer Even now?

Julia Well, yes because there is a special thing about reading a book that you loved as a child it takes you back to that time. You, typically if you ask people about their favourite book as, as a child or the book that made them a reader, which I think is another way of looking at it, they can remember a fantastic amount about it, they can often remember who gave it to them or who read it to them or where they read it or, and I have exactly that experience with, with that book.

Interviewer When you were a small child, who read to you, your mother or your father?

Julia Well, I'm third of four children and I, this is a terrible thing to say, I don't think anybody read to me, I think I remember listening in on my older sisters being read to, so I was the youngest of three girls and then I've got a younger brother. And I very much remember my mother reading the Laura Ingalls Wilder, *Little House on the Prairie* sequence to my brother and that's when I heard them too, I certainly never had them read to me. And then my father read me Rumer Godden's *Mouse House*, and again this is a very profound memory, probably because he didn't actually very often read aloud, so it's logged in my brain as something that he read to me.

Interviewer And who read to your children, you or your husband?

Julia Well, that's interesting because if I think back to it, I think, perhaps because I worked in books and my husband didn't, he seems to have done more of the reading aloud than I did, um, he loved reading aloud, he has incredible stamina for it and he would read for an hour quite happily, I think, at the end of a working day it was quite a nice thing for him to do.

Interviewer Do you have a favourite children's writer?

Julia I think my favourite author at the moment is Philip Pullman. I think he gave us a classic book in *Northern Lights*, the first of *His Dark Materials* trilogy which opened up to a very wide range of children, what imaginative fiction can be at its best and there's nothing that Philip has written that isn't interesting, beautifully crafted, um, surprising and a story that you reflect on. He, he raises so many questions, giving openings for children to think, that's the best kind of writing as far as I'm concerned. So if you ask me now of a contemporary writer, he would be the person who I think is the greatest.

2 24

Part 2

Interviewer What do you think is the one big thing that helps to make a child a reader?

Julia One of the extraordinary things about reading that isn't talked about enough, I think, there's a lot of, of talk about how children learn to read and all of this but actually, and what strategy might be best, but actually what makes a reader, a book, it's finding the book that you really want to read, and so that's the chemistry, that's the chemical moment when a child finds something that they really want to read.

Interviewer Teenagers can also be quite negative about reading, what do you think can help inspire teenagers to read?

Julia Well, I think the biggest inspiration that I, I would, I mean I would like to say again, to get back to the idea that it is the right book, but I think there are lots of ways into reading and one of the things that's very evident is that, um, good films, far from putting children off reading the book often take children or teenagers to read the book. You take a book like *The Beach*, all right it wasn't a book that was written for children, but it was a, you know, it was a great teen novel, it was a sort of almost a teen anthem novel and um, a lot of teenagers read the book after they'd seen the film.

Interviewer How do you feel about children reading books which are badly written?

Julia What I certainly wouldn't do is make judgements about quality of writing. One of the weirdest things that happens in children's books is that as soon as a child finds an author that they love the parents tend to think it's not suitable because they think if the child is loving it, it's too easy or too trivial or too whatever and Jacqueline Wilson is a very good example of this, she is an author who, girls, particularly, found and loved for years and it's taken the parents a very long time to realize that she is a very good author. And what do you say about someone like JK Rowling who is, you know, not a great literary stylist but has some really remarkable qualities in her books and will be credited over probably three more generations for having made children readers. I wouldn't want to say children shouldn't have read her books because they're not a great literary quality.

2 25

Part 3

Interviewer For the most part do you read paper books or e-books?

Julia Ah, I'm, I'm almost entirely a print book reader but that is not out of prejudice that's just out of, um the fact that I get sent all the books, so it's easy for me to find the book I want to read and pick it up. Um, I read on my, um, iPad, sometimes, um, I think we are, ought to, sort of, stop seeing the two in polarity I think, you know, everybody is going to read both, I read the newspaper online and I read it in print at the weekends. I think we are all just going to get very used to reading in different ways.

Interviewer Has all the new media made young people read less?

Julia When television first hit, as it were, everyone said children would stop reading, and the curious thing is that children's books and even books for teenagers are stronger now, much stronger than they were when television, children's television, first took hold. Children's television has slightly dwindled, books have increased. So the book has always been under threat from these other media but somehow reading survives, so there must be something very important about it or it would have gone, we would all have taken to seeing things in film which is a much easier way of accessing the same wonderful stories or, I, I always think the thing that really threatens reading is listening to music, I know you can do both but most people don't, but you know, even with the explosion of music that children have access to they still have found time for reading.

Interviewer Do you still read for pleasure?

Julia Well I still do read for pleasure, um, but it's harder to get back to that magical experience, which I do remember very clearly from childhood, I do remember that being totally absorbed in the book, but as you get older it's just harder to carve out time like that and there's always something else pressing and of course, that's got more so with, you know, I have a BlackBerry I look at it all the time, and, er, I have to stop myself doing that, if I'm going to enter this amazing fictional world, so for me the place that, that it really works best is a long train journey, 'cause I don't have to look at anything. I can be out of my ordinary life and I can just have that experience of getting completely lost in the story. But it only really works when the story comes to you and you have that kind of chemical moment when the story grabs you and you know you're not going to stop until you've got to the end of it or whatever, you know, you know you want to read it as long as possible. So I can still read for pleasure but I have to find the right book.

2 27

Interviewer What was your favourite book when you were a child?

Charlie My favourite book was *Dear Zoo*.

Interviewer Why did you like it so much?

Charlie I liked the fact that the boy got lots of different animals through the post and that, actually, all he wanted was a dog, um, for a pet. And that growing up, my parents wouldn't let me have a pet, so it was quite a nice idea of, you know, lots of animals coming to stay and then having to go backwards and forwards.

Interviewer Was there a character in a children's book that you identified with?

Charlie Err, yes, George, um, in Enid Blyton's *The Famous Five* was a girl, and it was just, she was like a tomboy so I quite liked the idea of being quite adventurous and doing things that boys tended to do when I was growing up.

Interviewer What was your favourite book when you were a child?

Sean Probably *The Lion, The Witch and The Wardrobe*.

Interviewer Why did you like it so much?

Sean Um, I remember we had a teacher at school who read it aloud to us, and um, when I was probably six or seven, when I was too young to read it myself, um, and I remember getting the book and then sitting down by myself and reading it. I think it was the first time I realized how much you could get out of a book, I think.

Interviewer Was there a character in a children's book that you identified with?

Sean I can't think of any specific characters. I think I was quite a scruffy child. I always had dirty knees and torn clothes and things like that, so whenever there was a, a boy who got into lots of trouble, I usually thought that was a little bit like me, but I can't think of one particular one.

Interviewer What was your favourite book when you were a child?

Lucy Um, I really loved anything by Michael Morpurgo, um, all the Roald Dahl books and the *Northern Lights* series by Philip Pullman.

Interviewer Why did you like them?

Lucy I really enjoyed the Roald Dahl books because of the great illustrations that Quentin Blake did, um, I just found them really inventive and vivid and they really kind of contributed to my understanding of those stories. And the *Northern Lights* I loved because it just offered a really detailed other world, to just dive into, and this kind of idea of alternative universes and weird futures that could possibly happen.

Interviewer Was there a character in a children's book that you identified with?

Lucy Um, not really sure, I used to love reading, um, school stories, like books about boarding schools off in the, um Swiss Alps or anything like that, and while I didn't necessarily identify with a specific character, I liked the kind of general idea of it, I suppose, and, um, the kind of jolly japes that they would get up to, so I kind of identified with them in a more general way as a schoolgirl, I suppose.

2 36

1 It was a few years ago now, I think, ah, it was 2010, my wife and I had booked to spend New Year's Eve in a pub in Yorkshire in the north of England. It's a very famous pub because it's supposed to be the highest pub in the UK, and it has beautiful views. Well, we knew that the weather wasn't going to be good – the forecast said it would snow, but it didn't really worry us – we're from the north and we're used to the snow. Anyway, we arrived in the afternoon and then we got dressed up for dinner. There were about, um, 30 guests and we were having a great time, but as it got nearer to midnight I noticed that it had started snowing very heavily. We went to bed late, of course – I mean it was New Year's Eve – but when we woke up the next morning there was so much snow that we realized it was going to be impossible to leave the pub. The roads were completely blocked and our cars were buried under mountains of snow. Everybody was stuck there in the pub for two more nights. But it wasn't a problem at all. There are worse places to be stuck than in a pub! In fact, we had a great time. We all helped a bit with preparing the food and we did the washing up after the meals. And in the evenings we organized quizzes and we all got to know each other. On January 3rd they finally cleared the roads with snow ploughs and we were able to leave. But I have to say that it was one of the best New Year's Eves ever.

2 This was in the summer of 2003 and there was a terrible heat wave in London. I remember it really well because it was my daughter's 6th birthday on the 7th of August and we'd invited some of her friends round to our house for a party in the garden. When the children arrived that afternoon, it was just unbearably hot – I mean it was about 36 degrees which is absolutely scorching for us – it was just too hot to be outside, and it was too hot to be inside, too, because we didn't have air conditioning – very few houses do in Britain. And all the little girls were starting to get really exhausted from the heat and I just didn't know what to do with them. But then my husband said, 'Why don't we all go to my clinic?' He's a doctor and his private clinic is just down the road and the clinic has air-conditioning. So we took the children to the clinic and had the party there. It was lovely and cool there and the girls played party games in the waiting room, but then they started running around the clinic as well and I got really worried that they were going to break something. The whole day was a bit of a nightmare, to tell the truth.

3 In October 1987 I was 16 and I was at a girls' boarding school, a school in Kent in the south-east of England. It was a big old house and it had really beautiful grounds. That night I woke up in the middle of the night because our bedroom window was rattling loudly. We could also hear very loud banging outside. I looked outside and I could see that it was incredibly windy. The wind was howling and trees were bending right over and things were being blown all over the place. I'd never seen such a strong wind. Soon all the girls in my dormitory had woken up, and the room was full of confused, sleepy teenagers. Suddenly, a group of girls came running in from the room next door – a tree had fallen and broken

the window by one of the beds and had covered it in glass.

It was quite scary but it was exciting as well. Then a teacher came in and told us not to worry and to go back to sleep but it was very difficult to get to sleep because of the noise of the wind, and we were awake for hours until finally the wind died down and we could get to sleep.

The next day when we woke up we looked outside. It looked as if somebody had dropped a bomb. There were fallen trees and branches everywhere. Just in our school grounds 200 trees had been blown down. On the radio they said that it had been a hurricane and that 18 people had been killed. Later we found out that all over Britain 15 million trees had blown down during the night.

2 38))

1 Yes, I think I am, or anyway more than I used to be. I think my attitude to risk has changed as I've got older, for example I'm more open to risking a change in appearance, because I think I'm less self-conscious now. I often change hairstyles and colour but when I was younger I had the same hairstyle for years and years. I also think I would take more risks travelling now because I'm more self-confident, so I'm pretty sure I could cope with any problems.

2 Yes, I'm definitely a risk taker. I take risks to do things that I enjoy like skiing or cycling in London, which is pretty dangerous. In fact I think the element of risk probably makes them even more enjoyable. The only time I wouldn't take a risk would be if I couldn't see that I was going to get any pleasure from it – I wouldn't do something risky just for the sake of it.

3 I'm the sort of person who likes to know exactly what I'm doing and when I'm doing it, so there's not much room for risk in my life. For me, risk means not being completely in control and that can make me feel really nervous. For example, if I'm meeting a friend for dinner, I always make sure we have a table booked somewhere nice. I wouldn't risk just turning up and hoping that there was a table. And I never buy clothes online because I don't want to run the risk of them being the wrong size and having to send them back.

4 I'm definitely not a risk taker. I might like to think that I am, as it seems exciting, but I'm not. I live in a suburb of London and I'd never walk home on my own in the evening when it's dark, as that just seems like an unnecessary risk to take. And I'd never get into a taxi on my own at night. But on the other hand, I would love to do something like bungee jumping or paragliding which other people would probably think is risky.

5 I don't see myself as a risk taker. I've done a lot of mountain climbing, and everyone assumes, because of this, that I'm attracted to risk, but it isn't really true. In fact when you're climbing high mountains you're always trying to minimize the risk. The biggest risk I've ever taken in my life was a professional one – after 20 years in the same job, I left and set up my own company – and that's given me a lot more sleepless nights than climbing in the Andes or the Himalayas.

6 I am happy to take risks. I love driving fast, in fact I bought myself a sports car when I had some money and I got quite a few speeding tickets – though probably not as many as I deserved! I also take risks with money, like lending to people who probably won't pay me back, or spending all I have on something a bit unnecessary. Last year I went on a balloon ride and I was amazed that so many people said, 'Ooh, I wouldn't do that!' I loved it and I'd happily do it again – it was fantastic!

2 44))

Presenter For most of us, the riskiest thing we ever do is to get into a car and drive. And as this is something that we do almost every day of our lives, we need to take the risks involved in driving very seriously. Sandra, you're an expert in road safety. How dangerous is driving compared to other ways of getting around?

Sandra Driving gets a lot of bad publicity. Statistics show that, mile for mile, it's riskier to be a pedestrian or a jogger than to drive a car or ride a motorbike.

Presenter But car accidents do happen. What's the main reason?

Sandra Fifty per cent of all fatal accidents occur because someone has broken the law. The most frequent cause of fatal accidents in the UK is driving

too fast, and the second most frequent is drink-driving. And the third major cause of fatal accidents is when a driver falls asleep at the wheel.

Presenter Is that very common?

Sandra Yes, it is. A surprising ten per cent of accidents are caused by this.

Presenter Tell us about some of the other factors that can increase our chances of having an accident.

Sandra Well, the time of day we're on the road is a very significant factor. Generally speaking, driving at night, for example, is four times as dangerous as during the day. This is mainly because visibility is so much worse when it's dark. By day, a driver's visibility is roughly 500 yards, but at night, driving with headlights, it can be as little as 120 yards.

Presenter Are there any times of day or night that are particularly risky?

Sandra Research shows that you're most likely to have an accident between five and seven p.m. during the week, that's to say during the evening rush hour, and especially in the winter when it's dark. And the day of the week when you're most likely to have an accident is Friday. In the UK, more accidents happen on a Friday between 5.00 and 7.00 pm than at any other time.

Presenter Why do you think that is?

Sandra It's probably because people are finishing work for the week and are rushing home to start their weekend. Their mind may already be on what they're planning to do, and they may not be concentrating 100 per cent on the road. So this is a time of the week when car drivers need to be especially careful.

Presenter Which brings us to where accidents happen.

Sandra Sixty per cent of accidents happen within two miles of where we live. Statistically the most common kind of accident is crashing into a parked car near our home. Research shows that drivers concentrate less well when they're driving on familiar roads. Fortunately most of these accidents are not fatal.

Presenter So what about fatal accidents? Where do these tend to happen?

Sandra As far as fatal accidents are concerned, the riskiest kind of road to drive on is a country road. Almost half of all fatal car crashes in the UK take place on country roads. In fact you're twice as likely to have an accident on a country road than on an urban road.

Presenter And why is that?

Sandra Drivers often think that it's OK to break the speed limit on these roads because there's less traffic and consequently they take more risks.

Presenter And the safest kind of road to drive on?

Sandra A motorway is by far the safest kind of road.

Presenter People – usually men – say that women have more accidents than men. Is that true?

Sandra Well, it is true that, mile for mile, women have more minor accidents than men, but a man is twice as likely to be killed in a car accident as a woman.

Presenter So men really are more dangerous drivers then?

Sandra Women, by nature, are usually much more careful and cautious drivers than men. In general men take far more unnecessary risks when they're driving than women.

Presenter The age of a driver must be an important factor, too?

Sandra Yes, in fact it's probably the most important factor. A driver aged between 17 and 24 has double the risk of having an accident than an older driver. The reasons for this are obvious. This is the age when drivers have very limited experience of driving but it's also when they're most likely to drive too fast and take unnecessary risks, particularly if there are other young people in the car.

Presenter Which is why a lot of people would like to see the age limit for having a driving licence raised to 21?

Sandra I think it would be a very good idea.

Presenter Well, that's all we have time for. Thank you very much for coming into the studio today, Sandra. And to all you drivers out there who are listening… drive safely!

3 6))

Yossi and Kevin soon realized that going by river was a big mistake. The river got faster and faster, and soon they were in rapids.

The raft was swept down the river at an incredible speed until it hit a rock. Both men were thrown into the water. Kevin was a strong swimmer and he managed to swim to land, but Yossi was swept away by the rapids.

But Yossi didn't drown. He was carried several kilometres downriver by the rapids but he eventually managed to swim to the river bank. He was totally exhausted. By an incredible piece of luck he found their backpack floating in the river. The backpack contained a little food, insect repellent, a lighter, and most important of all… the map. But the two friends were now separated by a canyon and six or seven kilometres of jungle.

3 7))

Kevin was feeling desperate. He didn't know if Yossi was alive or dead, but he started walking downriver to look for him. He felt responsible for what had happened to his friend because he had persuaded him to go with him on the river.

Yossi, however, was feeling quite optimistic. He was sure that Kevin would look for him so he started walking upriver calling his friend's name. But nobody answered.

At night Yossi tried to sleep but he felt terrified. The jungle was full of noises. Suddenly he woke up because he heard a branch breaking. He turned on his flash light. There was a jaguar staring at him…

Yossi was trembling with fear. But then he remembered something that he had once seen in a film. He used the cigarette lighter to set fire to the insect repellent spray and he managed to scare the jaguar away.

3 8))

After five days alone, Yossi was exhausted and starving. Suddenly, as he was walking, he saw a footprint on the trail – it was a hiking boot. It had to be Kevin's footprint! He followed the trail until he discovered another footprint and then another. But suddenly he realized that the footprints weren't Kevin's footprints. They were his own. He had been walking around in a circle. At that moment Yossi realized that he would never find Kevin. In fact he felt sure that Kevin must be dead. He felt totally depressed and on the point of giving up.

3 9))

But Kevin wasn't dead. He was still looking for Yossi. But after nearly a week he was also weak and exhausted from lack of food and lack of sleep. He decided that it was time to forget Yossi and try to save himself. He had just enough strength left to hold onto a log and let himself float down the river.

Kevin was incredibly lucky – he was rescued by two Bolivian hunters who were travelling down river in a canoe. The men only hunted in that part of the rainforest once a year, so if they had passed by a short time earlier or later, they wouldn't have seen Kevin. They took him back to the town of San José where he spent two days recovering.

3 10))

As soon as Kevin felt well enough, he went to a Bolivian army base and asked them to look for Yossi. ('My friend is lost in the jungle. You must look for him.') The army officer he spoke to was sure that Yossi must be dead, but in the end Kevin persuaded them to take him up in a plane and fly over the part of the rainforest where Yossi might be. But the plane had to fly too high over the rainforest and the forest was too dense. They couldn't see anything at all. It was a hopeless search. Kevin felt terribly guilty. He was convinced that it was all his fault that Yossi was going to die in the jungle. Kevin's last hope was to pay a local man with a boat to take him up the river to look for his friend.

3 11))

By now, Yossi had been on his own in the jungle for nearly three weeks. He hadn't eaten for days. He was starving, exhausted, and slowly losing his mind. It was evening. He lay down by the side of the river ready for another night alone in the jungle.

Suddenly he heard the sound of a bee buzzing in his ear. He thought a bee had got inside his mosquito net. But when he opened his eyes, he saw that the buzzing noise wasn't a bee…

It was a boat. Yossi was too weak to shout, but Kevin had already seen him. It was a one-in-a-million chance that Kevin would find his friend. But he did. Yossi was saved.

When Yossi had recovered, he and Kevin flew to the city of La Paz and they went directly to the hotel where they had agreed to meet Marcus and Karl.

But Marcus and Karl were not at the hotel. The two men had never arrived back in the town of Apolo. The Bolivian army organized a search of the rainforest, but Marcus and Karl were never seen again.

3 21))

1. The only thing I really regret is, is not having had the courage to chat up a girl who I met at a party last summer. I really fancied her – she was very attractive – but I just wasn't brave enough to start a conversation. I wish I'd tried. I'm absolutely positive we would have got on well. Now it's too late – she's engaged to another guy!

2. At the risk of sounding really negative, I think the one thing I really regret in my life is getting married, and I wished I had listened to my sister, who said to me in the car on the way to the registry office 'Someone has to say to you that you really don't have to do this you know' and, um, I really wish I'd listened to her because it was the biggest mistake of my life, and in fact the next day when I woke up I realized it was a terrible mistake, and I spent the next 15 years trying to get out of it. So, and I would never do it again. So that's probably my biggest regret.

3. Um, I really wish I'd been able to know my grandmother better. She died when I was 12, and since then I've discovered that she must have been a really fascinating person, and there are so many things I would love to have been able to talk to her about. She was Polish but she was in Russia, in St Petersburg, during the Russian Revolution and she knew all sorts of interesting people at the time: painters, writers, people like that. I was only a child so I never asked her much about her own life. Now, I'm discovering all about her through reading her old letters and papers, but I wish she'd lived longer so that I could have talked to her about those times face-to-face.

4. When I was 15 I had a Saturday job, um, in a supermarket – stacking shelves and that kind of thing. My friend also worked there, and he persuaded me one day to help him steal a carton of cigarettes, 200 cigarettes, from the stock room. It was a crazy idea, and totally out of character for me to do something like that. I'd always been very honest until then. Anyway, the manager of the shop found where we'd hidden the cigarettes – and he called the police. So when we came to work that evening the police were waiting for us. Although we got off with just a warning – we were only kids – the police came to my house and talked to my mum. I felt so awful. But in the long run it was probably a good thing because it meant that I never, ever thought about stealing something again.

5. When I was 16 I got the chance to change schools and go to a better school to do my last two years. My parents were really keen for me to change because they thought I'd probably get better marks in the university entrance exams and so have a better chance of going to university. But I was totally against the idea because I didn't want to leave all my friends behind and I didn't know anyone at the other school. So, in the end I managed to convince them and I stayed at my old school. I did OK in my exams but not brilliantly. Um, now I regret not listening to my parents because I think it would have been better for my future career, but at the time I just couldn't see it.

3 23))

Part 1

Interviewer What were you hoping to do by making the film *Trashed*?

Candida Well, I think, um, the role of the film, um, for me was to raise awareness, um, on the topic and get it into the press so that people could start having a, a meaningful conversation about waste which, um, is not a particularly, um, attractive subject, let's say.

Interviewer How many countries did you film in?

Candida We ended up actually filming in 11 countries, um, but the stories that I've chosen are universal and obviously I spoke to, to people in communities, um, in more countries, um, than we actually filmed in, um, but their stories are certainly not isolated, they were repeated around the world, sadly wherever you kind of want to pick actually.

Interviewer How did you persuade Jeremy Irons to get involved in the film?

Candida I had worked with Jeremy some years ago on a, on a different film and I was generally aware that he doesn't like waste either, um, he will, you know, wear his jumpers until they're worn out, he'll keep his cars until they're falling apart, you know, he'll repair

everything, so he's always seen, you know, um, the value in reusing things, it's just something natural to him as well, so he just felt like a natural, um, first approach, and, and so I sent him the treatment and amazingly he, um, he loved it.

Interviewer How did you get Vangelis to write the soundtrack?

Candida Well, Jeremy and Vangelis have been friends for years, so, um, Jeremy sent him the um, rough cut of the film and Vangelis absolutely loved it, he, he is also a committed environmentalist, so he's always been aware, um, he was aware 'cause he'd worked with, um Cousteau, sort of various people, you know, he was aware of issues for the seas and so on, um, but generally again he was very shocked, um, by the film and really wanted to get involved, so…

Interviewer What research did you do before you started making the film?

Candida I spent about a year, um, talking to communities, talking to experts, um, you know, obviously reading an awful lot, um, and, um, just ingesting it all because obviously again it's such an enormous topic to take on.

3 24))

Part 2

Interviewer Rubbish isn't very attractive visually. Was that a problem for you as a film maker?

Candida Er, yes and no, um, strangely enough. Obviously I had a wonderful, um, DOP, Director of Photography so, um he can pretty much make anything look beautiful, I think, but, um, I wanted to choose, as I've, as I've said earlier, um, you know, I did a lot of research and so sadly these things were repeatable and, and in every country around the world, so I wanted to choose, um, beautiful places wherever possible, um, that had been ruined unfortunately by, um, man-made rubbish, so, um, the ancient port of Saida in Lebanon, um, the fact that, you know, you've got this huge mountain of waste which was formerly a flat sandy beach.

Interviewer Documentaries about how we're destroying the planet can be very depressing, was that also a challenge for you?

Candida A huge challenge, yes, um, I would have preferred to have made a much more cheerful, um, documentary than, um, I think *Trashed* is, I think it has got hope, um, I think we were very much aware that we wanted to offer solutions at the end of it, but you are, um, the subject is not a cheerful subject, um, I could have gone further I think with it but I didn't want to because actually, you know, you could sort of end up feeling that you just want to go and shoot yourself which is not what I wanted, I wanted to feel, that you know, people feel that they can make a difference to this topic.

Interviewer In the film you focus on air pollution, land pollution, and water pollution, which do you think is the most worrying?

Candida Um, if I had to pick one, um, which I would be reluctant to do, er, it would be water without a doubt, I think that what has happened to all of the oceans and beaches actually as well, um, in the world in the last 30 years is astonishing in the scale and the speed, um, you know, there are certain places in the world, that you know, you have to dig down on a beach, um, over a foot, before you'll find sand that doesn't have plastic in it. Unfortunately what's happened with the way that soft plastic degrades in water is that, um, the pieces become so fragmented that they're the same size as the zooplankton, um, which obviously is in the food chain.

3 25))

Part 3

Interviewer Who do you think is mostly to blame for the problems we have with waste?

Candida I tried very hard actually not to blame one person or things, um, in the film, actually quite deliberately because I think in a way, um, it lets us off the hook, um, and it also, um, I think we all need to work on, the, the problem together because it's too complicated to blame one person or one thing or one act or, um, you know, I think it's, it's multi-faceted unfortunately.

Interviewer Your film finishes on an optimistic note with the example of San Francisco's zero waste policy. Can you tell us a bit about that?

Candida Well, I, I actually in the film ended up, um,

using San Francisco as, ah, the example because I wanted to show, er, that zero waste could be achieved on a big scale. When you go and stay in San Francisco in your hotel room, you'll have four different bins and you'll have signs on the wall of what goes into each bin, so it's very, very easy to, to recycle and I think that's a huge part of what we should be doing.

Interviewer Has the film changed your own habits regarding waste?

Candida I don't think the film has particularly changed my own habits dramatically, um, because I've always been thrifty, um, by nature because, um, I was lucky enough to spend a lot of time with my grandparents when I was growing up and the post war, sort of, philosophy of never wasting anything it just, you know, it was instilled in me. I ride the same bicycle that I've had since I was 15 years old and I've, over the years obviously had it repaired and repaired, but I take tremendous pride in the fact that I've always, um, ridden the same bike and you know I, I have lovely memories of it, so and with it, so, um I think, I think we need a sort of slight change of mind set to make things cool the longer you have them in a way, than actually this perpetual thing of buying new things for the sake of it.

3 27))

Interviewer How much recycling do people in your country do?

Sally I don't think we do enough, I think we could do a little bit more. I'm not wonderful myself but we try and do a little bit of recycling.

Interviewer How responsible are you personally?

Sally Well, we probably do about, probably about 30% we recycle.

Interviewer What do you think the government, or individuals, could do to make people recycle more?

Sally Well, they could give you all these, um, boxes and bins and things at home to help you recycle, the Germans seem to do it quite well.

Interviewer How much recycling do people in your country do?

Jo I think people are quite good at recycling, I think, um, now that the, the waste companies come and collect recycling from the houses, people haven't really got an excuse not to recycle any more.

Interviewer How responsible are you personally?

Jo Err, I, I recycle as much as I can.

Interviewer What do you think the government, or individuals, could do to make people recycle more?

Jo Um, well maybe they could offer a financial incentive for, for recycling, um, or maybe for producing less rubbish that can't be recycled.

Interviewer How much recycling do people in your country do?

Jill I think that recycling is getting better in this country, I think we still have a long ways to go. I think it's still done largely in pockets and not necessarily nationwide as much as it could be.

Interviewer How responsible are you personally?

Jill Actually, in the town where I live we have a very strong recycling program and so I participate um, in, filling it up with cans and bottles, newspapers and all kinds of stuff, and they come and get it every other week, so. Easy, too.

Interviewer What do you think the government, or individuals, could do to make people recycle more?

Jill Well, incentives always work. Um, besides, above and beyond monetary incentives, just incentives to promote, you know, benefits to the environment.

Interviewer How much recycling do people in your country do?

Pranjal I don't think people in the US recycle enough. I think we should recycle more and I'm even, uh, you know, I'm even guilty of not recycling enough, but I don't think we recycle enough.

Interviewer How responsible are you personally?

Pranjal Personally, I'm not really that responsible in cycling, I'll be honest, I don't really recycle that often, but if I do get the opportunity to recycle, I will.

Interviewer What do you think the government, or individuals, could do to make people recycle more?

Pranjal Well, I think it's important for individuals to realize that even the smallest difference makes a big difference, and so if everyone could just get in that mindset that the smallest change they can make in their lives makes a big difference. I think that will, in fact, make a big difference.

3 34
I think it's very interesting that human beings are the only animals which listen to music for pleasure. A lot of research has been done to find out why we listen to music, and there seem to be three main reasons. Firstly, we listen to music to make us remember important moments in the past, for example when we met someone for the first time. Think of Humphrey Bogart in the film *Casablanca* saying 'Darling, they're playing our song'. When we hear a certain piece of music, we remember hearing it for the first time in some very special circumstances. Obviously, this music varies from person to person.

Secondly, we listen to music to help us change activities. If we want to go from one activity to another, we often use music to help us make the change. For example, we might play a certain kind of music to prepare us to go out in the evening, or we might play another kind of music to relax us when we get home from work. That's mainly why people listen to music in cars, and they often listen to one kind of music when they're going to work and another kind when they're coming home. The same is true of people on buses and trains with their iPods. The third reason why we listen to music is to intensify the emotion that we're feeling. For example, if we're feeling sad, sometimes we want to get even sadder, so we play sad music. Or we're feeling angry and we want to intensify the anger then we play angry music. Or when we're planning a romantic dinner, we lay the table, we light candles, and then we think, 'What music would make this even more romantic?'

3 35
Let's take three important human emotions: happiness, sadness, and anger. When people are happy they speak faster, and their voice is higher. When they are sad they speak more slowly and their voice is lower, and when people are angry they raise their voices or shout. Babies can tell whether their mother is happy or not simply by the sound of her voice, not by her words. What music does is it copies this, and it produces the same emotions. So faster, higher-pitched music will sound happy. Slow music with lots of falling pitches will sound sad. Loud music with irregular rhythms will sound angry. It doesn't matter how good or bad the music is, if it has these characteristics it will make you experience this emotion. Let me give you some examples. For happy, for example, the first movement of Beethoven's *Seventh Symphony*. For angry, say *Mars*, from *The Planets* by Holst. And for sad, something like Albinoni's *Adagio for Strings*.

Of course the people who exploit this most are the people who write film soundtracks. They can take a scene which visually has no emotion and they can make the scene either scary or calm or happy just by the music they write to go with it. Think of the music in the shower scene in Hitchcock's film *Psycho*. All you can see is a woman having a shower, but the music makes it absolutely terrifying.

3 40
1
I Why do you have problems sleeping?
S Well I'm Spanish but I moved to London a few years ago when I married a British woman. I've been living here for three years now. I have a lot of problems getting to sleep at night because our bedroom just isn't dark enough. I can't get used to sleeping in a bedroom where there's light coming in from the streetlights outside. In Spain I always used to sleep in complete darkness because my bedroom window had blinds and when I went to bed I used to close the blinds completely. But here in England our bedroom window just has curtains and curtains don't block out the light properly. It takes me a long time to get to sleep at night and I always wake up more often than I used to do in Spain.
I So why don't you just get thicker curtains?
S Because my wife doesn't like sleeping in a completely dark room. She says that she feels claustrophobic if the room is too dark.
I Ah, yes, a lot of people do feel like that.

3 41
2
I Why do you have problems sleeping?
S Well, I'm a policeman and so I have to do shift work which means I work at night every other week, so I start work at 10 o'clock at night and finish at 6.00 in the morning the following day. The main problem is that my body's used to sleeping at night, not during the day. So it's very hard to get used to being awake all night and trying to work and concentrate when your body is just telling you to go to bed.
I But isn't it something you get used to?
S Actually no, because I work during the day for one week and then the next week I work at night which means that just when my body has got used to being awake at night then I go back to working in the day and then of course I can't get to sleep at night because my body thinks it's going to have to work all night. The other problem is that when I get home after working a night shift, everyone else is just starting to wake up so that means that it can be really noisy. The neighbours put the radio on, and bang doors and shout to wake their children up. So even though I'm really tired it's just very hard to get to sleep.
I How many hours do you usually sleep?
S Before I became a policeman I used to sleep about eight or nine hours a night but I think now I probably don't sleep more than six hours.

3 42
3
I Why do you have problems sleeping?
S I have a lot of problems sleeping because of jet lag. I have to travel a lot in my job and I take a lot of long haul flights. I fly to New York quite often and I arrive maybe at 6.00 in the evening my time, but when it's only one o'clock in the afternoon in New York. So at 5.00 in the afternoon local time, I'll be feeling tired and ready for bed because it's my bed time. But I can't go to sleep because I'm probably still working or having dinner with my American colleagues. Then when I do finally get to bed at say midnight local time, I find that I wake up in the middle of the night because my body thinks that it's morning because it's still working on UK time.
I And can you get back to sleep when you wake up?
S No, that's the problem I can't get back to sleep. And then the next day when I have meetings I feel really sleepy. It's very hard to stay awake all day. And just when I'm finally used to being on New York time, then it's time to fly home. And flying west to east is even worse.
I Oh! Why's that?
S Because when I get off the plane it's early morning in the UK. But for me, on New York time, it's the middle of the night. It takes me four or five days to recover from one of these trips.
I Gosh, that must be really difficult for you.
S Yes it is.

3 47
Presenter And finally today the story of a sleepwalker from Fife in Scotland who gets up in the middle of the night and goes to the kitchen and starts…you've guessed it, cooking. Robert Wood, who's 55 years old, used to be a chef until he retired last year. We have Robert and his wife, Eleanor, with us in the studio today. Robert, tell us what happens.
Robert Well, I've been a sleepwalker for about 40 years now. I think it first started when I was about 14 or so. Anyway these days I get up about four or five times a week and I always end up in the kitchen and I start cooking something.
Presenter Do you always cook?
Robert No, not always. I've done other things, too. I remember once I put the TV on – at full volume – and once I filled the bath with water, although I didn't get in it. But I usually cook.
Presenter Eleanor, do you wake up when this happens?
Eleanor Yes, I usually wake up because he's making a noise. I go downstairs and usually I find him in the kitchen. Once he was just laying the table but other times he's been cooking.
Presenter What sort of things does he cook?
Eleanor All sorts of things. I've caught him cooking omelettes and spaghetti bolognaise, and I even caught him frying chips once. That was a bit scary because he could easily have burnt himself or started a fire.
Presenter Do you ever eat the things that Robert cooks?
Eleanor No. It always looks lovely but I must admit I've never tried it – not at three o'clock in the morning. And the trouble is he always leaves the kitchen in a terrible mess. The last time he sleepwalked he spilt milk all over the place.
Presenter So, Robert, you have no idea that you're cooking?
Robert No, I haven't. I really am asleep and afterwards I just have no recollection of having cooked anything.
Presenter You're getting some help to see if you can cure your sleep walking, aren't you?
Robert Yes, I've been going to a sleep clinic in Edinburgh where they think they'll be able to help me.
Presenter Well good luck with that, and thank you both for coming into the studio today. Now we're going to a break, but join us again in a few minutes.

3 48
Presenter We've been talking to Robert, the sleepwalking cook and his wife, Eleanor. And we're now joined by Professor Maurice from Rochester, New York, who is an expert in sleepwalking. Hello. Welcome, Professor Maurice, does this story surprise you?
Professor No, it doesn't, not at all. I've treated people who have driven cars, ridden horses, and I had one man who even tried to fly a helicopter while he was asleep.
Presenter Do people usually have their eyes open when they sleepwalk?
Professor Yes, sleepwalkers do usually have their eyes open. That's why sometimes it's difficult to know if someone is sleepwalking or not.
Presenter How common is sleepwalking?
Professor More common than you might think. Research shows that about 18 per cent of the population have a tendency to sleepwalk. But it's much more common in children than in teenagers or adults. And, curiously, it's more common among boys than girls. Adults who sleepwalk are normally people who used to sleepwalk when they were children. They might do it after a stressful event, for example, after a traffic accident.
Presenter People always say that you should never wake a sleepwalker up when they're walking. Is that true?
Professor No, it isn't. People used to think that it was dangerous to wake up a sleepwalker. But in fact this isn't the case. You can wake a sleepwalker up without any problem, although if you do, it is quite common for the sleepwalker to be confused, so he or she probably won't know where they are for a few moments.
Presenter So, if we see someone sleepwalking, should we wake them up?
Professor Yes, you should remember that another of the myths about sleepwalkers is that they can't injure themselves while they are sleepwalking. But this isn't true. If a sleepwalker is walking around the house, they might trip or fall over a chair or even fall down stairs. There was a case a while ago of a nine-year-old girl who opened her bedroom window while she was sleepwalking and fell 30 feet to the ground. Luckily, she wasn't seriously injured. So you see, Eleanor, you're quite right to worry that Robert might burn himself when he's cooking. You need to wake him up and get him back to bed.
Presenter How long does sleepwalking usually last?
Professor It can be very brief, for example, a few minutes. The most typical cases are people getting up and getting dressed, or people going to the bathroom. But it can occasionally last much longer, maybe half an hour or even more, as in Robert's case.
Presenter And what happens when sleepwalkers wake up? Do they remember the things they did while they were sleepwalking?
Professor No, as Robert says, a sleepwalker usually doesn't remember anything afterwards.
Presenter So, is a sleepwalker responsible for his or her actions?
Professor That's a very good question, actually. A few years ago a man from Canada got up in the middle of the night and drove 20 miles from his home to the house where his parents-in-law lived and, for no apparent reason, he killed his mother-in-law. The man was charged with murder but he was found not guilty because he had been asleep at the time he committed the crime.

4 2
Conversation 1
Female student Where's my milk? It's not here.
Male student I haven't seen it. You must have finished it.

Female student I definitely didn't finish it. I was keeping a bit for my cereal this morning. You must have used it.
Male student Me? I never take anything from the fridge that isn't mine. You might have given it to the cat last night and then forgotten about it.
Female student The cat drinks water not milk, so I can't have given it to the cat. Last night there was half a carton of milk in the fridge. MY milk.
Male student Well, I don't know what's happened to it.
Female student What are you drinking?
Male student Just coffee.
Female student Yes, white coffee. That's where my milk went. Well, you can go to the supermarket and get me some more.
Male student OK, OK, calm down. I'll go and get you some milk...

Conversation 2
Satnav voice At the roundabout, take the second exit.
Woman Why are you taking the third exit? She said the second exit.
Man I'm sure it's this one. I remember when we came here last time.
Woman According to that sign this is the A245.
Man The A245? Oh no! We must have gone wrong.
Woman Of course we've gone wrong. We should have taken the second exit at the roundabout. What's the point of having a Satnav if you don't do what it says?
Man OK, I may have made a mistake. But if you knew the way to your cousin's house, then we wouldn't have to use the Satnav.
Satnav voice Turn round as soon as possible...

4 7
In life, we sometimes have disagreements with people. It could be with your partner, with your boss, with your parents, or with a friend. When this happens, the important thing is to try not to let a difference of opinion turn into a heated argument. But, of course, it's easier said than done.

The first thing I would say is that the way you begin the conversation is very important.

Imagine you're a student and you share a flat with another student who you think isn't doing her share of the housework. If you say, 'Look, you never do your share of the housework. What are we going to do about it?' the discussion will very soon turn into an argument. It's much more constructive to say something like, 'I think we'd better have another look about how we divide up the housework. Maybe there's a better way of doing it.'

My second piece of advice is simple. If you're the person who's in the wrong, just admit it! This is the easiest and best way to avoid an argument. Just apologize to your flatmate, your parents, or your husband, and move on. The other person will have much more respect for you if you do that.

The next tip is don't exaggerate. Try not to say things like, 'You always come home late when my mother comes to dinner' when perhaps this has only happened once before, or, 'You never remember to buy the toothpaste.' This will just make the other person get very defensive because what you're saying about them just isn't true.

If you follow these tips, you may often be able to avoid an argument. But if an argument does start, it's important to keep things under control and there are ways to do this.

The most important thing is not to raise your voice. Raising your voice will just make the other person lose their temper, too. If you find yourself raising your voice, stop for a moment and take a deep breath. Say, 'I'm sorry I shouted, but this is very important to me' and continue calmly. If you can talk calmly and quietly, you'll find the other person will be more ready to think about what you're saying.

It's also very important to stick to the point. Try to keep to the topic you're talking about. Don't bring up old arguments, or try to bring in other issues. Just concentrate on solving the one problem you're having, and leave the other things for another time. So, for example, if you're arguing about the housework, don't start talking about mobile phone bills as well.

And my final tip is that, if necessary, call 'Time out' like in a sports match. If you think that an argument is getting out of control, then you can say to the other person, 'Listen, I'd rather talk about this tomorrow when we've both calmed down.' You can then continue talking about it the next day when perhaps both of you are feeling less tense and angry. That way, there's much more chance that you'll be able to reach an agreement. You'll also probably find that the problem is much easier to solve when you've both had a good night's sleep.

But I want to say one last thing which I think is very important. Some people think that arguing is always bad, but that isn't true. Conflict is a normal part of life, and dealing with conflict is an important part of any relationship, whether it's three people sharing a flat, a married couple, or just two good friends. If you don't learn to argue properly, then when a real problem comes along, you won't be prepared to face it together. Think of the smaller arguments as training sessions. Learn how to argue cleanly and fairly. It will help your relationship become stronger and last longer.

4 11
I love this photo, especially the way she's using her hands...and the expression in her eyes and her mouth. Here she is in the role of a young single mother, who has just heard a noise in the kitchen in the middle of the night. You can see the fear in her eyes, that she's worried about her child. I think she suggests all that beautifully...

4 14
A Here's actress Cheryl Hines. If you think she looks furious, that's because she is! She's playing a wife who's opening the door to her husband at one o'clock in the morning. Her husband forgot that she was giving a dinner party, and he went off to play poker with his friends and turned his phone off. She looks as if she's going to tell him to leave and never come back.
B I love this one. This is Jason Schwartzman and he's playing a five-year-old boy. He's in the process of quietly putting his pet rat into his seven-year-old sister's clothes drawer. He looks pretty confident about what he's doing, and as if he's really looking forward to hearing her scream when she finds it!
C Here, Ellen Burstyn is playing a high school drama teacher. She is in the audience at the Oscar ceremony and one of the winners is an ex-student of hers. Her ex-student actually mentions her name when she makes her winner's speech. You can see how proud she is, and how moved she is to have been mentioned.
D In this photo I see pure horror and fear. This is the actor Dan Hedaya. He's playing the part of a long distance truck driver who was tired and closed his eyes for a few moments. He opens them to see that he's – you've guessed it, on the wrong side of the road, with cars racing towards him. Do you think he looks as if he's going to react in time? I think probably not.
E Here the actress Jane Lynch was given the role of a child. She's swallowing a spoonful of medicine that her mom promised would taste good. Of course it didn't, and now she's telling her that if it didn't taste awful it wouldn't work. She looks as if she's about to spit it out! I can remember reacting just like that when I was kid, and my mom saying those exact same words!
F When you look at this last one of Steve Guttenberg, I think you can immediately see from his expression that he's worried, and maybe nervous. Look at the way he's holding his hands, almost as if he were praying. He's playing the role of a married man, who's begging his wife to give him one more chance. But I think he looks as if he's done something bad, and is pretty desperate, so I'm not sure if his wife is going to forgive him!

4 15
Interviewer How difficult is it to express feelings when you can't use body language?
Tim Well, radio acting is a different style of acting from visual acting because, obviously, you only have your voice to, to use. But you can use your voice and you can use timing to convey everything. When I started off as a radio actor somebody said to me 'you have to be able to raise one eyebrow with your voice', which I loved. Because you haven't got your body, you have to put it into your voice and so therefore the way that a radio actor works isn't totally naturalistic in the way that it would be on the television or on film.
Interviewer What techniques do you use to help you to express emotions, feelings?
Tim Mmm, well, there's a big difference between speaking with a smile, and not speaking with a smile. There's a huge difference between being happy, and being really sad, and really angry.
Interviewer Is it hard for actors who don't have experience in radio to do radio acting?
Tim Well, people don't realize that it is a different technique. You would get famous people coming in, not realizing that there was a technique to radio acting and thinking that you could do total naturalism, and it isn't totally naturalistic. It's as naturalistic as you can make it sound – to lift it off the page, to make it sound as though you're not reading it.

4 23
1 Touching or stroking their neck is a very typical sign that a person is nervous, and is trying to calm themselves down. A woman may also play with a necklace, and a man may tighten his tie.
2 When somebody's standing and they point one of their toes upwards, this is a clear sign that the person is in a good mood, often because they are thinking about, or have just heard, something positive. If you see someone standing talking on the phone and they suddenly point one foot up, you can be sure that they have just been told some good news.
3 Crossing their legs, whether they're sitting or standing, is a sign that a person feels relaxed and comfortable. If the person is sitting with their legs crossed and their feet towards another person, that shows that they are interested in this person. However, if someone they don't like appears, you may find that they quickly uncross their legs.
4 This position, standing with your hands on your hips and your elbows pointing out, is a pose used to show dominance. If you watch police officers or soldiers you'll notice that they often use this pose. Men tend to use it more than women, and it's something we teach women executives to do in meetings where there are a lot of men present, to show that they are confident and won't be bullied.
5 We all know that thumbs up is a positive sign, meaning we feel good or approve of something. But what about when somebody puts their thumbs downwards, in their pockets? As you might guess, this usually means that their confidence is low, and they are feeling unsure of themselves. So try not to do this if you are in a situation where you need to look confident and in control.
6 Putting their head to one side is a powerful sign that a person feels friendly and interested in someone or something. It's an automatic, genuine gesture, unlike a smile, which might be artificial, and so it's a good sign of real interest. It's also very difficult to do naturally around people you don't like.
7 If you look at people in a stressful situation, for example witnesses who are answering questions in courts, you'll often see that it looks as if their lips have disappeared inwards. In fact this is one of the most universal signs of stress, as if a person wanted to disappear completely.

4 24
Part 1
Interviewer How did you get into acting?
Simon I was about 18, it was my first real job and it was a very unusual job because I was working in the box office of the Old Vic Theatre. Then not only did I get to see an awful lot of plays but I also met the actors and I was able to sneak into rehearsals, in the theatre, quite illegally, and I became fascinated by the work of the theatre.
Interviewer What in particular fascinated you?
Simon The thing that fascinated me, as I said, was, was when I was in rehearsals there was this, the work of the theatre, the sort of work it was, so I'd stand at the back of the Old Vic Theatre when the actors were rehearsing, but mostly it consisted of people sitting rather glumly about saying 'Well, I don't know how to do this, I don't know how to do this, I don't know how to make this scene work, I don't understand my character' and the Director would try to help them to understand the character or suggest a move here or a move there or maybe they'd try walking in a different way or putting on a different hat, and bit by bit it started to fall into place and I thought what a wonderful job, what a fantastically interesting job to wrestle with these kinds of problems, try to understand the characters, try to find out how best to express them and show them off, so I, I came to acting very much from that point of view.
Interviewer The role that first made you famous as a young actor was playing Mozart in the original

theatre production of *Amadeus*, which later went on to become a film. What was the most challenging thing about playing the part of Mozart?

Simon What was a challenge was that Mozart was a person who'd actually lived and was indeed one of the greatest artistic geniuses of the whole of Western civilization, and I was a great lover and admirer of Mozart's music, so there was a tremendous, er, challenge to bridge the character that Peter Shaffer had written, Peter Shaffer knows all about Mozart, he could so that Mozart was, was, er, er, sort of a smutty, er, hysterical child really, er, in a lot of the play. My job was to reconcile that with the fact that he wrote *The Marriage of Figaro* and that was tremendously hard.

Interviewer Was Mozart one of your most satisfying roles?

Simon No, I wouldn't say that, that it was the most satisfying, it was the most exciting because its, its fame er, almost from the moment it was announced was overwhelmingly greater than anything I had ever done, or to be honest ever have done since. The fact that the play was very, very controversial when it opened proved to be, er, very, um, um, shocking for many people, only increased the excitement around it, and it was, er, er astonishing to look out into the auditorium every night and to see Paul Red-Newman or, or, or, or Robert Redford or or, or Ava Gardner, or Margaret Thatcher sitting out there because everybody had to see that play.

4 25

Part 2

Interviewer Over your career you have acted in the theatre, and you have also acted in many films. Which do you prefer?

Simon They're absolutely different media, they require different things from you as an actor, I love them both. But they are each of them completely different, you bring completely different things to them. Obviously the crucial difference with the theatre is that there's an audience and that's such an important aspect of it in every way. It's uh, important because you have to reach out to them, make sure that everybody can hear and see what you're doing. The beauty of the theatre is that every single performance is utterly different from every other one.

Interviewer How do you motivate yourself to play the same character again night after night?

Simon I think as you get older you realize that, um, you never get it right, I, I mean I've, I've probably about half a dozen times in my 40 years of acting have thought well that was a really good performance, er, but it can always be better. And so one goes to the theatre every day hoping that it will be in someway better, er, er, you know there is always the possibility you might get it right, I mean you never do, you never can.

Interviewer So what for you is the main difference with film acting?

Simon Er, in movies or, or television film which is what almost all television is nowadays um, a lot of those responsibilities are, lie with the Director and the Editor. And having directed a film myself I know perfectly well that you can make a sad scene funny, you can make a slow scene fast, er, er, in the editing suite, it's, it's an astonishing, er, power that a Director and Editor have. Um, er, you can make a character seem stupid just by editing them a certain way or make them seem brilliant by editing them in a different way. So in that sense the actor is rather powerless.

Interviewer Anything else?

Simon The other thing that's very hard about acting on film is that hilariously it's regarded as a sort of naturalistic medium but in no sense is it that for the actor, because you're, you're, you know, first of all there are some, you know, little metal objects right in front of you, sort of, staring at you as you're doing your love scene or whatever else it might be.

4 26

Part 3

Interviewer Do you enjoy watching other actors acting?

Simon I love watching other actors acting, I, I, I've been obsessed by acting since I was a child and I'm a great connoisseur of it and I think I'm quite a good judge of it, and so I, I adore watching other actors work when it's good, when it's not it's a great pain to me.

Interviewer Who were the first great actors you saw?

Simon As a young man, and a boy, I was extraordinarily lucky to see that fabled generation of actors, of, of, of Gielgud and Richardson, Olivier, Edith Evans, Peggy Ashcroft, people now, almost all completely forgotten. Er, er, er even if they made movies it's unlikely that people of a younger generation know who they are, but, but er, when, when they were alive and kicking and, er doing their extraordinary work on stage it, it, it was something quite, quite remarkable, I mean it was, it was the sort of thing that nobody attempts any more.

Interviewer Do any modern actors come close to that golden generation?

Simon In ah, movies, not always but, but sometimes Daniel Day-Lewis does, er, I think probably approach a role in the way that a lot of them might have approached it.

Interviewer Is there anything you don't like about acting?

Simon I don't much like wearing make-up, I sweat a lot, it comes off, it's uncomfortable, it's sticky, and I do everything I can to avoid wearing make-up.

Interviewer Do you still get stage fright?

Simon I don't get stage fright but I do get self-conscious and I hate that and I wish I didn't, particularly at events like first nights, because I don't know how it's impossible to ignore the fact that there are at least 100 people sitting out there judging you, you know, I think almost all actors feel tremendous longing for the first night to be over, but it has to happen, it's like a sort of operation, it's, you, you know it's got to happen, it's going to hurt but you will feel better afterwards.

4 28

Interviewer What actors do you particularly enjoy watching?

Nathan Err, Kevin Spacey, um, Robert De Niro, Matt Smith, um, Olivia Colman, um, Jodie Foster.

Interviewer Why do you like them?

Nathan I think, well there's two things with actors, one is the ability to take on another character and perform it outside of themselves but also I think you tend to find that, that actors who are that famous have some sort of star quality, for want of a better expression, a pull towards them, like great sport stars.

Interviewer Which performances particularly?

Nathan Ow, um, err, well Robert De Niro in *Taxi Driver* is something to be beheld, um, I've seen Kevin Spacey a few times on stage and he's been incredibly impressive, um, so, yeah.

Interviewer What actors do you particularly enjoy watching?

Sean I don't really have a favourite actor I don't think, but, um, I always enjoy watching Robert De Niro.

Interviewer Why do you like him?

Sean I think he just has an intensity, and a presence that makes you want to watch him, makes you want to think about why he's doing what he's doing, I think even if it's something quite silly, um, it's still always interesting to watch.

Interviewer What performance of his do you particularly enjoy?

Sean I think my favourite film and my favourite performance of all time is *The Deer Hunter*.

Interviewer What actors do you particularly enjoy watching?

Jo I really like Judi Dench and I also like Russell Crowe.

Interviewer Why do you like them? What is it about them that you like?

Jo Um, I think they show a lot of emotion when they're acting.

Interviewer What roles in particular do you enjoy watching them in?

Jo Um, I like Judi Dench in her role, um, in the Bond films and I really enjoyed, um, Russell Crowe in *Gladiator*.

Interviewer What actors do you particularly enjoy watching?

Mairi Um, Audrey Hepburn and Natalie Portman.

Interviewer Why do you like them?

Mairi Um, I like Audrey Hepburn because I think she was very genuine and I feel like she put her heart into everything, I especially like watching films where she dances because she looks very happy. Um, I like Natalie Portman because, um, I feel like she is a very good actor, um, I don't think 'oh that's Natalie Portman in a film' I think 'Oh that's, that's a character' and I like that she does diff, a lot of different characters, um, and doesn't just stick to the same kind of film all the time.

Interviewer Which of their performances did you particularly enjoy?

Mairi Um, for Audrey Hepburn I like, err, her performance in *Funny Face* and for Natalie Portman I like Back… *Black Swan*.

4 30

Presenter So, welcome to the programme, Danny. Now you're an ex-burglar yourself so you can obviously give us the inside story here. Tell me, how long does a burglar usually take to burgle a house?

Danny I'd say that an experienced burglar would never spend more than 20 minutes in a house. Twenty minutes maximum and then out.

Presenter And how much would they probably take in that time?

Danny Maybe 2,000 or 3,000 quid's worth of goods. It depends on the house.

Presenter And what are the favourite things for burglars to steal?

Danny Well, these days they're usually looking for things like laptops and tablets. They're easy to sell, you see, and not so easy for the owner to identify if, you, if the burglar later gets caught.

Presenter What one thing would be likely to stop a burglar from breaking into a house?

Danny I'd say definitely a dog, especially a noisy one. Burglars don't like dogs because they're unpredictable.

Presenter What kind of things would actually make a burglar choose a particular house to break into?

Danny Well it's got to look like a house where there'll be things worth taking, so a burglar will normally go for a house that looks quite expensive, in a good area. And they'll also often choose a house where there are trees or bushes outside which are good places to hide while they're watching the house before they break in – and also where they could hide when they come out of the house. That way there's less chance of neighbours seeing them. And, obviously, they'll normally wait for the house to be empty before they break in.

Presenter So a burglar wouldn't break in if they thought the owners were at home?

Danny Not usually, no, though there are some burglars who actually prefer it if the owners are at home in bed. That way they won't get surprised by them suddenly coming home when they're in the middle of things.

Presenter Oh, not a very nice thought. What's the most common time of day for a burglar to break into your house?

Danny People always think of burglars as working at night, and of course some do but the majority of burglaries happen between around 10.00 in the morning and lunchtime. A burglar will watch a house and then wait for the adults to go to work and the kids go to school and then he can be sure the house is empty.

Presenter What's the easiest way for a burglar to break into a house?

Danny The easiest way is just taking out a window or a patio door, usually at the back of the house. You can do this really quickly and it doesn't make much noise if you've got good equipment, which a serious burglar would usually have.

Presenter And finally what's the safest room to hide your valuables in? What's the last place a burglar would look?

Danny There's a typical order burglars use when they search a house. They start with the main bedroom, because that's often where people leave their valuables, and then the living room. Um, after that probably the dining room if there is one, the study, and then the kitchen. The last place would probably be a kid's bedroom. You wouldn't normally expect to find anything worth taking there.

Presenter So a child's bedroom is the best place to hide things?

Danny Well, in theory, though of course if any burglars out there have been listening to this programme, they might start looking there first…

4 35

And last on our crime news stories from round the world, a burglar who's been fooling even the most intelligent students. The area between Broadway and 9th Street in New York is where students often head to when they're looking for a flat share. This was something well known to Daniel Stewart Cooper, who also knew that students in a shared house often go out and leave the door unlocked, maybe thinking that another flatmate is still inside. This situation suited Cooper perfectly, and he is thought to have committed between 50 and 100 burglaries in the area. It is believed that he was mainly interested in finding drugs, but that if he found electronics or other gadgets lying around, he took those, too. And he didn't just steal things. Cooper is also said to have made himself at home in the houses, helping himself to food from the fridge and even having a shower. Although he normally tried to make sure that the residents were out, if he did meet people, it's thought that he would pretend to know someone there, and so was able to leave without raising suspicions.

However on September 5th, Cooper was finally caught after two students saw him in the area with a laptop and a backpack which he had just stolen from their house. Dylan John, one of the victims, told CBS news that Cooper had taken some food, too. Cooper, who ran off as soon as he realized that the students suspected him, was found by the police hiding behind some nearby bushes.

4 38

And for our last story today, have you ever wondered what would it be like to be eaten by a tiger? Well, now we know, thanks to Soundari, a seven-year-old Siberian tiger living at Longleat Safari Park in Wiltshire. Last week when it snowed, the animal keepers decided to build some snowmen, to entertain the tigers, and they hid a tiny video camera inside one of the snowmen to film the tigers' reactions. At first, the tigers just sniffed at the snowman, but then one of them, called Soundari, began attacking the snowman and started to eat it and the camera. However she didn't like the taste of the camera, so after a while she spat it out. Amazingly, the camera had never stopped recording, and was still working when the animal keepers recovered it. The film that the hidden camera had taken was incredible. For the first time you could feel what it would be like to be attacked by a tiger, and see its open mouth coming at you and see its enormous razor sharp teeth and its rough tongue. In fact a spokesman for the safari park said that the shots of Soundari's teeth were so clear that it gave them the opportunity to have a quick health check on her mouth, gums, and teeth!

4 46

Interviewer Brad Pitt said recently, 'They call my kids by their names. They shove cameras in their faces. I really believe there should be a law against it.' He was talking, of course, about paparazzi. But are the paparazzi really as bad as Brad Pitt says they are? Today in the studio with me is Jennifer Buhl, who is an actual – is it paparazzi or paparazzo?

Jennifer Buhl Paparazzo for a man, paparazza for a woman. Paparazzi is the plural.

Interviewer So Jennifer are you good, bad, or in between?

Jennifer Well, I think I'm a good girl. But some people would probably not like me.

Interviewer A lot of people say there's a working relationship between celebrities and paparazzi. Would you say that was true? That celebrities actually tell you where they're going to be?

Jennifer Yes, of course. That happens all the time. But I think that's what a lot of the public doesn't realize. You know, people shout at us and insult us when there's a big crowd of us around, let's say, Britney Spears or Lindsay Lohan. I just want to tell them that they called us. And, after we've sold the photos, we split the money between the stars and us.

Interviewer I've often thought that must be true. I mean, nobody just goes to the gym with their hair done and make-up on unless they're actually expecting to be photographed.

Jennifer Exactly. But don't get me wrong, it's not like all the celebrities want to be photographed. If a celebrity wants to go out and avoid the paparazzi, it's pretty easy to do. Celebrities that don't like it rarely get photographed, they very rarely get photographed.

Interviewer Give me some example of celebrities who genuinely don't want to be photographed? Like, who really hates it?

Jennifer Julia Roberts hates it. Kate Bosworth hates it.

Interviewer Are photos of them worth more money if they hate it?

Jennifer It depends. No, not necessarily. Because they don't get photographed often, then nobody sees them in magazines, and they lose interest in them. Because they become boring.

Interviewer What shot have you taken that you got the most money for?

Jennifer Probably one of the shots that sold the best, that I didn't expect, didn't even know, was Paris Hilton carrying the Bible right before she went to jail. There were lots of paparazzi there but I was the only one that got the Bible.

Interviewer Do you think we need stricter laws to keep paparazzi away?

Jennifer There are already enough laws. We don't need more laws, or anti-paparazzi laws or anything else. There are places where celebrities can go to where they know they won't be followed, and places where they know they will be.

Interviewer For example?

Jennifer We don't go into restaurants, we don't go into stores, and of course we don't go into people's homes. That's private property. But a beach or a park isn't.

Interviewer So you don't think that being followed and photographed by the paparazzi is really stressful for celebrities?

Jennifer I think there are only a few people for whom it's really and truly stressful. I'd say that in most cases the star not only doesn't mind, but has actually told the paparazzi, 'This is where I'm going to be this afternoon.'

Interviewer Fascinating. Thank you very much for coming in to the studio. Jennifer Buhl everybody!

5 2

The first point to bear in mind is that nothing, but nothing, is ever free. How often have you seen adverts saying things like 'Get a free mp3 player when you subscribe to our magazine for six months'. There's something about the word 'free' that immediately attracts us – I want it! It makes us feel clever, as if we're going to get something for nothing. But, of course, that mp3 player (which, incidentally, will probably break the second time you use it) wasn't free at all. In spite of what the advert said, its price was really included in the magazine subscription. So don't trust any advert which offers something for free.

A second trick which advertisers use is when they tell us, 'There are only a few left! Buy now while stocks last!' What happens to us when we read or hear these words? Even though we don't really need the products, and maybe don't even like them, we immediately want to be among the lucky few who have them. But – let's be clear about this – companies just don't run out of products. Do you *really* think the manufacturers couldn't produce a few more, if they thought they could sell them? Of course they could.

When it comes to new products we, the consumers, are like sheep and we follow each other. So another way advertisers have of getting us to use something is to tell us, 'Everybody's using it'. And of course, we think everybody can't be wrong, so the product must be fantastic. So as to make us believe it, they use expressions like, 'It's a must-have' or 'It's the in thing', and they combine this with a photograph of a large group of people, so that we can't fail to get the message. But don't be fooled. Even if it everybody *is* using it (and they may not be), everybody *can* be wrong.

Another favourite message is 'You, too, can look like this', accompanied by a photo of a fabulous-looking man or woman. But the problem is, you can't look like this because actually the woman or man in the photo is a model and also because he or she doesn't really look like that, either. The photo has been airbrushed in order to make the model look even slimmer, with perfect skin, and even more attractive than they are in real life.

Finally, what most annoys me is, 'Trust me, I'm a doctor' or 'Trust me, I'm a celebrity'. The idea is that if a celebrity is using the product, it must be fantastic, or if a doctor recommends it, it must really work. But be careful. Although the actress is holding the product in the photo, do you *really* think she colours her hair with it at home? And the doctor in the advert, is he really a doctor or just an actor wearing a white coat? Adverts also often mention a particular organization which recommends their product – for example things like, 'Our dog biscuits are recommended by the International Association of Dog Nutritionists' – well, that's probably an organization which the company set up themselves. Or, 'A recent independent study found that our toothpaste cleans your teeth better than any other brand'. What study was it? Who commissioned the study? It was probably produced for the company itself, and paid for by them, too.

5 6

When Paul Feldman started his business, you know, he really thought that at least 95 per cent of the people would pay for their bagels. This was presumably because that was the payment rate that he got in his own office. But, in fact, this rate wasn't representative at all. I mean, in his office, most people paid probably just because Feldman worked there himself, and they knew him personally, and probably liked him.

So when Feldman sold his bagels in other offices, he had to accept less. After a while, he considered that a company was 'honest' if over 90 per cent of the people paid. Between 80 and 90 per cent was what he considered to be normal, you know, the average rate. He didn't like it, but he had to accept it. It was only if a company habitually paid less than 80 per cent – which luckily not many did – that he would feel he had to do something. First he would leave a note, sort of giving them a warning, and then, if things didn't improve, he would simply stop selling there. Interestingly, since he started the business, the boxes he leaves to collect the cash have hardly ever been stolen. Obviously in the mind of an office worker, to steal a bagel isn't a crime, but to steal the money box is.

So, what does the bagel data tell us about the kind of offices that were not honest, the ones that *didn't* pay? Well, first of all, it shows that smaller offices are more honest than big ones. An office with 20 to 30 employees generally pays three to five per cent more than an office with two to three hundred employees. This seems to be because in a smaller community people are more worried about being dishonest – probably because they would feel worse if they were caught.

The bagel data also suggests that your mood, how you feel, affects how honest you are. For example, the weather is a really important factor. When the weather is unusually good, more people pay, but if it's unusually cold or rainy, fewer people pay. And people are also affected by public holidays, but in different ways – it depends *which* public holiday. Before Christmas and Thanksgiving, people are less honest, but just before the 4th of July and Labour Day they are *more* honest. This seems to be because holidays like the 4th of July are just a day off work, and people always look forward to them. But Christmas and Thanksgiving are holidays where people often feel quite stressed or miserable. So their bad mood makes them less honest.

The other thing Feldman believes affects how honest people are is the morale in an office. When employees like their boss and like their job, then the office is more honest. He also thinks that the higher people are promoted, the less honest they are. He reached this conclusion because, over several years, he'd been delivering three baskets of bagels to a company that was on three floors. The top floor was the executive floor, and the lower two floors were people who worked in sales, and service, and administrative employees. Well, it turned out that the least honest floor was the executive floor! It makes you wonder whether maybe these guys got to be executives because they were good at cheating!

But in general the story of Feldman's bagel business is a really positive one. It's true that some people *do* steal from him, but the vast majority, even though no one is watching them, are honest.

5 17

I So, Miles, you're going to tell us about your top five cities.

M Yes. It was a difficult question for me because, of course, as a travel writer I've been to so many places. But, in the end, I decided that if I was making a personal choice, they had to be cities that meant something to me personally, that had a personal connection. So, these aren't necessarily big tourist cities, though some of them are, but the cities that are my own personal top five. Incidentally, these five aren't in any particular order.

I So, what's the first one in your top five?

M Well, the first one is Sydney. The personal connection is that my son and his family live there, so of course my wife and I have been there quite often and got to know it well. Of course, there are lots of amazing things about Sydney. For one thing it's a waterfront city, it has the sea all around it; there's wonderful surfing on Bondi beach and plenty of great little bays for sunbathing and swimming. It's also a very cosmopolitan city. Sydneysiders – which is what people from Sydney are called – come from all corners of the world, so for example the choice of places to eat is endless. You can find everything from simple soup kitchens to elegant, world-class restaurants so you can choose to eat Thai, Vietnamese, Greek, Italian and many, many other kinds of cuisine.

I And your second city?

M My wife and I spent our honeymoon in Edinburgh so it's always been a special place for me. But I think it's especially exciting during the Festival, which happens every August. Of course, there's a fantastic programme of music, and dance, and the arts. But what gives the city a special buzz during the Festival is 'the Fringe'. The Fringe is a massive alternative festival, and it has literally hundreds of events – comedy, theatre, amateur student groups, street entertainers. And, of course, the pubs stay open until much later than usual during the Festival and that adds to the atmosphere too. However, it's really hard to get accommodation during the Festival so you need to book well in advance.

I I must say, I've never been to the Festival, though I've often thought about going. Next year I must really try to get there. What about your third city?

M My third city is Cairo. We lived there for five years in the 70s and both our sons were born there, beside the River Nile. People always associate Cairo with the Pyramids, and of course they are amazing, but for me the best thing about it is the museums, which are absolutely fantastic. The Egyptian Museum has the world's largest and best collection from Pharaonic times. Then the Coptic museum, which is in the suburb of Al Fustat has the best of Egypt's Christian culture. And the Museum of Islamic Art has a whole lot of exquisite pieces from Muslim times. So if you're someone who likes museums and antiquities, my advice is go to Cairo.

I I must say that I *have* been to Cairo and I completely agree with you. And your next one?

M For my next one we're back in Europe in Italy. I've chosen Lucca, in Tuscany. Tuscany's two major tourist towns, Florence and Pisa, are absolutely jam-packed with tourists all year round, but most of them never get to Lucca. You can only really explore it on foot, which is the way I like to move around a town, and in about an hour you can do the four-kilometre circuit all around its Renaissance town walls. These walls are amazing – they're completely intact, and you can peer into people's living rooms as you walk past. Or you can walk from one end of the town to the other along Via Fillungo. Also, Lucca is the birthplace of Puccini, who's one of my all-time favourite composers. He played the organ of the town's magnificent cathedral when he was a young man, and there's a wonderful open-air festival every year where they perform his operas at a place called Torre del Lago, which is just nearby.

I And your last city?

M My last city is one that not many people have been to – it's not on the usual tourist route. I'd just finished university and I was curious about the wider world, so I went to Laos in South East Asia. Laos and its capital, Vientiane, were my first experience of living and working outside western Europe. The Laotians are a lovely, gentle, laid-back people. They taught me to relax. And they showed me how it's quite possible to be happy with very little money. The scenery is spectacular, too. The impressive Mekong River flows far away over the sands in the dry season and speeds by the city like a wide, rushing torrent once the rainy season begins. I remember looking down on it from one of the restaurants along its banks, and feeling that it was sweeping away all my troubles.

5 21))
Part 1
Interviewer What first drew you to advertising as a career choice?

George What drew me to advertising was actually, in a weird way, I had no choice, um, um I'm a third generation advertising guy. My, my father's brother, my uncle, who was 15 years older than he, was in advertising believe it or not in the 1940s, um, in Philadelphia. My father kind of took the baton from him and was in advertising and I grew up with it, so

I've been making a living in the business since 1984. It's a long time. It's 30 years.

Interviewer Do you still remember any commercials from your childhood?

George So I remember a lot of commercials, you know, growing up, um um, in an advertising household as we did, um, TV was more of a social event in those days. There wasn't a TV in every room like the family would gather to watch television. And um, we were told not to talk, you know, during the commercials, we could talk during the shows, so I grew up kind of watching commercials. I remember a lot of commercials. I bet you most people of my, um, generation would remember a lot of, I feel kind of guilty saying this because they're, they're usually decried as not very creative, but I remember a lot of jingles.

Interviewer What do you think makes jingles memorable?

George Among purists in the field jingles are, you know, laughed at, scoffed at, but God you remember them. You know they, what do they call them, ear worms? They get into your head and you can't get them out sometimes and you add that to almost everyday exposure six times a day, it's going to get in there. I can do, there was a, there was a, you know, there was a, there was a, I could sing one for you, there was a kids hot cereal, a hot cereal for children called H. O. Farina and it was an animated cartoon, it was very rudimentary. If you saw it today you wouldn't believe it was like a nationally broadcast cartoon and it was a little story of Willie and Wilhelmina and Willie trips on a rock and he goes, 'Every day I trip over that rock Wilhelmina.' And she says, 'Move it Willie.' And he says, 'Can't, too big.' And I bet you I'm getting this word for word if you could find it. And she says, 'I will.' And he says, 'Huh, you're a girl.' And she picks it up and then the jingle comes up and it goes 'Strong Wilhelmina eats her Farina.' Like I said, I probably heard that 500 times, maybe more, when I was growing up because it was, it was, every weekend for about eight years.

5 22))
Part 2
Interviewer What elements of a commercial are the most important?

George To me, um, a commercial basically is built in three parts. If you think of it as a pyramid, the top part of the pyramid I would say is impact. I have to intrude upon your life because you're probably working on your computer while you're watching TV or you're doing something, and when I'm talking about a TV commercial it's the same for a web ad or an app. So you have to get impact, you have to intrude, you have to kind of knock on the door. The second thing is communication, what do you want the person to know. And, and, that needs to be clear and precise. And um, the third thing is the hardest, it's persuasion because ultimately you're running a commercial to get people to do something, so it's that amalgamation. Another way of talking about it – um, and this is old school – but there's an acronym that probably comes from *Mad Men* era that is called AIDA, you know like the opera: um, Attention, Interest, Desire, Action.

Interviewer How do you feel about using celebrities to sell things?

George Sometimes it's a short, using a celebrity is a short cut to, ah, intrusion because people pay attention to celebrities. Hopefully, it's a celebrity that has some bearing on the brand. I don't think, if I was working on a depilatory, I would want to use Tommy Lee Jones, but um, that would just be gross. But you know if you find the right person, they can have special um, meaning, I think, and we do live in a celebrity culture, and people, you know their ears perk up when they see a celebrity. So, if you go back to the pyramid I drew, it's a way of getting, ah, impact. I'm not a giant fan of it, but sometimes you do things you're not a giant fan of.

Interviewer On your website you say, 'I can make people laugh.' How important is humour in advertising?

George I tend not to be funny in TV commercials, I'm just, partly because I'm a kind of cerebral guy and I wind up having to use that more than humour, but I think humour is incredibly important in, in, in the business and a lot of the commercials that really resonate with people I think are funny, a lot of the movies, a lot of everything, you know.

5 23))
Part 3
Interviewer With all the technology, viral advertising, etc, do you think billboards and TV commercials have had their day?

George Um, have billboards and TV commercials had their day? You know what, I don't think so. I mean, I can tell you empirically that 75% of all media dollars is spent on broadcast, and I know it's like, current to say, 'I don't have a TV,' or 'I never watch TV.' But people do. And the fact is, TV viewership is at an all-time high. So I don't think TV is dead and I don't think billboards will be, you know, something as kind of passé as a, as a billboard will be dead as long as, like, the highways are crowded, because you've got a captive audience, and until we can kind of pixelize ourselves and beam ourselves to work, I think there'll be billboards. They can be effective.

Interviewer As a consumer, and obviously as an advertiser, does advertising influence the decisions you make?

George Yes, um, you know, I'm very, I'm very susceptible to advertising. Um, I think because I tend to notice it. You know, I think I am very sensitive to, I think I'm very sensitive to um, stuff that isn't true. But when I see something that's well crafted and um, appeals, I think to both my head and my heart, I think, I think I register those things

Interviewer Is there an existing advertising campaign you wish you'd come up with, and why do you think it is so effective?

George Um, is there an existing advertising campaign? Yes, that I wish I did? There's a few. Um, I think the stuff that is being done for Nike just in general for, for 30 years has been exemplary, um, you know. They tapped into a mind set, and they made everyone feel like they were athletic, and, and they became kind of the gold standard, and they rarely hit a false note. The same thing with Apple, though people are just stressed in the industry about the latest direction Apple's been taking, which seems less sincere.

Interviewer Why do you think the Apple campaign is so effective?

George You know Apple took…I think Apple is effective because they looked at an industry and they said, 'Here's what's wrong with the industry um, and everything that industry does we're going to do differently.' So, that industry for years and years and years and years was talking about speeds and feeds, and they're talking about 697 megahertz and 4 megabytes of RAM or gigabytes of RAM, whatever it is, and Apple just said, 'It works.' And what they did was to say, 'You want to be creative? This machine makes you creative.' And they simplified, they simplified, and they were compelling, um, and they, they never lied, yeah.

5 25))
Interviewer Do you think you're influenced by advertising campaigns?
Jeanine Most definitely.
Interviewer Is there any product that shouldn't be advertised, in your opinion?
Jeanine Um, alcohol and junk food to children.
Interviewer Why should those ads be banned?
Jeanine Because it's promoting something that's unhealthy and that, especially junk food for children, when they see it they're very susceptible to the adverts and then they want it immediately and it's a problem.

Interviewer Do you think you're influenced by advertising campaigns?
Dustin I'm sure I am, probably not consciously but I'm sure subconsciously.
Interviewer Is there any product that shouldn't be advertised, in your opinion? Why should those ads be banned?
Dustin I mean I, I don't care for, for cigarette ads or alcohol ads, but should they be ad…, or should they not be advertised? That is not a decision I should make, so, I don't think so.

Interviewer Do you think you're influenced by advertising campaigns?
Elvira I'm not very influenced by ad campaigns, I'm influenced by reviews.

Interviewer Is there any product that shouldn't be advertised, in your opinion? Why should those ads be banned?

Elvira The only thing that comes to mind that should be banned from advertisements is, I think they tend to use the female body, um, inappropriately to sell things and items. That's pretty much the only thing that I can think of.

Interviewer Do you think you're influenced by advertising campaigns?

Ivan I think that everyone is somewhat influenced by advertising campaigns, even on a minor level.

Interviewer Is there any product that shouldn't be advertised, in your opinion? Why should those ads be banned?

Ivan Perhaps cigarettes shouldn't be advertised because children, um, probably shouldn't be seeing them advertised in a cool or exciting manner.

Interviewer Do you think you're influenced by advertising campaigns?

Yasuko I think a lot of people are usually influenced, you know, a little by advertisement, especially because we've, there's so much advertisement on media. And we watch a lot of TV, you know, internet. Um, I try not to be, I try to research the product on my own using internet or whatnot, and choose the, and try to choose the best product. Not because of the advertisement.

Interviewer Is there any product that shouldn't be advertised, in your opinion? Why should those ads be banned?

Yasuko Advertisements for, for cigarettes, I think should be banned. Um, I don't think there's anything positive about cigarette smoking, so I think that anything that causes health issues or bad influences or addiction should be banned from being on commercials.

5 27

Let's start with the first one about the coin. Many people think that a coin dropped from the top of the Empire State building, for example, would be travelling so fast that if it hit a person on the ground it would kill them. However this just isn't true. Coins are not aerodynamic and they are also relatively small and light so, although a person on the ground would certainly feel the impact, the coin wouldn't kill him – it wouldn't even hurt him very much!

Number two is one of the most popular scientific myths, that we only use ten per cent of our brains. Perhaps this is because people would like to think that they could be much more intelligent if they were able to find a way to use the other 90 per cent! In fact, neurologists haven't been able to find any area of our brains which isn't being used for something.

Number three. The dark side of the moon? Well, that only exists as the title of a Pink Floyd album. People used to think that there was a side of the moon that was always dark, that never got the sun, but, of course, that isn't true. The sun illuminates every part of the moon at some point during the 24-hour cycle. It is true that there's a side of the moon that we never see, that's to say we always see the same side of the moon, but the other side isn't always dark.

Now number four, the one about rubber tyres. A lot of people think that rubber tyres on a car will protect you from lightning in the same way that wearing rubber shoes will protect you from an electric shock. Well, it's certainly true that if you're caught in a thunderstorm, it's much safer to be inside a car than outside. But the tyres have nothing to do with it. When lightning strikes a car, it's actually the car's metal body that protects the passengers. It acts as a conductor and passes the electrical current down to the ground.

Number five. Poor old Einstein! Over the years he's often been used as an example to show that you can do very badly at school and still be very successful in life. And people have actually said that he wasn't very good at maths or science. But, in fact, records show that the young Albert, as you would expect, got very high marks in maths and science.

Number six. Antibiotics don't kill viruses. No, they don't, and it's a waste of time taking them if you have a virus. Antibiotics help your body to kill bacteria, not viruses. What's more, you can't exactly 'kill' a virus at all, since a virus is not really alive to begin with. Stick to your doctor's advice and only take antibiotics when he or she specifically prescribes them. The problem is that it's often very difficult for a doctor to know if you're suffering from a virus or from a bacterial infection.

Number seven. I love the idea that a full moon can make people go mad, but I think this is only true for werewolves. For centuries, nearly all cultures have attributed special mystical powers to the full moon, and in fact the English word 'lunatic', which can be used to describe a mad person, comes from the word 'lunar' – which means 'to do with the moon'. But, in spite of a lot of scientific research, nobody has found any link at all between the full moon and insanity or crime.

And finally, number eight, are bats really blind? Most British people probably think that they are, because we have the expression in English 'as blind as a bat'. But it's just not true. In fact, bats can see just as well as humans, even if they don't depend on their sight in the same way. Like dogs, bats rely heavily on other senses like hearing and smell. They have a very advanced sound-based system called echolocation, which allows them to know where they are when they're flying at night. But they can certainly see.

5 36

Presenter When Neil Armstrong became the first man to walk on the Moon on July 20th 1969, a global audience of 500 million people were watching and listening. As he climbed down the steps from the spacecraft and stepped onto the moon they heard him say, 'That's one small step for man, one giant leap for mankind'. It seemed like the perfect quote for such a momentous occasion. But from the moment he said it, people have argued about whether Armstrong got his lines wrong and made a mistake. James, tell us about it.

James Well, Armstrong always said that he wrote those words himself, which became some of the most famous and memorable words in history, during the time between landing on the moon and actually stepping out of the capsule onto the moon. That was nearly seven hours.

Presenter And so what is the controversy about what Armstrong said when he stepped down the ladder onto the moon?

James The question is, did he say, 'one small step for man' or 'one small step for a man'? That's to say did he use the indefinite article or not? It's just a little word but there's a big difference in meaning. Armstrong always insisted that he wrote 'one small step for a man, one giant leap for mankind,' Of course this would have been a meaningful sentence. If you say 'a man' then it clearly means that this was one small step for an individual man, i.e. himself, but one giant leap for mankind, that's to say, men and women in general. But what everybody actually heard was, 'One small step for man, one giant leap for mankind', with no indefinite article, and that sentence means, 'One small step for people in general, one giant leap for people in general.' And that doesn't really make sense.

Presenter So, did he just get the line wrong when he said it?

James Well, Armstrong himself was never sure if he actually said what he wrote. In his biography *First Man* he told the author James Hansen, 'I must admit that it doesn't sound like the word 'a' is there. On the other hand, certainly the 'a' was intended, because that's the only way it makes sense.' He always regretted that there had been so much confusion about it. But, almost four decades later, Armstrong was proved to be right. Peter Shann Ford, an Australian computer expert, used very hi-tech sound techniques to analyse his sentence and he discovered that the 'a' was said by Armstrong. It's just that he said it so quickly that you couldn't hear it on the recording which was broadcast to the world on 20th July 1969.

Presenter Was Armstrong relieved to hear this?

James Yes, he was. I think it meant a lot to him to know that he didn't make a mistake.

5 41

1 I was doing a tour of Asia where I was giving a presentation about database programs. I assumed the audiences would understand English – the organizers knew that I couldn't speak Chinese – and I knew they would be familiar with the, um, with the technical language of the products I was going to talk about, which were dbase and Clipper.

Well, for most of the tour the talks seemed to go extremely well; there were big audiences and the venues were great. The questions I was asked by the audience at the end of the talks showed that, um, everyone had really understood what I was saying.

When we arrived in the penultimate city, whose name I'm not going to mention, I started my session as I, as I usually did with a few questions to get to know something about the audience. So, first I asked them "How many of you use dbase?" I raised my own hand, because I use it myself and pretty much the whole audience raised their hands. So then I asked, 'How many of you here use Clipper?' And, once again, nearly 100 per cent of the audience raised their hands. This was, um, this was extremely unusual – in fact almost impossible. With a sinking feeling I then asked them, 'How many of you want to be an astronaut?' and I watched as everyone's hands went up. I might as well have been speaking to a group of aliens – as it turned out most of the audience spoke Chinese, and only Chinese. But I could see that two or three people in the audience spoke English, because they were practically rolling on the floor laughing.

2 I was giving a talk in Hungary to a group of about 200 English teachers. I got to the place where I was giving the talk a bit late, only about ten minutes before I was supposed to start. I rushed to the room, and saw that everything was set up and most of the audience were already waiting and I told the organisers that I just needed to quickly go to the toilet and then I would start. They pointed me in the right direction but, when I got to the toilets, I saw that there were two doors with words on them in Hungarian but no signs. I looked at the words and decided that one of them must be the men's toilet and I went in and went into a cubicle. Suddenly I heard voices of other people coming in – but, to my horror, they were women's voices, and I realized that I had guessed wrongly and had gone into the women's toilets. I guessed that these women must be teachers coming to my talk, so there was no way I could open the door and come out. I waited and waited, getting more and more stressed by the minute and worrying about being late to start my talk. After about five minutes or so, everything went quiet and I was able to rush out and go back to the room where the audience was waiting for me to start as it was already five minutes past the start time. Thank goodness nobody saw me…

3 My first ever presentation was at a conference for English teachers in Spain in about 1988. I wanted to show the audience some good ideas for using video in the classroom. I explained one of the ideas and then I went to turn on the video player and nothing happened...and then again... nothing…and again. By this time I was so stressed and annoyed that in the end I said, 'OK, if it doesn't work this time, I'm leaving', and I really meant it. Amazingly, almost as if it had heard me, it worked. I never forgot that talk and it taught me to never rely 100 per cent on technology in a presentation.

4 Some years ago, I had to do a presentation to a group of construction workers about health and safety at work. When I was getting dressed that morning I put on a silk skirt, and as I was doing it up, the button at the waist broke. I didn't bother to change, because the skirt had a zip and anyway I was in a hurry.

During the presentation, as I walked backwards and forwards across the stage, I started to feel something silky hit the back of my ankles. My skirt was falling down! The audience was absolutely entranced – and not by what I was saying. I quickly pulled it up and said, 'Now that I have your attention…'. The audience roared with laughter, and one of them shouted out, 'I thought that was part of your presentation!' I felt terribly embarrassed, and I could hear my mother's voice in my ear saying, 'You should always wear nice underwear, in case you are ever in an accident.' I managed to finish my presentation and I rushed outside and started to shake. That audience may never remember a thing I said, but I'm sure they won't forget me.

1A

question formation

1 2))

1 **Should we** buy her a present? How long **have you** been waiting? How many children **does your sister** have?
2 Why **didn't you** like the film? **Isn't this** a beautiful place?
3 **What** are they talking **about**? **Who** does this bag belong **to**?
4 **Who lives** in that house? **How many people follow** you on Twitter?

1 We make questions with modal verbs and with tenses where there is an auxiliary verb (*be, have*, etc.) by inverting the subject and the modal / auxiliary verb. With the present and past simple, we add the auxiliary verb *do / does* or *did* before the subject.
2 We often use negative questions to show surprise or when we expect somebody to agree with us.
3 If a verb is followed by a preposition, the preposition comes at the end of the question, not at the beginning NOT ~~About what are you talking?~~
 • We often just use the question word and the preposition, e.g. **A** *I'm thinking.* **B** *What about?*
4 When *who / what / which*, etc. is the **subject** of the question, we don't use *do / did*, e.g. *Who wrote this?* NOT ~~Who did write this?~~

indirect questions

1 3))

Could you tell me **what time the shop next door opens**? Do you know if **(whether) Mark's coming to the meeting**?

We use indirect questions when we want to ask a question in a more polite way, and begin with *Can | Could you tell me…?* or when we introduce a question with, e.g. *Do you know…? Do you remember…?*

Compare
What time does the shop next door open? (direct question), and
Could you tell me what time the shop next door opens? (indirect question)

 • In indirect questions the order is subject + verb. *Can you tell me where it is?* NOT ~~Can you tell me where is it?~~
 • We don't use *do / did* in the second part of the question. *Do you know where he lives?* NOT ~~where does he live.~~
 • You can use *if* or *whether* in questions underline{without} a question word (*What, How many*, etc.) and after *Can you tell me, Do you know*, etc.

> ### Other expressions followed by the word order of indirect questions
> The word order of indirect questions is used after:
> I wonder…, e.g. **I wonder** why they didn't come.
> I'm not sure…, e.g. **I'm not sure** what time it starts.
> I can't remember…, e.g. **I can't remember** where I left my phone.
> I want to know…, e.g. **I want to know** what time you're coming home.
> Do you have any idea…?, e.g. **Do you have any idea** if (whether) James is on holiday this week?

---

a Order the words to make questions.

tomorrow can't Why come you ?
Why can't you come tomorrow?

1 I Should her tell I feel how ?
2 friend known long best have How you your ?
3 tell when you train next leaves the Could me ?
4 housework family in Who your the does ?
5 are What about you thinking ?
6 at don't weekend you What doing the like ?
7 music to does What Jane kind like listening of ?
8 you time film know finishes Do what the ?
9 class students yesterday to many came How ?
10 you remember is where Do the restaurant ?

b Complete the questions with the words in brackets.

Where *did you go* on holiday last year? (you / go)

1 How often _____ exercise? (you / usually do)
2 Who _____ *Oliver Twist*? (write)
3 Could you tell me how much _____? (this book / cost)
4 I can't remember where _____ my car this morning. (I / park)
5 _____ your trip to Paris last weekend? (you / enjoy)
6 What kind of work _____? (your sister / do)
7 Who _____ the last biscuit? (eat)
8 Do you know what time _____ on a Saturday? (the swimming pool / open)
9 _____ the present you gave her? (your sister / not like)
10 _____ play your music so loud? I can't concentrate. (you / have to)

◄ p.5

auxiliary verbs

1 I like cats, but my husband **doesn't**.
Sally's coming tonight, but Angela **isn't**. **1 13**))
2 **A** I loved his latest novel.
B So did I.
A I haven't finished yet.
B Neither (Nor) have I.
Andrew's a doctor and **so is his wife**.
3 **A** I don't like shopping online.
B I do. I buy a lot of my clothes online.
4 **A** I went to a psychic yesterday.
B Did you?
A I'll make the dinner.
B Will you? That's great!
5 **A** You didn't lock the door!
B I did lock it, I know **I did**.
A Silvia isn't coming.
B She **is** coming. I've just spoken to her.
6 You won't forget, **will** you? She can speak Italian, **can't** she?

We use auxiliary verbs (*do*, *have*, etc.) or modal verbs (*can*, *must*, etc.):
1 to avoid repeating the main verb / verb phrase, e.g. NOT *I like cats but my husband doesn't ~~like cats~~*.
2 with *so* and *neither* to say that someone or something is the same. Use *so* + auxiliary + subject with a positive verb, and *neither* (or *nor*) + auxiliary + subject with a negative verb.
3 to say that someone or something is different.
4 to make 'reply questions', to show interest or surprise.
5 to show emphasis in a positive sentence, often when you want to contradict what somebody says. With the present / past simple, we add *do* / *does* / *did* before the main verb. With other auxiliaries, e.g. *be, have, will* the auxiliary verb is stressed and not contracted.
6 to make question tags, usually to check information. We use a positive auxiliary with a negative verb and a negative auxiliary with a positive verb.
- Question tags are often used simply to ask another person to agree with you, e.g. *It's a nice day, isn't it?* In this case the question tag is said with falling intonation, i.e. the voice goes down.
- Question tags can also be used to check something you think is true, e.g. *She's a painter, isn't she?* In this case the question tag is said with rising intonation, as in a normal *yes* / *no* question.

a Complete the mini-dialogues with an auxiliary or modal verb.

A You didn't remember to buy coffee.
B I *did* remember. It's in the cupboard.
1 **A** He's booked the flights, _____ he?
B Yes, I think so.
2 **A** It's hot today, _____ it?
B Yes, it's boiling.
3 **A** Why didn't you go to the meeting?
B I _____ go to the meeting, but I left early.
4 **A** I wouldn't like to be a celebrity.
B Neither _____ I.
5 **A** Emma doesn't like me.
B She _____ like you. She just doesn't want to go out with you.
6 **A** Mike's arriving tomorrow!
B _____ he? I thought he was arriving today.
7 **A** What did you think of the film?
B Tom liked it, but I _____. I thought it was awful.
8 **A** Are you a vegetarian?
B Yes, I am and so _____ my boyfriend.
9 **A** You'll remember to call me, _____ you?
B Yes, of course!
10 I really want to go to Egypt, but unfortunately my husband _____. He hates the heat.

b Complete the conversation with a suitable auxiliary verb.

A You're Tom's sister, [1]*aren't* you?
B Yes, I'm Carla.
A It's a great club, [2]____ it?
B Well, it's OK. But I don't like the music much.
A [3]____ you? I love it! I've never been here before.
B Neither [4]____ I. I don't go clubbing very often.
A Oh [5]____ you? I [6]____. In fact, I usually go most weekends.
B [7]____ you? I can't afford to go out every weekend.
A I didn't see you at Tom's birthday party last Saturday. Why [8]____ you go?
B I [9]____ go, but I arrived really late because my car broke down.
A Oh, that's why I didn't see you. I left early.
B I fancy a drink. I'm really thirsty after all that dancing.
A So [10]____ I. Let's go to the bar.

◀ p.9

2A

present perfect simple and continuous

present perfect simple: *have / has* + past participle

> 1 **Have** you **ever written** a blog?   **①37**》
> 2 We**'ve** just **landed** but we **haven't got off** the plane yet. I**'ve** already **told** you three times.
> 3 It's the best book I**'ve** ever **read**.
> 4 My computer**'s crashed**! Look, it**'s started** snowing.
> 5 I**'ve known** Miriam since I was a child. My sister **has had** flu for ten days now.
> 6 How many Agatha Christie novels **have** you **read**? They**'ve seen** each other twice this week.

We use the present perfect simple:
1 to talk about past experiences when you don't say when something happened.
2 with *just*, *yet*, and *already*.
3 with superlatives and *the first, second, last time*, etc.
4 for finished actions (when no time is specified) which have present results.
5 with non-action verbs (= verbs not usually used in the continuous form, e.g. *be, have, know, like*, etc.) to say that something started in the past and is still true now.
   - This use is common with time expressions like *How long…?, for* or *since, all day | evening*, etc.
   - Don't use the present simple or continuous in this situation: NOT *I know Miriam since I was a child*.
6 when we say or ask *how much | many* we have done or *how often* we have done something up to now.

present perfect continuous: *have / has* + *been* + verb + *-ing*

> 1 How long **have** you **been feeling** ill?   **①38**》
> He**'s been chatting** online all evening.
> 2 I **haven't been sleeping** well. It**'s been raining** all day.
> 3 I**'ve been shopping** all morning. I'm exhausted.
> **A** Take your shoes off. They're filthy.
> **B** Yes, I know. I**'ve been working** in the garden.

We use the present perfect continuous:
1 with action verbs, to say that an action started in the past and is still happening now.
   - This use is common with time expressions like *How long…?, for* or *since, all day | evening*, etc.
   - Don't use the present simple or continuous in this situation. NOT *I know Miriam since I was a child*.
2 for repeated actions, especially with a time expression, e.g. *all day, recently*.
3 for continuous actions which have just finished (but which have present results).

> 1 I**'ve been learning** French for the last three   **①39**》
> years. He**'s liked** classical music since he was a teenager.
> 2 She**'s been having** piano lessons since she was a child. They**'ve had** that car for at least ten years.
> 3 We**'ve lived** in this town since 1980. We**'ve been living** in a rented flat for the last two months.
> 4 I**'ve painted** the kitchen. I**'ve been painting** the kitchen.

1 To talk about an unfinished action we normally use the present perfect continuous with action verbs and the present perfect simple with non-action verbs.
2 Some verbs can be action or non-action depending on their meaning, e.g. *have piano lessons* = action, *have a car* = non-action.
3 With the verbs *live* or *work* you can often use the present perfect simple or continuous. However, we normally use the present perfect continuous for shorter, more temporary actions.
4 The present perfect simple emphasizes the completion of an action (= the kitchen has been painted). The present perfect continuous emphasizes the duration of an action, which may or may not be finished (= the painting of the kitchen may not be finished yet).

a Circle the correct form of the verb. Tick (✓) if both are possible.

Have you ever *tried* | *been trying* caviar?
1 She's *worked* | *been working* here since July.
2 Your mother has *phoned* | *been phoning* three times this morning!
3 The kids are exhausted because they've *run* | *been running* around all day.
4 Tim and Lucy haven't *seen* | *been seeing* our new house.
5 I've never *met* | *been meeting* her boyfriend. Have you?
6 It's *rained* | *been raining* all morning.
7 Bill has just *gone* | *been going* to work. He won't be back till this evening.
8 My sister has *lived* | *been living* alone since her divorce.

b Complete the sentence with the best form of the verb in brackets, present perfect simple or continuous.

I've bought a new car. Do you like it? (buy)
1 We _____ Jack and Ann for years. (know)
2 You look really hot. _____ at the gym? (you / work out)
3 Emily _____ her homework yet, so I'm afraid she can't go out. (not do)
4 They don't live in London, they _____. (move)
5 I _____ time to cook anything. (not have)
6 We _____ for hours. Is this the right way? (walk)
7 _____ you _____ my diary again? (read)
8 Oh no! I _____ my finger on this knife. (cut)

◄ *p.15*

134

adjectives as nouns, adjective order

adjectives as nouns

1 **The English** are famous for
drinking tea. 1 43))
The Chinese invented paper.
The Dutch make wonderful cheeses.
2 **The poor** are getting poorer and **the rich** are
getting richer.
The government needs to create more jobs for
the unemployed.

• You can use *the* + some adjectives to talk about groups of people, e.g.
  1 nationalities that end in *-ch*, *-sh*, *-ese*, and *-ss*, e.g. *the French*, *the Spanish*, *the British*, *the Japanese*, *the Irish*, *the Swiss*, etc. (**but** the Czechs)
  (most other nationality words are nouns and are used in the plural, e.g. *The Brazilians*, *the Poles*, *the Turks*, *the Hungarians*, *the Argentinians*, etc.)
  2 specific groups in society, e.g. *the young*, *the old* (or *the elderly*), *the sick* (= people who are ill), *the blind*, *the deaf*, *the homeless*, *the dead*.
• To talk about one person use, e.g. *a Japanese woman*, *a rich man*, etc. NOT ~~a Japanese, a rich~~
  You can also use adjective + *people* to talk about a group of people, e.g. *poor people*, *homeless people*, *old people*, *French people*.

adjective order

We've got a **lovely old** cottage just outside Bath.   1 44))
She has **long fair** hair.
I bought a **beautiful Italian leather** belt.

• You can put more than one adjective before a noun (often two and occasionally three). These adjectives go in a particular order, e.g. NOT ~~an old lovely cottage~~
• Opinion adjectives, e.g. *beautiful*, *nice*, *lovely*, always go <u>before</u> descriptive adjectives, e.g. *big*, *old*, *round*.
• If there is more than one descriptive adjective, they go in this order:

OPINION	SIZE	AGE	SHAPE	COLOUR	PATTERN
expensive	little	brand new	long	purple	striped
beautiful					

ORIGIN / PLACE	MATERIAL	NOUN
French	silk	**scarf**
Italian		**car**

a Re-write the <u>underlined</u> phrase using *the* + an adjective.

<u>People from Spain</u> enjoy eating out. *The Spanish*

1 <u>People from the Netherlands</u> tend to be good at languages.
2 Florence Nightingale looked after <u>the people who weren't well</u> during the Crimean war.
3 The system of reading for <u>people who can't see</u> is called Braille.
4 <u>People from France</u> think that their cuisine is the best in the world.
5 Ambulances arrived to take <u>the people who had been injured</u> to hospital.
6 <u>People from Switzerland</u> are usually very punctual.
7 The worst season for <u>people without a home</u> is winter.
8 There is a discount for students and <u>people without a job</u>.
9 The monument was erected to honour <u>the people who died</u> from the Second World War.
10 There are special TV programmes for <u>people who can't hear</u> which use sign language.

b Write the adjectives in brackets in the right place. Change *a* to *an* where necessary.

a big car park (empty)   *a big empty car park*

1 a man (young / attractive)
2 shoes (old / dirty)
3 a velvet jacket (black / beautiful)
4 a woman (fat / short / American)
5 a beach (sandy / long)
6 a country house (lovely / old)
7 a leather bag (Italian / stylish)
8 eyes (huge / dark)
9 a dog (black / friendly / old)
10 a T-shirt (striped / cotton)

◀ *p.19*

3A

narrative tenses: past simple, past continuous, past perfect, past perfect continuous

narrative tenses

> 1 We **arrived** at the airport and **checked in**. ② 8))
> 2 We **were having** dinner when the plane hit some turbulence.
>   At nine o'clock most people on the plane **were reading** or **were trying** to sleep.
> 3 When we arrived at the airport, we suddenly realized that we **had left** one of the suitcases in the taxi.
> 4 We**'d been flying** for about two hours when suddenly the captain told us to fasten our seat belts because we were flying into some very bad weather.

1 We use the **past simple** to talk about consecutive actions or situations in the past, i.e. for the main events in a story.
2 We use the **past continuous** (*was | were* + verb + *-ing*) to describe a longer continuous past action or situation which was in progress when another action happened, or to describe an action or situation that was not complete at a past time.
3 We use the **past perfect** (*had* + past participle) to talk about the 'earlier past', i.e. things which happened <u>before</u> the main event(s).
4 We use the **past perfect continuous** (*had been* + verb + *-ing*) with action verbs to talk about longer continuous actions or situations that started before the main events happened and have continued up to that point. Non-action verbs (e.g. *be, have, know, like*, etc.) are not normally used in the past continuous or past perfect continuous.

past perfect simple or continuous?

> Lina was crying because she**'d been reading** a ② 9))
> very sad book.
> Lina didn't want to see the film, because she**'d** already **read** the book.

- The past perfect continuous emphasizes the <u>continuation</u> of an activity. The past perfect simple emphasizes the <u>completion</u> of an activity.

---

a Circle the correct verb form.

Meg and Liam McGowan (got) | *were getting* a nasty surprise when they [1] *had checked in* | *were checking in* at Heathrow airport yesterday with their baby Shaun. They [2] *had won* | *won* three free plane tickets to Rome in a competition, and they [3] *were looking forward to* | *had been looking forward to* their trip for months. But, unfortunately, they [4] *had been forgetting* | *had forgotten* to get a passport for their son, so Shaun couldn't fly. Luckily, they [5] *had arrived* | *were arriving* very early for their flight, so they still had time to do something about it. They [6] *had run* | *ran* to the police station in the airport to apply for an emergency passport. Meg [7] *was going* | *went* with Shaun to the photo machine while Liam [8] *had filled in* | *was filling in* the forms. The passport was ready in an hour, so they [9] *hurried* | *were hurrying* to the gate and [10] *got* | *had got* on the plane.

b Put the verb in brackets in the past perfect simple (*had done*) or continuous (*had been doing*). If you think both are possible, use the continuous form.

His English was very good. He*'d been learning* it for five years. (learn)

1 I was really fed up because we <u>had been queuing</u> for hours. (queue)
2 She went to the police to report that someone <u>had stolen</u> her bag. (steal)
3 It <u>had been raining</u> all morning. The streets were wet, and there were puddles everywhere. (rain)
4 She got to work late because she <u>had left</u> her phone at home and <u>had had to</u> go back and get it. (leave, have to)
5 I almost didn't recognize Tony at the party. He <u>had changed</u> a lot since I last saw him. (change)
6 The tourists' faces were very red. They <u>had been sitting</u> in the sun all morning and they <u>hadn't put on</u> any sun cream. (sit, not put on)
7 I could see from their expressions that my parents <u>had been arguing</u>. (argue)
8 Jess had a bandage on her arm because she <u>had fallen</u> off her bike that morning. (fall)
9 I was amazed because I <u>had never seen</u> such an enormous plane before. (never see)
10 How long <u>had you been</u> <u>walking</u> before you realized that you were lost? (walk)

◀ p.26

the position of adverbs and adverbial phrases

1 He walks very **slowly**. I speak five languages **fluently**. The driver was **seriously** injured in the accident. (2 13))
2 I **hardly ever** have time for breakfast. Liam's **always** late for work. I would **never** have thought you were 40.
3 My parents will be **here in half an hour**. It rained **all day yesterday**.
4 I've **nearly** finished. We're **incredibly** tired. My husband works **a lot** but he doesn't earn **much**.
5 **Unfortunately**, the parcel never arrived. **Ideally**, we should leave here at 10.00.

My parents will be here in half an hour.

Adverbs can describe an action (e.g. *he walks **slowly***) or modify adjectives or other adverbs (e.g. *it's **incredibly** expensive, he works **very** hard*). They can either be one word (e.g. *often*) or a phrase (e.g. *once a week*).

1 **Adverbs of manner** describe how somebody does something. They usually go after the verb or verb phrase, however, with passive verbs they usually go in mid-position (before the main verb but after an auxiliary verb).

2 **Adverbs of frequency** go before the main verb but after the verb *to be*.
   - *Sometimes, usually,* and *normally* can also be put at the beginning of the phrase or sentence for emphasis.
   - If there are two auxiliary verbs, the adverb goes after the first one.
3 **Adverbs of time and place** usually go at the end of a sentence or clause. Place adverbs normally go before time adverbs. NOT *My parents will be in half an hour here.*
4 **Adverbs of degree** describe how much something is done, or modify an adjective.
   - *extremely, incredibly, very,* etc. are used with adjectives and adverbs and go before them.
   - *a lot* and *much* are often used with verbs and go after the verb or verb phrase.
   - *a little | a bit (of)* can be used with adjectives or verbs, e.g. *I'm a bit | a little tired. We rested a bit of | a little after the flight.*
5 **Comment adverbs** (which give the speaker's opinion) usually go at the beginning of a sentence or clause. Other common comment adverbs are *luckily, basically, clearly, obviously, apparently, eventually,* etc.

> 🔍 **Other adverbs**
> Most other adverbs go in mid-position, e.g. I **just** need ten more minutes. She didn't **even** say goodbye. She'll **probably** come in the end.

a Underline the adverbs or adverbial phrases and correct the sentences where the order is wrong.

> We're going to be <u>unfortunately</u> late. ✗
> *Unfortunately, we're going to be late.*
> He can speak German <u>fluently</u>. ✓

1 She liked very much the present.
2 Mark came last night very late home.
3 The ambulance arrived at the scene of the accident after a few minutes.
4 A young man was injured badly and was taken to hospital.
5 I was extremely tired last night.
6 She's lazy a bit about doing her homework.
7 I forgot your birthday almost, but fortunately my sister reminded me.
8 We luckily had taken an umbrella, because it started to rain just after we'd left.
9 Mary doesn't always eat healthily, because she often has snacks between meals.
10 Jack has been apparently sacked.

b Put the adverbs in brackets in the normal position in these sentences.

> *seriously*
> She wasn't ⋏ injured when she fell. (seriously)

1 Their house was damaged in the fire. (badly, last week)
2 Ben is at his friend's house. (often, in the evening)
3 My father has a nap. (usually, in the afternoon)
4 Julia left and she didn't say goodbye. (early, even)
5 Martin talks fast. (always, incredibly)
6 His brother died in a skiing accident. (apparently, nearly)
7 We're going to the cinema. (probably, tonight)
8 I send emails. (rarely, nowadays)
9 I've bought a beautiful new coat. (just, really)
10 Karen realized that she was going to learn to drive. (eventually, never)

◀ p.29

4A

future perfect and future continuous

future perfect: *will have* + past participle

> The decorators **will have finished** painting by (2) 29))
> Tuesday, so we can move back into the flat then.
> The football club say that they **'ll have built** the new stadium
> in six months.
> Laura **won't have arrived** before dinner so I'll leave some
> food in the oven for her.
> When **will they have learnt** enough English to be able to
> communicate fluently?

We use the future perfect (*will have* + past participle) to say
something will be finished before a certain time in the future.

- This tense is frequently used with the time expressions **by**
  Saturday | *March* | *2030*, etc. or **in** *two weeks* | *months*, etc.
- *By* + a time expression = at the latest. With *in*, you can say
  in six months or *in six months' time*.
- We form the negative with *won't have* + past participle and
  make questions by inverting the subject and *will* | *won't*.

future continuous: *will be* + verb + *-ing*

> Don't phone between 7.00 and 8.00 as we **'ll be** (2) 30))
> **having** dinner then.
> Good luck with your test tomorrow. **I'll be thinking** of you.
> This time tomorrow **I'll be sitting** at a café **drinking** a beer.
> Come at 7.00 because **we won't be starting** dinner until 8.00.
> **Will you be waiting** for me when I get off the train?
> **I'll be going** to the supermarket later. Do you want anything?

- Use the future continuous (*will be* + verb + *ing*) to say that an
  action will be in progress at a certain time in the future.
  Compare:
  We'll have dinner at 8.00 (= we will start dinner at 8.00)
  We'll be having dinner at 8.00 (= at 8.00 we will already
  have started having dinner)
- We sometimes use the future continuous, like the present
  continuous, to talk about things which are already planned or
  decided.
- We form the negative with *won't be* + verb + *ing* and make
  questions by inverting the subject and *will* | *won't*.

---

a Complete the sentences using the future perfect or
future continuous.

> The film starts at 7.00. I will arrive at 7.15. When I
> arrive at the cinema the film *will have started*. (start)

1 The flight to Geneva takes off at 9.00 and lands at 10.30.
  At 10.00 they'll be flying to Geneva. (fly)

2 I usually save €200 a month.
  By the end of the year, I will have saved €2,400. (save)

3 Rebecca leaves at 6.30. It takes her an hour to get to
  work.
  At 7.00 tomorrow she will have driven / be driving to work.
  (drive)

4 The meeting starts at 2.00 and finishes at 3.30.
  Don't call me at 2.30 because we will be having a
  meeting. (have)

5 Sam is paying for his car. The last payment is in May.
  By June he will have paid for his car. (pay)

6 Their last exam is on May 31st.
  By the end of May they will have finished their exams.
  (finish)

7 She writes a chapter of her novel a week. This week
  she's on chapter five.
  By the end of this week she will have written five
  chapters. (write)

8 Sonia is usually at the gym between 6.30 and 7.30.
  There's no point phoning Sonia now. It's 7.00 and she
  will be working out at the gym. (work out)

9 The film started downloading at 7.30. It will take
  another hour.
  The film will have downloaded at 8.30. (download)

b Complete the dialogue with the verbs in brackets in the
future perfect or continuous.

> **A** Well, it looks like we'll be having very
>   different weather in the future if climate
>   change continues.
> **B** What do you mean?
> **A** Well, they say *we'll be having* much | (have)
>   higher temperatures here in London, as
>   high as 30°. And remember, we
>   1_____ on the beach, | (not lie)
>   we 2_____ | (work)
>   in 30°, which is quite different.
>   And islands like the Maldives
>   3_____ by 2150 | (disappear)
>   because of the rise in the sea level. They
>   say the number of storms and tsunamis
>   4_____ by the middle | (double)
>   of the century too, so even more people
>   5_____ by then to | (move)
>   the cities looking for work. Big cities
>   6_____ even bigger by | (grow)
>   then. Can you imagine the traffic?
> **B** I don't think there will be a problem
>   with the traffic. Petrol
>   7_____ completely by | (run out)
>   then anyway, so nobody will have a car.
>   Someone 8_____ | (invent)
>   a new method of transport, so we
>   9_____ around in | (fly)
>   air cars or something.

◀ p.35

zero and first conditionals, future time clauses (with all present and future forms)

zero conditional

If you **want** to be fit, you **need to** do some exercise every day. **② 39))**

If people **are wearing** headphones in the street, they often **don't notice** other people.

If you **haven't been** to New York, you **haven't lived**.

To talk about something which is always true or always happens as a result of something else, we use *if* + present simple, and the present simple in the other clause.

- You can also use the present continuous or present perfect in either clause.

if + present simple *(handwritten: if + present simple, present continuous, present perfect (+) present simple)*

first conditional

If the photos **are** good, **I'll send** them to you. **② 40))** *(handwritten: P,S will)*

If you**'re not going** to Jason's party, **I'm not going to go** either.

If **I haven't come back** by 9.00, **start** dinner without me.

I'll have finished in an hour if you **don't** disturb me. *(handwritten: future perfect / present simple)*

To talk about something which will probably happen in the future, we use *if* + a present tense, and a future tense in the other clause.

- You can use any present form in the *if*-clause (present simple, continuous, or perfect) and any future form (*will*, *going to*, future perfect, future continuous) or an imperative in the other clause.

future time clauses

I'll be ready as soon as **I've had** a cup of coffee. **② 41))**

Send me a message when your train's **coming into** the station.

I'm not going to buy the new model until the price **has gone down** a bit.

I'm not going to work overtime this weekend unless I **get** paid for it.

Take your umbrella in case it's **raining** when you leave work.

When you are talking about the future, use a present tense after these expressions: *as soon as, when, until, unless, before, after,* and *in case*. This can be any present form, e.g. present simple, present continuous, present perfect.

- We use *in case* when we do something in order to be ready for future situations / problems. Compare the use of *if* and *in case*:

  I'll take an umbrella if it rains. = I won't take an umbrella if it doesn't rain.

  I'll take an umbrella in case it rains. = I'll take an umbrella anyway because it might rain.

a Circle the correct form.

Don't worry. Rob *will have passed* / *has passed* the exam if he's studied enough.

1 If you*'re not feeling* / *won't be feeling* better tomorrow, you should go to the doctor's.

2 If we're lucky, we*'ll have sold* / *'ve sold* our house by Christmas.

3 I'll pay for dinner – if I *have* / *'ll have* enough money!

4 If we carry on playing like this, we*'ll have scored* / *have scored* ten goals by half time.

5 Don't call Sophie now. If it's 8 o'clock, she*'ll bath* / *'ll be bathing* the baby.

6 If you don't hurry up, you *don't get* / *won't get* to school on time.

7 You can be fined if you *aren't wearing* / *won't be wearing* a seat belt in your car.

8 If you go out with wet hair, you*'ll catch* / *'ll be catching* a cold.

9 My suitcase *always gets* / *will always get* lost if I have a connecting flight.

10 I *won't go* / *don't go* to work on Monday if my daughter is still ill.

b Complete the sentences with a time expression from the list. You have to use some words more than once.

after   as soon as (x2)   before   if
in case (x2)   unless (x2)   until   when

I'll call you *as soon as* my plane lands.

1 I'm going to pack my suitcase ___before___ I go to bed.

2 Do you want to borrow my satnav ___in case___ you get lost?

3 I'll be leaving work early tomorrow ___unless___ my boss has a crisis.

4 I'll be meeting an old friend ___when___ I'm in London next week.

5 Don't worry. I'll call you ___as soon as___ I open the letter with my exam results.

6 ___unless if___ I'm late tomorrow, start the meeting without me.

7 Lily will have packed some sandwiches ___in case___ we get hungry.

8 The children will be playing in the park ___until___ it gets dark.

9 ___After___ we've had lunch we could go for a walk.

10 Don't call the emergency number ___unless___ it's a real emergency.

◄ p.39

5A

unreal conditionals

second conditional sentences: if + past simple, would / wouldn't + infinitive

> 1 If there **was** a fire in this hotel, it **would be** very   **3 12**))
>   difficult to escape.
>   I **wouldn't have** a car if I **didn't live** in the country.
> 2 If you **weren't** making so much noise, I **could concentrate** better.
> 3 If I **were** you, I'**d make** Jimmy wear a helmet when he's cycling.

1 We use second conditional sentences to talk about a hypothetical or imaginary situation in the present or future and its consequences.
2 In the *if*-clause you can also use the past continuous. In the other clause you can use *could* or *might* instead of *would*.
3 With the verb *be* you can use *was* or *were* for *I*, *he*, and *she* in the *if*-clause, e.g. *If Dan was / were here, he would know what to do.* However, in conditionals beginning *If I were you…* to give advice, we always use *were*.

third conditional sentences: if + past perfect, would / wouldn't have + past participle

> 1 If you **had come** to class more often, you **would have done**   **3 13**))
>   better in the exams.
>   I **wouldn't have been** late if I **hadn't overslept**.
> 2 He **would have died** if he **hadn't been wearing** a helmet.
>   If the jacket **had been** a bit cheaper, I **might have bought** it.

1 We use third conditional sentences to talk about a hypothetical past situation and its consequences.
2 You can also use the past perfect continuous in the *if*-clause. You can also use *could have* or *might have* instead of *would have* in the other clause.

second or third conditional?

> 1 If you **came** to class more often,   **3 14**))
>   you **would** probably **pass** the exam.
> 2 If you **had come** to class more often, you
>   **would** probably **have passed** the exam.

Compare the two conditionals.
1 = You don't come to class enough. You need to come more often if you want to pass the exam.
2 = You didn't come to class enough, so you failed.

> 🔎 **Mixed conditionals**
> We sometimes mix second and third conditionals if a hypothetical situation in the past has a present / future consequence, e.g. *You wouldn't be so tired if you had gone to bed earlier last night.*
> *If he really loved you, he would have asked you to marry him.*

---

a Complete with the correct form of the verb in brackets, using a second or third conditional.

> If Tim *hadn't got injured*, he would have played in the final. (not get injured)

1 I ~~wouldn't have made~~ so much food if you'd told me you weren't hungry. (not made)
2 If I were you, I ~~'d~~ wouldn't lend money to members of your family. (not lend)
3 I'd ask Jack to help me if he wasn't so busy. (ask)
4 Joe ~~wouldn't had had~~ an accident if he hadn't been driving so fast. (not have)
5 I'd run the marathon if I were a bit fitter. (be)
6 If you had looked where you were going, you wouldn't have fallen over. (look)
7 I'm sure you'd enjoy dancing if you came to the classes with me. (enjoy)
8 We'd go to the local restaurant if they changed the menu from time to time. (change)
9 Nina wouldn't have gone abroad if she had been able to find a job here. (be able)
10 If you had asked for a discount in the shop, they might have given you one. (ask)

b Complete using a second or third conditional.

> You didn't wait ten minutes. You didn't see Jim.
> If *you'd waited ten minutes, you would have seen Jim*.

1 Luke missed the train. He was late for the interview.
  If Luke hadn't missed the train, he wouldn't have been late for the interview.
2 Millie didn't buy the top. She didn't have any money.
  Millie would buy the top if she had some money. ¿?
3 It started snowing. We didn't reach the top.
  If it hadn't started snowing, we would have reached the top.
4 Rebecca drinks too much coffee. She sleeps badly.
  If Rebecca didn't drink so much coffee, she wouldn't sleep badly.
5 I don't drive to work. There's so much traffic.
  I would drive to work if there wasn't so much traffic.
6 Matt doesn't treat Sue well. She won't stay with him.
  If Matt treated his girlfriend better, she would stay with him.
7 You don't do any exercise. You don't feel healthy.
  You would feel a lot healthier if you did some exercise.
8 The taxi driver had satnav. He found the street easily.
  The driver wouldn't have found the street if he hadn't had satnav.
9 Jim bought the wrong size. I had to change the sweater.
  If Jim had bought the right size, I wouldn't have had to change the sweater.
10 You get up late. You waste half the morning.
  If you had got up earlier, you wouldn't have wasted half the morning.

structures after *wish*

wish + would / wouldn't

I wish cyclists **wouldn't cycle** on the pavement! (3 15)))
I wish you**'d spend** a bit more time with the children.
I wish the bus **would come**. I'm freezing.
I wish you **wouldn't leave** your shoes there. I almost fell over them.

We use *wish* + person / thing + *would* to talk about things we want to happen, or stop happening because they annoy us.
• You can't use *wish* + *would* for a wish about yourself, e.g. NOT ~~I wish I would…~~

wish + past simple or past perfect

1 I wish **I was** ten years younger! (3 18)))
  I wish **I could** understand what they're saying.
2 I wish **I hadn't bought** those shoes.
  I wish **you'd told** me the truth.

1 We use *wish* + past simple to talk about things we would like to be different in the present / future (but which are impossible or unlikely).
  • After *wish* you can use *was* or *were* with *I*, *he*, *she*, and *it*, e.g. *I wish I was / were taller*.
2 We use *wish* + past perfect to talk about things that happened or didn't happen in the past and which you now regret.

> 🔍 **If only…**
> We can also use *If only* instead of *I wish* in all these structures, e.g. *If only he'd hurry up! If only I had a bit more money. If only she hadn't told him about the affair!*

a Write sentences with *I wish…would / wouldn't.*

It annoys me that… you don't put away your clothes.

I wish you'd put away your clothes!

It annoys me that…

1 shop assistants aren't more polite
  I wish shop assitants would be more polite

2 you turn the heating up all the time
  I wish you wouldn't turn the heating up all the time.

3 my sister doesn't tidy our room
  I wish my sister would tidy our room.

4 the neighbour's dog barks at night
  I wish the neighbours' dog wouldn't barts at night

5 it doesn't stop raining
  I wish the raining would stop.

6 Jane talks about her boyfriend so much
  I wish Jane wouldn't talks about her boyfried so much.

7 my dad sings in front of my friends
  I wish my dad wouldn't sing in front of my friends.

8 you drive so fast!
  I wish you wouldn't drive so fast

9 my husband doesn't do the washing-up
  I wish my husband would do the washing-up

10 the bus doesn't come
  I wish the bus would come.

◀ p.48

b Complete with the verb in the past simple or past perfect.

I wish I _was_ a bit thinner! My clothes don't fit me! (be)

1 I wish I __had__ naturally blonde hair! (have)

2 Suzanne wishes her parents _didn't live_ so far away. (not live)

3 I wish I _had started_ learning English when I was a child! (start)

4 This flat's so cold! I wish it ___had___ central heating. (have)

5 I wish we_'d bought_ more expensive seats. I can't see a thing. (buy)

6 The party sounds as if it was great fun. I wish I ~~was been~~ had been there. (be)

7 Is it only five o'clock? I wish it ~~hadn't got~~ didn't get dark so early in winter. (not get)

8 I wish I _could_ speak French. It would be useful in this job. (can)

9 This suitcase is too heavy. I wish I hadn't _packed_ so many clothes! (not pack)

10 I'm really tired. I wish we ~~~~ had gone by car instead of deciding to walk. (go)

11 I wish I ~~been~~ hadn't been an only child. I'd love to have brothers and sisters. (not be)

12 I'd love to be able to play the piano. I wish I _learnt_ had when I was a child. (learn)

◀ p.51

6A

gerunds and infinitives

verbs followed by the gerund and verbs followed by the infinitive

> 1 I **enjoy listening** to music. I **couldn't help laughing**.　　(3) 37)))
> 2 I **want to speak** to you. They **can't afford to buy** a new car.
> 3 It **might rain** tonight. I'**d rather eat in** than go out tonight.

When one verb follows another, the first verb determines the form of the second. This can be the gerund (verb + -ing) or the infinitive (with or without to).

1 Use the **gerund** after certain verbs and expressions, e.g. *enjoy, can't help*.
  • When a phrasal verb is followed by another verb, the verb is the **gerund**, e.g. *carry on, keep on, give up, look forward to*, etc.
2 Use the **infinitive (with to)** after certain verbs and expressions, e.g. *want, afford*.
3 Use the **infinitive (without to)** after modal verbs and some expressions, e.g. *might, would rather*, and after the verbs *make* and *let*.
  • In the passive, *make* is followed by the infinitive with *to*. Compare *My boss **makes us work** hard. At school we were **made to wear** a uniform.*

▶ p.164 Appendix Verb patterns: verbs followed by the gerund or infinitive

> 🔍 **like, love, hate, and prefer**
> *like, love, hate*, and *prefer* are usually used with the gerund in British English but can also be used with the infinitive.
> We tend to use the gerund when we talk generally and the infinitive when we talk specifically e.g.
> *I like swimming* (general)
> *I like to swim first thing in the morning* when there aren't many people there (specific)
> *I prefer cycling to driving* (general)
> *You don't need to give me a lift to the station. I prefer to walk* (specific)
> When *like, love, hate*, and *prefer* are used with *would*, they are always followed by to + infinitive, e.g. *I'd prefer to stay at home tonight, I'd love to come with you.*

verbs that can be followed by either gerund or infinitive with *to*

> 1 It **started to rain**. It **started raining**.　　(3) 38)))
> 2 **Remember to lock** the door.
>   I **remember going** to Venice as a child.
>   Sorry, I **forgot to do** it.
>   I'll never **forget seeing** the Taj Mahal.
>   I **tried to open** the window.
>   **Try calling** Miriam on her mobile.
>   You **need to clean** the car.
>   The car **needs cleaning**.

1 Some verbs can be followed by the gerund or infinitive (with to) **with no difference in meaning**. The most common verbs like this are *start, begin*, and *continue*.
2 Some verbs can be followed by the gerund or infinitive (with to) **with a change of meaning**.
  – *remember* + infinitive = you remember first, then you do something. *Remember* + gerund = you do something then you remember it.
  – *forget* + infinitive = you didn't remember to do something.
     forget + gerund = You did something and you won't forget it. It is more common in the negative.
  – *try* + infinitive = make an effort to do something.
     try + gerund = experiment to see if something works.
  – *need* + gerund is a passive construction, e.g. *needs cleaning* = needs to be cleaned NOT ~~needs to clean~~.

---

a Complete with a gerund or infinitive verb (with or without *to*) from the list.

> carry call come do drive eat out go out take
> tidy wait work

I'm exhausted! I don't fancy *going out* tonight.

1 I suggest *taking* a taxi to the airport tomorrow. It'll be much quicker.
2 Even though the snow was really deep, we managed *to drive* to the local shop and back.
3 We'd better ___*do*___ some shopping – there isn't much food for the weekend.
4 I'm very impatient. I can't stand *waiting* in queues.
5 I wasn't well and a young man offered *to carry* my bags.
6 My parents used to make me ___*tidy*___ my room.
7 We threatened *calling to call* the police if the boys didn't stop throwing stones.
8 Do you feel like *coming* to the gym with me?
9 I'd prefer ___*drive*___ instead of getting a takeaway. *eat out*
10 I don't mind *waiting* late tonight if you want me to.

b (Circle) the correct form.

Your hair needs ((cutting)/ to cut. It's really long!

1 I'll never forget *to see /(seeing)* the Grand Canyon for the first time.
2 I need *to call /(calling)* the helpline. My computer has crashed.
3 Have you tried *to take /(taking)* a tablet to help you sleep?
4 I must have my keys somewhere. I can remember *to lock /(locking)* the door this morning.
5 I had to run home because I had forgotten *(to turn)/ turning* the oven off.
6 Our house needs *to paint /(painting)*. Do you know any good house painters?
7 Did you remember *(to send)/ sending* your sister a card? It's her birthday today.
8 We tried *(to learn)/ learning* to ski last winter, but we weren't very good at it.

◀ p.57

6B

used to, be used to, get used to

used to / didn't use to + infinitive

1 I **used to sleep** for eight hours every night, (3 43))
   but now I only sleep for six.
   I didn't recognize him. He **didn't use to have** a beard.
2 When I lived in France as a child we **used to have**
   croissants for breakfast. We **would buy** them every
   morning from the local baker.

1 We use *used to | didn't use to* + infinitive to talk about past
   habits or repeated actions or situations / states which have
   changed.
   • *used to* doesn't exist in the present tense. For present habits,
     use *usually* + the present simple, e.g. *I usually walk to work*.
     NOT ~~I use to walk to work~~.
2 We can also use *would* to refer to repeated actions in the past.
   However, we don't use *would* for non-action verbs (e.g. *be,
   have, know, like*, etc.). NOT ~~I didn't recognize him. He wouldn't
   have a beard~~.

be used to / get used to + gerund

1 I'm **not used to sleeping** with a duvet. I've always (3 44))
   slept with blankets.
   Carlos has lived in London for years. He's **used to driving**
   on the left.
2 **A** I can't **get used to working** at night. I feel tired all the
      time.
   B Don't worry, you'll soon **get used to it**.

1 Use *be used to* + gerund to talk about a new situation which is
   now familiar or less strange.
2 Use *get used to* + gerund to talk about a new situation which is
   becoming familiar or less strange.

[The difference between *be used to* and *get used to* is exactly the
  same as the difference between *be* and *get* + adjective.]

a Right (✓) or wrong (✗)? Correct the mistakes in the
       highlighted phrases.

   I can't get used to getting up so early. ✓
   She isn't used to have a big dinner in the evening. ✗
   isn't used to having

1 When we were children we used to playing football in ✗
   the road. (*we used to play*)
2 When we visited our British friends in London we
   couldn't get used to drink tea with breakfast. ✗ (*drinking*)
3 Have you got used to live in the country or do you still
   miss the city? (✗) *living*
4 I'm really sleepy. I'm not used to staying up so late. I'm
   usually in bed by midnight. ✓
5 There used to be a cinema in our village, but it closed
   down three years ago. ✓
6 Paul is used to having very long hair when he was younger. (✗) (*have*)
7 **A** I don't think I could work at night.
   B It's not so bad. I'm use to it now. (✗) *I'm used*
8 Did you use to wear a uniform to school? (✗) *used* ✓
9 It's taking me a long time to be used to living on my own. ✗ *get*
10 When I had exams at university I used to stay up all ✓
   night revising.

   Questions and did we drop de "d"

b Complete with *used to, be used to*, or *get used to* (positive
       or negative) and the verb in brackets.

   My boyfriend is Spanish, so he *isn't used to driving* on
   the left. (drive)

1 When Nathan started his first job he couldn't
   _____ at 6 a.m. (get up)
2 I didn't recognize you! You _____ long hair,
   didn't you? (have)
3 Isabelle _____ a flat when she was at university,
   but now she has a house of her own. (rent)
4 When we were children we _____ all day
   playing football in the park. (spend)
5 Jasmine has been a nurse all her life, so she _____
   nights. (work)
6 I've never worn glasses before, but now I'll have to
   _____ them. (wear)
7 Amelia is an only child. She _____ her things.
   (share)
8 Although I've lived in Spain for years, I've never
   _____ dinner at 9 or 10 o'clock at night. (have)
9 I _____ spinach, but now I love it. (like)
10 If you want to lose weight, then you'll have to _____
   less. (eat)

◄ p.58

7A

past modals

must / might / may / can't / couldn't + have + past participle

1 I **must have left** my phone at Anna's. I definitely (4·4)》
   remember having it there.
   You **must have seen** something. You were there when the
   accident happened.
2 Somebody **might have stolen** your wallet when you were
   getting off the train.
   He still hasn't arrived. I **may not have given** him the right
   directions.
3 She **can't have gone** to bed. It's only ten o'clock!
   You **can't have seen** their faces very clearly. It was too dark.

- We use *must | may | might | can't* + *have* + past participle to
  make deductions or speculate about past actions.

1 We use *must have* when we are almost sure that something
   happened or was true.

> 🔍 The opposite of *must have* is *can't have* – see 3 below
> NOT ~~mustn't have~~

2 We use *might | may have* when we think it's possible that
   something happened or was true. We can also use *could have*
   with this meaning, e.g. *Somebody could have stolen your wallet
   when you were getting off the train.*
3 We use *can't have* when we are almost sure something didn't
   happen or that it is impossible. We can also use *couldn't
   have* when the speculation is about the distant past, e.g. *You
   couldn't have seen their faces very clearly*, e.g. *She couldn't have
   gone to bed. It's only ten o'clock.*

should have / ought to have + past participle

We've gone the wrong way. We **shouldn't have** (4·5)》
turned left at the traffic lights.

It's my fault. I **ought to have told** you earlier that my mother
was coming.

- Use *should have* + past participle to say that somebody
  didn't do the right thing, or to express regret or criticism.
- You can use *ought to have* as an alternative to *should have*,
  e.g. *I ought to have told you earlier.*

---

a Rewrite the **bold** sentences using *must | might (not) |
   can't* + *have* + verb.

> **I'm certain I left my umbrella at home**. It's not in
> the office.
> I *must have left my umbrella at home*.

1 Holly's crying. **Perhaps she's had an argument with
   her boyfriend**. *She…*
2 **I'm sure Ben has read my email**. I sent it first thing
   this morning. *Ben…*
3 **I'm sure Sam and Ginny haven't got lost**. They have
   satnav in their car. *Sam and Ginny…*
4 **You saw Ellie yesterday? That's impossible**. She
   was in bed with flu. *You…*
5 **Perhaps John didn't see you**. That's why he didn't
   say hello. *John…*
6 **I'm sure Lucy has bought a new car**. I saw her driving
   a blue VW Golf! *Lucy…*
7 **I'm sure Alex wasn't very ill**. He was only off work
   for one day. *Alex…*
8 They didn't come to our wedding. **Maybe they didn't
   receive the invitation**. *They…*
9 This tastes very sweet. **I'm sure you used too much
   sugar**. *You…*
10 **It definitely wasn't my phone** that rang in the
   cinema. Mine was on silent. *It…*

b Respond to the first sentence using *should | shouldn't
   have* or *ought | oughtn't to have* + a verb in the list.

buy	come	eat	go	invite	~~learn~~	sit	write	take

   A We couldn't understand anybody in Paris.
   B You *should have learnt* some French before you went.
   A Sue is in bed with a stomach ache.
   B She *oughtn't to have eaten* so much chocolate cake
        yesterday.
1 **A** Tom told me the date of his party, but I've forgotten it.
   B You _____ it down.
2 **A** I was late because there was so much traffic.
   B You _____ by car. The metro is much faster.
3 **A** Amanda was rude to everyone at my party.
   B You _____ her. You know what she's like.
4 **A** I don't have any money left after going shopping
        yesterday.
   B You _____ so many shoes. Did you really
        need three pairs?
5 **A** You look really tired.
   B I know. I _____ to bed earlier last night.
6 **A** The chicken's still frozen solid.
   B I know. You _____ it out of the freezer earlier.
7 **A** I think I've burnt my face.
   B I'm not surprised. You _____ in the sun all
        afternoon without any sunscreen.

◀ p.64

7B

verbs of the senses

look / feel / smell / sound / taste

1 You **look tired**.
   That cake **smells good**!
   These jeans don't **feel comfortable**.
2 Tim **looks like his father**. This material **feels like silk** – is it?
   Are you sure this is coffee? It **tastes like tea**.
3 She **looks as if she's been crying**. It **smells as if something's burning**. It **sounds as if it's raining**.

1 Use *look, feel*, etc. + adjective.
2 Use *look, feel*, etc. + *like* + noun.
3 Use *look, feel*, etc. + *as if* + clause.

- You can use *like* or *as though* instead of *as if*, e.g.
  It sounds like | as though it's raining.

> 🔎 **Feel like**
> *feel like* can also be used as a verb meaning *'want' / 'would like'*. It is followed by a noun or a verb in the gerund, e.g. *I **feel like pasta** for lunch today* (= I'd like pasta for lunch today). *I don't **feel like going** to bed* (= I don't want to go to bed).

a Match the sentence halves.

1 That group sounds like   [F]   A her mother.
2 That boy looks   [   ]   B awful! You need to tune it.
3 Nora looks like   [   ]   C very soft.
4 That guitar sounds   [   ]   D someone has been smoking in here.
5 Tom looks as if   [   ]   E really sweet.
6 Our car sounds as if   [   ]   F ~~Coldplay.~~
7 Your new jacket feels   [   ]   G too young to be drinking beer.
8 This apple tastes   [   ]   H it's burnt.
9 It smells as if   [   ]   I roses.
10 Your perfume smells like [   ]   J it's going to break down any moment.
11 This rice tastes as if   [   ]   K he's just run a marathon.

b Circle the correct form.

   Your boyfriend *looks* / *looks like* a rugby player. He's huge!

1 You've gone completely white. You *look* / *look as if* you've seen a ghost!
2 What's for dinner? It *smells* / *smells like* delicious!
3 I think John and Megan have arrived. That *sounds* / *sounds like* their car.
4 Have you ever tried frogs' legs? Apparently they *taste like* / *taste as if* chicken.
5 Are you OK? You *sound* / *sound as if* you've got a cold.
6 Can you put the heating on? It *feels* / *feels like* really cold in here.
7 You *look* / *look like* really happy. Does that mean you got the job?
8 Your new bag *feels* / *feels like* real leather. Is it?
9 Let's throw this milk away. It *tastes* / *tastes like* a bit off.
10 Can you close the window? It *smells* / *smells as if* someone is having a barbecue.

◀ p.68

8A

the passive (all forms); *it is said that..., he is thought to...,* etc.

the passive (all forms)

present simple	Murderers **are** usually **sentenced** to life imprisonment.	(4)36))
present continuous	The trial **is being held** at the moment.	
present perfect	My car **has been stolen**.	
past simple	Jim **was arrested** last month.	
past continuous	The cinema **was being rebuilt** when it was set on fire.	
past perfect	We saw that one of the windows **had been broken**.	
future	The prisoner **will be released** next month. The verdict **is going to be given** tomorrow.	
infinitive with *to*	People used **to be imprisoned** for stealing bread.	
infinitive without *to*	You can **be fined** for parking on a yellow line.	
gerund	He paid a fine to avoid **being sent** to jail.	

- Use the passive when you want to talk about an action, but you are not so interested in saying who or what does / did the action.

- If you also want to mention the person or thing that did the action (the agent), use *by*. However, in the majority of passive sentences the agent is not mentioned.

it is said that..., he is thought to..., etc.

active	passive	
1 They say that the fire was started deliberately. People think that the mayor will resign.	**It is said that** the fire was started deliberately. **It is thought that** the mayor will resign.	(4)37))
2 People say the man is in his 40s. The police believe he has left the country.	**The man is said to be** in his 40s. **He is believed to have left** the country.	

- This formal structure is used especially in news reports and on TV with the verbs *know, tell, understand, report, expect, say,* and *think*. It makes the information sound more impersonal.

You can use *It is said, believed,* etc. + *that* + clause.
You can use *He, The man,* etc. (i.e. the subject of the clause) + *is said, believed,* etc. + *to* + infinitive (e.g. *to be*) or perfect infinitive (e.g. *to have been*).

---

a Rewrite the sentences in the passive, without the agent.

The police caught the burglar immediately.
The burglar was caught immediately.

1 Police closed the road after the accident.
The road…

2 Somebody has stolen my handbag.
My handbag…

3 They are painting my house.
My house…

4 They'll hold a meeting tomorrow to discuss the problem.
A meeting…

5 If they hadn't found the bomb in time, it would have exploded.
If the bomb…

6 The police can arrest you for driving without a licence.
You…

7 Miranda thinks someone was following her last night.
Miranda thinks she…

8 I hate somebody waking me up when I'm fast asleep.
I hate…

9 They're going to close the local police station.
The local police station…

b Rephrase the sentences in two ways to make them more formal.

People think the murderer is a woman.
It *is thought that the murderer is a woman.*
The murderer *is thought to be a woman.*

1 Police believe the burglar is a local man.
It…
The burglar…

2 People say the muggers are very dangerous.
It…
The muggers…

3 Police think the robber entered through an open window.
It…
The robber…

4 Police say the murderer has disappeared.
It…
The murderer…

5 Lawyers expect that the trial will last three weeks.
It…
The trial…

◄ p.76

8B

reporting verbs

structures after reporting verbs

1 Jack **offered to drive** me to the airport. **4 39**))
  I **promised not to tell** anybody.
2 The doctor **advised me to have** a rest.
  I **persuaded my sister not to go out** with George.
3 I **apologized for being** so late.
  The police **accused Karl of stealing** the car.

To report what other people have said, you can use *say* or a specific verb, e.g. *'I'll drive you to the airport.'*

  Jack **said** he would drive me to the airport.
  Jack **offered** to drive me to the airport.

- After specific reporting verbs, there are one to three different grammatical patterns (see chart on the right)
- In negative sentences, use the negative infinitive (*not to do*) or the negative gerund (*not doing*), e.g. *He reminded me not to be late. She regretted not going to the party.*

1 + *to* + infinitive	agree offer refuse promise threaten	**(not) to do something**
2 + person + *to* + infinitive	advise persuade ask remind convince tell encourage warn invite	**somebody (not) to do something**
3 + *-ing* form	apologize (to sb) for insist on accuse sb of recommend admit regret blame sb for suggest deny	**(not) doing something**

> **Verbs that use a *that* clause**
> With *agree, admit, deny, promise, regret*, you can also use *that* + clause.
> *Leo admitted stealing the watch.*
> *Leo admitted that he had stolen the watch.*

a Complete with the gerund or infinitive of the verb in brackets.

  The garage advised me *to buy* a new car. (buy)
1 Jamie insisted on _____ for the meal. (pay)
2 Lauren has agreed _____ late next week. (work)
3 I warned Jane _____ through the park at night. (not walk)
4 The man admitted _____ the woman's handbag. (steal)
5 The doctor advised Lily _____ drinking coffee. (give up)
6 The boss persuaded Megan _____ the company. (not leave)
7 Freya accused me of _____ to steal her boyfriend. (try)
8 I apologized to Evie for _____ her birthday. (not remember)
9 Did you manage to convince your parents _____ tonight instead of tomorrow? (come)
10 My neighbour denies _____ my car, but I'm sure it was him. (damage)

b Complete using a reporting verb from the list and the correct form of the verb in brackets. Use an object where necessary.

  accuse   invite   ~~offer~~   promise   recommend   refuse   remind   suggest   threaten

  Diana said to me, 'I'll take you to the station.'
  Diana *offered to take* (take) me to the station.
1 Ryan said, 'Let's go for a walk. It's a beautiful day.'
  Ryan _____ (go) for a walk.
2 'You copied Anna's exam!' the teacher said to him.
  The teacher _____ (copy) Anna's exam.
3 Sam's neighbour told him, 'I'll call the police if you have any more parties.'
  Sam's neighbour _____ (call) the police if he had any more parties.
4 The children said, 'We're not going to bed. It's much too early.'
  The children _____ (go) to bed.
5 Simon said to me, 'Would you like to have dinner with me?'
  Simon _____ (have) dinner with him.
6 Molly said to Jack, 'Don't forget to phone the electrician.'
  Molly _____ (phone) the electrician.
7 Ricky said, 'I'll never do it again.'
  Ricky _____ (do) it again.
8 Sarah said, 'You really must try Giacobazzi's. It's a fantastic restaurant.'
  Sarah _____ (try) Giacobazzi's. She said it was fantastic.

◀ p.78

9A

clauses of contrast and purpose

clauses of contrast

> 1 **Although** the advert said it would last **5 4**))
> for years, mine broke after two months.
> I went to work **even though** I wasn't feeling very well.
> I like Ann, **though** she sometimes annoys me.
> 2 **In spite of** (**Despite**)
> her age, she is still very active.
> being 85, she is still very active.
> the fact that she's 85, she is still very active.

Use *although*, *though*, *even though*, and *in spite of* or *despite* to express a contrast.

1 Use *although*, *though*, *even though* + a clause.
   Although and *even though* can be used at the beginning or in the middle of a sentence.
   • *Even though* is stronger than *although* and is used to express a big or surprising contrast.
   • *Though* is more informal than *although*. It can only be used in the middle of a sentence.

2 After *in spite of* or *despite*, use a noun, a verb in the *-ing* form, or *the fact that* + subject + verb.
   • Remember not to use *of* after *despite* NOT ~~Despite of the rain…~~

clauses of purpose

> to **5 5**))
> 1 I went to the bank **in order to** talk to my bank manager.
> **so as to**
> 2 I went to the bank **for** a meeting with my bank manager.
> 3 I went to the bank **so that** I could talk to the manager in person.
> 4 I wrote down what he said **so as not to** forget it.

Use *to, in order to, so as to, for,* and *so that* to express purpose.
1 After *to, in order to,* and *so as to,* use an infinitive.
2 Use *for* + a noun, e.g. *for a meeting.* You can also use *for* + gerund to describe the exact purpose of a thing, e.g. *This liquid is for cleaning metal.*
3 After *so that*, use a subject + modal verb (*can, could, would,* etc.).
4 To express a negative purpose, use *so as not to* or *in order not to*, e.g. *I wrote down what he said in order not to forget it.* NOT ~~to not forget it~~.

---

a Complete the sentences with *one* word.

> We're very happy in our new house, *though* there's a lot to do.

1 We loved the film _____ the fact that it was nearly three hours long!
2 Carl doesn't like spending money _____ though he's very well off.
3 They went down to the harbour _____ see if they had fresh fish.
4 I'll put your number straight into my phone so _____ not to forget it.
5 My mother called the doctor's in _____ to make an appointment.
6 The cake tasted good in _____ of not looking like the photo in the recipe book.
7 I've put the heating on quite high so _____ the house will warm up quickly.
8 I must say that _____ the service was poor, the meal was delicious.
9 I stopped at a motorway café _____ a quick meal before continuing on my journey.
10 _____ not being very fit, he managed to walk the three miles to the village.

b Rewrite the sentences.

> Despite not getting very good reviews, I thought the book was fantastic.
> Even though *the book didn't get very good reviews, I thought it was fantastic.*

1 We stayed at a bed and breakfast so as not to spend too much money on accommodation.
   We stayed at a bed and breakfast so that…
2 Despite earning a fortune, she drives a very old car.
   Although…
3 Everyone enjoyed the film even though the ending was sad.
   Everyone enjoyed the film in spite of…
4 The plane managed to land despite the terrible weather conditions.
   The plane managed to land even though…
5 I told her I enjoyed the meal she had cooked me so that I wouldn't offend her.
   I told her I enjoyed the meal she had cooked me so as…
6 The manager called a meeting so as to explain the new policy.
   The manager called a meeting in order…

◀ *p.85*

uncountable and plural nouns

uncountable nouns

1 The **weather** is fantastic there, and there's very   (5) 19))
   little **traffic** so you can walk everywhere.
   The **scenery** is beautiful here, but it's spoiled by all the
   rubbish people leave.
2 Could you give me **some advice** about where to stay?
   One useful **piece of advice** is to get a travel card.
3 The new opera house is made mainly of **glass**.
   Can I have **a glass** of tap water please?

1 The following nouns are always uncountable: *behaviour,*
   traffic, weather, accommodation, health, progress, scenery,
   rubbish, work, politics (and other words ending in *-ics,* e.g.
   athletics, economics).
   • They always need a singular verb, they don't have plurals,
     and they can't be used with *a | an.*
2 These nouns are also uncountable: *furniture, information,*
   advice, homework, research, news, luck, bread, toast, luggage,
   equipment. Use *a piece of* to talk about an individual item.

3 Some nouns can be either countable or uncountable, but
   the meaning changes, e.g. *glass* = the material used to make
   windows, *a glass* = the thing you drink out of. Other examples:
   iron, business, paper, light, time, space.

plural and collective nouns

1 One of the best museums is on **the outskirts** of   (5) 20))
   the city.
   My **clothes are** filthy. I'll put on **some clean trousers** |
   I'll put on **a pair of clean trousers**.
2 The hotel **staff are** very efficient.
   The **cabin crew are coming round** with the drinks
   trolley in just a few minutes.

1 *Arms* (= guns, etc.), *belongings, clothes, manners, outskirts,*
   scissors, trousers | shorts are plural nouns with no singular.
   They need a plural verb and they can't be used with *a | an.*
   • If they consist of two parts, e.g. *scissors, trousers, shorts,* etc.
     they can be used with *a pair of* or *some.*
2 *Crew, police, staff,* etc. are collective nouns and refer to a group
   of people. You can use a singular or plural verb with these,
   except *police,* which needs a plural verb.

---

a Right (✓) or wrong (✗)? Correct the
mistakes in the highlighted phrases.

   Our accommodation isn't satisfactory. ✓
   The news are good. ✗ *The news is*

1 We had a beautiful weather when we were
   on holiday.
2 They've got some lovely furnitures in their
   house.
3 My brother gave me a useful piece of advice.
4 Do you have a scissors? I need to wrap this
   present.
5 I need to buy a new trousers for my
   interview tomorrow.
6 The staff is very unhappy about the new
   dress code.
7 Your glasses are really dirty. Can you see
   anything?
8 The homeworks were very difficult last
   night.
9 There isn't any more space in my suitcase.
   Can I put this jacket in yours?
10 The police is sure that they know who was
   responsible for the vandalism.

b (Circle) the correct form. Tick (✓) if both are correct.

The traffic (is) | *are* awful during the rush hour.
1 Athletics *is | are* my favourite sport.
2 I bought *a pair of | some* new jeans.
3 Harvey's clothes *look | looks* really expensive.
4 The flight crew *work | works* hard to make passengers comfortable.
5 I found out *some | a piece of* useful information at the meeting.
6 Could I have *a paper | a piece of paper* to write down the new words?
7 I think I'll have *a | some* time after lunch to help you with that report.
8 I've got *a | some* good news for you about your job application.
9 We've made a lot of *progress | progresses* this term.
10 Hello, Reception? Do you have *an | some* iron I could use?

◀ p.91

10A

quantifiers: *all, every, both, etc.*

all, every, most

1 **All** animals need food. **All** fruit contains sugar. (5)31))
   All (of) the animals in this zoo look sad.
   The animals **all** look sad.
2 **Everybody** is here. **Everything** is very expensive.
3 **Most people** live in cities.
   Most of the people in this class are women.
4 **All of us** work hard and **most of us** come to class every week.
5 **Every** room has a bathroom. I work **every** Saturday.

1 We use *all* or *all (of) the* + a plural or uncountable noun.
   All = in general, *all (of) the* = specific.
   All can be used before a main verb (and after *be*).
2 We use *everything* | *everybody* (= all things, all people) + singular
   verb, e.g. *Everything is very expensive.* NOT ~~All is very expensive~~.
3 We use *most* to say the majority; *most* = general, *most of* = specific.
4 We often use *all* | *most of* + an object pronoun, e.g. *all of us, most of*
   them, all of you, most of it.
5 Use *every* + singular countable noun to mean 'all of a group'.

> 🔍 **every and all + time expressions**
> Note the difference between *every* and *all* + time expressions.
> *Every day* = Monday to Sunday. *All day* = from morning to night

I usually go running every day.

...but today I'm ill, so I stayed in bed all day.

no, none, any

1 Is there any milk? (5)32))
   Sorry, there's **no** milk. There **isn't any** (milk).
2 **A** Is there any food?
   B No, **none**. / There's **none**. But **none of us** are hungry.
3 Come **any** weekend! **Anyone** can come.

1 We use *no* + a noun after a ⊞ verb, or *any* + noun after
   a ⊟ verb to refer to zero quantity. *Any* can also be used
   without a noun.
2 We use *none* in short answers, or with a ⊞ verb to refer
   to zero quantity. You can also use *none* + *of* + pronoun /
   noun.
3 We use *any* (and *anything, anyone,* etc.) and a ⊞ verb to
   mean it doesn't matter what, who, etc.

both, neither, either

1 **Both** Pierre **and** Marie Curie were scientists. (5)33))
   Neither Pierre **nor** Marie was (were) aware of the
   dangers of radiation. Marie Curie wanted to study
   either physics **or** mathematics. In the end she studied
   both at the Sorbonne in Paris.
2 She and her husband **both** won Nobel prizes.
   Pierre and Marie were **both** interested in radium.
3 **Neither of them** realized how dangerous radium was.

1 We use a ⊞ verb with *both* and *neither*. The verb is plural
   with *both*, and either singular or plural with *neither*.
2 When *both* refers to the subject of a clause, it can also be
   used before a main verb but after *be*.
3 We often use *both* | *either* | *neither* + *of* + object pronoun,
   e.g. *us, them,* etc. or + *of the* + noun.

---

a (Circle) the correct word or phrase.

   We've eaten (all the) / all cake.

1 *Most of* | *Most* my closest friends live near me.
2 You can come round at *any* | *no* time on Saturday. We'll
   be home all day.
3 *All* | *Everything* is ready for the party. We're just
   waiting for the guests to arrive.
4 *Most* | *Most of* people enjoy the summer here, but for
   some it's too hot.
5 Gina goes dancing *all* | *every* Friday night.
6 We haven't got *any* | *no* onions for the soup.
7 *Any* | *None* of us want to go out tonight. We're all broke.
8 *Nobody* | *Anybody* can go to the festival. It's free.
9 I've got two very close friends, but unfortunately
   either | *neither* of them lives near me.
10 I'd like to have a bigger table, but there's *no* | *none* room
   in my kitchen.

b Right (✓) or wrong (✗)? Correct the wrong sentences.

   Both Mike and Alan passed the exam. ✓
   He neither watches the news or reads a newspaper. ✗
   He neither watches the news nor reads a newspaper.

1 Both the kitchen and the bathroom needs cleaning.
2 The food wasn't cheap nor tasty.
3 We can go on holiday either in July or in August.
4 Both the journey was long and boring.
5 It's or Jane's or Karen's birthday today. I can't
   remember which.
6 My brother has neither the energy nor the stamina to
   run a marathon.
7 Her aunt and her cousin came to visit both.
8 We can walk either or take the bus.
9 I have two children but neither of them look like me.
10 My parents love horses, and both of they ride every day.

◄ p.97

articles

basic rules: a / an / the, no article

> 1 My neighbour has just bought **a** dog. **The** dog is **an** Alsatian.   5 37 »)
> He got into **the** car and drove to **the** Town Hall.
> 2 **Men** are better at parking than **women**.
> I don't like **sport** or **classical music**.
> I stayed **at home last** weekend.

1 Use *a* or *an* when you mention somebody or something for the first time or say who or what somebody or something is. Use *the* when it's clear who or what somebody or something is (e.g. it has been mentioned before or it's unique).
2 Don't use an article to speak in general with plural and uncountable nouns, or in phrases like *at home | work, go home | to bed, next | last (week)*, etc.

institutions

> My father's **in hospital**.   5 38 »)
> They're building **a new hospital** in my town.
> He was sent **to prison** for two years.
> My grandmother used to work in **the prison** as a cleaner.

With words like *prison, church, school, hospital,* and *university,* don't use an article when you are thinking about the institution and the normal purpose it is used it for. If you are just thinking about the building, use *a* or *the*.

more rules: geographical names

> 1 **Tunisia** is in **North Africa**.   5 39 »)
> 2 **Selfridges**, one of London's biggest department stores, is in **Oxford Street**.
> 3 **Lake Victoria** and **Mount Kilimanjaro** are both in **Africa**.
> 4 **The River Danube** flows into **the Black Sea**.
> 5 **The National Gallery** and **the British Museum** are London tourist attractions.

We **don't normally use** *the* with:

1 most countries, continents, regions ending with the name of a country / continent, e.g. *North America, South East Asia,* islands, states, provinces, towns, and cities (exceptions: *The USA, the UK | United Kingdom, the Netherlands, the Czech Republic*).
2 roads, streets, parks, bridges, shops, and restaurants (exceptions: motorways and numbered roads, *the M6, the A25*).
3 individual mountains and lakes.

We **normally use** *the* with:

4 mountain ranges, rivers, seas, canals, deserts, and island groups.
5 the names of theatres, cinemas, hotels, galleries, and museums.

---

a (Circle) the correct article.

James bought **a** / *the* / (–) new suit at the weekend.

1 The weather was awful, so we stayed at *a | the | (–)* home.
2 *A | The | (–)* dishwasher we bought last week has stopped working already.
3 I love reading *a | the | (–)* historical novels.
4 Sarah had had an exhausting day, so she went to *a | the | (–)* bed early.
5 I saw a man walking with a woman in the park. *A | The | (–)* woman was crying.
6 The teachers are on strike, so the children aren't going to *a | the | (–)* school.
7 Turn left immediately after *a | the | (–)* church and go up the hill.
8 My neighbour's in *a | the | (–)* prison because he didn't pay his taxes.
9 People are complaining because the council have refused to build *a | the | (–)* new hospital.
10 Visitors will not be allowed to enter *a | the | (–)* hospital after 7 p.m.

b Complete with *the* or (–).

They're going to *the* USA to visit family.

1 _____ Sicily is the largest island in _____ Mediterranean.
2 Cairo is on _____ River Nile.
3 We didn't have time to visit _____ Louvre when we were in Paris.
4 _____ south west England is famous for its beautiful countryside and beaches.
5 _____ Mount Everest is in _____ Himalayas.
6 The largest inland lake is _____ Caspian Sea.
7 We stayed at _____ Palace Hotel while we were in Madrid.
8 *Romeo and Juliet* is on at _____ Globe Theatre.
9 Mont Blanc is the highest mountain in _____ Alps.
10 I've always wanted to visit _____ India.

◀ p.98

Illnesses and injuries

1 MINOR ILLNESSES AND CONDITIONS

a Match the sentences with the pictures.

She has / She's got...
- [ ] a cough /kɒf/
- [ ] a **head**ache /ˈhedeɪk/ (**ear**ache, **stom**ach ache, **tooth**ache, etc.)
- [1] a rash /ræʃ/
- [ ] a **tem**perature /ˈtemprətʃə/
- [ ] **sun**burn /ˈsʌnbɜːn/
- [ ] She's being sick / She's **vom**iting /ˈvɒmɪtɪŋ/.
- [ ] She's **snee**zing /ˈsniːzɪŋ/.
- [ ] Her **ank**le is **swol**len /ˈswəʊlən/.
- [ ] Her back hurts /hɜːts/ / Her back aches /eɪks/.
- [ ] Her **fin**ger is **bleed**ing /ˈbliːdɪŋ/.

b (1 29)) Listen and check.

c Match the illnesses and conditions with their symptoms or causes.

1 [B] He has **a sore throat** /sɔːθrəʊt/.
2 [ ] He has **diarrhoea** /daɪəˈrɪə/.
3 [ ] He **feels sick** /ˈfiːlz sik/.
4 [ ] He's **fainted** /ˈfeɪntɪd/.
5 [ ] He has a **blister** /ˈblɪstə/ on his foot.
6 [ ] He has **a cold** /ə kəʊld/.
7 [ ] He has **flu** /fluː/.
8 [ ] He feels **dizzy** /ˈdɪzi/.
9 [ ] He's **cut himself** /kʌt hɪmˈself/.

A He has a temperature and he aches all over.
B It hurts when he talks or swallows food.
C It's so hot in the room that he's lost consciousness.
D He's been to the toilet five times this morning.
E He feels that he's going to vomit.
F He's sneezing a lot and he has a cough.
G He feels that everything is spinning round.
H He's been walking in uncomfortable shoes.
I He's bleeding.

d (1 30)) Listen and check.

2 INJURIES AND MORE SERIOUS CONDITIONS

a Match the injuries with their causes or symptoms.

1 [C] He's **unconscious** /ʌnˈkɒnʃəs/.
2 [ ] He's had an **allergic** reaction /əˈlɜːdʒɪk/.
3 [ ] He's **twisted** his ankle /ˈtwɪstɪd/ / He's **sprained** his ankle /spreɪnd/.
4 [ ] He has **high** (low) **blood pressure** /ˈblʌd preʃə/.
5 [ ] He has **food poisoning** /ˈfuːd pɔɪzənɪŋ/.
6 [ ] He's **choking** /tʃəʊkɪŋ/.
7 [ ] He's **burnt** himself /bɜːnt/.

A He spilt some boiling water on himself.
B He fell badly and now it's swollen.
C He's breathing, but his eyes are closed and he can't hear or feel anything.
D It's 18 over 14 (or 180 over 140).
E He ate some prawns that were off.
F He was eating a steak and a piece got stuck in his throat.
G He was stung by a wasp and now he has a rash and has difficulty breathing.

> **Common treatments for...**
> **a cut** minor: put a plaster on it (*AmE* band aid) and antiseptic cream, major: have stitches
> **headaches** take painkillers
> **an infection** take antibiotics
> **a sprained ankle** put ice on it and bandage it
> **an allergic reaction** take antihistamine tablets or cream

b (1 31)) Listen and check.

3 PHRASAL VERBS CONNECTED WITH ILLNESS

a Match the **bold** phrasal verbs to their meanings.

Please **lie down** on the couch. I'm going to examine you.
I'd been standing for such a long time that I **passed out,** and when I **came round** I was lying on the floor.
It often takes a long time to **get over** flu.
A few minutes after drinking the liquid I had to run to the bathroom to **throw up**.

1 _____ faint
2 _____ put your body in a horizontal position
3 _____ vomit, be sick
4 _____ get better / recover from sth
5 _____ become conscious again

b (1 32)) Listen and check.

◄ p.14

Clothes and fashion

1 DESCRIBING CLOTHES

a Match the adjectives and pictures.

Fit

2 loose /luːs/

1 tight /taɪt/

Style

6 hooded /'hʊdɪd/

4 long sleeved /lɒŋ sliːvd/ (*also* short sleeved)

3 sleeveless /'sliːvləs/

5 V-neck /'viː nek/

Pattern

11 checked /tʃekt/

9 patterned /'pætənd/

7 plain /pleɪn/

10 spotted /'spɒtɪd/

8 striped /straɪpt/

b ⓵46)) Listen and check.

c Match the phrases and pictures.

Materials

4 a cotton vest /ə 'kɒtn vest/

9 a denim waistcoat /ə 'denɪm 'weɪskəʊt/

5 a fur collar /ə fɜː 'kɒlə/

3 a lace top /ə leɪs tɒp/

1 a linen suit /ə 'lɪnɪn suːt/

7 a lycra swimsuit /ə 'laɪkrə 'swɪmsuːt/

8 a silk scarf /ə sɪlk skɑːf/

6 a velvet bow tie /ə 'velvɪt bəʊ 'taɪ/

2 a wool(len) cardigan /ə 'wʊl(ən) 'kɑːdɪgən/

11 leather sandals /'leðə 'sændlz/

10 suede boots /sweɪd buːts/

d ⓵47)) Listen and check.

> 🔍 **wear and dress**
> Be careful with the difference between *wear* and *dress*. Compare:
> *The English don't **dress** very stylishly. She usually **dresses** in black.*
> *I usually **wear** a skirt and jacket to work. She always **wears** black clothes.*

2 ADJECTIVES TO DESCRIBE THE WAY PEOPLE DRESS

> 🔍 **trendy, stylish, and fashionable**
> *Fashionable* is a general adjective, and means following a style that is popular at a particular time. *Trendy* is very similar, but is more informal. *Stylish* means fashionable and attractive.

a Complete the sentences with an adjective.

> fashionable /'fæʃnəbl/ old-fashioned /əʊld 'fæʃənd/
> scruffy /'skrʌfi/ smart /smɑːt/ stylish /'staɪlɪʃ/
> trendy /'trendi/

1 Long skirts are really *fashionable* now.

2 She's very ~~trendy~~. She always wears the latest fashions.

3 The Italians have a reputation for being very ~~stylish~~ – they wear fashionable and attractive clothes.

4 He looks really ~~scruffy~~. His clothes are old and a bit dirty.

5 Jane looked very ~~stylish~~ smart in her new suit. She wanted to make a good impression.

6 That tie's a bit ~~old-fashioned~~! Is it your dad's?

b ⓵48)) Listen and check.

3 VERB PHRASES

a Match the sentences.

1 C I'm going to **dress up** tonight.

2 ☐ Please **hang up** your coat.

3 ☐ These jeans don't **fit** me.

4 ☐ That skirt really **suits** you.

5 ☐ Your bag **matches** your shoes.

6 ☐ I need to **get changed**.

7 ☐ Hurry up and **get undressed**.

8 ☐ Get up and **get dressed**.

9 ☐ That tie doesn't really **go with** your shirt.

A Don't leave it on the chair.

B I've just spilt coffee on my shirt.

C I'm going to a party.

D They don't look good together.

E It's bath time.

F They're too small.

G They're almost the same colour.

H You look great in it.

I Breakfast is on the table.

b ⓵49)) Listen and check.

◄ p.20

Air travel

1 AT THE AIRPORT

a Match the words and definitions.

1 [A] **Airport terminal**   6 [B] **Departures board**
2 [D] **Bag(gage) drop off**   7 [G] **Gate**
3 [I] **Baggage reclaim**   8 [H] **Runway**
4 [C] **Check-in desk**   9 [E] **Security** E
5 [J] **Customs** J   10 [F] **VIP lounge**

A a building at an airport divided into **Arrivals** and **Departures** (**domestic** and **international flights**)

B an electronic display showing **flight times** and if the flight is **on time**, **boarding**, **closed**, or **delayed**

C where you give in any checked-in **luggage (**bags, cases, etc.) and are given a **boarding pass**

D where you take your luggage to check it in if you already have your boarding pass

E where they check that you are not trying to take prohibited items (e.g. **liquids** or **sharp objects**) onto the plane, by **scanning** your **hand luggage**, and making you walk through a metal detector

F where passengers who are travelling **business** or **first class** can wait for their flight

G where you show your boarding pass and ID and **board** your flight

H where planes **take off** and **land**

I where you **collect** your luggage on arrival, and there are usually **trolleys** for carrying heavy cases

J where your luggage may be **checked** to see if you are bringing **illegal goods** into the country

b (2 3)) Listen and check.

2 ON BOARD

a Complete the text with the words in the list.

aisle /aɪl/   cabin crew /ˈkæbɪn kruː/   seat belts /ˈsiːt belts/
connecting flight /kəˈnektɪŋ flaɪt/   turbulence /ˈtɜːbjələns/
direct flights /dəˈrekt flaɪts/   jet lag /ˈdʒet læg/
long-haul flights /lɒŋ hɔːl flaɪts/

I often fly to Chile on business. I always choose an ¹_aisle_ seat, so that I can get up and walk around more easily. Sometimes there is ²_turbulence_ when the plane flies over the Andes, which I don't enjoy, and the ³_cabin crew_ tell the passengers to put their ⁴_seat belts_ on. There aren't any ⁵_direct flights_ to Chile from London, so I usually have to get a ⁶_connecting flight_ in Madrid. Whenever I take ⁷_long-haul flights_ I always suffer from ⁸_jet lag_ because of the time difference and I feel tired for several days.

b (2 4)) Listen and check.

3 TRAVEL, TRIP, OR JOURNEY?

a Complete the sentences with *travel* (verb or noun), *trip*, or *journey*.

1 We're going on a five-day _trip_ to the mountains.
2 **A** Did you have a good _journey_ here?
   B No, my flight was delayed for six hours.
3 Do you have to _travel_ much in your job?
4 Have a good _trip_. See you when you get back.

b (2 5)) Listen and check.

c What are the differences between the three words?

4 PHRASAL VERBS RELATED TO AIR TRAVEL

a Complete the sentences with a phrasal verb from the list in the past tense.

check in   ~~drop off~~   fill in   get off   get on   pick up
take off

1 My husband _dropped_ me _off_ at the airport two hours before the flight.
2 I _checked in_ online the day before I was going to fly.
3 As soon as I _got on_ the plane I sat down in the first empty seat.
4 The plane _took off_ late because of the bad weather.
5 I _filled in_ the immigration form for the US, which the cabin crew gave me shortly before landing.
6 When I _got off_ the plane I felt exhausted after the long flight.
7 When I _picked up_ my luggage at baggage reclaim I bumped into an old friend who had been on the same flight.

b (2 6)) Listen and check.

◀ p.24

Adverbs and adverbial phrases

1 CONFUSING ADVERBS AND ADVERBIAL PHRASES

a Match each pair of adverbs with a pair of sentences. Then decide which adverb goes where and write it in the adverb column.

- **5** at the **moment** / **actually**
- **4** **especially** / **specially**
- **8** **ever** / **even**
- **1** **hard** / **hardly**
- **3** in the **end** / at the **end**
- **2** **late** / **lately**
- **6** **near** / **nearly**
- **7** **still** / **yet**

1 He trains very ____ – at least three hours a day.
  It's incredibly foggy. I can ____ see anything.
2 I hate it when people arrive ____ for meetings.
  I haven't heard from Mike ____. He must be very busy.
3 ____ of a film I always stay and watch the credits roll.
  I didn't want to go, but ____ they persuaded me.
4 I love most kinds of music, but ____ jazz.
  My wedding dress was ____ made for me by a dressmaker.
5 She looks younger than me, but ____ she's two years older.
  ____ they're renting a flat, but they're hoping to buy one soon.
6 I've ____ finished my book. I'm on the last chapter.
  Excuse me, is there a bank ____ here?
7 Have you found a job ____ ?
  He's 35, but he ____ lives with his parents.
8 Have you ____ been to the USA?
  I've been all over the USA – I've ____ been to Alaska!

Adverbs

hard
hardly
late
lately
At the end
in the end
especially
specially
actually
at the moment
nearly
near
yet
still
ever
even

b **2 15**)) Listen and check.

2 COMMENT ADVERBS

a Read the sentences. Then match the **bold** adverbs with definitions 1–8.

✓ I thought the job was going to be difficult, but **in fact** it's quite easy.

✓ It took us over five hours to get there, but **eventually** we were able to relax /ɪˈventʃuəli/.

✓ **Ideally** we would go to Australia if we could afford it /aɪˈdiːəli/.

✓ **Basically** it's quite a simple idea /ˈbeɪsɪkli/.

✓ I thought they'd broken up, but **apparently** they're back together again /əˈpærəntli/.

✓ …so you can see it was a really awful weekend. **Anyway**, let's forget about it and talk about something else /ˈeniweɪ/.

✓ She's only 14, so **obviously** she can't stay at home on her own /ˈɒbviəsli/…

✓ She's been ill for weeks, but **gradually** she's beginning to feel better /ˈɡrædʒuəli/.

1 _ideally_ — in a perfect world
2 _in fact_ — the truth is; actually (used to emphasize something, especially the opposite of what was previously said)
3 _Basically_ — in the most important ways
4 _obviously_ — clearly (used to give information you expect other people to know or agree with)
5 _gradually_ — little by little
6 _apparently_ — according to what you have heard or read
7 _anyway_ — in any case (used to change or finish a conversation)
8 _eventually_ — in the end; after a series of events or difficulties

b **2 16**)) Listen and check.

◀ p.29

Weather

1 WHAT'S THE WEATHER LIKE?

a Put the words or phrases in the right place in the chart.

below zero /bɪ'ləʊ 'zɪərəʊ/   boiling /'bɔɪlɪŋ/   breeze /briːz/   chilly /'tʃɪli/   cool /kuːl/   damp /dæmp/   drizzling /'drɪzlɪŋ/
freezing /'friːzɪŋ/   humid /'hjuːmɪd/   mild /maɪld/   pouring /'pɔːrɪŋ/ (with rain)   showers /'ʃaʊəz/   warm /wɔːm/

1 It's *cool* . (quite cold) 2 It's _freezing_ (unpleasantly cold)	5 It's _mild_ . (pleasant and not cold) 6 It's _warm_ . (a pleasantly high temperature)	8 It's _humid_ . (warm and wet but not raining) 9 It's _damp_ . (slightly wet) 10 It's _drizzling_ . (raining lightly)	13 There's a _breeze_ . (a light wind)
It's cold.	It's hot.	It's raining / wet.	It's windy.
3 It's _chilly_ . (very cold) 4 It's _below zero_ . (−10°)	7 It's _boiling_ / It's scorching. (unpleasantly hot)	11 There are _showers_ (raining intermittently) 12 It's _pouring_ . (raining a lot)	

b Complete the sentences with *fog*, *mist*, and *smog*.

When the weather's foggy or misty, or there's smog, it is difficult to see.
1 _fog_ isn't usually very thick, and often occurs in the mountains or near the sea.
2 _mist_ is thicker, and can be found in towns and in the country.
3 _smog_ is caused by pollution and usually occurs in big cities.

c (2 31))) Listen and check **a** and **b**.

2 EXTREME WEATHER

a Match the words and definitions.

blizzard /'blɪzəd/   drought /draʊt/   flood /flʌd/
hail /heɪl/   heatwave /'hiːtweɪv/   hurricane /'hʌrɪkən/
lightning /'laɪtnɪŋ/   monsoon /mɒn'suːn/   thunder /'θʌndə/

1 *heatwave* n a period of unusually hot weather
2 _drought_ n a long, usually hot, dry period when there is little or no rain
3 _hail_ n and v small balls of ice that fall like rain
4 _lightning_ n a flash of very bright light in the sky caused by electricity
5 _thunder_ n and v the loud noise that you hear during a storm
6 _blizzard_ n a snow storm with very strong winds
7 _flood_ v and n when everything becomes covered with water
8 _hurricane_ n a violent storm with very strong winds (also *cyclone*, *tornado*)
9 _monsoon_ n the season when it rains a lot in southern Asia

b (2 32))) Listen and check.

3 ADJECTIVES TO DESCRIBE WEATHER

a Complete the weather forecast with these adjectives.

bright /braɪt/   changeable /'tʃeɪndʒəbl/   clear /klɪə/
heavy /'hevi/   icy /'aɪsi/   settled /'setld/ (= not likely to change)
strong /strɒŋ/   sunny /'sʌni/   thick /θɪk/

In the north of England and Scotland it will be very cold, with 1*strong* winds and 2 _heavy_ rain. There will also be 3 _thick_ fog in the hills and near the coast, though it should clear by midday. Driving will be dangerous as the roads will be 4 _icy_ . However, the south of England and the Midlands will have 5 _clear_ skies and it will be 6 _bright_ and sunny, though the temperature will still be quite low. Over the next few days the weather will be 7 _changeable_ , with some showers, but occasional 8 _sunny_ periods. It should become more 9 _clear_ over the weekend.

b (2 33))) Listen and check.

◀ p.36

Feelings

1 ADJECTIVES

a Match the feelings and the situations.

1 J 'I'm very **offended** /əˈfendɪd/.'
2 F 'I feel a bit **homesick** /ˈhəʊmsɪk/.'
3 E 'I'm a bit **disappointed** /dɪsəˈpɔɪntɪd/.'
4 G 'I'm very **lonely** /ˈləʊnli/.'
5 I 'I'm incredibly **proud** /praʊd/.'
6 H 'I'm really **nervous** /ˈnɜːvəs/.'
7 C 'I'm very **grateful** /ˈɡreɪtfl/.'
8 A 'I'm **shocked** /ʃɒkt/.'
9 D 'I'm so **relieved** /rɪˈliːvd/.'
10 B 'I feel a bit **guilty** /ˈɡɪlti/.'

A You discover that you have a brother you had never known about.
B You haven't visited your grandparents for a long time.
C A stranger gives you a lot of help with a problem.
D You are abroad and you think someone has stolen your passport, but then you find it.
E You don't get a job you were hoping to get.
F You go to study abroad and you're missing your family and friends.
G You move to a new town and don't have any friends.
H You are going to talk in public for the first time.
I Someone in your family wins an important prize.
J A friend doesn't invite you to his wedding.

> 🔍 **fed up** and **upset**
>
> *fed up* = bored or frustrated and unhappy (especially with a situation which has gone on too long)
> *I'm really <u>fed up</u> with my job. I think I'm going to quit.*
> *upset* = unhappy when something bad happens
> *Kate was terribly upset when her dog disappeared.*

b 🔊 (3 2)) Listen and check.

2 STRONG ADJECTIVES

a Match the strong adjectives describing feelings with their definitions.

√astonished /əˈstɒnɪʃt/   bewildered /bɪˈwɪldəd/   √delighted /dɪˈlaɪtɪd/
√desperate /ˈdespərət/   √devastated /ˈdevəsteɪtɪd/   √horrified /ˈhɒrɪfaɪd/
√overwhelmed /əʊvəˈwelmd/   √stunned /stʌnd/   thrilled /θrɪld/

1 *stunned* very surprised and unable to move or react
2 devastated extremely upset
3 delighted incredibly pleased
4 thrilled very excited
5 bewildered (*amazed*) / very surprised
6 desperate with little hope, and ready to do anything to improve the situation
7 overwhelmed feeling such strong emotions that you don't know how to react
8 astonished extremely confused
9 horrified extremely shocked or disgusted

> 🔍 **Modifiers with strong adjectives**
>
> Remember you <u>can't</u> use *a bit*, *quite*, or *very* with these adjectives. NOT *I was very astonished*. If you want to use an intensifier, use *really / absolutely / totally / completely*.

b (3 3)) Listen and check.

3 INFORMAL OR SLANG WORDS AND EXPRESSIONS

a Look at the highlighted words and phrases and try to work out their meaning.

1 B I was scared stiff when I heard the bedroom door opening /skeəd stɪf/.
2 A You look a bit down. What's the problem?
3 D I'm absolutely shattered. I want to relax and put my feet up /ˈʃætəd/.
4 F I was completely gobsmacked when I heard that Tina was getting married /ˈɡɒbsmækt/!
5 E I'm sick of hearing you complain about your job.
6 C When he missed that penalty I was absolutely gutted /ˈɡʌtɪd/.

b Match the words and phrases to the feelings.

A sad or depressed   D exhausted
B terrified   E fed up or irritated
C very disappointed   F astonished

c (3 4)) Listen and check.

◀ *p.45*

Verbs often confused

a Complete the **verbs** column with the correct verb in the right form.

	verbs
argue / discuss	
1 I need to ▢ the problem with my boss.	_____ (= talk about sth)
2 I often ▢ with my parents about doing housework.	_____ (= speak angrily to sb)
notice / realize	
3 I didn't ▢ you were so unhappy.	_____ (= understand fully, become aware of sth)
4 I didn't ▢ that Karen had changed her hair colour.	_____ (= see, observe)
avoid / prevent	
5 Jack always tries to ▢ arguing with me.	_____ (= try not to do something)
6 My dad can't ▢ me from seeing my friends.	_____ (= stop)
look / seem	
7 I've spoken to her husband twice and he ▢ very nice.	_____ (= general impression)
8 Carol doesn't ▢ very well. I think she's working too hard.	_____ (= physical appearance)
mind / matter	
9 My parents don't ▢ if I stay out late.	_____ (= get annoyed or upset)
10 It doesn't ▢ if we're five minutes late.	_____ (= be a problem)
remember / remind	
11 Can you ▢ me to call my mum later?	_____ (= help sb to remember)
12 ▢ to turn off the lights before you go.	_____ (= not forget)
expect / wait	
13 I ▢ that Daniel will forget our anniversary. He always does.	_____ (= think that sth will happen)
14 We'll have to ▢ half an hour for the next train.	_____ (= stay where you are until something happens)
wish / hope	
15 I ▢ I was a bit taller!	_____ (= want sth to be true even if it is unlikely)
16 I ▢ that you can come on Friday. I haven't seen you for ages.	_____ (= want sth to happen)
beat / win	
17 Arsenal ▢ the match 5–2.	_____ (= be successful in a competition)
18 Arsenal ▢ Manchester United 5–2.	_____ (= defeat sb)
refuse / deny	
19 Tom always ▢ to discuss the problem.	_____ (= say you don't want to do sth)
20 Tom always ▢ that he has a problem.	_____ (= say that sth isn't true)
raise / rise	
21 The cost of living is going to ▢ again this month.	_____ (= go up)
22 It's hard not to ▢ your voice when you're arguing with someone.	_____ (= make sth go up)
lay (*past* laid) / lie (*past* lay)	
23 Last night I came home and ▢ on the sofa and went to sleep.	_____ (= put your body in a horizontal position)
24 I ▢ the baby on the bed and changed his nappy.	_____ (= put sth or sb in a horizontal position)
steal / rob	
25 The men had been planning to ▢ the bank.	_____ (= take sth from a person or place by threat or force)
26 If you leave your bike unlocked, somebody might ▢ it.	_____ (= take money or property that isn't yours)
advise / warn	
27 I think I should ▢ you that Liam doesn't always tell the truth.	_____ (= tell sb that sth unpleasant is about to happen)
28 My teachers are going to ▢ me what subjects to study next year.	_____ (= tell sb what you think they should do)

b **4 9))** Listen and check.

◀ p.67

The body

1 PARTS OF THE BODY AND ORGANS

a Match the words and pictures.

     <u>an</u>kle /ˈæŋkl/

 1   calf /kɑːf/ (*pl* calves)

     heel /hiːl/

     <u>el</u>bow /ˈelbəʊ/

     fist /fɪst/

     nails /neɪlz/

     palm /pɑːm/

     wrist /rɪst/

     <u>bott</u>om /ˈbɒtəm/

     chest /tʃest/

     hip /hɪp/

     thigh /θaɪ/

     waist /weɪst/

     brain /breɪn/

     heart /hɑːt/

     <u>kid</u>neys /ˈkɪdniz/

     <u>li</u>ver /ˈlɪvə/

     lungs /lʌŋz/

b **4 17**)) Listen and check.

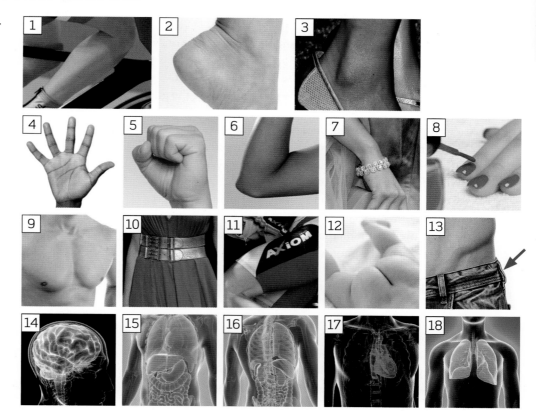

2 VERBS AND VERB PHRASES

a Complete the verb phrases with the parts of the body.

> arms   <u>eye</u>brows   hair (x2)   hand   hands
> head   <s>nails</s>   nose   <u>shoul</u>ders   teeth
> thumb   toes

1   **bite** your <u>*nails*</u>   /baɪt/

2   **blow** your _____ /bləʊ/

3   **brush** your _____ |
    brush your _____ /brʌʃ/

4   **comb** your _____ /kəʊm/

5   **fold** your _____ /fəʊld/

6   **hold** somebody's _____ /həʊld/

7   **touch** your _____ /tʌtʃ/

8   **suck** your _____ /sʌk/

9   **shake** _____ /ʃeɪk/

10   **shrug** your _____ /ʃrʌg/

11   **shake** your _____

12   **raise** your _____ /reɪz/

b **4 18**)) Listen and check.

c Read the sentences. Write the part of the body related to the **bold** verb.

1   He **winked** at me to show that he was only joking. *eye* _____
    /wɪŋkt/

2   The steak was tough and difficult to **chew**. _____ /tʃuː/

3   When we met, we were so happy we **hugged** each other.
    _____ /hʌgd/

4   Don't **scratch** the mosquito bite. You'll only make it worse.
    _____ /skrætʃ/

5   She **waved** goodbye sadly to her boyfriend as the train left the
    station. _____ /weɪvd/

6   Some women think a man should **kneel** down when he proposes
    marriage. _____ /niːl/

7   The teacher **frowned** when she saw all the mistakes I had made.
    _____ /fraʊnd/

8   The painting was so strange I **stared** at it for a long time.
    _____ /steəd/

9   She got out of bed, and **yawned** and **stretched**.
    _____ | _____ /jɔːnd/stretʃt/

10   If you don't know the word for something, just **point** at what you
    want. _____ /pɔɪnt/

d **4 19**)) Listen and check.

◀ p.70

Crime and punishment

1 CRIMES AND CRIMINALS

a Match the examples to the crimes in the chart.

A They took away a rich man's son and then asked for money for his safe return.

B She went to her ex-husband's house and shot him dead.

C Two passengers took control of the plane and made the pilot land in the desert.

D After the party, the man made the woman have sex against her will.

E We came home from holiday and found that our TV had gone.

F A teenager got into the Pentagon's computer system and downloaded some secret data.

G Someone tried to sell me some marijuana during a concert.

H When the border police searched his car, it was full of cigarettes.

I Someone threw paint on the statue in the park.

J He said he'd send the photos to a newspaper if the actress didn't pay him a lot of money.

K An armed man in a mask walked into a shop and shouted, 'Give me all the money in the till!'

L The company accountant was transferring money into his own bank account.

M The builder offered the mayor a free flat in return for giving his company permission to build new flats on a piece of green land.

N They left a bomb in the supermarket car park which exploded.

O Somebody stole my car last night from outside my house.

P A man held out a knife and made me give him my wallet.

Q A woman followed a pop singer everywhere he went, watching him and sending him constant messages on the internet.

	Crime	Criminal	Verb	
1	blackmail /ˈblækmeɪl/	blackmailer	blackmail	
2	bribery /ˈbraɪbəri/	–	bribe	
3	burglary /ˈbɜːɡləri/	burglar	break in / burgle	
4	drug dealing /drʌɡ ˈdiːlɪŋ/	drug dealer	sell drugs	
5	fraud /frɔːd/	fraudster	commit fraud	
6	hacking /ˈhækɪŋ/	hacker	hack (into)	
7	hijacking /ˈhaɪdʒækɪŋ/	hijacker	hijack	
8	kidnapping /ˈkɪdnæpɪŋ/	kidnapper	kidnap	A
9	mugging /ˈmʌɡɪŋ/	mugger	mug	
10	murder /ˈmɜːdə/	murderer	murder	
11	rape /reɪp/	rapist	rape	
12	robbery /ˈrɒbəri/	robber	rob	
13	smuggling /ˈsmʌɡlɪŋ/	smuggler	smuggle	
14	stalking /ˈstɔːkɪŋ/	stalker	stalk	
15	terrorism /ˈterərɪzəm/	terrorist	set off bombs, etc.	
16	theft /θeft/	thief	steal	
17	vandalism /ˈvændəlɪzəm/	vandal	vandalize	

b (4 32)》 Listen and check.

2 WHAT HAPPENS TO A CRIMINAL

a Complete the sentences with the words in the list.

The crime

arrested /əˈrestɪd/   questioned /ˈkwestʃənd/
charged /tʃɑːdʒd/   committed /kəˈmɪtɪd/
investigated /ɪnˈvestɪɡeɪtɪd/   caught /kɔːt/

1 Carl and Adam *committed* a crime. They robbed a large supermarket.

2 The police _____ the crime.

3 Carl and Adam were _____ driving to the airport in a stolen car.

4 They were _____ and taken to a police station.

5 The police _____ them for ten hours.

6 Finally they were _____ with (= officially accused of) armed robbery.

The trial

accused /əˈkjuːzd/   acquitted /əˈkwɪtɪd/
court /kɔːt/   evidence /ˈevɪdəns/
guilty (opposite *innocent*) /ˈɡɪlti/
judge /dʒʌdʒ/   jury /ˈdʒʊəri/   proof /pruːf/
punishment /ˈpʌnɪʃmənt/   sentenced /ˈsentənst/
verdict /ˈvɜːdɪkt/   witnesses /ˈwɪtnəsɪz/

7 Two months later, Carl and Adam appeared in _____.

8 They were _____ of armed robbery and car theft.

9 _____ told the court what they had seen or knew.

10 The _____, (of 12 people) looked at and heard all the _____.

11 After two days the jury reached their _____.

12 Carl was found_____. His fingerprints were on the gun used in the robbery.

13 The _____ decided what Carl's _____ should be.

14 He _____ him to ten years in prison (jail).

15 There was no _____ that Adam had committed the crime.

16 He was _____ and allowed to go free.

b (4 33)》 Listen and check.

◀ p.75

The media

1 JOURNALISTS AND PEOPLE IN THE MEDIA

a Match the words and definitions.

agony aunt /ˈægəni ɑːnt/   commentator /ˈkɒmənteɪtə/   critic /ˈkrɪtɪk/   editor /ˈedɪtə/   freelance journalist /ˈfriːlɑːns ˈdʒɜːnəlɪst/
newsreader /ˈnjuːzriːdə/   paparazzi (pl) /pæpəˈrætsi/   presenter /prɪˈzentə/   reporter /rɪˈpɔːtə/

1   _critic_____ a person who writes (a **review**) about the good / bad qualities of books, concerts, theatre, films, etc.
2   _____ a person who describes a sports event while it's happening on TV or radio
3   _____ a person who collects and reports news for newspapers, radio, or TV
4   _____ a person in charge of a newspaper or magazine, or part of one, and decides what should be in it
5   _____ a person who introduces the different sections of a radio or TV programme
6   _____ a person who writes articles for different papers and is not employed by any one paper
7   _____ a person who reads the news on TV or radio
8   _____ photographers who follow famous people around to get photos of them to sell to newspapers and magazines
9   _____ a person who writes in a newspaper or magazine giving advice to people in reply to their letters

b **4 43))** Listen and check.

2 ADJECTIVES TO DESCRIBE THE MEDIA

a Match the sentences.

1 ☐ The reporting in the paper was very **sensational** /senˈseɪʃənl/.
2 ☐ The news on Channel 12 is really **biased** /ˈbaɪəst/.
3 ☐ I think *The Observer* is the most **objective** /əbˈdʒektɪv/ of the Sunday papers.
4 ☐ The film review was quite **accurate** /ˈækjərət/.
5 ☐ I think the report was **censored** /ˈsensəd/.

A It said the plot was poor but the acting good, which was true.
B It bases its stories just on facts, not on feelings or beliefs.
C The newspaper wasn't allowed to publish all the details.
D It made the story seem more shocking than it really was.
E You can't believe anything you hear on it. It's obvious what political party they favour!

b **4 44))** Listen and check.

3 THE LANGUAGE OF HEADLINES

> 🔍 **The language of headlines**
> Newspaper headlines, especially in *tabloids, often use short snappy words. These words use up less space and are more emotive, which helps to sell newspapers.
> *newspapers with smaller pages that print short articles with lots of photos, often about famous people

a Match the highlighted 'headline phrases' with their meaning.

1   A Famous actress in restaurant bill **row**
2   ☐ United boss **to quit** after shock cup defeat
3   ☐ Prince **to wed** 18-year-old TV soap star
4   ☐ Prime minister **backs** his Chancellor in latest scandal
5   ☐ Tarantino **tipped** to win Best Director
6   ☐ Thousands of jobs **axed** by UK firms
7   ☐ Stock market **hit** by oil fears
8   ☐ Police **quiz** witness in murder trial
9   ☐ Astronaut **bids** to be first man on Mars
10 ☐ Ministers **clash** over new car tax proposal
11 ☐ Bayern Munich boss **vows** to avenge defeat
12 ☐ Footballer and wife **split** over affair with cleaner

A argument   G is going to marry
B have been cut   H promises
C question, interrogate I is predicted
D is going to attempt   J disagree
E is going to leave   K has been badly affected
F separate   L supports

b **4 45))** Listen and check.

◀ p.81

Business

1 VERBS AND EXPRESSIONS

a Complete the sentences with a verb from the list in the right form (present simple, past simple, or past participle).

> become /bɪ'kʌm/   close down /kləʊz daʊn/   drop /drɒp/
> grows /grəʊz/   expand /ɪk'spænd/   export /ɪk'spɔːt/
> import /ɪm'pɔːt/   launch /lɔːntʃ/   manufacture /ˌmænjʊ'fæktʃə/
> market /'mɑːkɪt/   merge /mɜːdʒ/   produce /prə'djuːs/
> set up /set ʌp/   take over /teɪk 'əʊvə/

1   Although GAP stands for Genuine American Product, most of its clothes are *manufactured* in Asia.

2   In 1989 Pepsi-Cola _____ **a new product** called *Pepsi A.M.*, which was aimed at the 'breakfast cola drinker'. It was an immediate flop.

3   The Spanish airline Iberia _____ **with** British Airways in 2011.

4   Apple is considered one of the best companies in the world for the way they _____ **their products**.

5   *Prosciutto* is a kind of Italian ham. Two of the best known kinds are San Daniele and Parma, which are _____ in the Friuli and Emilia regions of Italy, and are _____ all over the world.

6   The Royal Bank of Scotland _____ NatWest Bank in 2000, even though it was in fact a smaller rival.

7   The supermarket chain Tesco _____ **the market leader** in 1995, and is still the UK's biggest-selling chain.

8   Zara shops were opened in Spain in 1975, but the company soon _____ internationally.

9   Nowadays it is quite a risk to _____ **a new business**. In the UK, 20% of businesses fail in their first year.

10 The cost of living in Iceland is so high because so many food products have to be _____.

11 During a boom period, the economy _____ quickly and living standards improve.

12 During a recession, many companies _____ and living standards _____.

b **5 7**)) Listen and check.

c *Do* or *make*? Put the phrases in the right column.

> business (with) /'bɪznəs/   a deal /diːl/ (= business agreement)
> a decision /dɪ'sɪʒn/   a job /dʒɒb/   a loss (opposite *profit*) /lɒs/
> market research /ˌmɑːkɪt rɪ'sɜːtʃ/   money /'mʌni/
> somebody redundant /rɪ'dʌndənt/ (= sack somebody because he / she isn't needed any more)   well / badly

do	make
business (with)	

d **5 8**)) Listen and check.

2 ORGANIZATIONS AND PEOPLE

a **Organizations** Match the words and definitions.

> a business /'bɪznəs/ (or firm / company)
> a branch /brɑːntʃ/   a chain /tʃeɪn/   head office /hed 'ɒfɪs/
> a multinational /mʌltɪ'næʃnəl/

1   *a chain* _____ a group of shops, hotels, etc. owned by the same person or company

2   _____ an organization which produces or sells goods or provides a service

3   _____ a company that has offices or factories in many countries

4   _____ the main office of a company

5   _____ an office or shop that is part of a larger organization, e.g. a bank

b **People** Match the words and definitions.

> the CEO /siː iː 'əʊ/ (= chief executive officer)
> a client /'klaɪənt/   a colleague /'kɒliːg/   a customer /'kʌstəmə/
> a manager /'mænɪdʒə/   the owner /'əʊnə/   the staff /stɑːf/

1   _____ the group of people who work for an organization

2   _____ someone who buys goods or services, for example from a shop or restaurant

3   _____ someone who receives a service from a professional person, for example from a lawyer

4   _____ a person who works with you

5   _____ the person with the highest rank in a company

6   _____ the person who owns a business

7   _____ the person in charge of part of an organization, for example a shop or a branch

c **5 9**)) Listen and check your answers to **a** and **b**.

◀ p.87

Word building

1 PREFIXES AND SUFFIXES WHICH ADD MEANING

a Match the **bold** prefixes in sentences 1–11 to their meanings A–K.

1 G Mumbai is a very **over**crowded city.
2 ☐ Tokyo is one of 20 **mega**cities.
3 ☐ This part of the city is very poor and **under**developed.
4 ☐ London is a very **multi**cultural city, with many different races and religions.
5 ☐ The quickest way to get around New York is on the **sub**way.
6 ☐ Montreal is probably the most **bi**lingual city in the world – most inhabitants speak English and French.
7 ☐ If you want to avoid the traffic jams in Bangkok, get the **mono**rail.
8 ☐ The **auto**pilot was switched on after the plane had taken off.
9 ☐ Vandalism, especially breaking public property, is very **anti**social behaviour.
10 ☐ I **mis**understood the directions that man gave me, and now I'm completely lost.
11 ☐ He's doing a **post**graduate degree in aeronautical engineering.

A against
B many
C big
D not enough
E one
F by (it)self
G ~~too much~~
H two
I after
J under
K wrongly

b 🔊 (5 12)) Listen and check.

c Match the **bold** suffixes to their meaning.

1 ☐ There are a lot of home**less** people in this city. The situation is hope**less**.
2 ☐ Be care**ful** how you drive! The instructions were very use**ful**.
3 ☐ The police usually wear bullet**proof** vests. My watch is water**proof**.
4 ☐ Their new laptops are completely unbreak**able**. I don't think the tap water here is drink**able**.

A with   B can be done
C resistant to   D without

d 🔊 (5 13)) Listen and check.

2 NOUNS FORMED WITH SUFFIXES

> 🔍 **Noun suffixes**
> **Common endings for nouns made from verbs:**
> **-ion / -(a)tion**   <u>alienate – alienation</u>
> **-ment**   <u>employ – employment</u>
> **Common endings for nouns made from adjectives:**
> **-ness**   <u>lonely – loneliness</u>
> **-ence / -ance**   <u>violent – violence</u>
> **Common endings for abstract nouns made from nouns:**
> **-hood**   <u>neighbour – neighbourhood</u>
> **-ism**   <u>vandal – vandalism</u>

a Make nouns from the words in the list and put them in the right column.

> absent /ˈæbsənt/ ~~accommodate~~ /əˈkɒmədeɪt/ alcohol /ˈælkəhɒl/
> brother /ˈbrʌðə/ child /tʃaɪld/ cold /kəʊld/ convenient /kənˈviːniənt/
> distant /ˈdɪstənt/ entertain /entəˈteɪn/ excite /ɪkˈsaɪt/ friendly /ˈfrendli/
> govern /ˈgʌvn/ ignorant /ˈɪɡnərənt/ improve /ɪmˈpruːv/ intend /ɪnˈtend/
> pollute /pəˈluːt/ race /reɪs/ reduce /rɪˈdjuːs/ ugly /ˈʌɡli/ weak /wiːk/

-ion / -(a)tion	-ment	-ness	-ence / -ance	-ism	-hood
accommodation					

b 🔊 (5 14)) Listen and check.

3 NOUNS WHICH ARE DIFFERENT WORDS

> 🔍 **Noun formation with spelling or word change**
> Some nouns made from verbs or adjectives are completely different words, e.g. *choose – choice, poor – <u>poverty</u>*.

a Write the verb or adjective for the following **nouns**.

			Noun
1	_____	verb	loss /lɒs/
2	_____	verb	death /deθ/
3	_____	verb	success /səkˈses/
4	_____	verb	thought /θɔːt/
5	_____	verb	belief /bɪˈliːf/
6	_____	adj	heat /hiːt/
7	_____	adj	strength /streŋθ/
8	_____	adj	hunger /ˈhʌŋɡə/
9	_____	adj	height /haɪt/
10	_____	adj	length /leŋθ/

b 🔊 (5 15)) Listen and check.

◀ p.89

Appendix

Verb patterns: verbs followed by the gerund or infinitive

Gerund

admit	In court the accused admitted (to) stealing the documents.
avoid	I always try to avoid driving in the rush hour.
be worth	It isn't worth going to the exhibition. It's really boring.
can't help	We can't help laughing when my dad tries to speak French. His accent is awful!
can't stand	I can't stand talking to people who only talk about themselves.
carry on*	We carried on chatting until about 2.00 in the morning.
deny	Miriam denied killing her husband but the jury didn't believe her.
enjoy	I used to enjoy flying, but now I don't.
fancy	Do you fancy seeing a film this evening?
feel like	I don't feel like going out tonight.
finish	Have you finished writing the report yet?
give up*	Karen has given up eating meat, but she still eats fish.
keep (on)	I keep (on) telling my husband to lose some weight, but he just won't listen.
look forward to	We are really looking forward to seeing you again.
imagine	I can't imagine living in the country. I think I would get bored after a week.
involve	My boyfriend's job involves travelling at least once a month.
mind	I don't mind doing housework. I find it quite relaxing.
miss	Does your father miss working now that he has retired?
postpone	We'll have to postpone going to the beach until the weather improves.
practise	The more you practise speaking English the more fluent you'll get.
recommend	I recommend doing a double-decker bus tour as the best way to see London.
regret	I regret not travelling more before I got my first job.
risk	If were you, I wouldn't risk walking through the park at night.
spend	I spent half an hour looking for my glasses this morning.
stop	Once I open a box of chocolates, I can't stop eating them.
suggest	A friend of mine suggested visiting London in the autumn.

* All phrasal verbs which are followed by another verb, e.g. *carry on*, *give up*, etc. are followed by the gerund.

Infinitive (with *to*)

afford	I can't afford to go on holiday this summer.
agree	I have agreed to pay David back the money he lent me next week.
appear	The results appear to support the scientist's theory.
arrange	I've arranged to meet Sally outside the restaurant.
be able	I won't be able to work for two weeks after the operation.
can't wait	We can't wait to see your new flat – it sounds fantastic.
choose	I chose to study abroad for a year, and it's the best thing I've ever done.
decide	They've decided to call off the wedding.
deserve	Kim deserves to get the job. She's a very strong candidate.
expect	We're expecting to get our exam results on Friday.
happen	Tom happened to be at Alan's when I called in, so I invited him to our party as well.
help*	The organization I work for helps young people to find work abroad.
hesitate	Don't hesitate to ask a member of staff if you need anything.
hope	I'm hoping to set up my own company if I can get a bank loan.
learn	I wish I had learnt to play the guitar when I was younger.
make	When I was at school, we were made to wear a uniform. It was awful.
manage	Did you manage to get to the airport in time?
offer	Lucy has offered to give me a lift to the station.
plan	We're planning to have a big party to celebrate.
pretend	I pretended to be enthusiastic, but really I didn't like the idea at all.
promise	Sarah always promises to help me in the kitchen, but she never does.
refuse	My neighbour refused to turn down the music and I had to call the police.
seem	Something seems to be wrong with the washing machine.
teach	Jack's father taught him to drive when he was 17.
tend	My boss tends to lose her temper when she's feeling stressed.
threaten	The teacher threatened to call my parents and tell them what I had done.
want	The police want to interview anyone who witnessed the crime.
would like	Would you like to try the dress on? The changing rooms are over there.

* *help* can be followed by the infinitive with or without *to*.
The organization I work for helps young people (to) find work abroad.

Infinitive (without *to*)

can	Can you help me carry these suitcases?
may	There's a lot of traffic today, so we may be a bit late.
might	It might rain tomorrow, so please bring an umbrella or a raincoat.
must	I must remember to phone Harry – it's his birthday today.
should	Should we book a table for tomorrow night? It's a very popular restaurant.
had better	You'd better leave now if you want to catch that train.
would rather	You look tired. Would you rather stay in this evening and watch a film?
make	Sue makes her two teenagers do the washing-up every evening after dinner.
let	Let me pay for coffee – it must be my turn.

◄ *p.142*

Irregular verbs

Infinitive	Past simple	Past participle
be /bi/	was / were /wɒz/ /wɜː/	been /biːn/
beat /biːt/	beat	beaten /ˈbiːtn/
become /bɪˈkʌm/	became /bɪˈkeɪm/	become
begin /bɪˈgɪn/	began /bɪˈgæn/	begun /bɪˈgʌn/
bite /baɪt/	bit /bɪt/	bitten /ˈbɪtn/
break /breɪk/	broke /brəʊk/	broken /ˈbrəʊkən/
bring /brɪŋ/	brought /brɔːt/	brought
build /bɪld/	built /bɪlt/	built
burn /bɜːn/	burnt /bɜːnt/ (burned) /bɜːnd/	burnt (burned)
buy /baɪ/	bought /bɔːt/	bought
can /kæn/	could /kʊd/	–
catch /kætʃ/	caught /kɔːt/	caught
choose /tʃuːz/	chose /tʃəʊz/	chosen /ˈtʃəʊzn/
come /kʌm/	came /keɪm/	come
cost /kɒst/	cost	cost
cut /kʌt/	cut	cut
deal /diːl/	dealt /delt/	dealt
do /duː/	did /dɪd/	done /dʌn/
draw /drɔː/	drew /druː/	drawn /drɔːn/
dream /driːm/	dreamt /dremt/ (dreamed /driːmd/)	dreamt (dreamed)
drink /drɪŋk/	drank /dræŋk/	drunk /drʌŋk/
drive /draɪv/	drove /drəʊv/	driven /ˈdrɪvn/
eat /iːt/	ate /eɪt/	eaten /ˈiːtn/
fall /fɔːl/	fell /fel/	fallen /ˈfɔːlən/
feel /fiːl/	felt /felt/	felt
find /faɪnd/	found /faʊnd/	found
fly /flaɪ/	flew /fluː/	flown /fləʊn/
forget /fəˈget/	forgot /fəˈgɒt/	forgotten /fəˈgɒtn/
get /get/	got /gɒt/	got
give /gɪv/	gave /geɪv/	given /ˈgɪvn/
go /gəʊ/	went /went/	gone /gɒn/
grow /grəʊ/	grew /gruː/	grown /grəʊn/
hang /hæŋ/	hung /hʌŋ/	hung
have /hæv/	had /hæd/	had
hear /hɪə/	heard /hɜːd/	heard
hit /hɪt/	hit	hit
hurt /hɜːt/	hurt	hurt
keep /kiːp/	kept /kept/	kept
kneel /niːl/	knelt /nelt/	knelt
know /nəʊ/	knew /njuː/	known /nəʊn/

Infinitive	Past simple	Past participle
lay /leɪ/	laid /leɪd/	laid
learn /lɜːn/	learnt /lɜːnt/	learnt
leave /liːv/	left /left/	left
lend /lend/	lent /lent/	lent
let /let/	let	let
lie /laɪ/	lay /leɪ/	lain /leɪn/
lose /luːz/	lost /lɒst/	lost
make /meɪk/	made /meɪd/	made
mean /miːn/	meant /ment/	meant
meet /miːt/	met /met/	met
pay /peɪ/	paid /peɪd/	paid
put /pʊt/	put	put
read /riːd/	read /red/	read /red/
ride /raɪd/	rode /rəʊd/	ridden /ˈrɪdn/
ring /rɪŋ/	rang /ræŋ/	rung /rʌŋ/
rise /raɪz/	rose /rəʊz/	risen /ˈrɪzn/
run /rʌn/	ran /ræn/	run
say /seɪ/	said /sed/	said
see /siː/	saw /sɔː/	seen /siːn/
sell /sel/	sold /səʊld/	sold
send /send/	sent /sent/	sent
set /set/	set	set
shake /ʃeɪk/	shook /ʃʊk/	shaken /ˈʃeɪkən/
shine /ʃaɪn/	shone /ʃɒn/	shone
shut /ʃʌt/	shut	shut
sing /sɪŋ/	sang /sæŋ/	sung /sʌŋ/
sit /sɪt/	sat /sæt/	sat
sleep /sliːp/	slept /slept/	slept
speak /spiːk/	spoke /spəʊk/	spoken /ˈspəʊkən/
spend /spend/	spent /spent/	spent
stand /stænd/	stood /stʊd/	stood
steal /stiːl/	stole /stəʊl/	stolen /ˈstəʊlən/
swim /swɪm/	swam /swæm/	swum /swʌm/
take /teɪk/	took /tʊk/	taken /ˈteɪkən/
teach /tiːtʃ/	taught /tɔːt/	taught
tell /tel/	told /təʊld/	told
think /θɪŋk/	thought /θɔːt/	thought
throw /θrəʊ/	threw /θruː/	thrown /θrəʊn/
understand /ʌndəˈstænd/	understood /ʌndəˈstʊd/	understood
wake /weɪk/	woke /wəʊk/	woken /ˈwəʊkən/
wear /weə/	wore /wɔː/	worn /wɔːn/
win /wɪn/	won /wʌn/	won
write /raɪt/	wrote /rəʊt/	written /ˈrɪtn/

Vowel sounds

	usual spelling		! but also
fish	**i**	linen silk trip fit fill pick	pretty women guilty decided village physics
tree	**ee** **ea** **e**	bleed sneeze beat steal even medium	people thief key relieved receipt
cat	**a**	rash back ankle match hang travel	
car	**ar** **a**	scarf smart sharp hardly calf branch	aunt laugh heart
clock	**o**	cotton top drop cost off on	watch want because cough
horse	**(o)or** **al** **aw**	sore floor stalker wall yawn draw	warm warn pouring thought caught exhausted launch
bull	**u** **oo**	full put hooded woollen stood good	could should would woman
boot	**oo** **u*** **ew**	loose cool argue refuse chew news	suit juice shoe prove through queue
computer		Many different spellings. /ə/ is always unstressed. co<u>ll</u>ar <u>p</u>atterned a<u>d</u>vise <u>c</u>omp<u>l</u>ain infor<u>m</u>ation <u>s</u>andals	
bird	**er** **ir** **ur**	verdict prefer dirty skirt hurt burn	research worker worth worse journey
egg	**e**	denim dress trendy belt ever yet	friendly leather deaf threaten anybody said

	usual spelling		! but also
up	**u**	cut scruffy lungs stunned upset discuss	money someone enough touch flood blood
train	**a*** **ai** **ay**	ache lace faint plain may lay	break steak great weight suede obey grey
phone	**o*** **oa**	choke chose froze fold toast approach	throw elbow below although shoulders
bike	**i*** **y** **igh**	striped ice lycra stylish tight flight	buy eyes height aisle
owl	**ou** **ow**	hour mouth proud around showers frown	drought
boy	**oi** **oy**	boiling avoid point avoid enjoy employer	
ear	**eer** **ere** **ear**	career volunteer here we're nearly clear	realize ideally seriously zero
chair	**air** **are**	airport upstairs fair hair scared stare	their there wear area
tourist		A very unusual sound. euro jury sure plural	
/i/		A sound between /ɪ/ and /iː/. Consonant + *y* at the end of words is pronounced /i/. windy sunny foggy	
/u/		An unusual sound between /ʊ/ and /uː/. education usually situation	

* especially before consonant + *e*

○ short vowels　　● **long** vowels　　○ diphthongs

Consonant sounds

	usual spelling		! but also
parrot	**p**	postpone polluted	
		hope damp	
	pp	disappointed kidnapping	
bag	**b**	brain bribe	
		objective biased	
	bb	robbery hobby	
key	**c**	court critic	choir orchestra
	k	kidneys shake	stomach-ache
			question
	ck	shocked homesick	expect accuse
girl	**g**	regret grateful	
		colleague forget	
	gg	hugged mugging	
flower	**f**	fist theft	enough laugh
	ph	physicist symphony tough	
	ff	offended staff	
vase	**v**	velvet vandalism	of
		nervous prevent	
		evidence review	
tie	**t**	taste tend	produced
		stand chest	passed
	tt	matter bottom	
dog	**d**	deny murder	failed bored
		editor redundant	
	dd	addictive suddenly	
snake	**s**	stops suck	science scenery
	ss	witness loss	fancy
	ce/ci	notice censored	
zebra	**z**	breeze freezing	
	zz	dizzy blizzard	
	s	nose raise spends agrees	
shower	**sh**	shrug brush wish clash	sugar sure chic
	ti (+ vowel)		
		ambitious sensational	
	ci (+ vowel)		
		spacious sociable	
television	An unusual sound.		
	decision confusion usually genre		

	usual spelling		! but also
thumb	**th**	thunder thick	
		healthy thigh	
		death teeth	
mother	**th**	the that with	
		further brotherhood	
chess	**ch**	checked chilly	
	tch	scratch stretch	
	t (+ure)	departure	
		temperature	
jazz	**j**	jet-lag hijack	
	g	suggest manager	
	dge	knowledge judge	
leg	**l**	lie liver	
		heel lonely	
	ll	colleague pillow	
right	**r**	rise ride	written
		risky pretend	wrong
	rr	terrorism arrested	
witch	**w**	win waste	one once
		waist wave	
	wh	while wherever	
yacht	**y**	yet yearly	
		youth yourself	
	before u	university argue	
monkey	**m**	mild remind	comb
		seem remember	
	mm	commit commentator	
nose	**n**	nails honesty	kneel
	nn	announce beginning	knew
singer	**ng**	length arranging	
		hang bring	
	before g / k	wink sink	
house	**h**	humid hail	who
		behaviour inhabitants	whose
		inherit perhaps	whole

○ voiced   ○ unvoiced

OXFORD
UNIVERSITY PRESS

Great Clarendon Street, Oxford, OX2 6DP,
United Kingdom

Oxford University Press is a department of the University of Oxford. It furthers the University's objective of excellence in research, scholarship, and education by publishing worldwide. Oxford is a registered trade mark of Oxford University Press in the UK and in certain other countries

© Oxford University Press 2014

The moral rights of the author have been asserted

First published in 2014

2018 2017

10 9 8 7 6

No unauthorized photocopying

ISBN: 978 0 19 455840 2

ISBN: 978 0 19 455848 8 (with Oxford Online Skills)

Printed in China

This book is printed on paper from certified and well-managed sources.

ACKNOWLEDGEMENTS

The authors would like to thank all the teachers and students round the world whose feedback has helped us to shape English File.

The authors would also like to thank: all those at Oxford University Press (both in Oxford and around the world) and the design team who have contributed their skills and ideas to producing this course.

A very special thanks from Clive to Maria Angeles, Lucia, and Eric, and from Christina to Cristina, for all their support and encouragement. Christina would also like to thank her children Joaquin, Marco, and Krysia for their constant inspiration.

The publisher and authors would also like to thank the following for their invaluable feedback on the materials: Robert Anderson, Elif Barbaros, Kinga Belley, Brian Brennan, Rachel Buttery-Graciani, Erika Edit, Mónica Gómez Ruiz, Gill Hamilton, Jane Hudson, Deborah Keeping, Petra Krasser, Rebecca Lennox, Martin Mani, Beatriz Martín Garcia, Magdalena Miszczak-Berbec, Daniela Moren, Magdalena Muszyńska, Wayne Rimmer, Graham Rumbelow, Louise Rutter, Rachael Smith, Joanna Sosnowska, Raphael Stoll, Pavlina Zoss.

The Publisher and Authors are very grateful to the following who have provided information, personal stories, and/or photographs: Ryan Judd (pp.12–13), Julia Eccleshare (pp.32–33), Candida Brady (pp.42–43), Simon Callow (pp.52–53), and George Tannenbaum (pp.62–63) for agreeing to be interviewed for the Class DVD and iTutor; John Sloboda (p.56) and Miles Roddis (p.90) for agreeing to be interviewed for the Class DVD and iTutor; Krysia Cogollos for her invaluable research; Fran Drescher, Cheryl Hines, Jason Schwartzman, Ellen Burstyn, Dan Hedaya, Jane Lynch, and Steve Guttenberg (pp.68–69) for giving us permission to print their *Actors Acting* photographs; Joe Navarro (p.71) for allowing us to use the photographs from his book.

The authors would also like to thank Alicia Monge for her help with interpreting handwriting material. We would also like to thank all the friends, colleagues and people in the street who have constantly answered surveys and questions for us.

The authors and publisher are grateful to those who have given permission to reproduce the following extracts and adaptations of copyright material: p.5 Extract from "Q&A: Elisabeth Moss" by Rosanna Greenstreet, first published in The Guardian, 31 March 2012. Reproduced by kind permission. p.4 Extract from "Q&A: Benedict Cumberbatch" by Rosanna Greenstreet, first published in The Guardian, 6 January 2012. Reproduced by kind permission. p.6 Adapted extract from "Big beasts fail 'extreme interviews'" by James Gillespie and Lou Stoppard, The Sunday Times, 11 March 2012. Reproduced

by permission of News Syndication. p.14 Adapted extract from "British Red Cross First Aid Quiz", redcross.org.uk/firstaid. Reproduced by permission of British Red Cross. p.16 Adapted extract from "Confessions of a cyberchondriac" by Anita Chaudhuri, The Sunday Times, 26 April 2009. Reproduced by permission of News Syndication. pp.18–19 Adapted extract from "Older and wiser" by Liz Gill, The Times, 10 August 2004. Reproduced by permission of News Syndication. p.23 Adapted extract from "Rise of the shamans" by Atul Sethi, The Times of India, 21 August 2011. Copyright © 2013, Bennett, Coleman & Co. Ltd. All Rights Reserved. Reproduced by permission. pp.24–25 Adapted extract from Air Babylon by Imogen Edward-Jones. Published by Bantam Press. Reprinted by permission of The Random House Group Limited and Furniss Lawton. p.26 Adapted extract from "Mini Sagas" by Brian Aldiss, The Daily Telegraph, © Telegraph Media Group Limited 2013. Reproduced by permission. pp.28–29 Adapted extract from "Rampage" by Lewis Cole, fiftywordstories.com. Reproduced by permission of Lewis Cole (www.coleshideyhole. blogspot.com). p.30 Adapted extract from "Lazy Susan" by Nancy Pickard, copyright © 1991 by Nancy Pickard, adapted from Sisters in Crime 4, edited by Marilyn Wallace. Used by permission of Nancy Pickard and The Berkley Publishing Group, a division of Penguin Group (USA) LLC. p.34 Adapted extract from "Little habits rack up big eco-guilt" by Mary Schmich, Chicago Tribune, 23 April 2008 © 2008 Chicago Tribune. All rights reserved. Used by permission and protected by the copyright Laws of the United States. The printing, copying, redistribution, or retransmission of this Content without express written permission is prohibited. p.36 Adapted extract from "Why we always warm to the weather" by William Langley, The Daily Telegraph, 1 October 2011 © Telegraph Media Group Limited 2011. Reproduced by permission. p.40 Adapted extract from "I'm Dave, I'm a speedaholic" by Emma Smith, The Sunday Times, 24 June 2007. Reproduced by permission of News Syndication. p.43 Adapted extract from "They Believe They Can Fly" by Douglas Quenqua, New York Times, 14 December 2012 © 2012 New York Times. All rights reserved. Used by permission and protected by the copyright Laws of the United States. The printing, copying, redistribution, or retransmission of this Content without express written permission is prohibited. p.45 Adapted extract from The Survivor's Club by Ben Sherwood (Michael Joseph, 2009) . Copyright © 2009 by Ben Sherwood. By permission of Grand Central Publishing and Penguin UK. All rights reserved. p.55 Adapted extract from "What music would you play an alien?" by Rhys Blakely, The Times, 3 October 2012. Reproduced by permission of News Syndication. p.60 Adapted extract from "Sleepwalking chef's recipe for disaster" by Kirsty Scott, The Guardian, 31 March 2006. Copyright Guardian News & Media Ltd 2006. Reproduced by permission. p.63 Adapted extract from "Survival tastes so sweet for rescued British backpacker" by Alexi Mostrous, The Times, 15 February 2013. Reproduced by permission of News Syndication. p.65 Adapted extract from "Why men and women argue differently" by Damian Whitworth, The Times, 30 October 2007. Reproduced by permission of News Syndication. pp.70–71 Adapted extract from What Every Body Is Saying by Joe Navarro and with Marvin Karlins, PhD. Copyright © 2008 by Joe Navarro. Reprinted by permission of HarperCollins Publishers. p.77 Adapted extract from "Freeloaders and the internet" by Caitlin Moran, The Times, 22 September 2012. Reproduced by permission of News Syndication. p.80 Adapted extract from 24 Hours in Journalism by John Dale. John Dale Publishing Limited. Reproduced by permission. p.84 Adapted extract from "The 10 biggest lies ever told in advertising" by Jim Edwards, CBS News Website, 21 July 2011. Reproduced by permission of CBS News. p.86 Abridged extract from "What the Bagel Man Saw" by Stephen J. Dubner and Steven D. Levitt. Copyright © by Stephen J. Dubner & Steven D. Levitt. From The New York Times (June 6, 2004). Reproduced by permission. p.103 Adapted extract from "How's that for good karma? Homeless man is given $100,000 by well-wishers after he returned diamond engagement ring to bride after it fell into his cup" by David McCormack, Daily Mail, 23 February 2013. Reproduced by permission of Solo Syndication. p.112 Adapted extract from "Choking dog saves its own life by dialling 999" by Alistair Taylor, The Sun, 28 March 2012. Reproduced by permission of News Syndication. All rights reserved. Any unauthorised copying, reproduction, rental, or communication to the public of the material contained in this product is a violation of applicable laws.

The publisher would like to thank the following for their kind permission to reproduce photographs: Advertising Archives p.84 (Luckies) 85 (Loreal); Alamy 12 (Ian Dagnall/kit kat, Erkan Mehmet/ Facebook, Life on White/horse), 21 (Leila Cutler/boy with tattoo), 23 (Hemis/shaman), 24 (Image Source Plus/luggage), 25 (Alfonso de Tomas/paper aeroplane), 34 (Oleksiy Maksymenko/car, Studiomode/bag),35 (Johan H/tall wind turbines), 36 (H Lansdown/ drake, Lugris/duck), 41 (imagebroker), 46 (Bruce Coleman/jaguar, Mode Images/footprint, Jacques Jangoux/canoe), 57 (Sergey Galushko/earphones), 70 (Richard Heyes/hammer), 78 (Bernd Mellmann/bus), 88 (Delphotos/flats), 90 (Mike V/Sydney Beach, Jeremy Sutton-Hibbert/Edinburgh Festival, Manfed Gottschalk/ Vientiane), 91 (Tibor Bognar/Cairo), 92 (Jeremy Sutton-Hibbert/ BOSS ad), 94 (Clive Rivers/coins, Marvin Dembinsky Photo Ass/ Dog howling) 115, 118 (Bubbles), 119 (Janine Wiedel Photolibrary/ Fast food, Hemis/Empty restaurant, Mark Dyball/pub), 159 (Simon Balson/calf, David Taylor/thigh), 162 (Clynt Garnham Food & Drink/Pepsi can); Associated Press/Press Association 55 (Grant Hindsley/Austin Chapman); Aviation Images 24 (air crew); Barcroft Media 38–9 (Jun Ahn); Stephen Bettles 18 (Karoline

Bell and Nick Sydney); Cris Burgess 40 (key ring); Captainbijou. com 92 (MOM Brands/Farina cereal); Cartoonstock 36 (weather); Corbis Images 16 (Tetra Images), 18 (Ocean/park), 24 (Thom Lang/ mobile phone), 47 (jungle), 63 (Splash News/Sam Woodhead), 72 (Ocean/rehearsal), 73 (Hulton Deutsch Collection/Laurence Olivier), 88 (Colin McPherson/Andrew Marr), 153 (Daisy Cooper/ vest), 162 (Mike Segar/Reuters/Apple); Jon Fletcher 10 (pen); Frasers Autographs 10 (Leo Tolstoy, Shulz, Charles Dickens, Elijah Wood, Damien Hirst); Kevin Gale 47 (photo of Yossi and friends); Getty Images 4, 5, 6 (couple), 7 (Reza Estakhrian), 12 (Focus-on-nature/landscape), 12 (H Lansdown/drake), 13 (Izabela Harbur), 17 (Stocklib), 20 (Film Magic/Adele, WireImage/Jane Fonda), 21 (Image Source/grey haired man), 24–25 (David Joyner/Aircraft landing), 26 (James Lauritz/Pilot), 34 (Gotografia Basica/bottles), 35 (solar panels, Gamma-Rapho/wind turbines on houses, AFP/ snow machine), 40 (Maurice Marquardt/motorbike), 43 (Anders Blomqvist/wingsuit), 45 (Joe Petersburger/elephant), 47 (aeroplane shadow), 50 (Peter Widmann), 51 (Hill Street Studios), 54 (Tetra Images/bass guitar background, Hans Neleman/choir, Classic Rock Magazine/female guitarist, drummer, Redferns/flutist), 55 (Brand X Pictures/bass guitarist), 56 (AFP/John Sloboda, Ben Richardson/notebook), 60 (Stocktrek Images/Luis Argerich), 70 (Stephen Stickler/gun), 77 (Tetra Images/mouse, Chris Cheadle/ grafitti), 79 (Roman Okopny/Globe, chefs), 81 (Wireimage/Britney Spears, Lindsay Logan, PCA/Paris Hilton), 89 (Artem Vorobiey/ Tokyo), 93 (Bloomberg/Nike ad, Hulton Archive/Apple ad), 94 (Tetra Images/large moon, Einstein, Ingram Publishing/brain, Sean Murphy/lightening, Allan Barredo/bats), 98, 99 Emmeline Pankhurst, Gama-Keystone/Winston Churchill, AFP/Nelson Mandela, AFP/Barak Obama), 105, 108 (Blend Images), 110 (AFP), 111 (Vincenzo Lombardo/jasmine), 112 (AFP), 117 (Hans Neleman/ family, Leland Bobbe/texting) 153 (Trish Gant/sandals), 159 (Ian Sanderson/heel, Film Magic/ankle, JazzIRT/fist, WireImage/wrist, waist), 161 (Ian McKinnell), 162 (Bloomberg/Gap, Cover/Iberia airlines, UK Press/Tesco bag); Istockphoto 46 (raft) 153 (bow tie), 159 (hip); KCTV5 News 103; Kobal Collection 32(20th Century Fox/The Beach), 72 (Polygram/Channel 4/Working Title/Four Weddings film still), 73 (Miramax/Dimension Films/Gangs of NY film still); Ben Lack 78 (dog); Steve Mytton 78 (Longleat/tiger); N.I. Syndication 6 (The Sun/Dinosaur head); Oxford University Press Picture Bank 48 (portraits), 70 (knife), 85 (stop watch), 94 (small moon), 111 (cat, Vinegar); Ross Parry Agency p.37 (Jonathan Pow); Rex Features 10 (Barak O'Bama, Startraks Photo/Paris Hilton, Sipa Press/Usain Bolt, Peter Brooker/Paul McCartney, Ken McKay/Sean Connery), 20 (David Hartley/Gareth Malone, Dave J Hogan/Mick Jagger), 24 (Alex Segre/life jkt demo, Eric Vidal/ Emergency exit demo), 26 (Action Press/Air traffic controller), 32 (Jacqueline Wilson, JK Rowling), 52 (Everett Collection), 54 (Reg Wilson/Jacqueline Du Pre), 70 (Miramax/everett/The Queen), 72 (Alisdair Macdonalds/Old Vic, Graham Wiltshire/Amadeus), 80–81 (paparazzi), 81 (Dupuy Florent/Sipa/Brad Pitt, Broadimage/ Julia Roberts, Startraks Photo/Kate Bosworth), 83, 89 (Patrick Frilet/Mexico), 91(Image Broker/Lucca), 94 (Eye Ubiquitous/ Empire State Building, Garo/Phanie/pills); Science Photo Library 159 (Ian Hooton/bottom, kidneys, brain, lungs, heart, liver); Shutterstock 21 (pink hair, striped skirt), 34 (Shower head, Ingram Publishing/filling bottle), 35 (electric car) 107 (cabbage, mango, rose, lolly, coat), 111 (camembert, chilli), 153 (cardigan, lace top, fur collar, silk scarf, boots), 159 (palm, elbow, fingernails, chest,); Thomson Reuters 89 (Tim Bravo/Band); Universal Uclick 11; Mark Wemple 70 (Joe Navarro), 71; 32 Cover image of Warrior Scarlet by Rosemary Sutcliff (Oxford University Press, 1958), reproduced by permission of Oxford University Press; 32 Cover image of Northern Lights Text Copyright © Philip Pullman 1995, Cover Design by Crush Design, 2011 Reproduced by permission of Scholastic Ltd. All rights reserved.; 47 Cover image of Lost in the Jungle by Yossi Ghinsberg is reproduced by kind permission of Summersdale Publishers; 90 cover image of Blue Guide Istanbul by kind permission of Blue Guides; 90 cover Reproduced with permission of Lonely Planet. © 2011 Lonely Planet; The photographs of Fran Dresher on page 68 and Ellen Burstyn, Dan Hedaya and Steve Guttenberg on page 69 are reproduced by kind permission of Howard Schatz from In Character: Actors Acting (published 2006 by Bulfinch Press) © Howard Schatz and Beverly Ornstein 200.; The photographs of Cheryl Hines, Jason Schwartzman and Jane Lynch are reproduced by kind permission of Howard Schatz from Caught in the Act: Actors Acting (published 2013 by Glitterati, Inc.) © Howard Schatz and Beverly Ornstein 2013.

Pronunciation chart artwork: by Ellis Nadler

Illustrations by: The Art Market/David McConochie pp.8, 9, 44, 56–57, 157; Colagene/Jerome Mirault p.60, 100; Dutch Uncle Agency/Atsushi Hara pp.27, 132, 133, 135, 136, 137, 139, 141, 143, 144, 145, 148, 149, 150, 151; Good Illustration/Oliver Latyk pp.74, 75, 160; Illustration Ltd/Matthew Hollings pp.14, 30–31, 105, 109, 116, 152, 153; Tim Marrs pp.48–49; Joe Mclaren p.58–59; Roger Penwill p.156; Peppercookies/Lisa Billvik pp.28, 29, 66, 67, 96, 97, 114, 155.

Commissioned photography by: Gareth Boden: p.64; MM Studios: pp: 32 (bookcovers), 57 (bookcovers), 61, 70 (ice pick), 86/7, 90 (bookcovers) 153 (suit; swimming costume; waistcoat).

Although every effort has been made to trace and contact copyright holders before publication, this has not been possible in some cases. We apologise for any apparent infringement of copyright and, if notified, the publisher will be pleased to rectify any errors or omissions at the earliest possible opportunity.